ONCE UPON A MIND
THE STORIES AND SCHOLARS OF GIFTED CHILD EDUCATION

ONCE UPON A MIND
THE STORIES AND SCHOLARS OF
GIFTED CHILD EDUCATION

JAMES R. DELISLE

Kent State University

HARCOURT BRACE COLLEGE PUBLISHERS

Fort Worth   Philadelphia   San Diego   New York   Orlando   Austin   San Antonio
Toronto   Montreal   London   Sydney   Tokyo

Publisher	Earl McPeek
Executive Editor	Carol Wada
Developmental Editor	Christine Abshire
Project Editor	Laurie Bondaz
Art Director	Vicki Whistler
Production Manager	Andrea Archer

Cover image by Mary Thelen

ISBN: 0-15-503192-9
Library of Congress Catalog Card Number: 98-88540

Address for Domestic Orders
Harcourt Brace College Publishers, 6277 Sea Harbor Drive, Orlando, FL 32887-6777
800-782-4479

Address for International Orders
International Customer Service
Harcourt Brace & Company, 6277 Sea Harbor Drive, Orlando, FL 32887-6777
407-345-3800
(fax) 407-345-4060
(e-mail) hbintl@harcourtbrace.com

Address for Editorial Correspondence
Harcourt Brace College Publishers, 301 Commerce Street, Suite 3700, Fort Worth, TX 76102

Web Site Address
http://www.hbcollege.com

Printed in the United States of America

9 0 1 2 3 4 5 6 7 8 016   9 8 7 6 5 4 3 2 1

Harcourt Brace College Publishers

ACKNOWLEDGMENTS

When this book was first envisioned as a possibility, I knew that it was one I did not want to complete alone. The energy that would be entailed in the research would be work enough for two authors, but this book was going to have even more—it was going to be composed of many interviews and excerpts from people's work and their lives.

In the entire field of gifted child education, there is no one who does a better job at getting to the heart of an issue (and an individual) than my wonderful friend and colleague Dr. Felice Kaufmann. Perhaps it is her love of soap operas or her genuine fondness for uncovering the frailties and strengths of the human condition, but Felice knows how to interview people; Felice knows how to move souls.

And that is exactly what she did for *Once Upon a Mind.* Spending countless hours interviewing the individuals whose lives unfold in this book and then transcribing the tapes so that portions could be used in this text, Felice deserves a coauthorship, but that is something she chose not to take.

But I want Felice to know that her name and her work are written all over this book. I want Felice to know that her telephone calls, E-mails, and postcards from Iceland kept me going when this project seemed not worth the effort—and there were many of those times. I want Felice to know that this book would not have been completed without her input and without her stamina, both physical and psychological. And finally, I want Felice to know that she is my best friend and my finest colleague.

For all you do, for all you are—Felice, thank you.

The other individuals I wish to thank are those who gave so much of their valuable time and insight in responding to questions that make up the sidebars of this book. Their expertise is surpassed only by their generosity, and this book's content is richer because of the lives they have led and the work they have shared with us all.

Last, I thank my friend and colleague Bob Schultz, whose work on behalf of this manuscript was instrumental in the book's completion. Bob, thanks for always being there.

DEDICATION

This book is dedicated to my life partner, Deb.
She and I share everything,
and we know that we have always been together.

Bunny bunny

INTRODUCTION: A READER'S GUIDE

AN ODE TO TEXTBOOKS

Generally, there is nothing quite as dry as the reading of a textbook. For the most part, a textbook is something you are told to buy, rather than a volume you choose of your own volition. It is often overpriced and underused, stuffy and pretentious in its presentation of ideas, with much of the content seemingly directed to those with a penchant for the esoteric. Readers of textbooks, once the book is completed, are often left asking a most important question about the book's content: "So what?"

Another thing working against textbooks is that your absorption of its content is often gauged by an outsider—a professor—who checks the accuracy of your reading by assigning projects or administering tests on the book's main ideas. There is nothing quite as inhibiting to a flow of good thoughts than to have to interrupt your thinking by highlighting a quote or fact in fluorescent yellow or pink for fear that you might be tested on it.

Then, there is the writing of the textbook itself. Chapter after chapter includes fact after fact and reference after reference. By mid-book, the reader is often left wondering who said what, and when, and (most important) why. If you're lucky, all the pieces come together at the end, and the subject of the textbook is revealed as much more cohesive than it originally seemed. If you are not so lucky, the textbook appears to be a series of disjointed ideas with only the glue and a binding holding them together.

It was these negative ideas about what textbooks are and how they are used that I thought about when I decided to write *Once Upon a Mind*. Let's face it: It wasn't too long ago that I was on the receiving end of textbooks, reading others' writings as you are about to read mine. I recall the drudgery and the memorization, and I longed to turn a page and find something fun or interesting—a cartoon, a song passage, a personal story, or a quote. When these were present, I stopped reading the main text and devoured, instead, the piece on the side. These written or visual diversions gave life and fullness to the text's main body; in some cases, they were the most meaningful parts of all.

That's when the "AHA!" went off in my brain. What if a textbook was written that appealed to the senses as well as the mind? What if the facts and figures were accompanied by stories and images of the people who derived these facts and figures? What if a textbook were . . . personal?

If I have succeeded as an author, then that is what you are now holding and reading: a textbook that tells the rest of the story.

Once Upon a Mind: The Stories and Scholars of Gifted Child Education is intended to be a book that is not written like any other I have seen on this topic. Inside these pages, you will read about the "major players" in gifted child education and the ideas and theories they have spawned. But you will also learn more. For example:

- James J. Gallagher, a leader in our field, went to a special program for gifted children in downtown Pittsburgh and, at the age of 6, had to change streetcars by himself to get to his school.

- Leta S. Hollingworth, one of our field's founders, wrote poetry about the pangs of being a brilliant woman in an era in which such intellectual powers were thought to be the bastion of males alone.
- Alexinia Y. Baldwin, a leader from Alabama in promoting the unique needs of African American gifted children, hitched her trailer to her car (and a star) in the late 1970s and drove north to Connecticut—a place she had never been—to pursue her goal of becoming an expert educator.

Stories of people; sagas of lives; situations of humor, heart, and depth: these are what make the field of gifted child education—or any field, for that matter—memorable and important for future generations to read about and understand. These stories and scholars are the main distinction between other textbooks in gifted child education and the one you are about to read now: *Once Upon a Mind.*

HOW TO READ THIS BOOK

Open to virtually any page of this book and you will find that the main text is interrupted by a box (or a "sidebar") or an extended quotation or passage. If you were to read this book chapter by chapter, page by page, my guess is that at least some of you would be distracted by what might appear as a "choppy" writing style. If that is the case, may I kindly submit that you are reading my book the wrong way. You are being too formal for its informal style.

Here is my advice: Begin reading a chapter by reviewing each of the sidebars first. Some will connect with one another; others will not. After you have taken the time to read all these, it is time for you to begin reading the actual text of the chapter itself—the material that is not in boxes or sidebars—the content that is written in the style of a more typical textbook. With any degree of luck, these seemingly disparate pieces will meld together into a technical and personal cohesion that resembles verbal choreography. That is, in fact, the intent.

If, at the end of a chapter, you find yourself wanting to know more about a specific topic that was not covered in the depth you desire, I would suggest you locate one of the main reference books cited in that particular chapter. In writing this book, and in including so many sidebars, something else had to be omitted so that this book did not resemble in size an A-to-Z encyclopedia. In some cases, what was omitted—and this was intentional—was the dissection of a topic into its smallest parts. But this is only one book, and its focus is to resemble a spotlight more than a laser. There are many other volumes out there for you to peruse, and many of them are cited in this text. So, see this book as the beginning of an intellectual journey rather than the entire trek. It is my hope that the contents enclosed—the stories, the scholars, the sidebars—will cause you to be curious enough to desire additional exploration elsewhere.

Best wishes as you weave your way through a most exciting field of pursuit: the psychology and education of children whom we have chosen to call "gifted."

Jim Delisle
Kent, Ohio

CONTENTS

ONCE UPON A MIND
THE STORIES AND SCHOLARS OF GIFTED CHILD EDUCATION

GIFTED CHILD EDUCATION

A HISTORY OF PEOPLE AND IDEAS

"Once upon a time . . ."

So many of our most beloved stories from childhood begin with those words. Fairy godmothers, evil witches, sleeping beauties, and stout-hearted knights all wove tales that caught and kept our attention. In time, though, we put away such childish notions as we realized that the dragons to be slain lurked not in deep, dark forests, but in the depths of our own psyches. We had only ourselves, not some brave rescuer on a sleek stallion, to whisk us away from the world's fears and evils. In time, the "once upon a time" tales became stories that we told to others who, as young as we once were, absorbed the lessons taught by the spun magic of words from wizards. We passed on to children truths that we no longer believed ourselves, hoping that these young people would live happily ever after.

But fairy tales are not the only prose for which the words *once upon a time* have meaning. Each of our lives fits somewhere into this scheme, and many of life's endeavors do as well. Take, for example, this story:

Once upon a time, in a kingdom of a thousand towns, there lived an emperor who feared that his land would be overrun by evil outsiders. He searched far and wide for someone who could help him to hold onto the land he loved and the people he served.

His cry was heard throughout the kingdom: "Bring me the most able subjects you can find. Look among the common and the poor, for among them, too, lies much talent."

But the emperor's henchmen were perplexed. "Sire, how will we find these people? What will we look for in them, and how will we know when we find it?"

The emperor was challenged by this request, but after much good thought and hard work, a plan was devised.

"Let us bring together many people who show promise of strength and wisdom, and let us give each of them a test of skill. Those who do the best shall take over my kingdom after I am gone."

And so it was. On one momentous day, huddled together to answer the same questions and perform the same tasks, people came from far and wide to take the emperor's challenge. Those who did well were rewarded with roles that allowed their leadership to bloom, those who did not do well went back to the lives they had already been leading, and those who cheated had a hand cut off, as a permanent reminder that leadership demands integrity and inner strength.

Even today, 2,000 years hence, this kingdom still exists thanks to an emperor who thought that, through intelligent leadership, his subjects could live happily ever after.

This story, far from being a fairy tale, is a (somewhat) accurate account of the first instance of standardized testing ever conducted, more than 2,000 years ago in China (Whitmore, 1980). The fascination with intelligence—especially extreme intelligence—has been present ever since, and our efforts to identify intellect, talent, and leadership have taken us far and wide and into a thousand towns and many kingdoms.

Gifted child education, the focus of this book and the people who have made this field a viable entity, is almost as ancient as humanity itself. Whether we look far back to the ancient Greeks and medieval Europeans, among whom "there existed a popular notion that great intellect is a divine gift, a touch of omniscience enabling one to penetrate to deep truths" (Tannenbaum, 1983, p. 2), or a bit more current, to 800 AD, when Emperor Charlemagne urged the state to finance the education of promising young children found among the common people (Galbraith & Delisle, 1996), we find a fascination with people, especially children, who seem to have detoured from the typical paths of childhood. As Feldman (1986) states,

> There is something uncanny about children who display talents that are only supposed to be the province of gifted and highly trained adults. When feats that are rare even among adults are performed by a mere child—composing a symphony, for example, or beating a chess master in a match—they seem to violate the natural order of things. (p. 4)

Yes, gifted child education is a series of stories; stories told and stories heard. From ancient attempts to find talent, we move to later attempts to develop it (Thomas Jefferson, founder of the University of Virginia, proposed that youth with potential be provided with a university education at public expense). From media portrayals of gifted children as nerds to ridicule (e.g., Steve Erkel on "Family Matters") we move to musical tributes to gifted children as precious gems to polish (Natalie Merchant's 1996 song "Wondrous"). There's no doubt about it: Gifted children, and the adults who care for and about them, have transfixed our imaginations since time began.

Giftedness is arguably the most precious natural resource a civilization can have. There are any number of resources, natural and man-made, that contribute to the development of a civilization. But if one looks back through history and asks just what it is that made certain civilizations great, or remembered, or esteemed, it is inevitably the gifts, whether individual or collective, of those who lived in them. These gifts are what give civilizations such as ancient Greece or the European Renaissance a special place in the history of humankind.
—*Sternberg & Davidson, 1986, p. ix*

A LITTLE BIT OF OLD STUFF

The clarion call for high intelligence continued to echo as the centuries passed. In the 15th century, Constantinople became the site of a palace school that was populated by boys who, without regard to social class, were given education that took advantage of the three criteria that determined their admission to this school: good looks, strength, and intelligence. Groomed to be warriors, leaders, and fathers, it was thought that both innate traits and learned skills contributed to one's capability to achieve.

A bit later, in the 17th century, John Amos Comenius, the son of a Czech miller, became fascinated with the minds of people like himself. Admitted to a Latin school at the age of 16, Comenius was none too pleased with the education that he and his classmates were receiving. Schools like his, Comenius writes,

> are the terror of boys, and the slaughterhouse of minds,—places where a hatred of literature and books is contracted, where ten or more years are spent in learning what might be acquired in one, where what ought to be poured in gently is violently forced in and beaten in, where what ought to be put clearly and perspicuously is presented in a confused and intricate way, as if it were a collection of puzzles,—places where minds are fed on words. (Laurie, 1892, p. 29)

In his lifelong effort to identify talents in children and then construct an education that took advantage of these strengths, Comenius was convinced that "a good education can be attained by everyone who is gifted with healthy senses, reason, memory and will" (Kozik, 1958, p. 63). Toward this end, Comenius designed principles of education that were precursors to the fields of developmental psychology and progressive education, as attested to by his own words from *Didactica Magna (The Great Didactic)* in 1657:

> Though . . . schools be different, we do not wish them to teach different things, but rather, the same things in a different manner. I mean, all things which can make men truly men, and the learned truly learned; they should be taught in consideration of the pupil's age and the standard of his prior preparation, which should always tend gradually upward.

The importance of matching teaching methods to the styles and strengths of the child is given further evidence when Comenius comments that "there have . . . been many instances in which those who are naturally stupid have gained such a grasp of the sciences as to excel those who were more gifted" (Comenius, 1657, p. 67). Too, his forward-thinking reference to gender equality makes him sound as contemporary as today's agenda of the National Organization for Women:

> No reason can be shown why the female sex . . . should be kept from a knowledge of languages and wisdom. For they are also human beings, an image of God, as we are; they are also partakers of the mercy and the kingdom of the future life; in their minds they are equally gifted to acquire

wisdom; indeed, in gentleness and understanding they are often more endowed than we. (Kozik, 1958, p. 8)

Move over, Betty Friedan; step aside, Howard Gardner: your thoughts are mere paraphrases of one of the world's greatest thinkers and teachers—John Amos Comenius.

And Benjamin Bloom, father of the *Taxonomy of Educational Objectives*? Perhaps he should have consulted Comenius's threefold method of explaining the processes involved in learning, which preceded Bloom by 300 years:

1. We become acquainted with the parts of anything by means of analysis.
2. We come to know them more completely if we also employ synthesis.
3. We come to know them most completely if, in addition, we employ syncrisis (translation: *evaluation*).

These comments, among many other time-forgotten gems, make up the 1657 volume of the *Didactica Magna,* arguably the first gifted child education text ever written. Although it is often said that Lewis Terman (more on him later) is the father of gifted child education, that title seems more aptly applied to Comenius, who connected giftedness and the need for a kind and relevant education 250 years before *Genetic Studies of Genius,* Terman's opus of giftedness, was ever published.

THREE HEROES AND THEIR STORIES

> *My*
> *dear*
> *Uncle*
> *we have*
> *got ducks. I know*
> *A Nest. I mean*
> *to make a*
> *Feast.*
>
> —*Sir Francis Galton, Age 4*

In the history of psychology and psychometrics, one of the earliest superstars was a man named Francis Galton. A late bloomer by any standard, his most famous book, *Hereditary Genius* (which presented the view that genetics is the source of all intelligence, especially genius), was published in the author's 50th year, and some of his most important work in psychology was accomplished when he was well into his 80s.

But his prodigious achievements as an adult were foreshadowed by his abilities as a youngster. Under the tutelage of his sister Adele, Francis learned about books, about numbers, about life:

She taught him his letters in play, and he could point to them all before he could speak. [Adele] taught herself Latin and Greek that she might teach him. She never had him learn by heart, but made him read his lesson, bit by bit, eight times over, when he could say it. He could repeat much of Scott's *Marmion* and understood it all by the time he was five.

—*From Elizabeth Ann Galton's* Reminiscences *in*
The Life, Letters and Labours of Francis Galton

Other early signs of Galton's of genius included

- He knew his capital letters at 12 months.
- He could read a book, *Cobwebs to Catch Flies,* at 2 1/2 years.
- He could sign his name at 3 years.
- At age 4, he could do any addition sum and most multiplication tables.
- At age 6, he was thoroughly conversant with *The Iliad* and *The Odyssey.*

Sent to a boarding school at age 8, where most of his classmates were 15 years old, Galton continued to excel, his intellect to surprise those around him. That he was able to intellectually handle this challenge is noted in the book *The Life, Letters and Labours of Francis Galton:*

In the first year at this school, we find Francis writing to his father in these words: "I am very glad that you have left off being a banker, for you will now have more time to yourself and better health." This little quotation certainly betokens a degree of filial solicitude by no means common to children of this age. Such altruism does not ordinarily develop so early. The words fit sixteen-year-old much better than eight-year-old intelligence. (Pearson, 1914, p. 14)

Galton's own intellect, the opportunity to visit and speak with his first-cousin, Charles Darwin, and his upbringing as the elite son of a physician certainly contributed to his propensity toward genetics as the source of all good, intellectually speaking. Making the analogy of a well-toned physical muscle being limited by its own composition, Galton believed the same to be true for mental capacity:

[Every student] glories in his newly developed mental grip and growing capacity for application and, it may be, fondly believes it to be within his reach to become one of the heroes who have left their mark upon the history of the world. The years go by: he competes in examinations of school and college, over and over again with his fellows, and soon finds his place among them. He knows he can beat such and such of his competitors; that there are some with whom he runs on equal terms, and others whose intellectual feats he cannot even approach. (Dennis & Dennis, 1976, p. 2)

Taking his zeal for genetics even further, Galton suggested that those adults who were not endowed with the proper intellectual equipment should refrain from procreation altogether (and, it appears, all sexual relations) and get themselves to celibate monasteries and sisterhoods.

Obviously, Galton's views would be grounds for a Title IX lawsuit today, but in the 1850s, his ideas were considered by noted authorities as useful, accurate, and on the cutting edge of science! It wasn't until much later, when the role of environment began to eke into the intelligence equation, that Galton's views were moderated by a world more prone to look at intelligence—genius—as a combination platter: a few genes, a rich environment, and the appropriate opportunity to transform the seeds of intellect into a rich bounty of talents.

Some elements of Galton's work do survive today; indeed, many of them helped to shape the field of intelligence testing. His emphasis on reaction time to physical tasks as a main predictor of mental acuity helped Alfred Binet to refine his thoughts on ways to measure the intellect, and Hans Eysenck (1985) cites that the use of physiologic measurements to determine IQ may, in fact, have more merit than current ideology allows. Also, anyone who has ever suffered through a statistics course involving the concepts of "regression to the mean" and "correlation" has Sir Francis to thank for coining those terms.

A Renaissance man whose work transcends generations, Galton probed areas of intellectual measurement and functioning that had previously been relegated to soothsayers and charlatans. He shaped the thinking of those who came after him—Alfred Binet and Lewis Terman, to name two—and his collected ideas were building blocks for the field of modern psychology.

A question remains, though: If Galton became the intelligent youngster that he was thanks, at least in part, to the tutelage of his sister Adele, whatever became of her, and what intellectual feats did she accomplish in adulthood? How sad that the sexism of an earlier age will probably leave that question unanswered.

THE TERMAN ERA. THE TERMAN ERROR?

Bodily functions that are already weak are dangerously undermined by the high pressure of the average school. The resulting nervousness shows itself in innumerable ways . . . the dull boy is injured no less than the bright one, for if he belongs to the higher classes he is pushed, crowded and tutored privately till he becomes either a nervous wreck or a helpless graduate. (Terman, 1905, pp. 156–157)

A mention of the name Lewis Terman in psychology circles, and especially within the realm of gifted children, gets an immediate "AHA!" response, as this Stanford professor of psychology conducted the most noted longitudinal examination of gifted children ever accomplished, *Genetic Studies of Genius.* In addition, others know Terman's work through his introduction and refinement of the intelligence test developed by French psychologist Alfred Binet. This refinement led eventually to the development of the Stanford-Binet Intelligence Test, the sine qua non of intellectual assessment for the past eight decades. Terman's own history, and his own early work in understanding precocity in its many dimensions, provide a fascinating template through which his later work should be analyzed. Let's examine how.

In Volume I of *Genetic Studies of Genius,* Terman examines the roots of human differences by exploring the variations existing within species of the animal kingdom:

> Compare the young of the quail with the young of the eagle. The former are a numerous progeny. They can run, utter alarms, feign death and peck grain almost at the very moment of their escape from the shell. Throughout life, these instinctive activities will meet all requirements. . . . The eaglet, on the other hand, is long helpless. With his one or two mates he keeps the nest for many weeks and is not mature for 6 to 10 years. As a bird of prey, he will have to fight numerous battles in which the degree to which he has acquired skill will be the determining factor. If, for a time, therefore, he is helpless and runs in debt to the world for his care, the mortgage he gives therefor is genuine. (Terman, 1905, p. 149)

Terman then goes on to explore how different human cultures allow for precocity, especially how "primitive" cultures require that young men and women develop physical and creative skills, like the quail's instinctive skills, if they are to survive into adulthood. These interindividual differences, and the rates at which children progress through developmental stages depending on the environment in which they are raised, appeared to guide Terman in his lifelong quest to determine the source of intelligence, as well as its appropriate caretaking. With his own subjects, 1,528 10- and 11-year-old children with a Binet IQ of 130 or higher (most were above 140 IQ) that he began studying in 1921, Terman himself seemed to arrive at more questions than answers as his research progressed. For example:

- Is a person's IQ constant throughout life, as Terman believed, and if so, what ramifications ensue for providing appropriate educations to *all* children?
- Because 31% of his subjects came from parents who were professional (a *very high* percentage, considering the era), did this imply a connection between social class and intellect? (Newland, 1976)
- Would early notice of and attention to one's intellectual gifts ensure a successful life? And by what standards would "success" be determined?
- Would the positive social and emotional adjustment common among his subjects as children (96% were noted as having positive social and emotional adjustment at the study's onset) continue throughout life, and if not, what factors would interfere?
- What educational factors caused some of his subjects to be more successful academically than others? (In 1959, Terman and Oden reported that "in connection with failures in college that in high school they found it so easy to make high marks that they underestimated the amount of study necessary in college" [p. 68].)
- Were Terman's results generalizable to other gifted children during his lifetime, or now, considering that "his primary basis of identification

could be regarded as a circuitous, self-fulfilling one: he selected those who already had, in effect, demonstrated that they had learned quickly; they, therefore, were likely to continue learning quickly" (Newland, 1976, pp. 323–324)?

The "Terman legacy," as some have come to call it (Tannenbaum, 1983; Winner, 1996), is a vast and varied pool of information, statistics, and interpretation of data that, to this day, is still being examined. Debates still focus on whether Terman was correct to see intelligence as a unitary trait that can be measured accurately and fully by a one-time IQ test (Winner, 1996). Others ask whether his work is valuable at all, as it was not based on an underlying theory of intelligence but, rather, on a mere practical application of Binet's intelligence test (Guilford, 1967). Still others (Renzulli, 1978) ask what Terman and Oden (1947) appeared to suggest themselves: whether the traits of (1) persistence in accomplishment of ends, (2) integration toward goals, (3) self-confidence, and (4) freedom from inferiority feelings are the actual seeds of intelligence and intelligent behavior, rather than a specific score on even the best intelligence test.

If nothing else, the critique of Terman's work 75 years after it began gives evidence of its complexity and its implications for parents and educators of gifted children. As Abraham Tannenbaum, a noted scholar and historian in gifted child education, wrote so aptly: "[Terman's work] suggests the need for special educational programs for the gifted, an idea that would be irrelevant if there were no developmental connection between early promise and later fulfillment" (1983, p. 73). A glance at some of Terman's earliest thoughts on the nature of giftedness (Figure 1.1) points out that he was a gentle giant; a grandfatherly patron to both his 1,528 "Termites" and those who came after these chosen few.

The day I became aware of the Terman study was the day I knew what I wanted to do with my career in gifted education. I remember thinking that no pursuit could be as meaningful or interesting as the study of the lives of gifted people over time. Everything about the study fascinated me—the scope of the data, the methodology, the quirkiness of Terman's life, the sheer numbers—even Catherine Cox's study of assigning eminent people an IQ score long after they were dead, which I thought was surely a satire. Though I later became aware of many of the flaws of the study, I still respected and admired the tenacity with which Terman and his colleagues maintained the project for so many years. That fervor, that desire to investigate one group from so many different directions, literally spoke volumes to me and taught me that it is just as important to find one subject and examine it elegantly as to explore many unconnected areas of study.

—*Felice Kaufmann is a consultant and author in gifted child education.*

THE LADY WITH THE LAMP

The Year: 1926

The Place: New York City, Public School #165

The Class: Children identified on the Stanford Binet as having an IQ of 130+

The Teacher: Leta S. Hollingworth

The Result: Some of the most remarkable insights ever gained about the education and psychology of gifted children

FIGURE 1.1

■ _____

Pre-Terman, Terman

Excerpts from "A Study in Precocity and Prematuration"

> Many who talk of precocity do not even realize that the assumption of some norm is necessary…when an Englishman writes that the children of the Negro race are precocious, he is evidently setting up his own race as a standard. The Negro child could just as well say of the English child that it is retarded in development. One statement means as much as the other. We simply have a disparity, which may be named from either end. (pp. 145–146)

ॐ

> The prodigy of encyclopedic learning at 10 years of age may conceivably be less precocious than the dullard of 20. It may require more pressure to place the latter on a low plane by 20 than to make a scholar of the former by 10. In short, precocity, in this sense, is simply a condition brought about by forced culture. (p. 147)

ॐ

> To designate a quality or character as "abnormal" is, in the popular mind, to condemn it. Hence children of unusually rapid development have sometimes been called "monsters." (p. 147)

ॐ

> Teachers of mixed schools in the Northern States are continually surprised at the rapid school progress made by the Negro child for the first few years, in many cases even outdoing his white competitors. But before long the tide turns and the negro child relapses into a state of chronic stupidity, while the white child pushes onto heights the former will never see. (p. 151)

ॐ

> All systems of education may be viewed only as means devised to help us get the full value of our bargain; and if man would live for the future rather than for the present, his chief concern must be to see that the younger generation comes to its full inheritance,—in other words, that it reaches the fullest possible maturity. (p. 152)

ॐ

> From a look into many of our schools, one is forced to view . . . that childhood is a necessary evil, that adulthood is the only perfect state, and that

continued on the following page

continued from the previous page

the chief business of the school is to make boys and girls into men and women by the shortest method possible. (p. 153)

The school curriculum attempts to answer the question *how,* long before the child asks or cares to know. . . . Instead of trying to find out what is indigenous to the human soul and how we could best build upon this, we rather consider it a blank page upon which to inscribe adult "proper conclusions." (p. 154)

It is well known that manhood and womanhood normally bring a certain amount of disillusionment. The real world as the adult finds it never measures up to the fairy tale world which the child has looked forward to. . . . But if, through the prematuring effects of a wrong education, the disillusionment comes too early, before the will has developed and while the passions are still explosive, we have the prime conditions for making the youthful suicide or criminal on one hand, or the cynic and pessimist on the other. (p. 155)

In no field of crime is the growing precocity more marked than in suicide. It would seem to be one of the strongest indictments against the prematuring effects of modern education as carried on by the leading nations, that what should be a period of veritable intoxication from the overflow of joyous animal spirits, is frequently burdened with sorrows so keenly felt that relief is purchased by suicide. (p. 161)

Heroic effort is made to boost every child just as near to the top of the intellectual ladder as possible, and to do so in the shortest possible time. Meanwhile, the child's own instincts and emotions, on which alone all volition is based, are allowed to wither away. No adjustment of clock wheels, however complicated and delicate, can avail if the mainspring is wrongly attached or altogether missing. (pp. 162–163)

School work is done too early and does not educate the child as a whole. . . . To build up the intellect at the expense of the rest of mentality robs it of every element that ennobles it. It becomes mechanical and has no life blood in it. (p. 163)

We must explore the child's natural interests and take our cue from them. Until the awakening of altruism it will be useless to try to force upon his comprehension a religion whose keynote is love and sympathy. The child is, and ought to be, an egoist. (p. 165)

The narrowing of interest and talents, even in adult life, to the close confines of a small department of one profession is rather an event to be deplored and to be postponed as long as possible. . . . The child, as the epitome of the race, ought to represent in miniature the sum total of all human endeavor and aspirations. But if he shows unusual talent in one particular direction and is made into a parade horse on account of it, there is a danger of developing a morbid conceit that will tinge the whole life. (p. 168)

The prime object of our education ought to be a delaying of mental maturity. Up to 10 at least, the smallest amount of mental together with the greatest bodily occupation should be the rule. The opposite course makes for morbidity, self-consciousness, nervousness, unbalance, religiosity and later cynicism, criminality, bad sexuality, or suicide—all owing to the physiological and neurological concords that are present to be played upon. . . . In neglect of all these things, we have lengthened the hours of school work and taken away largely the opportunity for physical development. (p. 182)

—*Terman, 1905, pp. 145–183*

While Terman was receiving much attention and many grant dollars for his work with gifted children at Stanford, a colleague of his on the other U.S. coast became interested in doing work with gifted children that, in some ways, paralleled Terman's own. However, rather than use a broad brush to examine the statistical differences and similarities of more than 1,500 children, Hollingworth took a different approach: She would examine just a few gifted children, but she would do so in great depth. Also, she would get to know the subjects as the psychologist she was and the teacher she would soon become. Leta S. Hollingworth, in analyzing the inner complexities of gifted children's minds and emotions, contributed as much to this emerging field of study as anyone ever did. Yet, sadly, her work was not highly valued until years after her death in 1943.

What caused this educational psychologist at Teachers College, Columbia University to come to devote her life to gifted children? The answer, in Hollingworth's own words, pinpoints a single incident, and a single child in the year 1916. Hollingworth observed an 8-year-old boy who had just scored a remarkably

Genius is not "politically correct." How does one justify the expenditure of funds on a child who "will learn no matter what we do," as at least one school board member has uttered? In St. Paul, the area school established for the gifted and talented was even refused permission to have the words "gifted and talented" in its name. It was "elitist."

It is a false joke on us all that the desire of our nation's founders, that all men would be equal before the law, has been so corrupted that those who show potential or ability above the common masses must be brought down or, at least, not allowed to rise too far.
—*Tighe, 1997, p. 20.*

high 187 IQ on the Stanford Binet, placing him in the top one-hundredth of 1 percent. As her previous experiences involved the testing of "thousands of incompetent persons," she became intrigued with this boy's talents: "I perceived the clear and flawless working of his mind against a contrasting background of thousands of dull and foolish minds. It was an unforgettable observation" (Hollingworth, 1942, p. xii) and one that caused her to approach the New York City School Board with a proposal to assemble a "special class" of highly able children, a classroom that would become her laboratory for all manner of educational innovations that, even today, would be considered enlightening.

The Board approved this class, and about 10 years later, she gained approval again to start another class, at P. S. #500 (Speyer School). Here, she herself would serve as the teacher with 50 children whose IQs ranged from 130 to 200—a daunting task, as would be attested to by anyone who has tried to teach even 15 highly gifted children simultaneously! She and her students designed a curriculum handbook titled *The Evolution of Common Things,* a sourcebook to be used by other teachers of gifted children—in effect, the world's first text on teaching gifted children. Each child learned to speak French; to do research by using the primary sources available at the Teachers College library; to study nutrition, music, dramatics, chess, and other intellectually and physically demanding subjects; and to complete extensive biographies at the rate of more than 100 per year. (The biographies were intended, in part, to let gifted children learn about themselves by studying the lives of others—an early form of today's concept of "bibliotherapy.")

But Hollingworth was more than a teacher; she was a life guide. As one of her former students, now an older adult, remarked on the influence of her class, "I would say that the Speyer School was the most influential aspect of all of my education. As I look back, I realize that by the time I was in high school, I had an attitude about learning that I did not get from a conventional school" (White & Renzulli, 1987, p. 94).

As one of our nation's earliest teachers of gifted children (and a remarkable teacher, from all accounts), Hollingworth should be a household name for anyone who claims this field as a passion. However, it was for Hollingworth's writing about two other areas—profoundly gifted children and the social and emotional problems of gifted persons—that she is most renowned—and rightly so.

PROFOUNDLY GIFTED CHILDREN: HOW DEVIATION CAN BECOME DEVIANT

Although Terman's study included children whose IQs were in the 180+ range, he did not study them specifically as a subgroup until many years after his study began. Perhaps he should have.

Hollingworth, with her now-assembled class of highly gifted children, found a total of only 12 children in 23 years of testing whose IQs were at 180 and above. She studied these children extensively; she interviewed them and their parents; she asked them complex questions about life and death and justice and joy. In the end, she began a manuscript that was completed, posthumously, by her husband, Harry Hollingworth. That book, *Children Above 180 IQ Stanford Binet* (1942), is a remarkable volume. Among her many findings worth mentioning are

- "This target group could be distinguished from the more 'typical' 130 IQ precocious population by virtue of its incredibly rapid intellectual advancement and, conversely, by its painful problems in social and emotional development" (Tannenbaum, 1983, p. 72).
- For this type of child, ordinary school is virtually a total waste of time, "viewed either with sheer indifference or positive distaste, especially if the demands are no more imaginative than requiring mastery of the multiplication tables and all the drudgery that goes with it" (Tannenbaum, 1983, p. 103).
- For this type of child, adult-sized concerns are common at an age when most children are asking merely how to tie their own shoes: "The higher the IQ, the earlier does the pressing need for an explanation of the universe occur; the sooner the demand for a concept of the origin and destiny of the self appears" (Hollingworth, 1942, p. 281).
- For this type of child, socialization is often a painful problem, as their interests are so different and their knowledge so much more extensive than that of their agemates. Such advanced insights predispose them to isolation and alienation; ironically, even from their less-gifted peers who, although intelligent, are still operating at a level, intellectually, that is far below these one-in-a-million children. As Newland (1976) states in an apt analogy,

> It takes considerable accommodation to establish a harmony between the walking pattern of a five-foot-tall youngster and that of his three-and-a-half-foot agemate. If the five-footer does not adapt his pace to that of his shorter friend, he soon is out far ahead, at least spatially alienated; if he does adapt to his shorter friend's pace, he must restrain himself, thereby being able to go less far. Bright children whose communication channels are restricted or grossly impaired because of a lack of reasonable reciprocity of conceptual levels have the social and educational cards stacked against them. (p. 104)

- For this type of child, there may be a keen but personally bothersome sense of disrespect for the judgments and actions of those in authority (Clark, 1992), if the highly gifted child sees contradictions in logic or arbitrariness in decision making. Often, Hollingworth found, adults need to teach these children to "suffer fools gladly" (Hollingworth, 1942,

p. 299), thereby remaining silent about these foibles of others for risk of alienating themselves even more from the mainstream culture if they were to speak out.

Children above 180 IQ may be a statistical rarity, yet the insight provided by Hollingworth as to the necessity to address their special social and emotional needs is something Terman barely touched on in his own research. In essence, when Terman studied his subjects, he used a spotlight; Hollingworth, a laser.

ISSUES OF SOCIAL AND EMOTIONAL DEVELOPMENT

Prior to her work with profoundly gifted children, Hollingworth studied those who were somewhat less precocious. Still, the issues many of these children faced were similar in kind, if not in intensity, to those with the highest IQs. Indeed, Hollingworth postulated that there was an "optimal IQ," somewhere between 135–150, and children at these levels hold certain advantages (she listed these advantages as superior size, strength, beauty, emotional balance, self-control, good character, and the ability to win the confidence of their contemporaries) over their less able agemates. An IQ higher than 150 might cause one to stand out like the proverbial sore thumb, risking being seen as "weird" rather than as "smart." Thus, being gifted can work to one's social advantage—as long as you are not *so* different than those around you that they see few commonalities when they compare themselves to you.

Among the categories of possible maladjustment of gifted children (Hollingworth, 1926) are

1. **Problems associated with play, friendship, and physique.** Gifted children often prefer complicated games with rules; less able agemates might not see the purpose behind such structure, frustrating both playmates. Further, gifted children may have intellectual ideas that cannot be expressed as well as they would like through writing and drawing—their finger muscles have not yet caught up to their mental ones. The ensuing frustration causes gifted children to feel something is "wrong" with them, when all that is occurring is that one body system (the mental one) is far outpacing another one (the physical one). Another reason that Hollingworth cited physique as an issue was that gifted children, in her day, were often grade skipped several times, thereby making them much smaller and weaker than their classmates. Today, with

How's your love life? If you are a "gifted and talented" student, probably not very good. After all, what is a love life? Intelligent people do not party, drink, or date; they are the ones that stay home and work the calculus problems so that everyone can copy the homework in the morning. Some people don't think that we "gifties" could be interested in mundane things like parties and the opposite sex. Well, we are! That's right, folks, "gifties" enjoy fun things, too!

—*American Association for Gifted Children, 1978, pp. 21–22*

extreme grade acceleration being less common, this issue is not as obvious.

2. **Problems associated with a lackluster school curriculum.** According to Hollingworth, children of IQs of 140 waste half of their time in the elementary classroom, and as reported earlier, those at 180 and above learn virtually nothing in a school day, spending their time in "various sorts of bizarre and wasteful activities" (Hollingworth, 1942, p. 299). This often leads to poor work habits, which, in later years, may make *true* learning difficult, as these students may not have the "tools" (e.g., organization skills, study habits) to pursue what they wish to learn.

3. **Problems associated with adjustment to occupation.** Gifted children, who are often so self-directed in their learning habits, may find it difficult to take orders from a "superior" (in an employment, not intellectual, sense of that word) who expects certain things to be done in certain ways and on a certain time line. Also, gifted children often have a vast number of interests, making career selection difficult, as they seem blessed with an "embarrassment of riches": too much to choose from and too little time to do it all.

4. **Problems associated with becoming negative with authority figures.** Alluded to above, this issue deals specifically with gifted children trying to "make good" the mistakes or misconceptions of others. She relates one anecdote of a young student who is chided by a teacher when the student argues that the Chinese, not the Germans, invented printing—even though the student could prove he was right. Another example comes from a youngster who was not allowed to use any section of the library except the juvenile section, even though he needed advanced resources to complete his learning. An example from today's schools would be students (or teachers) who are told they can't use certain books at particular

> It's kind of depressing to find out now, in my junior year of high school, that it's okay for me to ask for things in school. It just never occurred to me that I could. I'd always assumed that I didn't have the right to ask for anything to be different, and that adults always knew what was best for me.
> —*Galbraith & Delisle, 1996, p. 141*

> I've changed my major several times and worked in a wide range of jobs ranging from factory worker to family counselor. In my undergraduate years I tried literature, psychology, philosophy, the arts. Presently I am interested in clinical psychology and filmmaking. I'm engaged by the challenge of teaching and will be committed to it as long as I do it. My ambivalence about my career, however, is a constant source of stress.
> —*Simpson & Kaufmann, 1981, p. 42*

> Even now, I speak most comfortably with a pen, but my voice is strong. My fears have lessened. I wish I could have trusted more or asked someone for help. While I have fond memories of the sweet lady with the brogue (my kindergarten teacher), I must wonder—what if she had challenged me, asked more pointed questions, not accepted my well-constructed excuses? I wish Mrs. Feeney had recognized not just my potential but also my pain.
> —*Johnson, 1997, p. 63*

One thing I've regretted about passing from the high school–college phase of my intellectual life to the graduate school–professional phase is that a lot of the sense of discovery and trying new things has been lost. I had a much stronger sense of continual intellectual growth when I was younger and found that the opportunities for recognition were much more available and therefore reinforcing.

—*Kaufmann, 1981, p. 167*

Some people assume I'm conceited and untouchable, or impossible to get along with. They've heard of me but they don't know me in person; they've read the reviews and think they've read the book. . . . I may not get along as well as I'd like to with everyone, but the important thing is do I get along with myself? . . . On the whole, yeah, I guess I do get along with myself. I'm on speaking terms with myself to the point where I can decide what I *want* in life, and I know myself well enough to plan how I might *get* what I want in life. . . and those other guys don't know what they're missing.

—*American Association for Gifted Children, 1978, pp. 20–21*

grade levels, because "those are fifth grade books and authors." These issues often cause the student to react either violently or subversively need against "the system." Hollingworth gives but one reminder: "Many a reformer has died at the hands of a mob which he was trying to improve" (1942, p. 299).

5. **Problems associated with the tendency to be isolated in interests and goals.** Gifted children have more than one set of peers, and the intellectual peers may not be available to them in their classrooms or neighborhoods. Thus, when confined to working with other children of the same age but lesser abilities, boredom may result and intolerance may set in.

6. **Problems associated with using one's intellect to take advantage of others.** Hollingworth wrote that many of her highly able students were also highly skilled at "benign chicanery"—using their intellects to get their own way with others or to do a "Tom Sawyer"—to get someone else to whitewash the fence because you don't want to and making them believe it was their idea in the first place. Noting that such skills are often valued in adulthood, her main concern was that gifted children need to be *aware* of when they are using their intellects in a sneaky or rude manner. Otherwise, they may set themselves apart even more from classmates (and others) who eventually catch on to this intellectual bait-and-switch. By placing gifted children with their intellectual peers, such behaviors would probably be less effective, which, to Hollingworth, was a good lesson to learn: "Conceit was corrected, rather than fostered, by the experience of daily contact with a large number of equals" (Hollingworth, 1931, pp. 4–5).

As you can see by this extensive review of Hollingworth, her work was outstanding for her time and has lost very little luster and appeal over the ensuing decades. This last of Hollingworth's quotes, as true today as ever, speaks to the timelessness of her vision:

Where the gifted child drifts in school unrecognized, held to the lockstep which is determined by the capacities of the average, he has little to do.

He receives daily practice in habits of idleness and daydreaming. His abilities are never genuinely challenged, and the situation is contrived to build in him expectations of an effortless existence. (1931, p. 5)

From Hollingworth's vantage, schools in 1931 could have done a better job of educating gifted children. Some things, unfortunately, never change.

THE WORLD'S MOST INCONVENIENT CHILD

A little girl comes home from her first day in kindergarten with a frown on her face and a note from her teacher. This is *not* a good sign. Claiming she did nothing more than ask a question, this small child is seeking to discover why she is already in trouble. The note's contents read:

Dear Mr. and Mrs. Random:

Please discuss with your daughter the importance of following class procedures and listening to directions. Today, after we practiced our tornado and fire drill procedures, Sara asked me, "If we have a tornado and fire at the same time, do we go inside or outside?"

I told her that was a silly question because those two things would probably never happen together. Sara then asked if it was *possible* that these two events could occur at the same time. When I told her that it was possible but not likely, she asked me again where she should go if they did. Honestly, I just don't have time for silly questions like this.

I would appreciate if you would talk to your daughter about disrupting my class in this way.

Thank you,
Ms. Concrete

There is no greater struggle than that of a square-pegged child trying to fit into a round world. Sara, like millions before and after her, suffers from the ability to see everything in shades of gray. A sometimes lonely place, this "Ever Ever Land" of countless possibilities intrudes on the lives of those whose own limited imaginations and patience prefer the blacks and whites of issues, thoughts, questions, and morals. This creative child, this inconvenient child, is also the most at-risk child that our society harbors; for few want to be associated with someone who second guesses the obvious, and even fewer still see this amazing feat as an asset in a classroom where conformity is among the most prized of all assets.

However, there is one individual whose life and work celebrate the existence of originality in children. This man, as much a pioneer as Terman and Hollingworth

Emotional education is an idea whose time has come. Gifted children need exactly the kind of curriculum, programming and appreciation for their social and emotional development that Leta Hollingworth provided almost 70 years ago. Through her rediscovery in gifted education, I hope we will be able to implement many of her timeless ideas in modern programs for the gifted.
—*Silverman, 1990, p. 177*

in establishing a foundation for gifted child education, is E. Paul Torrance, the inconvenient child's best friend.

THE LIFE OF A MASTER

THE MAN . . .

My first year of teaching in a rural school had some very creative boys. There were two especially. One was W. J. Ursury, who later became the Secretary of Labor for the Ford administration and is known as one of the best negotiators in the world. The other was a very intelligent and creative boy named White Lawrence, who later became county super-intendent of schools. In fact, he established the first county high school that enrolled both boys and girls. I thought he was very imaginative in doing that.

. . . But they drove me crazy my first year of teaching with all of the creative things they used against me as a teacher. And I recognized at least something of what I had on my hands but I didn't know how to use it. And so it was very early that I recognized the necessity for a teacher know-ing how to use the creativity of his students, because that was their strength. (personal correspondence with Felice Kaufmann, 1995)

E. Paul Torrance, the crusader of the creative spirit that exists within us all, found out about the challenges of creativity the hard way: from a group of cre-ative youngsters who were in his class during his first year of teaching. How en-couraging to learn that even a genius such as Torrance could have felt at his wit's end with a group of creative young people! What hope that gives to the rest of us!

Torrance contributed so much to so many diverse fields of education, creativ-ity, and life that it would require at least a book to review them all. And, thanks to Garnet W. Millar, that is exactly what happened. In his authorized biography of Torrance's life (1995), Millar solicits testimony from those who have known Torrance for decades, including their memories of Torrance as an educator, re-searcher, and human being. Among the most poignant is a memory from Jack Presbury, a professor of psychology in Virginia, whose first visit with Torrance illustrates the man more than his mission:

In 1983, I wrote to Dr. T. and stated that if he would let me hang out with him for a month during the summer, that I would perform any work that he wished in return. He agreed, and I met him face to face for the first time in his large office in Aderhold Hall at the University of Georgia. I was prepared to meet someone who was a "distinguished professor" and I expected that he was from Minnesota, and so would be formal and some-what distant—sort of like Garrison Keilor's portrayal of the Norwegian

Lutheran. Instead, there was this fellow who looked for all the world like the Happy Buddha speaking in this thick southern accent! He approached me, somewhat stooped-shouldered, and warmly grasped my hand, seemingly delighted to see me. This infectious delight, which he communicates to all, is the most memorable aspect of his personality for me. (Millar, 1995, p. 225)

Others reflect on Torrance's demeanor, again through personal memories. June Maker, a gifted child specialist and professor at the University of Arizona, remembers sitting down for lunch at a meeting of the National Association for Gifted Children with a group of people whom she did not know. As people introduced themselves, she found she was sitting next to Paul Torrance, and a delightful conversation ensued. Later, Paul made a speech to the convention, during which time he took off his dress shirt to reveal the T-shirt underneath. On the front it read "I Am a Creative Child." Such playfulness, such warmth, are benchmarks of the personal relationship Paul Torrance establishes so quickly with so many.

. . . AND HIS WORK

Of course, it is his work that distinguishes him so prominently! His students recall him as someone who used a nondirective approach that put students in situations that were often new and potentially uncomfortable for them. Although some swam in the sea of indecision as to what steps to follow, others flew to new heights of their own creativity. As Kobus Neethling, creativity advisor to the government of South Africa, said of Torrance, "He has taken me to the edge of the cliff and showed me the wonder of wings." Harry Passow, a major contributor to gifted child education in his own right (more on him later in the book), mentioned that Torrance taught him to "think creatively about creativity." Also, Passow recalls looking for research citations for creativity in the 1950s and finding few. A decade later, the references were numerous, with many pointing to the work of one man: E. Paul Torrance. In yet another realm, Carol Schlichter, a professor of education from the University of Alabama, recalls how Torrance helped her in the 1960s when she was a graduate student in search of ways to stimulate children's thinking. After Torrance sent her some of his own work in this area, Schlichter went on to develop problem-solving strategies that did three things to help children learn to:

1. *Initiate activities* that puzzled and stimulated their interest in learning.
2. *Explore activities* in which they are encouraged (but not required) to continue thinking about their first ideas.
3. *Follow-through activities* that invite them to carry out their ideas in a hands-on fashion.

The Talents Unlimited Program, a nationally recognized method of tapping into the creative potential of all students, was the result of this early "long-distance mentoring" provided to Schlichter by Torrance. In retrospect, she calls Torrance her professional "lode star."

Arguably, the most well known of Torrance's many accomplishments is the creation and statistical validation of his Torrance Tests of Creative Thinking (TTCT) (1966), which, as even Torrance has admitted, have been misinterpreted as measuring that elusive concept called "creativity":

> Scientists studying creative behavior and its predictability characteristically have been unrealistic in their expectations of the predictability of tests of creative thinking. This itself may be a part of the Western world's penchant for short cuts and instant success. Many researchers and reviewers have expected a single test of creative thinking to correlate quite highly with some criterion of creative achievement. (Torrance, 1979, p. 11)

What Torrance attempted to accomplish with the TTCT was several things. First, he hoped to use a complex model of the intellect developed by J. P. Guilford (see chapter 4) to show that some separate "parts" of the intellect are very much linked to creative thinking and accomplishments. Second, he wanted to devise an instrument that could be used along with IQ tests to tap into elements of creative thinking that IQ tests did not. Third, he wanted to determine if creative *thinking* would lead to creative *production,* a research task that would take him years to complete.

These paper-and-pencil "tests" look like typical tests in some ways, and in other ways, they look like puzzle books. There are two forms of the TTCT, one requiring written responses (the "Verbal" test) and the other drawn responses (the "Figural" test; see samples of the Figural Test in Figure 1.2). Each test has two alternate forms, which have been used for pre/posttesting experiments, and the verbal and figural forms purport to be comparable in the results you would get. The TTCT can be given to young children, and they can be given to adults; statistical norms for various age groups are available.

But if the TTCT doesn't measure creativity directly, what *does* it measure? Again, Torrance takes us back to Guilford's view of the intellect and provides us with the answer—the TTCT measures four elements:

1. **Fluency:** How many responses can you come up with to a verbal or figural prompt?
2. **Flexibility:** How many different ways can you see the same object or the same idea? (E.g., a brick can be used to help build a house, as a weapon against an enemy, and as a piece of big, red chalk. Now *that's* flexibility!)
3. **Originality:** How statistically rare (without being bizarre) are the responses you provide?
4. **Elaboration:** How many little details do you add to the picture you are drawing or the verbal response you are giving?

The person scoring these tests (a difficult job that requires training) is able to report how the child or adult compares with others who have taken the TTCT

FIGURE 1.2

Sample Responses for the Torrance Test of Creative Thinking
(Figural Version)

Your Title: *Fountain of Youth*

Life Is Cruel

The Bubblemakers

—*Published with permission from the copyright holder, Creative Education Foundation, 1050 Union Road, Buffalo, NY 14224*

previously. Thus, a relative estimation of creative talent is available. (For examples of TTCT results, see Figure 1.2.)

The TTCT has been used for a variety of purposes, but one of the main ones is to identify children for gifted programs by using a means other than an IQ or achievement test score. However, this use does beg the question: If our gifted programs are designed to help children become more creative, why should a high score on the TTCT be a criterion for admission? Wouldn't it make more sense to use the TTCT at the beginning and end of a school year to note if children *have grown* more creative?

A second use of the TTCT, and one that occupied much of Torrance's energies through the years, was determining whether high scores on his tests predicted creative behaviors in future years. The short answer? Yes. In one study, Torrance looked at high school students who had taken the TTCT in 1959. He examined them in 1966 and again in 1971 to determine whether their "Quality of Creative Achievements" was rated highly by five judges who considered evidence

---

PAUL TORRANCE ON PAUL TORRANCE

On the Need for Creative Potential to Be Identified
By 1960, educators were already talking about the Space Age and what it meant. . . . Margaret Mead and I were the headline speakers at a conference. . . . Mead spoke of the changes that would have to be made because five-year-old children knew more about space than their parents and teachers. My job was to predict what would occur in the training of teachers and other educators. I predicted that in addition to the psychology of learning, we would need a psychology of thinking and problem solving. Mead challenged me and asked if creativity in education had any better chance than it had had at other times when it had been tried. I argued that we knew more about creativity than we did in other times and that we had some tests that were being validated. For scientific progress, we had to have valid measurement. (p. 3)

On Designing Two Forms for the Torrance Tests of Creative Thinking
I recognized at the outset that "creative thinking" is a very complex phenomenon. There are many ways in which a person may be creative. It seemed to me that a battery should sample these different modes. At first, the batteries were administered to a larger number of people and the scores were then factor analyzed and this information was used in deciding what tasks to retain. The verbal and figural tasks were quite different factorially, so we called one battery "verbal" and the other "figural." I was not surprised by this because we were dealing with two different modalities in thinking. (p. 83)

On Timing for Creativity Tests

The Torrance Tests for Creative Thinking could be given as an untimed test. This would probably be a good idea, but it would not be acceptable to most schools. Schools insist that the time allotted for testing fit within their schedules. (p. 84)

On Passions

Having a passionate love for something is probably the key to being courageous. (p. 129)

On the Need to Encourage "Disadvantaged" Children

In my 1968 keynote address before the National Association for Gifted Children, . . . I predicted then that in the future we shall have to depend upon creatively gifted members of the disadvantaged and minority cultures for most of our creative achievements. I explained that to be a part of the advantaged, mainstream culture, a person usually has to sacrifice too much of his or her perception of reality and search for the truth to make much of a creative contribution. Our creative achievers will be those who accept only those parts of the dominant culture that are true and hold to their individuality and their minority or disadvantaged culture. It will be they who possess the different element, the divine discontent, and the clearness of vision to see when the king wears no clothes. (p. 173)

On Gifted Children with Learning Disabilities

There are many people who cannot accept the fact that a person may be both learning disabled and creatively gifted. . . . In the third grade of one school, I tested a boy whose performance on the test was most impressive. . . . When I asked the teacher about him, I was told that the boy had just been tested and was brain damaged. In 1958, when I first tested this boy, I thought that brain damage was a misdiagnosis. Nevertheless, his parents engineered a change from a public school to the University of Minnesota Elementary School. There, his best friend was a boy who was equally creative and was a high achiever. He went ahead and earned his PhD in computer science. . . . His employer sent him and his five-person team to the University of Georgia. He remembered me and he and his family became good friends with me and my late wife. (pp. 359–360)

On a Personal Note

Now that I have had a stroke, suffered sòme brain damage, and done some research on hemisphericity, I can understand how he [the boy above] could have had some brain malfunctioning in the third grade and recovered by the fourth grade. I have recovered some of my left brain functions. The brain is a wonderful self-healing organism. (p. 360)

—*Excerpts from Torrance, 1995*

such as books, poems, and songs written or published; radio or TV scripts; musical compositions produced; original research conducted; in-service training of colleagues done; grants received; scientific papers presented; businesses begun, and patents, awards, and prizes received. What Torrance discovered was that a high score on the TTCT was even more predictive than measures of intelligence in forecasting creative achievements in adulthood. Further, the predictive value of these scores rose as the examinees matured. (Torrance, 1977) An additional (and larger) study conducted in 1981, with all students who had been enrolled in grades one through six in two elementary schools, yielded similar positive results.

Still, Torrance is the first to admit that a high score on the TTCT is not the ultimate reason that someone becomes creative. Rather, he asserts that the "motivation of the subject, his early life experiences, the immediate and long-range rewards, the richness of the environment, and other factors are important enough to make a difference in creative functioning" (Torrance, 1975, p. 285). This last comment is indicative of the type of thinking that causes others to value Torrance's work so highly. Joseph Renzulli, in discussing the TTCT, believes that they represent "a contribution to the literature that ranks along with the work of Alfred Binet, Hermann Rorschach, David Wechsler, and a few other true pioneers in measurement of human behavior" (Millar, 1995, p. 237). Also, Renzulli credits Torrance's ideas with directly influencing his own thoughts on the conception of giftedness and the need to expand our views of both who is gifted and how we should meet their needs.

The Good Life, *à la* Torrance: one that is both enriched and enriching, filled with surprises and glee and focused on accomplishing goals that are important and fun for the individual. It is obvious that Torrance accomplishes these goals regularly, both with children and expert educators who have, for decades, sought his personal, reflective guidance.

FUTURE PROBLEM SOLVING: TAKING CREATIVITY TO ITS HIGHEST HEIGHT

In 1974, in response to children's fears that they had about the world, and that they felt little control over being able to solve these crises, Paul Torrance initiated a program that has become international in scope and a common element of many schools: Future Problem Solving (FPS).

Using an organized system of creative thinking, Creative Problem Solving, developed by Alex Osborn in 1963, children in FPS are given an ethical, moral, or environmental situation (called "The Fuzzy") and are asked to tease out the main problem that they see within this situation. After brainstorming alternate solutions to the problem, the children use particular criteria (e.g., expense, feasibility, damage to others or environment) to judge their most acceptable solution. This solution, described in detail in writing, is then scored by judges for its merits.

The "teams" who arrive at the best solutions are invited to a state competition with other winning teams. There, they participate in other events involving creative thinking and the future, and the winning teams in each state (or nation) are invited to an international competition each May.

Open for children from all grade levels, only those in grades 4 and up participate in competitions. An especially intriguing adjunct to this is called Community Problem Solving, in which teams of children relate the FPS process to a community issue and act on the solution that they create.

If the truest test of creative thinking is to help others around you to improve their world, then FPS qualifies as an idea of Torrance's that may, indeed, change the course of time.

MENTORSHIPS AND FALLING IN LOVE

I'm not exactly sure why I dropped out of the honors math program. Part of it was my own fault. But I wished someone had counseled me to really stick it out. I think I would have liked a little more encouragement. For someone to say, "You can do it, Pam." My counselors seemed to accept it as perfectly natural that I would drop out of the math program and not take advanced biology. I think if I'd taken advanced biology in high school I would have realized how interesting I'd find it. (Arnold, 1993, p. 26)

Another of Paul Torrance's outstanding contributions is his emphasis on the importance of adult mentors for creative and gifted children. A significant someone who would encourage your interests and talents; who would ask you your preferences; and who would challenge you to explore options that you may not have considered previously—all elements sadly lacking in the case of Pam, presented above. Not wanting to see intelligent children select a career solely because of the salary and prestige it might bring, Torrance encourages mentorships so that exploration of a possible career path (or paths, most likely) will result in an intrinsic fulfillment, not just the extrinsic trappings of success.

Torrance's revealing longitudinal study of creative children and the career paths they chose (1980) showed to him that many subjects merely played "the games that others . . . presented, rather than using their own creative strengths" (p. 158). The sad conclusion that he drew was that both our society and its individuals lose out when one pursues passions that are not one's own. And because so many gifted and creative children are pulled toward careers that others deem to be good for them—law, medicine, business, computers—many of our most able youth are existing in fur-lined ruts: economically comfortable but emotionally barren way stations they call "careers."

Torrance's hope was that adults would take the time and care to instruct children to "play their own games and . . . engineer their lives so that they have a chance to do just this—play their own games in their own way, being the very best of whatever they are" (1980, p. 159).

More recently (1996), Torrance, Murdock, and Fletcher opened their book, *Creative Problem Solving Through Role Playing,* with Torrance's checklist, "How to Grow Up Creatively Gifted":

1. Don't be afraid to "fall in love" with something and pursue it with intensity. (You will do best what you like to do most.)
2. Know, understand, take pride in, practice, develop, use, exploit and enjoy your greatest strengths.
3. Learn to free yourself from the expectations of others and to walk away from the games they try to impose upon you.
4. Free yourself to "play your own game" in such a way as to make good use of your gifts.
5. Find a great teacher or mentor who will help you.
6. Don't waste a lot of expensive, unproductive energy trying to be well rounded. (Don't try to do everything; do what you can do well and what you love.)
7. Learn the skills of interdependence. (Learn to depend upon one another, giving freely of your greatest strengths and most intense loves.)

—*Preface*

An example of how valuable a relevant mentorship can be is Bob, a 28-year-old who took a "try before you buy" opportunity to explore a possible career path. He exemplifies all that Torrance hoped a mentorship would accomplish:

I think the most important thing I learned during my internship is that one's job doesn't have to be something that is only endured. It can also be pleasurable and fulfilling. When I first started working as an intern in an office, I had the notion that the rest of my life would be filled with jobs that I would take simply because I needed to pay my bills. I knew that some jobs would be better than others, but that the differences would be small because they were all work. I learned, by the example of the people I worked with, that this concept was wrong. I learned that people can care a lot more about work than how much money they make. I learned that a person's work is an extension of their mind and soul, and that the rewards are more than money. I learned that an office can be more than a workplace; it's a community of people. Work can be fun and interesting in ways I never could have imagined. (Galbraith & Delisle, 1996, p. 99)[1]

CONCLUSION

Willard Abraham, in his 1958 book *Common Sense About Gifted Children,* relates the story of a graduate student who took on the assignment of doing library research

[1]Excerpted from *The Gifted Kids' Survival Guide: A Teen Handbook* by Judy Galbraith, MA, & Jim Delisle, PhD, Copyright © 1996. Used with permission of Free Spirit Publishing, Minneapolis, MN.

to arrive at a definition of giftedness. He allowed himself 1 hour. One week and 113 definitions later, the student gave up this task.

It's a good thing that student didn't then take on the task of trying to define creativity, for surely, this would have been an even more arduous task. Still, thanks to the life and work of E. Paul Torrance, this elusive trait that we cannot define but we do recognize when we see it is more comprehensible than it ever would have been without his dedication and persistence. Also, the children and adult children who have benefited from his work on mentoring, Future Problem Solving, identification of culturally different gifted children, sociodrama, and so much more have seen their lives enriched in countless and important ways. If there ever was a Renaissance Man among researchers in gifted child education, it is E. Paul Torrance.

Paul Torrance is one of the few people I know who absolutely lives what he preaches. For example, I remember when he first got interested in future studies. He called me into his office and asked me to go to the library to see if there was anything written about the future. He told me that he had just read Alvin Toffler's *Future Shock* and wanted to explore more. He was practically giddy with excitement. And when I came back with an armload of books, the grin on his face just about stretched from one side of his office to the other. I could see his mind working overtime. He became obsessed with the future and all the possibilities for studying it. He could almost not think or talk of anything else for days. It was fluency, flexibility, originality and elaboration in action. A few days later, the Future Problem Solving Bowl was born and, with it, a whole new generation of futurists and their teachers."

—*Felice Kaufmann is a consultant and author
in gifted child education.*

. . . AND THE BEAT GOES ON

It is hard to imagine that thoughts and studies more original and purposeful than those done by Terman, Hollingworth, and Torrance will ever again be a part of gifted child education. This is not a slam on the intellectual descendants of these three pioneers in our field; rather, it is merely a realization that once a well is dug, there is little more to do than thank those who did the digging and continue to pursue the line of research that they unearthed. With few exceptions, that is what has occurred with the psychology and education of gifted children; the many good and sensitive individuals who have shaped our field as it exists today, did so on the backs of Hollingworth and Terman, and Torrance.

In the chapters that follow, you will be introduced to theorists, practitioners, researchers, parents, and others who have helped to shape the field of gifted child education into the somewhat cohesive field that exists today. You will be introduced to ideas that will startle you to think and, conversely, ideas that will simply startle you. You will read about ways to educate and understand gifted children that seem diametrically opposed to each other, and you will hear from the persons who put forth these ideas defending or explaining their points of view in their own words.

But here, in this chapter, you were introduced to the foundation of our field, which is, after all, a foundation of *people.* It is hard to imagine that this book on gifted children would have ever been written—indeed, any book on gifted children—were it not for the lives and work of three passionate individuals who took the time to fall in love with an idea and pursue it with intensity: Lewis M. Terman, Leta S. Hollingworth, and E. Paul Torrance.

GUIDING QUESTIONS FOR CHAPTER 1

1. When did the field of gifted child education begin?

2. How did the field of gifted child education emerge into a unique educational entity?

3. Whose work in gifted child education is the most groundbreaking of all?

CHAPTER 1 RESOURCES TO REMEMBER

Tannenbaum, Abraham J. (1962). *Adolescent attitudes toward academic brilliance.* New York: Bureau of Publications, Teachers College, Columbia University.

This monograph, designed to determine which type of student other high school students admire, is among the most interesting blends of education, psychology, and sociology that you will find anywhere. More than 600 students were asked which category of students they would prefer as friends—studious or nonstudious, athletic or nonathletic, brilliant or average in abilities. The results, hardly surprising, present a still-valid picture of the sometimes ambivalent attitudes that teenagers have toward others with extraordinary abilities. Well worth the search for it!

Terman, L. M., et al. *Genetic studies of genius.* Stanford, CA: Stanford University Press.

Volume 1: *Mental and physical traits of a thousand gifted children* (1925)
Volume 2: *The early mental traits of three hundred geniuses* (1926) by Catherine Miles Cox
Volume 3: *The promise of youth* (1930) by Barbara S. Burks, Dortha Jensen, and Lewis Terman
Volume 4: *The gifted child grows up* (1947) co-author: Melita Oden
Volume 5: *The gifted group at mid-life* (1959) co-author: Melita Oden

Trying to understand the history of gifted child education without knowledge of this body of literature is like trying to describe the taste of a fine Cabernet Sauvignon to someone used to drinking wine with twist-off caps: There will be only a vague comprehension of its depth and intensity. Do yourself a favor: Scan at least one volume of this series to get a "flavor" of the essence of this field of study.

Torrance, E. Paul. (1962). *Guiding creative talent.* Englewood Cliffs, NJ: Prentice Hall.

Of all the books available on the creatively talented person, this resource is my favorite. Torrance articulates clearly the societal benefits and drawbacks of being creative in a world that neither fully appreciates nor understands this type of individual. Poignantly, he articulates how and why educators and parents need to pay attention to the needs of the often-misunderstood child: the creative one.

UP, UP, AND AWAY

THE RISE OF THE FIELD
OF GIFTED CHILD EDUCATION

There is no doubt that the field of gifted child education was shaped initially by the great and extensive work of our fondest forebears, Terman, Hollingworth, and Torrance. However, as their individual and collective influence continued to be felt, more and different people, events, and coincidences began to take center stage, shaping this field of study into the diverse one that it is today. Often piggy-backing on each other's ideas and theories, gifted child educators have followed well the guidance of Sir Isaac Newton, who proclaimed that the reason that he knew what he knew about his world was because he had stood on the shoulders of giants who had come before him. In gifted child education, there have been many giants and more than enough shoulders to go around. This chapter intro-duces you to many of these people and their ideas.

THE RED SCARE

Perhaps no other single event catapulted gifted child education into public prominence as did a significant, and seemingly unrelated, occurrence in 1957: the Russian launch of the Sputnik satellite into space. During that Cold War era when the race to space occupied everyone's attention, the United States ended up on the short end of the scientific stick. There we were, the greatest na-tion on Earth, humiliated by a menacing enemy who, only a bit more than a decade before, had been our ally. That national amity, bitterly lost and now most reviled, pitted these two great nations—the United States and Russia—against one another in a spitting contest of global proportions. And with the Russians' successful launch of the first space satellite, they had won the brag-ging rights for spitting the farthest—all the way into outer space.

Tannenbaum, in recollecting the widespread, nationalistic panic in the United States present at the time, called the years immediately following Sputnik's launch, the years of the Great Talent Hunt, "a time when every possible effort was exerted at federal, state, and local levels to identify gifted children and to educate them to the limits of their potential" (Tannenbaum, 1983, p. 23). This spiraling of interest in anyone gifted was noted especially in the areas of science and mathematics, in which programs appeared almost overnight in an effort to train our young people to become the best thinkers of the next generation. Based more on fear and humiliation than on any altruistic sense that the intellectual needs of gifted children should be met, the sense of the time is summarized by Tannenbaum in a cogent, face-front manner: "Suddenly, the prestige and survival of a nation were jeopardized because the enemy's greatest minds of the day had outperformed ours, and the Russians capitalized on this coup by broadcasting to every nation on earth its success in reducing America to a second-class power at long last" (p. 17).

Thus began, in 1957, the most prominent and focused attention ever paid by our nation to the intellectual needs of its most gifted children. Also, the launching of Sputnik served as another first: the first time that gifted children entered the fray as political pawns for legislators and educators who could not decide (and still cannot decide today!) if the education of gifted children is the zenith of a society pledged to excellence or the nadir of a culture that was founded on the basis of egalitarianism.

But we're getting a little ahead of ourselves, because before reviewing in depth the influence of Sputnik and the rippling effect that it had on our nation's schools and psyche for more than a decade, let us return to calmer days, pre-Sputnik days, when the efforts to serve gifted children's needs were, at best, spotty and limited.

GOOD INTENTIONS OF A GROWING NATION

I wasn't ashamed of being a Quiz Kid, but talking about it (even to people who were genuinely interested) seemed like bragging. Once a kindly woman struck up a conversation with me on a train. "You sound like Ruthie Duskin," she said. I never let on that I was.

I wanted to be accepted for myself, not as a quiz whiz. I discounted my abilities; they seemed quite natural to me. The more I knew, the more I realized I did not know. Yet others seemed to assume I knew it all.

—*Personal reflection from "Ruthie," a long-running Quiz Kid from Chicago, in Feldman, 1982, p. 52*

One of the most fascinating aspects of gifted child education is the varied ways that it has been perceived through the decades due to the political, economic, and social climates present at the time. Consider these specifics:

- In the 1920s—the Roaring 20s— immigrants from other nations were beginning to leave permanent marks in their new-found home, America. The education of the many, rather than a select few able children, took top seed, despite a valiant effort by the Progressive Movement to make schools more accommodating for all levels of learners.

- In the 1930s, for a nation still reeling from an economic downturn that paralyzed even the powerful and moneyed, education was a luxury few could afford. It was work that brought in extra dollars, not education. Gifted education, with few exceptions, was regarded as a luxury for the lucky few who could afford a private school tuition.
- In the 1940s, with money more available (due, in part, to WWII's inclusion of the term *working mother* into our vernacular) and more children than ever being educated, enrichment for the masses was the norm. Gifted children, if they were not merely "grade skipped" (the most common provision of that era), were generally within classrooms grouped heterogeneously by ability. Little writing about gifted children and their education was done in the mid-1940s, our nation's attention and resources being directed elsewhere.
- In the 1950s, prior to Sputnik's launch, the special needs of gifted children were beginning to be addressed in various publications, with the implication that not enough was being done to serve the talents of these youngsters. Sputnik's launch catapulted this attention even more into the public's prominence. Also, the advent of television brought gifted children and adults into everyone's living room, with shows such as "Quiz Kids" and "The $64,000 Question." This was prime time for the field of gifted child education to rise from its long, quiet slumber.

> ## RULES FOR MAKING A QUIZ KID
>
> 1. Banish for all time the thought that the two-year-old chip off the block rates nothing but baby talk.
> 2. If three-year-old Johnny is always making a run for his father's fine coin collection, don't think you've done your part by slapping his hands.
> 3. There's not a mother or father who has not heard *What's that?* The stock answer is, "You're too young to understand." Maybe he is not too little to understand.
>
> —*Feldman, 1982, p. 21*

PRE-SPUTNIK ATTEMPTS AND INFLUENCES

Thanks again to the influence and success of Terman's and Hollingworth's work, some school-based provisions for gifted children began in earnest in some pockets of the United States. Edgar Dransfield was among the first to thoroughly investigate the benefits of enrichment programs for gifted children (Dransfield, 1933). In one experiment, Dransfield employed one highly trained teacher to work with gifted children—those with IQs of 110 and up. He also insisted that she take into account a child's home conditions and interests in setting up enrichment opportunities. Based on this information, the teacher then designed individual activities and readings that would broaden each child's knowledge of the world.

As reported by Burroughs (1979), Dransfield's conclusions about enrichment proved its benefits:

> School became an immensely interesting place for [these students]. The enrichment teacher was used to her very limit, class work improved, and at the same time the pupils were not removed from the social unit in which they were leaders and in which they continued to lead to the end of their elementary school years. (Dransfield, 1933, as reported by Burroughs, 1979, p. 28)

Dransfield's second experiment took the units of study developed by his enrichment teacher—units on myths, folklore, colonial life, migration, and others—and gave them to regular classroom teachers, to see if they could use them effectively with gifted children, by allowing them to work on the units independently. His results, although not as impressive as the results shown by his enrichment teacher, did show some student growth in academics, especially in the early elementary years.

Another program for gifted children, and certainly the nation's most extensive, began in Cleveland, Ohio, in the 1920s. Started at Denison School with noted educator Henry H. Goddard as a consultant, the program was called the "Major Work" program, the term coming from the fact that the children identified for these classes would be doing "major work projects" instead of the typical work required of them in their classroom environment, including acceleration in math, science, and foreign languages. In evaluating the need for such a program, Goddard wrote:

> Rarely has this work been carried below the fifth grade. In the Cleveland schools, while the work began in the fourth and fifth grades, gifted children are now often picked from the first grade. Thus these bright children do not wait for recognition until they have learned habits of idleness by being forced to mark time for three, four, or five years; they are given the opportunity at the very beginning. (1928, p. 4)

The long-term benefits of Major Work has been studied periodically, with two extensive reviews done by Walter Barbe of Major Work graduates (1955, 1957). He found that of the 456 graduates who had responded to his questionnaire about Major Work (representing a 15-year period), 91% of the men and 53% of the women had achieved at least some level of college education and nearly 44% of the entire group held college degrees. These remarkable results (even more impressive when considering the time period covered), coupled with the positive findings regarding the subjects' mental health and adjustment, showed the long-term benefits of such extensive, specialized services for gifted children.

The Major Work program, with its provision of self-contained classes for gifted children at the elementary level and magnet schools at the middle and high school levels, remains in effect today, more than 70 years after it began—a remarkable achievement by any yardstick measurement.

One study of the status of education of gifted children was released in 1941. This document, from the National Educational Association, analyzed the presence of gifted programs in several hundred U.S. high schools, yet the data, already outdated on its publication, did little to draw attention to the need for gifted education options in our nation's schools. However, another document, released in 1950 by the Educational Policies Commission, chastised our nation for paying scant attention to the needs of gifted children, calling this lack of special programming a "social waste." The commission made several recommendations for improving this sad educational lot, and the next year, thanks to one of our field's most forward thinkers, Paul Witty, positive changes for gifted students began to occur more rapidly.

"ALL CHILDREN ARE GIFTED" FINDS ITS FIRST ALLY

In 1951, under the auspices of the New York–based American Association for Gifted Children, a book called *The Gifted Child* was published. Its editor, Paul Witty, had gathered together prominent thinkers of the day to write about the characteristics of gifted children and how schools could best meet the needs of these able few.

. . . Except for one thing—to Paul Witty, the gifted were not few in number. To him, giftedness was a widely distributed human trait. In a sort of professional defiance of then-common logic, Witty arrived at a definition of giftedness far different from any that had been professed before. In 1958 he wrote, "We consider any child gifted whose performance in a potentially valuable line of human activity is consistently remarkable" (p. 62). What did this new definition, written by one of our field's most respected leaders, imply for a society that had heretofore relegated giftedness to jumping through test-based hoops with the greatest of ease? For one thing, because it came so soon after the Sputnik scare, it caused a rift between those who saw giftedness as a rare human trait and others, such as Witty, who believed it to be distributed to the population in far greater proportion. Also, it made special programs for gifted children a questionable endeavor, for if one could be gifted mathematically, artistically, linguistically, personally, or in any other way that was not socially deviant ("gifted

> The Cleveland Major Work Program should be credited with setting a standard for gifted education that has yet to be surpassed. Failure to recognize Dorothy Norris, longtime supervisor of the Program, is unfortunate, for she led a program where gifted children were recognized and provided for within the public school system. One particular factor that stands out, and one which I always believed deserved further study, was that even though a thorough evaluation was made to determine the gifted population at about the age of six, the process was repeated after several years—and still more children were identified as gifted. The question that arose in my mind was "How did this group, that had somehow escaped detection at the age of six but only several years later were deemed to be gifted, differ from the group who had been identified earlier?" Mrs. Norris used the analogy of removing cream from the top of milk which, of course, resulted in more cream rising to the top. My observation was that those identified earlier tended to be more verbal, perhaps right brained, while those identified later tended to be less verbal (glib?), but in many instances, actually brighter.
>
> —*Walter Barbe is a retired professor of reading and gifted child education.*

criminals" didn't qualify, presumably), then what kinds of programs would benefit this broad array of students? Perhaps *everyone* should be allowed to take advantage of the educational opportunities usually reserved for gifted children?

Witty did not suggest this conception of giftedness merely to incite controversy in a field already rife with it. Rather, he based his interpretation on experiences he had and experiments he conducted beginning in the 1920s. For example, it was Witty who began studying play habits of gifted children as a way to document their intellects (Witty & Lehman, 1927), and he was among the first to suggest that to find intelligence in Negro children or children whose life experiences were limited by economic disadvantage, observations would be more prudent criteria than test scores (Witty & Jenkins, 1934). It was Witty who reported in the first longitudinal study of its type that maladjustment among gifted boys and girls was possible, especially for boys, and especially as they matured (Witty, 1940). In this same study, Witty questioned the wisdom of identifying creative children with IQ tests:

> If by gifted children we mean those youngsters who give promise of creativity of a high order, it is doubtful if the typical intelligence test is suitable for use in identifying them. (p. 504)

And it was Witty who, in 1955, looked at the *behaviors* of gifted children that might lead others to suspect that, indeed, they held high promise. Among his characteristics to consider are

- the early use of a large vocabulary, accurately employed
- keen observation and retention of information about things observed
- early interest in calendars and clocks
- early discovery of cause-effect relationships
- ability to attend or concentrate for a longer period of time than is typical of most children

Witty's insights, and his clarion call to question what seemed so obvious, may have been heard for a longer period of time had Sputnik not arrived on the scene. However, in the mad scramble following this historic event, Witty's interpretation was just not, shall we say, politically correct anymore. It

---

My recollections of Paul Witty cover a period of more than 25 years, first as a student of his (from undergraduate through graduate school), to colleague and dear friend. Dr. Witty brought dignity to the teaching profession, for he was both a scholar and gentleman. But his respect for teachers would shine through so clearly that the Northwestern University campus in the summer was packed with teachers from throughout the country who had heard him speak and came to study with the master. One of the speakers at his retirement dinner said it best when she described him as truly a "gentle man."

I recall so well discussing with Dr. Witty his early articles on the gifted in which he reacted against Dr. Terman's use of the word "genius" in his studies of gifted children. Clearly, Dr. Terman had come around, for the 25-year follow-up avoided the word genius and was entitled "The Gifted Child Grows Up." Dr. Witty spoke, wrote and thought from a position of sensitivity, great knowledge and intelligence, combined with a secure background. His early studies on giftedness among Black Americans reflected his unwillingness to accept prejudice in his search for truth. His early article on drive, a neglected trait in the study of the gifted, continues to be vitally important, but is virtually unknown today.

—*Walter Barbe is a retired professor of reading and gifted child education.*

was the era of tests! It was the era of science! But it was an *error* to dismiss Witty's ideas as wholeheartedly as they were. In fact, when one looks at *today's* views of intelligence and intelligent behavior (see chapter 3), there are more parallels to Witty's work than at any other time since it was first published.

THE GUILFORD CHALLENGE

Around the same time that Paul Witty's remarks about giftedness were making the rounds in the educational community, another set of whispers turned into roars, thanks to three researchers who cried out for more attention to be given to a neglected area of study: creativity.

Joy P. Guilford, a man whose work on examining the structure of the intellect (SOI) gave the world a theoretical view of intelligence as being fluid and multifaceted, composed of at least 120 separate elements (more on SOI in chapter 4), was president of the American Psychological Association in 1950. As the focus of his keynote address to that year's APA convention, Guilford challenged his audience to do something that few others had suggested before: to study the area of human creativity. Specifically, he challenged his fellow psychologists to study how to identify creativity in children and, then, to develop ways to foster it in all individuals.

REFLECTIONS ON J. P. GUILFORD'S SOI MODEL

Guilford and I were walking across campus at the University of Southern California discussing my Master's thesis, "Developing Intellectual Abilities Through the Teaching of French," and I said to him, "I believe that your model may be more than a model. It may be a theory and if so, it is in the wrong discipline."

"What makes you say that, and in what other discipline?" He was surprised—he had not expected that the model could be used because that inferred one could "teach" intelligence.

"Education," I said, "not psychology. Teachers need a way of understanding how children learn. Because when children don't learn, teachers can fail them, and that is fatal for an identified gifted child."

"But Mary, these abilities have not been obtained on children."

"But children do have these abilities. I know. I've seen them in my children—some of them, at least—and in other students. Remember, until you began the factor analytic studies, these abilities were not known to exist in adults, either."

"Well, Mary, we must find out . . ."

continued on the following page

continued from the previous page

In 1965, Guilford retired, but he never stopped searching for more factors. Guilford had been a middle child, born on a farm in Nebraska. His brother wanted only to run the farm. His sister was considered "retarded" and was not accepted at the one-room school because she could not learn to read, yet she could remember recipes and change them arithmetically to feed all the farmhands. She ran the house efficiently. Guilford was the scholar and was graduated at sixteen.

He did live to see his model applied and to learn through the use of the SOI research findings, that his sister was not retarded but had severe semantic learning disabilities.

Guilford had studied under Thurstone and helped define factor analysis. He lived until 1987, to over 90 years of age. He lived to see his model applied to the gifted, to the learning disabled, and through the SOI tests, to see that career possibilities could be based on computerized profiles of intellectual abilities.

"That means a lot more to me than men walking on the moon," he said.

—*Personal reflections by one of J. P. Guilford's students, Mary Meeker*

FIGURE 2.1
■

Excerpts from J. P. Guilford's Speech, "Creativity," to the American Psychological Association at Pennsylvania State College, September 5, 1950

I discuss the subject of creativity with considerable hesitation, for it represents an area in which psychologists generally, whether they be angels or not, have feared to tread. It has been one of my long-standing ambitions, however, to undertake an investigation of creativity. (p. 444)

There are certain aspects of creative genius that have aroused questions in the minds of those who have reflected much about the matter. Why is creative productivity a relatively infrequent phenomenon? Of all the people who have lived in historical times, it has been estimated that only about two in a million have become really distinguished. Why do so many geniuses spring from parents who are themselves very far from distinguished? Why is there so little apparent correlation between education and creative productiveness? Why do we not produce a larger number of creative geniuses than we do, under supposedly enlightened educational practices? These are serious questions for thought and investigation. (pp. 444–445)

The neglect of this subject by psychologists is appalling. The evidences of neglect are so obvious that I need not give proof. But the extent of the neglect I had not realized until recently. To obtain a more tangible idea of the situation, I examined the abstracts of the *Psychological Abstracts* for each year since its origin. Of approximately 121,000 titles listed in the past 23 years, only 186 were indexed as definitely bearing on the subject of creativity . . . in other words, less than two-tenths of one percent. (p. 445)

Some of you will undoubtedly feel that the subject of creative genius has not been as badly neglected as I have indicated, because of the common belief that genius is largely a matter of intelligence and the IQ. But . . . I believe that creativity and creative productivity extend well beyond the domain of intelligence. (p. 445)

I am not opposed to the use of the multiple-choice or other objectively scorable types of test items in their proper places. What I am saying is that the quest for easily objectifiable testing and scoring has directed us away from the attempt to measure some of the most precious qualities of individuals and hence to ignore those qualities. (p. 445)

Various branches of the government, as you all know, are now among the largest employers of scientific and technical personnel. These employers, also, are asking how to recognize the individuals who have inventive potentialities. The most common complaint I have heard concerning our college graduates in these positions is that while they can do assigned tasks with a show of mastery of the techniques they have learned, they are much too helpless when called upon to solve a problem where new paths are demanded. (p. 446)

I am convinced that we do teach some students to think, but I sometimes marvel that we do as well as we do. In the first place, we have only vague ideas as to the nature of thinking. We have little actual knowledge of what specific steps should be taken in order to teach students to think. Our methods are shotgun methods, just as our intelligence tests are shotgun tests. It is time that we discarded shotguns in favor of rifles. (p. 448)

We all know teachers who pride themselves on teaching students to think and yet who give examinations that are almost entirely a matter of knowledge of facts. . . . Let us recognize where facts are important and where they are not. Let us remember, too, that the kinds of examinations we give really set the objectives for the students, no matter what objectives we may have stated. (p. 448)

By way of summary, it can be said that psychologists have seriously neglected the study of the creative aspects of personality. On the other hand, the social importance of the subject is very great. Many believe that creative talent is to be accounted for in terms of high intelligence or IQ. This conception is not only inadequate but has been largely responsible for the lack of progress in the understanding of creative people. (p. 454)

—*Guilford, 1950, pp. 444–454*

Of all the topics Guilford could have selected to address in his presentation, why creativity? At least one answer resided in his own recent experiences with the testing of pilots for WWII. Guilford found that when pilot candidates were examined for potential by the U.S. Army, the much-respected IQ tests qualified many who were still unable to pass their course work. However, when Guilford began testing people on measures other than IQ—he used assessments that were more related to what it took to actually fly airplanes—he found a much larger pool of qualified candidates who, once airborne, possessed the skills they needed to fly successfully.

This was the beginning of his career-long mission to break up the monopoly of intelligence as being measured by IQ alone and to get his research associates worldwide to do the same. What better forum, what larger audience, than APA?

Almost two decades later, Guilford's landmark book *The Nature of Human Intelligence* (1967) elaborated on research that was then available on how creativity, especially divergent production (which includes such abilities as flexible thinking, synthesizing, analyzing, reorganizing existing ideas, and evaluating them), must be used if our world is to benefit from the multiple talents possessed by people but not measured solely by IQ. He found this to be especially important when analyzing the abilities of individuals from other than the mainstream culture, as explained eloquently in a review of Guilford's work by Ernesto Bernal (1979), an expert on educating gifted children from diverse cultures:

> If one considers the 120 abilities represented in Guilford's Structure of the Intellect Model . . . is it so difficult to believe that no society is able to develop all of them to any great degree in all or most of its citizens? It is more reasonable to believe that every culture selectively reinforces a more limited number, thus producing in its members some specialization of cognitive abilities, leaving others to happenstance. (p. 398)

The rippling effect of the Guilford challenge to pursue the study of creativity and its measurement as assiduously as had been the study of IQ several decades before was astronomical. Study after study appeared in the ensuing years, making the 1950s a hotbed for the study of creativity as an important element in determining anyone's intellectual prowess.

If one study could be singled out as having the most impact of all—and, indeed, that *can* be done—it was the research led by Jacob Getzels and Philip Jackson in their 1958 article "The Meaning of 'Giftedness'—An Examination of an Expanding Concept." This study, surely one of the most cited in the history of our field, compared University of Chicago High School (a *very* high-powered place to be a student!) students who were highly creative but had lower IQs with those who had high IQs but lower scores on creativity measures. Among the findings of this study was that the students who were highly creative completed class assignments that were as exceptional as those of their higher-IQ counterparts. This finding added even more fodder to Guilford's contention that one must look beyond IQ to notice potential eminence. (Another not-so-surprising finding was that teachers preferred students who were highly intelligent to those who were highly creative. The reason seems pretty obvious: Intelligent kids, generally speaking, are more academically oriented than their creative classmates.)

The Getzels and Jackson study does have its detractors. Gallagher (1979) finds it odd that these high school students, with an average IQ of 127, would ever be considered "low"; indeed, such an IQ is very close to what generally qualifies one as gifted! Further, Newland (1976) pointed out the Getzels and Jackson used tests of divergent thinking to determine one's creativity level, "playing down the fact that such measures tended to correlate with test-measured 'intelligence' in the 30s" (p. 70).

Yet despite these justifiable questions and criticisms, there is no doubt that the field of giftedness and creativity was enriched by the research done in the 1950s focusing on the refinement of both of these concepts, a refinement that is still in process today.

THE ROEPER LEGACY BEGINS

In 1939, George and Annemarie Roeper emigrated to the United States, escaping the horror of the oncoming Nazi invasion of Europe. Two years later, they founded the Roeper City and Country School in Bloomfield Hills, Michigan. Basing its guiding philosophy on a boarding school in Germany run by Annemarie's parents, Drs. Max and Gertrude Bondy (and the school that both Annemarie and George attended), the Roeper School soon became known for its respect of children of all persuasions—in fact, it was one of the nation's first private schools ever to be racially integrated.

The curriculum of the school centered on the legacy given to the Roepers by Annemarie's parents. Her mother, a psychoanalyst, believed that the emotional well-being of children must be considered if they are to grow fully and in a

---

In 1967, E. Paul Torrance developed the Ideal Child Checklist, a list of descriptors of children that educators were asked to complete. In response to the question "What kind of person would you like the children you teach to become?" educators were to place one checkmark next to the qualities they felt were desirable in children, two checkmarks next to those most important, and to cross out any characteristics that they considered undesirable. A sample of the 66 characteristics include

•adventurous, testing limits •affectionate, loving •attempting difficult tasks •courteous, polite •critical of others •domineering, controlling •emotionally sensitive •guessing, hypothesizing •haughty and self-satisfied •intuitive •neat and orderly •never bored, always interested •popular, well liked •refined, free of coarseness •self-assertive •sense of humor •stubborn, obstinate •truthful, even when it hurts •unwilling to accept things on mere say-so •visionary, idealistic

Once completed, the Ideal Child Checklist begins to show teachers patterns of traits or behaviors that they consider important in educating children. Self-reflection on what this means for students in their classrooms who display *less than* ideal behaviors helps to give teachers some insights into potential biases that they bring into their classrooms.

—*A full copy of the Ideal Child Checklist can be found on page 161 in* Gifted and Talented Children in the Regular Classroom *by E. P. Torrance and D. Sisk (1997).*

DON'T HOLD SUMMITS WHEN YOU CAN HOLD AN HORIZON

George Roeper passed away in 1992, and many in the current Roeper community never had the opportunity to know him. George loved horizons, both natural and intellectual. He saw them as registers for the imagination, limits to be outrun, points of endless possibility. George was kind and wise and the most empathetic person I have ever seen. Talking with George was unlike talking to anyone else. It was as if he had known you forever, better than you knew yourself; it was as if he were listening for whatever there was behind the words, waiting to be understood.

George saw education as the defining act of what it means to be human. Educational theory for George was the theory of everything: psychology, philosophy, politics, history, and science were all drawn together in a vision of identity and relationships.

It is in the practice of imagining the next horizon that sets George apart from others, that makes The Roeper School such an extraordinary place, and that will prepare us to adapt successfully in a future we can make.

The horizons he held are there for us. Let's hold a horizon for George.

—*Personal reflections from Chuck Webster,*
former head of The Roeper School

healthy manner. Max Bondy, an art historian and educator, perceived the need for children to see themselves as a part of a global community, a community that emphasized art, culture, and philosophy. Thus, beginning with these traditions, the Roeper School started with high ideals but a humble enrollment—just a handful of nursery school children attending classes in the top floor of an old house.

As the reputation of the school grew, so did the enrollment. The Roepers created an educational program that gave equal emphasis to all areas of a child's development—physical, intellectual, social, emotional, and creative (Roeper, 1995). They instituted an ungraded structure, with children free to move between groups depending on their individual needs and strengths. The integrated school day, so common in the British system of teaching, was superimposed at Roeper. As Annemarie writes, "We had at last found a useful approach to education for life" (Roeper, 1995, p. 115).

Still, prior to the mid-1950s, Roeper was not a school exclusively associated with the education of gifted children. That change came as a result of a meeting in 1956 that took place between the Roepers and A. Harry Passow, one of one field's finest thinkers. As Passow recalls:

It was in June, 1956 that I first met Annemarie Roeper. At the invitation of Annemarie and George Roeper, I had arrived to spend a week at their City and Country School in Bloomfield Hills, Michigan, chairing a meeting that was to plan the "conversion" of the school to one for gifted children. I think there were about ten of us, including Annemarie and George, who spent that week together in what I still recall some 32 years later, as one of the most challenging, exciting activities I had ever been involved in.

Two years earlier, I had initiated the Talented Youth Project at Teachers College, Columbia University, and my colleagues and I had already designed and started to implement research and development in the field of the gifted. But, here we were being asked by the Roepers to design a school of our dreams! And dream we did that week as we explored every aspect of what a school for the gifted should be—from its guiding philosophy, to the selection of its students, to its curriculum design and instructional strategies, to its staffing, to its overall ethos and climate. . . . While the school is known as a school for the gifted . . . what [the Roepers] are advocating is appropriate for *all* children. The "cooperative, non-hierarchal philosophy and system of education" which is embodied in the Roeper School—the modern learning community—has meaning for *all* educators. (Passow, in Roeper, 1990, Preface)

The Roeper School, and the philosophy that undergirds it, were as ahead of their time then as they are now. Children are given options of classes that they may take, even in the earliest grades. "Town meetings" are scheduled frequently so that children can air their concerns—as can teachers—as to ways to improve the school climate. Teachers serve as interdisciplinary instructors and as counselors to children. Teams of teachers plan units of instruction. Staff and students participate in the hiring and firing of other staff members. Applicants are required to spend time in the classroom prior to admission—a high IQ is not the sole criterion to decide whether a child, even a very gifted one, will benefit from the Roepers' unique form of education.

In their own quiet ways, the Roepers have shown others how gifted children (all children?) can be educated in a respectful and legitimate manner. But their influence is not merely with the establishment of their school. As Linda Silverman (1995) recounts:

Eleanor Roosevelt visited the Roeper City and Country School, was impressed, and invited Annemarie and George to her apartment in Manhattan shortly afterwards. *Sesame Street* might not have existed without Annemarie. The creators of *Sesame Street* consulted with her in designing their grant application, and Annemarie's ideas were influential in getting the program funded. When studying medicine in Vienna, Annemarie lived across the street from Sigmund and Anna Freud, and after consulting with both of them, she became the youngest person accepted to study psychoanalysis with Anna Freud. Unfortunately, the course had to be canceled as both Annemarie and the Freuds were forced to flee Vienna when the Nazis invaded Austria. (p. x)

COMMENTS FROM CHILDREN WHO ATTENDED ROEPER SCHOOL

"I have been going to Roeper for 5 years and it is special to me because it is non-competitive and that affects me because it makes it so I can mess up and always try again."

"It makes me feel like I'm not just a little kid. When I was 7, I thought the only way to solve a problem was to fight it out. I now know that isn't a good way."

"In the future, I may put my children in Roeper, or if I build a school, I may make it like Roeper."

AND THEIR PARENTS

"My son can write a paper with 35 footnotes, and he also knows that everybody deserves his respect."

"There's no division between jocks and intellectuals. It's assumed everybody has a body and a mind."

—*Delisle, 1991, pp. 96–97*

In an era of Sputnik scares and a philosophy that seemed to treat gifted children as anything but the sensitive beings they were, the Roepers' commitment to the whole child remained intact. To this day, on their two school campuses in southeastern Michigan, more than 600 students, nursery school through twelfth grade, benefit from their lifelong commitment to educating gifted students with compassion.

WHAT SPUTNIK DID—AND DIDN'T—DO

One Russian satellite in 1957 launched more than the beginning of the space age; it also ushered in our nation's most extensive and orchestrated effort toward meeting the needs of gifted students within public schools.

This was the setting: Once Sputnik rocketed into the heavens, U.S. politicians did what they often do so well—they looked for a scapegoat to blame why an embarrassing event occurred. The easiest targets, of course, were schools and teachers, for if educators were doing the jobs they were hired to do, and students were learning courses that tested their mental muscles, then *we* would have been first in space.

There was some evidence to back up these claims that America was letting its greatest minds off too easy. For example, Wolfe's book *America's Resources of Specialized Talent* (1954) reported that not enough Americans were being prepared in the areas of natural sciences, health, teaching, and engineering. Also, with only one-half of all high school graduates in the top quarter of their class going to college, and with only 3% of those capable of completing a PhD choosing to do so, the "brain drain" seemed real. This information, coupled with the spurious "evidence" from a 1959 U.S. report on Soviet education (Tannenbaum, 1983) in which it was stated that the typical Soviet high school graduate had completed 10 years of math, 5 years of physics, 4 years of chemistry, 1 year of astronomy, 5 years of biology, and 5 years of a foreign language, caused U.S. citizens to question whether they were, indeed, doing enough to challenge all students, including the gifted. (Whether *every* Russian student received

A GIFTED WOMAN; A SPUTNIK SUBJECT

What began as a simple question—why had certain gifted women failed to fulfill the rich promise of childhood?—became a research project, then a counseling program for gifted girls and women, and finally a book: *Smart Girls, Gifted Women.* Identified as gifted soon after the launch of Sputnik in 1957, these girls (and myself as well, since I, too, was so singled out) were given, for the next seven years, a special curriculum designed to foster leadership and success. When we met for a reunion ten years after graduation from high school, their stories intrigued me, and my studies of their lives became the basis of *Smart Girls, Gifted Women.*

I have come to believe . . . that although women's socialization and education do indeed shape them to be more concerned with connectedness and intimacy, that gifted women still bear the responsibility for actualizing their talents. It is not an either/or world, and women do not have to choose between vocation and intimacy.

—*Kerr, 1985, pp. ix, xvi*

FIGURE 2.2

New York Times Newspaper Headline of Sputnik Launch

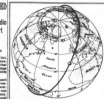

this rigorous education was questionable, but it would have been rude to ask during our time of national crisis.)

So, an explosion took place: an explosion of interest, an explosion of money, an explosion of programs. Gifted students' needs were finally going to get fully addressed within every one of America's schools!

Well . . . kind of.

Indeed, all-new forms of math and science curricula were developed, including the School Mathematics Study Group (SMSG), Physical Science Study Committee (PSSC), and Biological Science Curriculum Study (BSCS). In addition, many other new and intriguing courses were established for high school students, including "The Mathematics of Science," "Opera Production," "Integration of the Arts," "Structural Linguistics," and "World Affairs" (Tannenbaum, 1979). Surely, with this plethora of new and challenging options, more U.S. students than ever would become the standard bearers for the world, boldly going where no teen had gone before.

But several events conspired to work against Sputnik as having a long-term, positive impact for gifted children and their education. First, many of the schools in which these rigorous courses were to be taught still possessed antiquated equipment and laboratories—it's tough to teach astrophysics with little more than a Bunsen burner! Further, without adequate training on how to teach advanced content in new ways (and who had time for training when the Russians were nipping at our scientific heels!), teachers often found themselves unable to interpret this scientist-designed curriculum for their students. Third, it is difficult to impose brand new, different, and intensely rigorous material on students in high school (where most of the Sputnik-era programs were focused) without considering what students would have needed to learn in earlier grades to succeed in later years.

Yet it could be argued that these problems could have been overcome in time. The reason they were not may be because of one other flaw in the design of our Sputnik-inspired programs: America initiated them because it *had* to, not because it *chose* to. As a nation, we were scared, and the decisions made at times of crisis are often made to accommodate short-term fears rather than long-term needs. So, as the U.S. scientists worked overtime to get a satellite up to compete with Sputnik (they were, of course, successful) and as school-based programs crashed and burned due to the problems mentioned in the previous paragraph, interest in making wholesale changes in our schools—for gifted students or *any* student—waned as quickly as it had waxed.

Certainly, some of the innovations that took place in secondary schools have lasted even until today—advanced courses for the most academically able students, a comprehensive selection of courses to tap the interests and talents of many types of students, an emphasis on course selection as related to intended career goals—but who is to say that these changes would not have occurred *anyway,* as merely a natural transition from one generation's educational philosophy to the next?

Sputnik's influence on gifted education is analogous to the launch itself: a spectacular send-off, surrounded by excitement, followed by a mad rush to action, followed shortly thereafter by a return to more of the same. If only the Sputnik era had incorporated a *philosophic* rationale for educating gifted children to the best of their abilities in addition to its *political* agenda, its long-term impact may have been stronger.

Then again, maybe not, for America soon entered the tumultuous 1960s, a time when, indeed, it was *not cool* to promote gifted children and their education.

A SLICE OF AMERICAN PIE

The 1960s started out as calmly as the 1950s ended. Donna Reed was still everyone's favorite TV mom, Ricky Nelson still looked too young to shave yet he was old enough to lose his heart after saying hello to Mary Lou, and Elvis was still as thin as the plots of his too-many movies starring Shelly Fabares. But as Bob Dylan presaged, something was blowin' in the wind, and the societal changes that would ensue affected all aspects of American life, including our schools.

The early 1960s—the Camelot years—showed the nation and the world that it was okay to be smart. John F. Kennedy was young, savvy, and popular, and he surrounded himself with advisors who looked and acted very much as did he. The collective impression given was that academic success would be rewarded and intellectual pursuits were worth the energy that it took to achieve them. Even the moon was within reach, a promise made to our nation that although Russia may have won the first space skirmish, *we* would win the space race war: A man on the moon by 1970 was Kennedy's promise to a nation wanting so much for it to be so.

And then, the music died.

The changes that began to take place once an assassin's bullet killed our national innocence were frantic, almost schizophrenic. Where just years earlier the accepted societal standard was to locate future space scientists and give them whatever they needed to succeed, the new thinking was that this was self-serving and discriminatory. "Why give more to those who already have so much?" was a typical societal response when it was suggested that gifted children had special learning needs.

Now, attention was focused on children and families who struggled to maintain even the barest of minimums in their lifestyle and education. What emerged were two important movements that grew side by side and by leaps and bounds: special education and the Civil Rights movement. To some extent, these two issues were not new; rather, in the 1950s and before, they lay dormant, victims of a society whose energies and interests were directed elsewhere. But in their 1960s heyday, the aura surrounding these two powerful issues was enough to overshadow most progress made in Americans' collective thinking about gifted children. Indeed, anything that smacked of elitism or privilege didn't fit our

ALEXINIA BALDWIN: HER LIFE AND EXPERIENCES

On Identifying Gifted Children from Minority Groups

The first time that black students in Birmingham, Alabama were ever tested was when they were tested for special ability programs for the first gifted program that would be for black children. Children from the majority culture had been tested for gifted programs for years! When schools became integrated, teachers found out that there were different textbooks in the black community from those in the white community. So my students didn't have the kinds of information they needed in order to pass the tests which were designed to assess the material and skills in books they didn't even have!

On Her Experiences with Grade Skipping

I started to school when I was 4 years old and entered high school at age 11. I was pushed through and felt that I missed a lot. I got accelerated but didn't get the kinds of in-depth knowledge I needed. I missed a lot, but teachers assumed that I would be able to accommodate.

On a Dream Deferred

I was a solo cornetist in high school and college. Growing up in a segregated society, I would not be able to continue in the symphony orchestra of my city, but since there were no black symphony orchestras, I had no outlet for my ability. The alternative was that I could play in a jazz band at night, but my mom encouraged me not to do that, so I lost my interest and skill with the cornet and concentrated on the piano. I was always a child who worked outside of the usual lines and I dreamed dreams that my peers didn't dream.

On Teaching

I started teaching as a music and physical education teacher. The school was old and run down and soon to be torn down, but I always told my kids that in spite of their surroundings, they could be anything they wanted to be. Many were poor kids, but I was there to show them the possibilities of being great. I had them doing ballet, making their own costumes and writing their own music. I knew that many of these children had talents that were not being recognized. They had something on the ball . . . teaching music might have shaped my feeling about children within the classroom, because I could see a kid who might not have been so good in math but yet still had the ability to excel elsewhere.

On Receiving Her First Opportunity in Gifted Education

Federal money was available to provide programs for the gifted—it was 1965 or 1966—and the city school administrators needed to provide programs that included minority schools. Who would be the teacher of a class for the black gifted students? I was the one selected, perhaps because I had classes that involved students with hands-on items, and the outside world was brought into the classroom through their frogs, birds, turtles, and so forth. So, I tested and selected 25 students for the class, even though I didn't know a whole lot about education of the gifted. I used common sense and read books to start the first class for gifted black students in Birmingham.

On Beginning Her Doctoral Program in Gifted Child Education

A lot of programs for reading, math and science were receiving federal grants, but these were not of particular interest to me. And then, across my desk came this brochure from Joseph Renzulli, announcing an advanced graduate program for teachers of the gifted. I said, "This is what I want!" I had always wanted to get my doctorate and this was my opportunity! My daughter thought that her mother had lost her mind because she was so determined to take her away from her home, her grandmother and her friends, and go off to somewhere she had never heard of before.

My friends and neighbors were concerned that I was going to drive alone from Alabama to Connecticut. I had never driven out of the state by myself—had never driven more than 200 miles by myself—but I just hooked the trailer to my car, practiced how to back up in my driveway, and drove, scared to death, to Connecticut. And I never returned to Alabama to work.

On Human Abilities

There are some human characteristics that go across the board. You can conceptualize regardless of what color you are and the level of conceptual ability determines the amount of brain power you have. You might be conceptualizing on something that is not in the classroom, but you're still able to conceptualize.

On Being a Minority Leader in Gifted Education

The first thing needed for minority leaders in education of the gifted is to have confidence in themselves. They need to be aware of their own feelings about the whole concept of giftedness. They can't vacillate if they are going to make an impact. The next thing they will have to do is to be able to articulate their views. We need to be ready to argue with supportive evidence for the kid who can't measure up on an IQ test. There is also a need to help those with whom they are colleagues understand that within the African-American communities there is often just as much divergence as there is outside of these communities. Minority scholars who enter this field will need to have a tough outer shell and arm themselves with research skills to support their positions, because there will often be rejection along the way.

—Dr. Alexinia Baldwin is a full professor in the Department of Curriculum and Instruction at the University of Connecticut.

national psyche anymore, so, with few exceptions, gifted children and their education were exiled to a very cold back burner.

In hindsight, which is always 20/20, this de-emphasis on anything gifted should have been easy to foretell. The almighty IQ test was still the instrument of choice to identify (or, more important, to *not* identify) children as gifted, and then as now, very few persons from minority or poor backgrounds scored a 130+ IQ. Thus, gifted programs (then, as now) included a preponderance of children who looked very much like the 1950s sitcom families: white, middle class, intact. Also, gifted children fell victim to a seldom-discussed-in-polite-company-but-always-present reality: Few persons give sympathy to smart kids. Sure, it is easy to negate the needs of someone who is taking good advantage of his or her God-given talents when a child with physical or intellectual handicaps is vying for limited attention and dollars. How easy it is to deny access to special programs for highly talented children, when a class of inner-city youth with minimal resources and marginal dreams vies for equal attention. In the dog-eat-dog world that sets educational funding and program priorities, gifted children always fall short when they are compared with others who appear less fortunate.

Is this comparison *fair*? Is it *right* to pit one child's needs against another's, rather than seeing the needs as just being *different,* instead of more or less important? Of course not! Still, when reality is pitted against theory, it is often the latter that loses. As put so well by John Gowan, a 1960s leader of gifted child education of much renown: "Gifted education is a passionless issue in a society geared to emergencies."

So, although President Johnson's Great Society and the late-1960s backlash against anything elitist and middle class did not bode well for accelerated programs in our schools, there were still some who refused to allow the needs of gifted children to be denied completely. These people, as much pioneers as those who forged our field decades earlier, deserve recognition and r-e-s-p-e-c-t for choosing to act and talk at a time when silence was a more reasoned response.

GETTING SOME SATISFACTION

Throughout gifted child education's history, most of the emphasis was on teaching gifted children in ways that capitalized on their talents. Little attention, though, was paid to the needs of those who knew gifted children the best: their parents. This began to change in the 1960s, thanks to the work of several persons.

Ruth Strang, a Teachers College leader in the Leta Hollingworth tradition, emphasized the social and emotional needs of gifted children. Her 1960 book, *Helping Your Gifted Child,* provided parents with some reflective thoughts regarding the role that gifted children play both at home and in society. Specifically, she warned against

1. parental pressure and exploitation of a gifted child's talents, in which parents emphasize the intellect at the expense of the emotions
2. parental indifference to the fruition of their child's talents
3. financial limitation caused by poverty or the unwise expenditure of funds that might otherwise have enhanced a child's intellectual progress
4. parental desire for the child to be perfect or equally advanced in all areas—an unreasonable and potentially dangerous stance to assume
5. parental boasting and possessiveness, as parents live out their own unfulfilled dreams through their gifted children

Strang's advice to parents was to be sensible and realistic about the needs of gifted children and to believe that their own insights and observations of giftedness in their children were valid. Speaking more like a seasoned grandmother than the powerful researcher she was, Strang reminded parents that the gifted child "has to be himself; he must not become a martyr to your own unfulfilled ambitions" (1960, p. 29).

Gertrude Hildreth, another passionate leader whose career spanned several decades, including the 1960s, refuted the notion that giftedness was a trait or behavior that looked similar in all identified individuals. In *Introduction to the Gifted* (1966), she questioned the use of IQ alone to identify giftedness and proposed that specific talents be noted through teacher and parent observations of a child. Further, Hildreth's work focused on how gifted children do not constitute a single intact group; that, indeed, giftedness can be a very broad range of abilities, including those of profoundly gifted children and of children whose abilities, although strong, are not so extreme.

In relation to curriculum, the name that rose to the top in the 1960s is Virgil S. Ward, a no-nonsense writer who believed in, and applied, stringent standards to the field of gifted child education. Ward was (and is) an advocate of a rigorous curriculum that tested the intellectual mettle of even the strongest student. His *Educating the Gifted: An Axiomatic Approach* (1961) provided a philosophic rationale for *differential education of the gifted* (DEG) that included an emphasis on a classical curriculum by using a scientific approach to instruction as its basis. Thus, by using the laws of learning that govern all content domains—exposure, repetition, understanding, conviction, and application—Ward believed that all areas of a gifted child's education could be addressed: intellectual, emotional, physical, and social. Probably considered an "elitist" by some, Ward emphasized the importance of educating gifted students separately from others, of reminding them that they will assume leadership roles as adults, and ensuring that those who taught them were gifted themselves. Ward undergirded each of his instructional ideas with philosophic principles and corollaries, and his work is truly academic in nature. Also, it is the basis of much of the current emphasis in our field that education of gifted students provides a degree of differentiation that respects the knowledge that they possess and the characteristics that caused us to call these students "gifted" in the first place.

BORN TO BE WILD: FITTING IN AND ACTING OUT

Two other areas of interest that came alive in the socially conscious 1960s were the reaction to gifted children by others and an increased effort to comprehend the problem that has come to be called "underachievement."

First, how gifted children are accepted by others. Of all the labels that can be applied to children who learn differently than others—learning disabled, mentally retarded, gifted—the one that would seem to have the most positive reaction would be "gifted." After all, to be able to conceptualize beyond one's years or to use and understand vocabulary that classmates do not yet comprehend would surely be a social bonus; a "positive deviance" that sets one apart in a good way.

Guess again.

As Gallagher and Gallagher (1994) state, America has a love–hate relationship with gifted people. They are loved for what they can do to better society, but they are disliked because, in doing so, they make many others feel inferior. This dichotomous reaction is even present with children, as pointed out by researchers in the late 1950s and early 1960s. For example, Gallagher and Crowder (1957), while commenting on the overall superior adjustment of gifted children, implied that some gifted children are popular only when they downplay the presence or extent of their intellectual talents—in effect, they "play dumb," or more accurately, they "play average." Coleman's study (1961) of the adolescent culture showed that the pull of social acceptance is so strong among teenagers that many will sacrifice their academic achievement to fit into the mob psychology that anything different is weird.

Tannenbaum (1962), in a fascinating study with distinct sociologic overtones, described eight imaginary high school students in short, three-sentence descriptions. Each description included information on the student's academic ability (brilliant or average), school effort (studious or a slacker), and sports abilities (athletic or nonathletic). Thus, the eight combinations that emerged ranged from the brilliant, studious athlete to the average, nonstudious nonathlete, and every other triple combination in between. Then, Tannenbaum asked 615 eleventh graders from New York City

---

STUDENTS' VIEWS ON BEING SMART

So often I feel that gifted kids are defined by their smartness, by teachers, other kids, parents—Nobody should be defined solely by their intellect. (Paulita, 18 years old)

Some of the people I know care more about their hair than world hunger. They just aren't concerned about anything beyond their own little world. (Anonymous, 13 years old)

It's a great advantage to be gifted. Sometimes you feel like you're really alone, but you're not. It's great to be your own person, and you shouldn't try to be like everyone else just so people will like you. It's very important not to let your talents slip through your fingers by trying to fit in with everyone. Rather, you should find friends who complement your abilities. (Rene, 15 years old)

How can parents help gifted students? By lowering their expectations. That way they are always surprised! (Jonathan, 12 years old)

—*Excerpted from* The Gifted Kids' Survival Guide: A Teen Handbook *by Judy Galbraith, MA, & Jim Delisle, PhD, Copyright © 1996. Used with permission of Free Spirit Publishing, Minneapolis, MN.*

to rate these hypothetical classmates on 54 character traits. His results were fascinating: The composite student who was most socially acceptable was the *brilliant, nonstudious athlete* whereas the least admirable combination was the *brilliant, studious nonathlete*. His conclusion? Although academic ability *alone* did not appear to have an effect on one's peer status, it was more acceptable when accompanied by athletic prowess, but *far less* acceptable if embodied in a student who admitted to being studious. The obvious implication is that a gifted nonathlete who studies—which is, of course, the societal stereotype of the gifted nerd—is a social leper, removed from acceptance in an adolescent context in which taking pride in one's academic achievement is risky business. Hardly an anachronistic study, similar results were found in Calgary, Canada, by Mitchell (1974) and most recently by Schroeder-Davis (1995) in Minneapolis, Minnesota.

A second area of intense study in the 1960s was underachievement, wherein researchers formulated many studies to determine what it was that caused some students to succeed in school whereas others of similar ability fell by the academic wayside. Raph and Tannenbaum (1961) reported on more than 90 empirical studies of underachievement that had been conducted since 1931, yet the only conclusion they could come to was *no* conclusion. The results of the studies were contradictory, making generalizations about ways to prevent or reverse patterns of underachievement impossible. Throwing up their hands in empirical frustration, Raph and Tannenbaum concluded that the only accurate statement that could be divined from this research analysis was the obvious: Achievers succeeded in school; underachievers did not.

Several years later, Raph, Goldberg, and Passow (1966) tried again to understand the complexity of underachievement. In a 2-year, hands-on study of underachieving high school boys, the researchers split their group of 64 tenth-grade students into two separate classes. All the boys had IQs of at least 120 yet had ninth grade marks below an 80% average. Additional data about the boys' personalities, interests, and attitudes toward teachers and schools were also obtained. Then, the boys were placed in two different settings. One group was placed in the same social studies class with a teacher who was aware of their backgrounds and abilities and who showed a genuine interest in taking on the challenge of teaching 31 "underachievers." The other students were spread throughout the school's remaining social studies classes,

> Keeping in mind that developed talent exists only in adults, a proposed definition of giftedness in children is that it denotes their potential for becoming critically acclaimed performers or exemplary producers of ideas in spheres of activity that enhance the moral, physical, emotional, social, intellectual, or aesthetic life of humanity.
> —*Tannenbaum, 1983, p. 86*

> I would like to think that we have come to understand the multiple dimensions of cognitive and affective growth so that our goals for the gifted go beyond high academic achievement and include creative, productive behaviors of many kinds which represent the realization of potential in many socially valuable areas.
> —*A. Harry Passow, in a speech to the National Association for Gifted Children, 1986*

with no special attention provided or information given to their teachers about their underachieving status.

Ironically, at the end of the first term, the *nonselected* students had significantly higher grade point averages than did the experimental group! Still, the experimental teacher, thinking that good things take time, continued the study for another term. In the end, the experiment ended up lasting 2 full years, with 28 of the original 31 experimental students remaining in the intact class.

Still, the overall results were disappointing, as the final grades for the experimental subjects averaged a dismal 73%. Most of the students were not accepted by the colleges of their choice, several had already dropped out of school, and overall, few planned to continue their academic pursuits.

Interestingly, and with a generation of additional research on underachievement now under our belt, the study by Raph et al. yielded some fascinating and important results. First, the original instructor of the experimental group was replaced after 1 year by a more stringent, "toe-the-line" type of teacher. The resulting academic defeats of the majority of students seem to point to the importance of establishing a long-term relationship and rapport between teacher and student, especially for students at risk for academic failure. Second, the original teacher respected and understood each of the boys as an individual, a concern that did not seem particularly important to their tenth grade teacher. Surely, recent research on the importance of classroom climate that leads to student success implies that the students may have felt little urge to achieve, given the "factory" atmosphere present in their classroom—produce or get out! Last, this study shows the difficulty of intervening in a child's academic life once a problem has been allowed to fester for a number of years. Obviously, these students did not *begin* to underachieve in tenth grade but probably much earlier, perhaps even in the primary school years. Early intervention, preventive intervention, may have shown far different results with these poor lost boys.

Raph, Goldberg, and Passow contributed greatly to our understanding of the concept of underachievement and interventions that might take place to ameliorate it, even if the results of their 2-year study did not appear enlightening when it was first completed. As noted in later chapters, their important work underpins even today's study of this important topic.

UP, UP, AND AWAY: A MAN NAMED MARLAND USHERS IN THE 1970s

How ironic that the one individual who is often credited with changing the face of gifted child education in the 1970s was someone who had done very little direct work himself on behalf of gifted children! In a classic case of being in the right place at the right time, Sidney P. Marland prompted a resurgence of interest in gifted children that continues even today. Here's how it happened.

As the 1960s ended and gifted children, as a group, were as neglected a special population as any, the U.S. Congress added Section 806, "Provisions Related to Gifted and Talented Children" to the then-pending Elementary and Secondary Education Amendments of 1969. This congressional prodding mandated, among other things, that a national study be conducted to determine

FRED WEINTRAUB

On the Politics of Gifted Child Education

The Marland Report got started at a luncheon where I asked Roy Milleson, "What do you think about legislation for the gifted?"

"Let's get a bill together," he said to me.

That was 1968, and the "Gifted and Talented Children's Assistance Act," sponsored by Senator Jacob Javits, was planned. That's what led to the Marland Report.

On the Usefulness of Policy

I've looked at the relationship between government policy and practice. Policy is something that empowers, but you must have people locally who are willing to use that policy. If we want effective government policy, we need people who are willing to implement it.

On Infighting in the Gifted Education Field

In the 1970s, the Council for Exceptional Children wanted to include gifted and talented into educational policy. The problem was not any opposition outside the gifted and talented community, the problem was fighting *inside* the gifted and talented community! After the Marland Report was released, the fighting got worse, as everyone was playing "Who's King of the Hill?" That's always been part of the problem. When it's an issue of scarce resources, people fight each other over them instead of working together.

On the Current State of Education

The strength of American education is our diversity, and every time we try to standardize it, education goes downhill! I panic when people talk about "the program" instead of "the kids." Higher math just doesn't work for some kids, and some kids will never reach particular standards, while others will surpass the standards easily! Kids at the highest level of test performance can't drive scores up, because they can't score any higher. The issue is not standards, it's kids.

We inherited regular education from the Germans and special education from the French. *Vive la différence!*

—Fred Weintraub, now retired, served at the head of governmental relations at the Council for Exceptional Children.

Among the individuals who provided testimony to the U.S. Congress during the Marland Report hearings were Kay Bruch, Virgil Ward, Joseph Renzulli, Abraham Tannenbaum, James Gallagher, Jacob Getzels, A. Harry Passow, and William G. Vassar.

what was (and what was not) being done to meet the needs of the top 3 to 5% of the school-age population.

Enter Sidney P. Marland. As then-U.S. Commissioner of Education, he invited expert testimony to address the intellectual, social, and emotional well-being of gifted children. He also gathered statistics on how many gifted children were being served in special school programs and how school personnel ranked the importance of meeting the needs of the gifted population. Once these facts and opinions were gathered, the commissioner issued a 2-inch-thick, two-volume government document that presented back to Congress all that he had discovered. This report, known both then and now as the Marland Report, is actually a collection of the best thinking at the time about gifted children, a "Who's Who," and a "What's What," that prodded growth in the field of gifted child education. Not as splashy or meteoric a rise as caused by Sputnik, the Marland Report caused more of a slow burn: a gradual increase in our nation's acceptance that gifted children, too, have special educational needs.

Among the findings that Marland reported to Congress were

1. Only about 4% of the estimated 2 million gifted children nationwide were being served by special programs.
2. Differentiated educational programs had a very low priority in most schools. In fact, 57% of school administrators reported that *no* gifted children existed in their schools or school districts.
3. The lack of knowledge about gifted children—who they are and what they need—is widespread among educators (see #2 as proof).
4. State legislation to provide for gifted children was limited and, when present, most frequently merely represented intent, not mandates, for services.
5. Identification of gifted children was hampered by three factors: cost, apathy, and hostility on the part of some school personnel.

Given the scope of the problem, it might seem logical that millions of dollars would now flow into the coffers of gifted child advocates. Well, not exactly. Rather, what transpired was a series of inexpensive (by federal standards) priorities that primed the pump for local and state agencies that wished to improve services to gifted children. These provisions were

1. systematic in-service preparation of teachers and administrators about the nature and needs of gifted children
2. financial support—seed money—for both research and the development of experimental programs for gifted students
3. establishment of a federal Office of Gifted and Talented, to coordinate the above efforts and to serve as the clearinghouse (eventually, the ERIC Clearinghouse on the Gifted and Talented) from which information on exemplary programs would be funneled

The total funds available for the above services was $290,000 in 1972, growing to a whopping $1.1 million in 1974—this last figure representing an investment of about 60 cents per gifted child nationally, based on the figure of 2 million gifted school-age children.

Still, this was enough of an impetus to start a nationwide movement toward providing both in-school services and professional training options on the needs of gifted children. Indeed, where in 1972, only 10 states had any professional staff assigned part-time or more as a state consultant for gifted programs, by 1977, 40 full-time state consultants were employed. Also, by 1977, the percentage of gifted children being served in special programs had risen from the 4% figure of 1971 to 12%—still a small number, but a sizable increase, nonetheless (Burroughs, 1979). And Zettel and Ballard (1979) reported that 31 states had increased their financial appropriations for gifted programs by more than 50% since the release of Marland's report and that 42 states were providing some type of in-service training to its teachers and administrators about gifted children.

Whichever analogy seems most appropriate—"The Little Engine That Could," the Biblical saga of the loaves and the fishes, or "The Sound of Music"'s signature song "Climb Every Mountain," it is obvious that a little national emphasis and a few federal dollars returned self-respect to a field that had lost much of it and initiated programs that multiplied many times over the school

THE ISSUE OF SOCIETAL DISCOMFORT WITH GIFTED STUDENTS

People oppose gifted education because it is not democratic. It's the whole egalitarian attitude that an awful lot of folks still have, even today. This whole nonsense that we have currently about heterogeneous and homogeneous grouping in classrooms is an example. I can't believe it when high school principals tell me they cannot do homogeneous grouping of gifted students. Life is nothing but a group of homogeneous groups—whether political or religious or educational.

I met with parents in a very affluent school district one night. One woman was talking about how everyone should be treated equally. I asked her if she had trash collectors in her town. She said, "Oh, yes. And they are very good ones!" I said back to her, "That's fine. Now, tell me the last time that you invited those trash collectors to your Christmas cocktail party." Her face just fell.

If you believe in heterogeneous grouping of students, that's fine. If you believe in homogeneous grouping, that's fine, too. But if you're trying to tell me that you're going to equalize education by putting everyone together in the same place, you're wrong.

—*William G. Vassar is the former director of gifted education programs for the state of Connecticut.*

provisions available to our nation's most able youth. Sidney Marland, now deceased, provided a shot in the arm for a field in desperate need of a booster.

. . . AND ANOTHER THING

Marland's report prompted much growth in the field of gifted child education. Arguably, though, the report's most lasting impression was the definition of giftedness that it provided as a model for states searching for a new one. This definition, revised several times since, is still the basis of a majority of states' definitions of giftedness:

Gifted and talented children are those identified by *professionally qualified* persons and who, by virtue of outstanding abilities, are *capable* of high performance. These are children who *require* differentiated educational programs *and/or* services beyond those normally provided by the *regular* school program in order to realize their contribution to *self and society.*

Children capable of high performance include those with demonstrated achievement and/or *potential ability* in any of the following areas, singly or in combination:

1. General intellectual ability
2. Specific academic aptitude
3. Creative or productive thinking
4. Leadership ability
5. *Visual or performing arts*
6. Psychomotor ability

—Marland, 1971, p. ix; emphasis added

Taking apart this definition (the italicized words), we can note the following attributes:

- *Professionally qualified:* This *implies* that the teachers, psychologists, or others doing the identification of gifted children know something about their characteristics. This was still not always the case, but the notation of professional qualifications was an added and necessary bonus.
- *Capable:* Not only could you be gifted by *demonstrating* your abilities, you could be gifted if you showed the *potential* for high talent. A big change in thinking about giftedness as involving potential, not just production.
- *Require:* At last, a view of the development of giftedness that gets away from the stereotypic one that "gifted children will learn on their own." "Not so," say the Feds.
- *And/or:* One of the few negatives about this definition, as it allows schools *not* to provide special programs, but rather, a provision or two that may be less than satisfactory.
- *Regular:* The standard for what were determined to be "above and beyond" provisions for gifted students became the school's regular program. A good idea, for school districts' regular classroom options vary considerably nationwide, implying that gifted programs, likewise, will always differ from one community to another.
- *Self and society:* Finally, the Sputnik-era view of giftedness as something that is solely a societal commodity to be exploited for the betterment of our nation is softened. Now, "the self" becomes an important reason to progress as far as you can.
- *Potential ability:* Mentioned above under *capable,* here is a second iteration of giftedness as being something that could be hidden inside a child, not necessarily brimming over for all to see.

- *Visual and performing arts:* People often ask where the "talented" is in gifted child education. In this federal definition, at least it appears with equal weight with the headier interpretations of intellectual or academic ability.

After sifting through this definition, some researchers still found it too limiting or confusing. Renzulli (1978) argues that some of these six categories are observable through performance (e.g., visual and performing arts) whereas others are more process centered (creative thinking). Gallagher (1979) sees a danger that each of the six categories will be seen as totally separate when, in fact, much overlap might occur. Piirto (1994) questions why this definition of giftedness (and others) omits any mention of personality characteristics that might play a vital role in the fruition of gifts or talents.

Still, as a first attempt by a body as large as the federal government, this definition gave both a direction and a set of parameters that were certainly more generous than Terman's view of giftedness and far more specific than Witty's important but vague interpretation. Are there flaws in it? Many thought so. But it served as a launchpad for gifted programming efforts that, through the ensuing decades, were far more substantial than the one provided by Sputnik.

The Marland years were exciting, formative years in gifted education. It began in 1961 in Washington, DC, when at dinner Mr. Marland shared his vision of needed federal support with several of us state directors of gifted education. Later, we testified at regional hearings and wrote sections of his 1972 Report to Congress.

At my suggestion in 1962, the state directors formed the Council of State Directors of Programs for the Gifted, which became a national unifying force. After 1972, states and our nation benefited greatly from federal grants which enabled us to:

1. showcase *uniquely appropriate* and *qualitatively different* teaching and learning
2. train thousands of teachers to orchestrate the development of higher intellectual and creative skills
3. produce special frameworks and curriculum guides
4. persuade publishers to differentiate their materials, and
5. support legislative, school-board, and professional-organization efforts in combating mediocrity and promoting excellence.

—*Paul Plowman, specialist in gifted education and investigator for the California Department of Education*

ANOTHER BRICK IN THE WALL: THE REEMERGENCE OF UNIVERSITY RESEARCH ON GIFTED CHILDREN

In the 1930s, the bicoastal powerhouses of Stanford University and Teachers College, Columbia University, ruled the majority of research done in the area of gifted child education. Throughout ensuing decades, Teachers College continued to dominate, as Hollingworth was followed by Miriam Goldberg, Abraham Tannenbaum, A. Harry Passow, and others. Stanford, Terman's home, continued to provide some direction, but interest there remained targeted to the 1,528 "geniuses" who were now entering adulthood rather than to the gifted population in general.

But thanks to Marland's call for increased graduate-level programs for advanced training in gifted child education, several additional universities became "major players," offering Master's and doctoral programs to interested educators. Among the most prominent were Purdue University, the Universities of Georgia and Connecticut, Johns Hopkins University, and of course, Teachers College. Indeed, many among the crop of gifted child educators now holding leadership positions nationwide can trace their professional roots to one of these five universities.

DR. JOHN FELDHUSEN: WORLD-CLASS EDUCATOR

On His Introduction to the Field of Education

I never thought about being gifted and talented. In fourth grade, I was seated in class next to the encyclopedias, and I would read them when I finished my work. On the last day of school that year, my teacher gave me the old encyclopedias. . . . When I applied to college, I got into the University of Massachusetts and Cornell. I went to Cornell because at least I had heard of it! While there, I applied to West Point and got in. I entered in the summer of 1945. Realizing West Point was not for me, I returned to Carroll College in Waukesha, eventually getting my degrees at the University of Wisconsin. My first teaching job was in a military academy at Lake Geneva, Wisconsin. I took it because I knew I would have small classes—but the kids were bright, so it also became my first exposure to gifted children!

On Meeting the Giants

I began graduate school in 1954, and it was then that I first met Julian Stanley. Later, while I was teaching in Eau Claire, Wisconsin, I heard there would be a lecturer from the University of Minnesota. It was E. Paul Torrance. I'd not paid attention to his work previously, and I went with skepticism, but instead, I got captivated by him and his enthusiasm. My first forays into research involved creativity, nursing education and juvenile delinquency.

On Identification of Talents

This summer I am going to teach for the last time a course on identifying gifted children. That course has changed so drastically over the last several years toward more and more precise talk about how we can identify specific talents in children. The gifted movement depended so much on tests and rating scales. Now, the great shift is to more use of direct observation, portfolios, and a whole range of instruments, *but not just tests!* Tests are still good and helpful in the academic realm, but that is about all they are good for. . . . If a teacher or parent or uncle or aunt or grandfather or whoever it is says "Please give Donny a chance, I think he's got something going," we must never turn him away.

On Creativity Testing

I have been quite critical in recent years, particularly in the creativity testing realm. I think that we went through a period of incredible optimism that we were doing wonders or working miracles with creativity tests and training. Then we began to look more critically. I think the major shift that has occurred is the recognition that creativity, whatever it is, is a set of processes—cognitive, personal and social processes—but that beneath it is a knowledge base. In testing for creativity, we need to remember the importance of one's knowledge base.

On Talent Development

My faith has become very strong that if children have an opportunity, a challenging opportunity, in a focused kind of learning experience—a class in math, computers, nursing, astronomy, archeology—they may begin to think "maybe I've got something going here." And if they have a teacher who is attuned to recognizing developing talents, then something very worthwhile will happen, both in identifying talents and nurturing them.

On the Importance of Mentors

I am convinced that it would probably be worthwhile for people in the gifted area to go out of their ways to help children meet and have interactions with famous people, particularly people who might relate to their interests. I've seen very little effort in that direction. I think we are so sold on long-term mentoring, but the brief meetings with famous people is akin to mentoring. It's kind of like a mentor who sticks with you vicariously.

On Programming for Gifted Students

I am not an inclusionist with reference to gifted and talented kids. They need to be in environments that are high-powered and challenging if they are going to go on to high level achievement. I don't like pull-out programs, either. I know a boy who was identified as gifted and put in a pull-out gifted program. He told me, "I really love mathematics, but there's no math in our program. I can't see why they put me in it!" That case and similar experiences convinced me that pull-out programs often completely disregard students' talents. So, I advocate full-time classes for the gifted because there, you can identify individual talent strengths.

On His Life

My life has been such a magic carpet. I'm almost alarmed at times how neatly and productively things fall into place for me. If I make a mistake, the alternatives often turn out far better than the thing I began with!

—Dr. John Feldhusen is a Robert B. Kane Distinguished Professor
of Education at Purdue University.

A STUDENT RECALLS

I clearly remember the day in 1979 that I sat next to John Feldhusen at a rather uninspiring (okay, it was boring) meeting on the Purdue campus. I won't identify the group or the topic, but I will say that John was uncharacteristically disconnected from the discussions. He was busily making notes on small pieces of paper and passing them over to me. Although I can't recall the various titles, I do remember the words "Super Saturday." The next thing I knew, Ann Robinson, Pam Clinkenbeard and I were sitting on the living room floor of a friend's house shuffling through applications of 96 children from 14 counties who wanted to come to Purdue on Saturday mornings to attend challenging classes for bright children. This was one of the earliest activities of the Gifted Education Resource Institute. John had a vision—to create an organization to provide services to talented children, their parents, their teachers and other educators who were interested in this population of students. In GERI, John gathered a group of Purdue faculty and eager graduate students and set out to meet the varied needs of those groups. The adventures began!

—*Dr. Penny Britton Kolloff teaches, consults, speaks, writes, and mentors in areas of gifted education.*

At Purdue University, under the leadership of Dr. John Feldhusen, the emphasis is on the practical: What can schools and teachers do to best meet the needs of gifted children? Taking on an eclectic approach to answering this question, Feldhusen and his students examined the benefits of enrichment programs versus acceleration (grade skipping); the academic and social rewards of Saturday enrichment programs (Feldhusen & Wyman, 1980); and the role creativity played in the everyday curriculum presented by teachers (Feldhusen, 1981). Because Feldhusen had a strong background in educational psychology, his studies provided careful documentation of what worked best—and why. Combining these features into a program called the Gifted Education Resource Institute (GERI), Feldhusen and his students served (and continue to serve) as valuable resources for both educators and parents. GERI's "Super Saturday" enrichment programs for children have been the model for countless other enrichment programs that exist throughout the nation. Additionally, Feldhusen introduced his Three-Stage Model of Gifted Education, a model that emphasizes process thinking skills (creative and convergent thinking), creative problem-solving abilities, and the development of independent study skills that would allow the child to complete self-selected projects (Feldhusen & Kolloff, 1981). The Three-Stage Model was one of several similar models developed during the early rush for devising practical methods for working with gifted students in schools.

At the University of Georgia, long known for its work on creativity due to the presence of E. Paul Torrance, another emphasis started to emerge in the 1970s. Thanks to the presence of two other professors, Drs. Catherine (Kay) Bruch and Mary Frasier, the identification of gifted children from minority backgrounds, especially African Americans, became a prime focus. Bruch considered ways to find talent potential in African American students by asking their peers to name schoolmates whom they considered leaders outside of the school setting (Bruch & Curry, 1978). Also, Bruch initiated efforts to identify giftedness in minority populations by using an abbreviated form of the Stanford Binet Intelligence Test, focusing on those parts of the test that emphasized more creative responses. She found that African Americans excelled in nonverbal tasks of creativity and visual activities and were highly creative in the areas of move-ment, dance, and other physical activities (Bruch, 1975). From these findings, she suggested using these indices for pinpointing giftedness and creativity in African American children. Further, Bruch also was instrumental in assisting Torrance in planning and implementing the initial stages of the Future Prob-lem Solving Program.

Mary Frasier, a "new arrival" to the University of Georgia in the mid-1970s, conducted similar studies of identification of giftedness in black children, but she also addressed a seldom-discussed topic: the dilemma faced by many African American children who are being asked to succeed in a predominantly white, middle-class culture that may hold values different from their own. She sug-gested counseling for students who are caught in the bind of wanting to express their talents while remaining true to their own family and community values (Frasier, 1979).

The University of Connecticut is, today, the best known of the universities that focus on graduate-level programs for the gifted and talented. Home of the National Research Center for the Gifted and Talented (since renamed the Neag Center for Gifted Education) since the early 1990s and site of the internation-ally recognized "Confratute," a 2-week summer immersion into gifted child ed-ucation that began in 1978 and has served thousands of educators, the univer-sity's gifted program has been under the guidance of Dr. Joseph S. Renzulli for almost three decades.

In the early years of Renzulli's prominence, he focused his efforts on the fruition of creativity in a classroom setting. His workbooks, *New Directions in Creativity* (Renzulli, 1976a), were teacher-led activities that tapped into many of the elements of creativity that Guilford reviewed in his Structure of the In-tellect Model. Also, his *Scales for Rating the Behavioral Characteristics of Superior Students* (1976b) became the most commonly used rating form for identifying diverse talents in students. Among the 10 scales' categories are "learning char-acteristics," "creativity," "motivation," and "artistic abilities."

In later years, and continuing even today, Renzulli focused his efforts on con-ceptualizing giftedness as a set of behaviors, rather than a set of high test scores (more on this in chapter 3). Also, in relation to his new idea of what made gifted-ness, he designed a program model for gifted education called the Enrichment Triad Model, a three-part system of instruction based on student interest and focusing on the student production of professional-quality products (more on this in chapter 5). Most recently, he and his colleague Sally Reis have developed the Schoolwide Enrichment Model, an attempt to take the best of gifted educa-tion practices and infuse them into an entire school building and district.

Whether you agree with Renzulli or not—and he has many supporters and more than a few vocal detractors—there is no arguing that he is this genera-tion's most influential educator in the field of gifted child education, even if he does not fully believe in the concept of gifted *children,* but rather, gifted *behav-iors* of children.

Meanwhile, not too far away from Renzulli's rural Connecticut landscape, was situated a noted researcher and educator who was as far removed from Renzulli's line of thinking as one can be: Dr. Julian Stanley, of Johns Hopkins University. Not only did Dr. Stanley state that gifted children *existed,* he also believed that their brilliance was readily identified by standardized tests that challenged them and that enrichment programs did little, if anything, other than postpone their boredom slightly. Further, Stanley believed that once found, these highly able students should be allowed to progress through their formal schooling as quickly as possible. But how Dr. Stanley's interest in gifted children was first sparked is a fascinating story of happenstance.

In 1971, Stanley founded SMPY, the *S*tudy of *M*athematically *P*recocious *Y*outh, yet SMPY's genesis was prior to then. The reason for its founding was a serendipitous event that had occurred 3 years earlier: Dr. Stanley was presented the dilemma of a brilliant eighth-grade boy named Joe Bates. Joe was participating in a summer computer program at Towson State University in Maryland, when his instructor noticed Joe's extreme intellectual precocity. This instructor, Doris Lidtke, contacted Dr. Stanley, asking for help. As Dr. Stanley recalls, "I was somewhat hesitant and perhaps even reluctant at first to get involved: there were too many other pressing duties. But I did, and my life and career were never to be the same again."

What Dr. Stanley did was to administer to Joe the College Board Scholastic Aptitude Test (SAT), several College Board achievement tests, and some other exams, "because I felt that I needed to know more about Joe in order to work with him effectively. Joe was only 13 years old, yet he was taking college courses. My reasoning was that, if he could handle college level material, then why not college level tests?" Joe's scores were, in Dr. Stanley's words, "startlingly excellent," which sparked this lifelong interest and commitment in children who excelled academically.

Thus, as SMPY developed, its main purpose was to locate junior high school students within extraordinary talents in mathematics and provide them with vastly accelerated school options to take advantage of these gifts. Finding these mathematical geniuses was easy: Stanley continued to administer the Scholastic Aptitude Test-Mathematics, usually reserved for high school juniors and seniors, to seventh-grade students (over the objections of school principals and many of his colleagues). Those who scored at least 500, which was the 51st percentile of entering college freshman, represented the 99th percentile among their seventh-grade colleagues; they were invited to take summer classes in mathematics at the college level. It was Stanley's view that one of his 3-week courses, taught 5 to 6 hours per day, was equivalent to 1 to 2 years of high school algebra and geometry. By eighth grade, Stanley contended that his SMPY students were ready for calculus (Stanley, 1982).

This so-called radical acceleration allowed students a number of options: They could take college courses part-time, enter college early on a full-time basis, take Advanced Placement courses to earn college credit while still in high school, or skip one or more grades entirely, especially in junior high school.

Stanley's rationale for beginning SMPY was simple: Talented math students are bored in grade-level courses and, therefore, seldom have a positive view of the field of mathematics. As Stanley (1979) himself said, "Often, highly able youths are not aware of the extent of their slowdown, because it has been their lot from kindergarten onward."

Beginning in 1979, Stanley initiated a series of national "talent searches" in the hope of locating gifted students in math and in verbal areas (using the verbal portion of the SAT). Situated at universities in Arizona, California, Colorado, North Carolina, Illinois, Iowa, and Maryland, these ongoing searches give high-achieving youth the opportunity to use their summer to study in their areas of strength at some of the nation's most esteemed institutions—Duke, Northwestern, and Johns Hopkins, to name three.

The SMPY model is not without its critics. Some have questioned whether the price paid for such rapid advancement through one's adolescent school years has a detrimental effect on social and emotional development. Benbow, a colleague of Stanley who is now conducting a longitudinal study of early SMPY participants, argues vehemently that such is not the case and that "acceleration benefits students academically while not detracting from social and emotional development" (1992, p. 116). Other researchers, even those who are fans of acceleration,

THREE VIEWS ON ACCELERATION FROM STUDENTS WHO KNOW IT WELL

Although skipping a grade was advantageous in meeting my intellectual needs and was probably a good move in the long run, I often wonder what effect that experience had on me socially and emotionally. With hindsight, it seems to me that those who decided I should skip should have considered more carefully my emotional readiness to do so. I also feel that by skipping I may have lost time in which I could have developed other skills, including writing. (American Association for Gifted Children, 1978, pp. 79–80)

After skipping seventh grade, I took an introductory computer science course at the local university in the spring of my eighth grade. Considering the drudgery that I had encountered in much of my junior high school work, this fascinating course was a truly stimulating experience. (p. 81)

Although I have never skipped a grade, I did have the option to graduate after the eleventh grade. I was counseled by the guidance office to go ahead and graduate early but I chose not to. The main reason, although I hate to admit it, is that I was afraid. *In the regimentation of school, there is an odd security.* Skipping would be taking away your security blanket after it's been with you for eleven years. Which college? What are your future plans? What do you want in life? You've had to make no major decisions until now. . . . I felt I needed that last year to "get it all together." (pp. 83–84)

are not as effusive in their praise. For example, Southern and Jones (1991) and Piirto (1994) state that although it is easy to measure one's increased abilities in mathematics, it is much more difficult to pinpoint accurately any social or emotional problems that may have been exacerbated by such radical acceleration. Still, the lessons of SMPY continue today, having grown to include hundreds of thousands of children in annual talent searches all over the United States and in several foreign countries.

. . . and Joe Bates, the student who began it all? As Julian Stanley observes proudly, "Joe thrived and went on to receive his BA and Master's degrees in computer science at age 17. Then, still 17, he became a doctoral student at Cornell University. Today, more than 25 years later, Dr. Bates is an outstanding researcher and professor, striving at Carnegie Mellon to bring drama to 'virtual reality'" (Stanley, 1995, personal communication).

DR. JULIAN STANLEY: BEST FRIEND OF THE MATHEMATICALLY BRILLIANT

On Initial Reluctance to Promote Radical Acceleration

I began casting around for high schools, public or private, that would allow Joe Bates (then an eighth grader) to take mainly eleventh and twelfth grade Advanced Placement Program or honors courses. Principals and headmasters thought this a ridiculous suggestion . . . so—quite reluctantly—Joe, his parents, and I decided to let him try being a regular student at Johns Hopkins—seemingly an even more ridiculous suggestion. We feared that he would find the courses that seemed best for him initially (calculus, computer science, and physics) too difficult, but our options were severely limited. Yet, to our great surprise and pleasure, Joe thrived. So did many others who soon followed him.

How SMPY Was Founded—and Funded

My long-term but almost latent interest in intellectually talented youths made me receptive in 1970 to a call for grant proposals from the newly formed Spencer Foundation. It had plenty of money but no established list of potential grant seekers, whereas I had some tentative ideas about how to find "youths who reason exceptionally well mathematically." . . . My 4.5 page, double-spaced proposal won a $266,100 five-year grant, ending in 1976. Generously, the Spencer Foundation renewed its support until 1984, but at lower levels. With that, the Study of Mathematically and Scientifically Precocious Youth (SMSPY) was born. (Shortly thereafter, the "and Scientifically" was dropped, because mathematical reasoning ability is prerequisite for most scientific achievement nowadays.)

Outgrowths of SMPY

At first, verbally talented individuals were not served by SMPY. This was an omission with which we felt uncomfortable. Thus, we helped form at Johns Hopkins in 1972 another group, the Study of Verbally Gifted Youth (SVGY), to serve such students. It functioned until 1977. The Intellectually Gifted Child Study Group (IGCSG), created by Lynn H. Fox in 1975, also was an outgrowth of SMPY and is an integral part of its early story. It flourished for several years with Spencer Foundation support, focusing its work on gifted females and then on learning-disabled gifted students. IGCSG closed its doors upon Dr. Fox's departure from Johns Hopkins in 1982, but its legacy has continued.

Extensions of the SMPY Model

My wife of 32 years died in late 1978. She had been ill with metastasized breast cancer for nearly six years. I was exhausted from teaching my university classes, looking after her, expanding SMPY, and developing the SMPY model. Thus, in 1979, I went to President Steven Muller of Johns Hopkins and, in 15 minutes, arranged to create at Johns Hopkins, independent of SMPY, the Office of Talent Identification and Development (OTID) to take over operational aspects. . . . OTID took off like a rocket in January of 1980 with an expanded talent search, now including verbal and general ability. The first *residential* program of fast-paced courses followed that summer . . . [and] has expanded ever since, now serving over 75,000 young boys and girls each year. It's name changed to the Center for Talented Youth (CTY) and, more recently, to the Institute for the Academic Advancement of Youth (IAAY).

Lessons Learned from SMPY

1. It is crucial to find—via systematic, objective, well-focused procedures—youths who *reason* exceptionally well in the content domain of your specific interest. . . . If you want to make rabbit stew, first catch a rabbit.

2. Thus far, [the SATs] provide the most secure, appropriately difficult way to assess the quantitative aptitude of upper-3 percentability 12-year-olds.

3. Perhaps the virtually unique contribution of SMPY has been its emphasis on acceleration in its many forms and on fast-paced academic courses. . . . Appropriately gifted students can master a whole year of high school subject matter, such as algebra or biology, in three intensive summer weeks.

4. SMPY emphasizes subject-matter acceleration more than grade skipping. Yet they are only two of the approximately twenty main ways to accelerate one's educational progress. . . . In 1971, acceleration was anathema to most educators. Today it is endorsed by the National Association for Gifted Children. It has been shown to have a positive relationship with academic achievement up to 10 years after implementation.

5. Long-term longitudinal follow-ups of the youths who reason extremely well mathematically (and verbally) are highly important. Dr. Camilla Persson Benbow . . . and her colleague Professor David Lubinski are conducting such studies at Iowa State University. . . . To date, data have been collected via comprehensive questionnaires on individuals considered gifted using SMPY's criteria, at ages 13, 18, 23, and 33. This is truly a modern-day,

continued on the following page

continued from the previous page

multiple-cohort extension of Terman's classic, one-cohort longitudinal follow-up study.

Summary Thoughts from Dr. Stanley on SMPY

As yet, the impact of these ideas on national educational policy has been less than I had hoped. Perhaps this is due to our approach. Mostly, we have "burrowed under" the particular school in what I, coining an oxymoron, term a "benignly insidious" manner. SMPY has sent the SAT scores directly to the examinee, who then could work with his or her parents in the local school situation and community to secure needed curricular adjustments and other opportunities to move ahead faster and better in academic areas of his or her greatest precocity, thus establishing precedents. SMPY almost never tackles school boards directly. There are too many, and it is extremely difficult to effect long-term change in their stated policies. . . .

Mathematical precocity is an intriguing topic; it certainly captured my interest back in January 1969 when I first met Joe Bates, and continues to do so.

—Julian Stanley is professor of psychology at Johns Hopkins University and director of the Study of Mathematically Precocious Youth (SMPY).

Institutions such as SMPY and the gifted education specialists who have served in them since the 1970s caused a renaissance that was needed badly to resurrect our field from the depths of its 1960s slump. Of course, many other individuals contributed greatly to our understanding of gifted children during the 1970s, on both university campuses and in local public schools. As we were on a roll, it was not long before the picture changed drastically, as the politics of education again entered the picture, jeopardizing the hard-fought gains of so many. Once again, gifted children and their education would be challenged.

STAYING ALIVE: GIFTED EDUCATION FALLS BACK, TAKES OFF

Ah, the late 1970s!: a time of rampant inflation, 17% mortgage rates, and hostage takings of Americans in far-off lands. Attention was focused on issues related to economics and defense, with educational reform being nowhere in sight. America was depressed.

Then, with the impact of a freight train, a new administration was elected and the Great Communicator, Ronald Reagan, promised sweeping changes that would improve our lifestyles and our international reputation. People listened. They wanted a hero, and Reagan fit the bill. He told us something we wanted to hear: that we could spend now and pay later, resulting in a robust economy

DR. DOROTHY SISK: THE FEDERAL GOVERNMENT AND GIFTED EDUCATION

On Directing the Office of Gifted and Talented (OGT)

When I directed OGT, I had 2.56 million dollars and there were purported to be 2.56 million gifted children in our nation. I remember remarking to a reporter that "I've got one dollar per gifted child." Unfortunately, that was the only quote the woman used in her article. Of course, I really did get into hot water for that statement—but it was true! I had one dollar per gifted child!

So, what I did was call together directors of educational programs—the career education specialists, the Head Start people, and others—and invited them to sessions where they could talk about their initiatives. Then I would say, "Now, I would like to move us to the next stage: how can we collaborate and identify common interests?" One person said, "You want some of our money!" and I responded, "You're absolutely right!" Out of that came several co-operative projects, including one on career initiatives for the gifted.

On Being Among the Best

Our U.S. Commissioner of Education at the time, Ernest Boyer, had 144 projects to control. One of the things he did was to rank our programs from 1 through 144. So, all of the project directors were called together in this big auditorium, and each of us sat there thinking, "Oh God, *don't* let me be number 144!" In addition, Boyer was going to identify seven programs to spotlight, and as I sat there, I heard him call out OGT—I think we were number 5. The seven of us met with him weekly, discussing our goals and objectives. We stimulated each other's thinking and became very close. Ernie's singling out OGT set the tone for what I considered to be a sense of urgency for the gifted, a sense of what I was doing as being very important.

On Identifying Giftedness at an Early Age

In the 70s, we funded model projects and they were funded for three years with the idea that each needed a bit of start up time. One of the areas that we funded was early childhood education, because one of the problems that we had (and still have!) in gifted education is that people tend to want to protect the young child and NOT identify the gifted until they are 8 or 9 years old. We wanted to demonstrate that not only could you identify giftedness at a young age, but that you *should* do it. In a sense, we were ahead of our time.

continued on the following page

continued from the previous page

On the Importance of "Networking"

If I had to characterize what went on in those OGT days, it was the networking. I networked the 144 programs in such a way that we sent fliers and information to one another, we lunched together, found ways to collaborate, and we were truly, truly integrated. The leaders in gifted education who followed this same pattern in their states were extremely successful, and the ones who walked around by themselves were easily cut off.

On the Need for Diversity in Gifted Programs

One of the tragedies that I experienced and one of the disappointments that I had as I went around and looked at gifted programs was that they were so white. And they were so middle class. I thought to myself, "this can't be." To counteract this situation, I put together a wonderful conference with Dr. Mary Berry (Assistant Secretary of Education), Representative Shirley Chisholm, and Dr. E. Paul Torrance. I then invited educators in from all over and said, "Listen to this. We're going to send out grants for minority and economically disadvantaged children." Then we went back to the OGT and waited for the grants to come in. When they came in they were grants written to serve already identified gifted kids. It was probably one of the most disappointing things I've ever experienced. What happened? We didn't have the champions in the minority and economically disadvantaged groups step forward and say, "Let me tell you about the needs of these children." We really needed that.

On the Overall OGT Experience

As I look back on what we did with that $2.56 million, we ought to get some kind of award because there wasn't one dollar that was mismanaged or abused. I hate the slang term "bang for the buck," but we didn't bang that buck, we blew it up and made it ballistic!

—*Dr. Dorothy Sisk was the first director of OGT and is now a professor at Lamar University in Texas.*

that would grow on its own impetus. But as our economy grew, so did our national debt; warnings were beginning to sound that we were enjoying our present at the expense of our children's future. America became confused.

Scapegoats were needed. It had to be someone's fault that this economic revolution was a mile wide but only an inch deep. As so often before, blame fell on segments of society with less power than most. The poor were told to get off their duffs and depend more on themselves and less on their government, and public school educators were told to get serious about helping kids learn or else the government would allow the private sector to do the job right. The Statue of Liberty's invitation to "give us your tired, your poor, your huddled masses . . ." seemed a bit passé. America became greedy.

In the midst of this economic furor, schools fought for even fewer federal dollars, as programs that had earlier been targeted with special funds—including gifted education—were now thrown into a "block grant" system, in which a lump sum is given to a state and the main players are on their own to fight for their own piece of the economic pie. Gifted programs were in for the fight of their lives, for it became increasingly difficult to convince school boards that intelligent kids were as needy as others who could not read. At a time in our history when intellectual guidance was needed the most, federal funds for gifted education dried up, as did the federal Office of Gifted and Talented, which was eliminated under the Educational Consolidation and Improvement Act. Once again, the political chess game began, with gifted children (among others) being the expendable pawns.

And then, from out of nowhere, came what appeared to be our salvation. The National Commission on Excellence in Education released a report, *A Nation at Risk* (1983), a political document that focused on the sorry state of America's public schools. Science and math education were in abysmal shape, the report contended, and fully 50% of all gifted students did not perform to their tested potential. In one sound bite after another, a clarion call was obvious: We need to do more for our nation's gifted students!

. . . Do more, of course, with less money.

The 1980s: gifted education's most manic-depressive era, for every move made that looked positive and uplifting was followed shortly thereafter by the slap of reality and crunched budgets.

THE RICHARDSON REPORT

A definite highlight of this frenetic decade was a 4-year study of gifted child education conducted by the Sid W. Richardson Foundation of Fort Worth, Texas. June Cox and her able team of researchers began in 1981 to investigate three central questions:

1. What programs for able learners existed across America?
2. What program models were used, and which were most effective?
3. What recommendations could be made to assist all types of schools to serve able learners better?

—*Cox, Daniel, & Boston, 1985*

(It is important to note that Cox and her colleagues chose the term *able learners* instead of *gifted* throughout their study and its subsequent publications. This was a conscious choice, as it was believed by the researchers that the term *able learners* was all-encompassing and less volatile than the word *gifted*.)

To answer these questions, every one of the 16,000+ public and parochial school districts across the nation was sent a questionnaire regarding the extent of their options for able learners; 4,000 completed surveys were returned. Then, a more lengthy questionnaire, asking for more specific programmatic and identification information, was sent to these respondents; 1,572 districts completed and returned this form. Among the findings were

- The most common approach to serving gifted students (71% of respondents) was a part-time resource room, with able learners spending the majority of time in the regular classroom.
- Fewer than 5% of districts offered a special school for able learners (e.g., a school focused on science or the arts).
- Teacher recommendations and achievement and IQ tests were used most frequently for identification of able learners, although the cutoff scores varied considerably from one district to another (so, you could be gifted in one town, but not another).
- Goals and objectives in programs for able learners were weak and varied, and a comprehensive program of services for grades K to 12 was rare in districts.

These results, hardly uplifting, showed that the programs for able learners across America were splintered and sporadic. In effect, America was providing a part-time solution (the resource room) to a full-time problem when it came to educating its most able youth.

In response, the research team put together a series of recommendations for change. With continued funding, they were able to implement these changes in several school districts nationwide, to show what a comprehensive program for able learners might look like under the best of circumstances. Their plan was called "The Pyramid Project" (see Figure 2.3), and the continuum of services ranged from enrichment in all classrooms to specialized programs (e.g., the International Baccalaureate program or community mentorships) for selected students. Two key phrases that recur through the report of Cox et al. are "appropriate pacing" and "continuous progress," both of which would allow students to tackle academic content that matches their current learning needs. This accommodation could be made in a number of ways—special classes, independent study, in-classroom enrichment—but it needed to move beyond the "I'm gifted on Tuesday" approach too often offered by the ever-popular resource room.

In addition to recommendations related to comprehensive programs for able learners, the Richardson Study also suggested

- using counselors in the identification process and in various capacities for meeting the affective needs of able learners
- encouraging concurrent enrollment, in which students may attend elementary and middle schools simultaneously, or high school and college

FIGURE 2.3

Pyramid Project

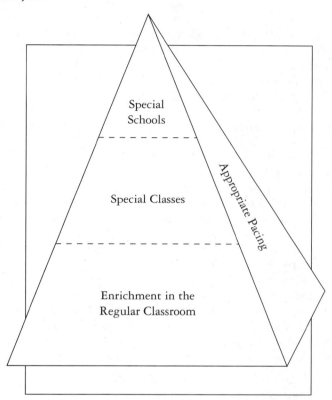

—*From* Educating Able Learners: Programs and Promising Practices
by June Cox, Neil Daniel, and Bruce O. Boston, Copyright © *1985.*
By permission of the University of Texas Press.

- making effective use of community resources (people, museums, businesses) within the schools
- realizing that able learners differ from one another and that no one program or provision will meet the needs of all able learners

The Richardson Study, the most comprehensive review of its type since the Marland Report of 1971, provides to this day a blueprint for attaining excellence in schools. Few school districts have had the commitment (or the dollars) to implement its provisions, but the guidelines that it suggests are as comprehensive as any that have ever been offered in the field of gifted child education.

TOTAL ECLIPSE OF THE HEART: PROGRAMS
AND PLANS FOR THE UNDERSERVED

In yet another ironic twist of 1980s logic, several populations of gifted children who had heretofore been neglected started to gain attention, at least from the research community. Even though our schools were doing only a half-hearted job at educating its "run of the mill" gifted students, there were several voices in the educational wilderness crying out for us to take another look at other groups of gifted children: those who do not achieve for reasons that we do not fully understand.

The most articulate and convincing voice was that of Joanne R. Whitmore, whose book *Giftedness, Conflict, and Underachievement* (1980) provided proof positive that children who underachieved in school did not do so on purpose and that their lack of academic progress had its roots in their psychological makeup. The first step in the remediation of underachievement was to treat the children with respect and to channel their energies and talents in directions that provided real challenges in a safe, secure atmosphere. Throughout her book, Whitmore discusses how she did this in her self-contained class for primary-age children who were performing far below what their IQs indicated they could. In relating how she structured her classroom in Cupertino, California, and how she adjusted her teaching style to accommodate the intellectual and emotional needs of gifted children, Whitmore provides at least some solutions to this most perplexing of problems. Also, by focusing on two personality elements that were present in all her students—perfectionism and supersensitivity—Whitmore established the need for the presence of a caring teacher who saw these children as the vulnerable beings that they were. As she writes:

> These gifted children had been very vulnerable to emotional disturbance because of their perceptions of having failed to meet the expectations of self or others, their tendencies to set unrealistically high goals, and their intense desires for perfection. That vulnerability was exacerbated by the individual's acute sensitivity to the responses, that is, the social feedback, of others. It was easy for these children to feel rejected and valueless. (Whitmore, 1980, p. 129)

Joanne R. Whitmore provided both research-based solutions and sensitive advice on how best to help gifted underachieving children. Not before or since has such eloquence been used to address the needs of this special population.

A related area of study that emerged in the 1980s was a concern for gifted children and adults who were also diagnosed with disabilities. Again, it was Joanne Whitmore who took the lead in gaining the public's attention that highly able people could also possess some learning deficiencies. For example, Whitmore writes (1981) about a child, Kim, who has cerebral palsy, no speech, and limited motor control. Placed in a class for severely handicapped students, it was hard to see Kim as anyone other than a low-functioning child. However,

ON DECIDING TO LEAVE SCHOOLCHILDREN AND TEACH AT THE COLLEGE LEVEL

In working with highly gifted young children who had failed to minimally succeed, much less thrive, in school, I gained profound respect for their abilities and sensitivities. So, when I was offered the opportunity to earn a doctorate and pursue a career in teacher education, I shared my dilemma with the class—hating to leave the joys and rewards of classroom teaching and yet drawn to the challenges and possibilities of higher education. The next day, one of my most rambunctious boys, age 8, burst into the classroom shouting to me that he had the answer for me. When asked, he drew out of his pocket a long, crumpled piece of paper on which he had calculated the impact of my work if I were to teach 25 teachers instead of children, each passing on the learning to their 25 students! With a glimpse of the potential impact of a teacher educator, I made my decision to accept the offer.

HOW CAN WE BEST HELP CHILDREN WHO ARE CALLED "UNDERACHIEVERS"?

The greatest lesson I learned from my class of young highly gifted underachievers was a tri-part perspective that became the core of my approach to helping them become high achievers in school:

1. *All* children, including the gifted, want to achieve success in school—academically and socially.
2. *None* of my children manifested low self-esteem and patterns of underachievement *before* entering school; their underachievement was content-specific.
3. Classroom conditions, social and academic in nature, had taught my children that non-engagement was safer and more rewarding than engagement. Appropriate classroom conditions with peers, curriculum and instructional approaches can reverse even the most severe patterns of underachievement in *young* children.

—*Joanne Rand Whitmore is professor and dean of education at Kent State University.*

Kim's parents thought otherwise and requested that she be placed in an openspace elementary school, where her abilities became apparent. In just 2 days, Kim learned to use Morse Code to communicate, and within 4 months she was reading on grade level, with subsequent testing revealing a superior intellect.

Whitmore and Maker (1985) combined first-person accounts similar to the one above with practical solutions for positive change in their ground breaking book *Intellectual Giftedness in Disabled Persons.* Other individuals did similar work. Susan Baum (1988), in working with gifted students with learning disabilities, found that such complex children require focused attention on the development of their particular gift or talent without undue time given over to remediation of skills that, indeed, they may never master. Also, she advocated providing them with strategies and techniques to compensate for their learning deficiencies and to be honest with them about both their obvious strengths and weaknesses. Again, as in Whitmore's work, the emphasis is on strengths and the psychological climate in which these children exist.

Unfortunately, the promise of program options for gifted children with learning or physical disabilities, or those who chronically underachieve, was not fully realized in the 1980s, nor has much more happened since. How sad; for now, with the knowledge that we have gained from research and practice about the best ways to serve these "twice-exceptional" individuals, few programs with a long-term commitment to reaching the talents of these students exist. Indeed, gifted children with disabilities will soon enter their third decade of being called "underserved."

I AM WOMAN, HEAR ME ROAR

As I travel around the country lecturing on giftedness and achievement in women, I have often been dismayed by the defensive postures of many gifted women in regard to their lifestyles. The seemingly simple question, "Why don't gifted girls achieve more in their careers?" has drawn angry questions and hostile retorts: "So, what's wrong with not having a career?" argue women who consider themselves traditional. "You're measuring women by masculine standards of achievement!" insist certain feminists. Some women have been offended because they believed I was devaluing homemaking; others, because I referred to research showing that gifted women earn less and have lower-status jobs than gifted men. . . . But I now realize that, gifted or not, most women in America—including myself— have felt defensive at one time or another about lifestyle choices and self-definitions.

——*Kerr,* Smart Girls: A New Psychology of Girls, Women and Giftedness, *1997, p. x*

Although no researchers have ever found that males are more intelligent, as a gender, than females, several researchers did find that gifted girls and women are not represented as fully as males in a variety of areas that deal with high intellect. For example, Gallagher and Gallagher (1994) report that women are underrepresented among high achievers and innovators in the arts, sciences, and humanities. Years earlier, Terman and Oden (1947) found that the gifted girls in their study turned out to be far less productive as adults than males in their careers. Callahan (1979) suggests that gifted girls and women suffer from some "cultural handicaps," including teacher behaviors that favor boys, organizational reward systems, and test bias as reasons that gifted females' talents, societally, have not been fully realized.

In *Smart Girls, Gifted Women* (1985), a very personal book that examined many of the reasons for this state of affairs with gifted girls, Barbara Kerr took us back to her 10-year high school reunion, an event she definitely was *not* looking forward to attending. Having been a part of a Sputnik-era accelerated program from grades 5 to 12, Kerr assumed that her "lowly" PhD in counseling psychology would pale in comparison with the success her female classmates must surely have attained—she assumed that they all became something important, such as scientists, which was one of the goals of her special program.

When she went to her reunion, Kerr was, indeed, surprised: Although most of the boys, now men, had continued their career aspirations in the sciences or mathematics, most of the highly intelligent girls, now women, had chosen to become housewives, not physicists, or entered "disposable careers" such as teaching or nursing, which could be done anywhere your husband received his next job transfer. Now it was Kerr's turn, as a gifted woman and psychologist, to find out why this occurred, why so much promise went unrealized (or "under"realized) among her female classmates.

Her book is a fascinating combination of research, sociology, and soap opera, and it caused other researchers (and herself) to examine the reasons behind the wholesale abandonment of high ideals and goals by too many gifted girls. Indeed, of all the "new" areas of research in gifted child education in the 1980s, the study of the special needs of gifted females was the most elaborate.

REELIN' IN THE YEARS: JAVITS, GARDNER, AND A SEARCH FOR PASSION

As evidenced by the previous discussion, each decade brought with it its own views on what giftedness is and how valuable an asset it is to the individual and the society. As the 1980s ended and the 1990s began, the conversations and controversies continued—indeed, they expanded! New players were brought into the game, many with only a passing knowledge of the field of gifted education, but a genuine concern for how well the concept of giftedness fit into an increasingly diverse American society.

A notable new player (actually, one brought out of retirement) was the federal government, which again assumed a role, albeit a small one, in the development of gifted programs nationally. This financial and philosophic impetus added credibility to a field always in search of respect and legitimacy.

Ironically, the 1990s were marked by as much dissension *within* the field of gifted child education as from outside interests. These "family squabbles" created a not-unhealthy tension, as evidenced by the continuing quest for ways to serve gifted children in ways that benefited their high abilities. As a field, few may have agreed on what to label the children (or whether they should be labeled at all!), but all agreed on one ideal: to allow every child to take full advantage of his or her innate gifts and developed talents.

JACOB J. JAVITS: THE GIFTED CHILD'S FAVORITE SENATOR

When the Office of Gifted and Talented in the U.S. Department of Education was eliminated in 1982, advocates sought ways to bring it back into existence. The Council for Exceptional Children and the National Association for Gifted Children, the two political machines behind this impetus, lobbied Capitol Hill in hopes of finding friends. They found several, among them Senator Bill Bradley of New Jersey and Senator Jacob J. Javits of New York. Javits, one of the most senior senators, was always ready to insert a line item for gifted and talented children in the proposed federal budget. However, the austerity of the era allowed for no new capital expenditures, so time and again Javits's efforts were rebuffed. It seemed that once a line item was in the federal budget, it was easy to maintain; the difficulty was in getting one's financial foot in the door initially.

That toehold took place in 1988, shortly after Javits's death. The Jacob J. Javits Gifted and Talented Students Education Program was authorized for funding under Title IV, Part B of the Hawkins-Stafford Elementary and Secondary Amendments of 1988. This legislation sponsored three separate activities: a program of grants and contracts to set up demonstration projects that would benefit gifted children; the establishment of a national research center for the study of the education of gifted children; and the reestablishment of a federal office for gifted and talented, to serve as a national clearinghouse for information dissemination (Ross, 1994).

The focus of this legislation, especially the grants and demonstration projects component, was one that would appease even the most vocal critic's concerns about elitism: 80 to 90% of the monies would be targeted toward students who were economically disadvantaged, limited English proficient, or disabled. Thus, the disenfranchised gifted children from past generations, the "hidden gifted" child, would be the main recipient of the government's beneficence.

. . . And that is exactly what happened. With nearly 100 multiyear projects funded up through 1997, the Javits Act has prompted action with types of gifted children who, truth be told, would probably not have been served otherwise. Among the projects that were funded were

- EAEP: The *Early Assessment for Exceptional Potential* Program, designed to identify young, at-risk talented children, primarily of poor or African American heritage, in the Cleveland, Ohio, public schools, by portfolio assessment and extensive staff development. (Funded at Kent State University, Ohio)
- Project Synergy, a New York City-based program designed to use a case study approach and extended observations to identify talents among young minority students. Once identified, these students were assigned mentors—achieving adolescents from their own ethnic group. (Funded at Teachers College, New York)

- APOGEE, *A*cademic *P*rograms for *G*ifted with *E*xcellence and *E*quity, in which the top 25% of students in various categories, such as disadvantaged, minority, underachievers, limited English speakers, and disabled, were placed in special language arts/reading classes with teachers who had received 45 hours of special training in how to challenge their talents. (Funded at Educational Information and Resource Center, Sewell, New Jersey)
- *Project Promise,* designed to provide leadership opportunities and information on careers and college to identified middle school students, especially those from low socioeconomic backgrounds in Arkansas, Kansas, and Missouri. In-school curricular options were supplemented with a home visitor, who served as a liaison between family and school. (Funded at Texas Education Agency)

Each grant was designed to identify and serve gifted students, their teachers, and/or their families. Each grant was responsible for disseminating information nationally so that others could adopt successful strategies to benefit other gifted children. Each grant was designed to plug in another piece in the completion of the complex puzzle that constitutes every gifted child.

Alexinia Y. Baldwin, a researcher in the Javits 7+ Gifted and Talented Program, which was designed to provide inner-city children with in-school opportunities that would prepare them for programs for gifted children, quoted Pablo Casals in introducing her Javits 7+ program (Baldwin, 1994):

> When will we also teach them who they are? . . . We should say to them you are unique, you are a marvel. In this whole world there is no one like you and there will never be again. (p. 80)

This quote represents the overall importance of the Javits grants and demonstration projects that have been conducted to date. In a diverse world where every gift, no matter how hidden, should be found, explored, and valued, these projects give evidence that there is still much to learn about giftedness and the children who wear this label.

THE NATIONAL RESEARCH CENTER ON THE GIFTED AND TALENTED (NRC/GT)

The competition was limited, but fierce: The federal government was going to fund a multiyear, multimillion dollar research center to conduct "consumer-oriented" research related to issues and problems relevant to the education of gifted and talented children (Renzulli, 1991). The few notable bidders included some of gifted child education's most respected authorities, but when the dust settled and the "winner" was announced, it was a consortium of universities, spearheaded by the University of Connecticut, that took top honors. Since that

It takes a perceptive person to look beyond what's out there to see something is going on. I don't think this has anything to do with race or color, it just has to do with the persons themselves—whether or not they are open-minded. . . . Sometimes, some of us who are trying to get a message across, we do it more out of anger and, therefore, we turn people off instead of really focusing in on the basic concepts.
—*Alexinia Y. Baldwin is a full professor at the University of Connecticut.*

TITLES AND AUTHORS OF SOME STUDIES SPONSORED BY THE NATIONAL RESEARCH CENTER ON THE GIFTED AND TALENTED

- *Self-Concept and the Gifted Child* by Robert D. Hoge and Joseph S. Renzulli (1991)
- *Issues and Practices Related to Identification of Gifted and Talented Students in the Visual Arts* by Gilbert A. Clark and Enid Zimmerman (1992)
- *Some Children Under Some Conditions: TV and the High Potential Kid* by Robert Abelman (1992)
- *Reading with Young Gifted Children* by Nancy Ewald Jackson and Cathy M. Roller (1993)
- *State Policies Regarding Education of the Gifted as Reflected in Legislation and Regulation* by A. Harry Passow and Rose A. Rudnitski (1993)
- *Creativity as an Educational Objective for Disadvantaged Students* by Mark A. Runco (1993)
- *Helping Gifted Children and Their Families Prepare for College: A Handbook Designed to Assist Economically Disadvantaged and First-Generation College Attendees* by Avis L. Wright and Paula Olszewski-Kubilius (1993)
- *Helping Your Child Find Success at School: A Guide for Hispanic Parents* by Candis Y. Hine (1994)
- *Recognizing Talent: Cross-Case Study of Two High-Potential Students with Cerebral Palsy* by Colleen Willard-Holt (1994)
- *The Recruitment and Retention of African-American Students in Gifted Education Programs: Implications and Recommendations* by Donna Y. Ford (1994)

—Copies of the above reports may be obtained by writing to NRC/GT, the University of Connecticut, 362 Fairfield Road, U-7, Storrs, CT 06269-2007.

time, NRC/GT has fulfilled its promise—and more. Dozens of publications and research studies have been funded on every aspect of educating gifted children, and remaining true to the overall focus of the Javits legislation, many of the projects have involved gifted children from historically underrepresented populations.

First, the basics: NRC/GT, directed by Joseph Renzulli, combined the Universities of Georgia and Virginia and Yale University into a four-site powerhouse. Two of Renzulli's former doctoral students, Mary Frasier and Carolyn Callahan, spearheaded the NRC/GT in Georgia and Virginia, respectively. Robert Sternberg, IBM Professor of Psychology and an expert on conceptions of intelligence, headed the NRC/GT at Yale. This combined university effort was enhanced by the collaboration of 54 state and territorial departments of education and nearly 300 public and private schools or districts. These "home-based" sites provided diverse locations and students to test out some of the ideas and practices generated by NRC/GT researchers. In addition, more than 200 content area specialists were selected for a "consultant bank," a storehouse of human knowledge that the NRC/GT staff could tap into regarding the consultants' specific areas of expertise. The roster of contributors was completed by including representatives of parent groups for gifted children, state and local legislators, business leaders, and others with expressed interest in pursuing the goals of gifted child education.

Once established, the NRC/GT sent 19,000 letters and surveys to persons involved in gifted child education, asking them what it was they wanted to know about identifying, understanding, educating, and evaluating gifted children. The responses, diverse yet not unexpected, included the usuals—"How do we know if our programs are making a difference?" "What are the best methods and practices to teach gifted children?" "How do you identify gifted children from diverse backgrounds?"—as well as some more focused and idiosyncratic questions: "How best do we serve artistically talented students?" "What staff development models have proved to have the most impact?" "What certification standards should there be for teachers of gifted children?"

Wasting no time in pursuing these and other issues, Renzulli and his colleagues published dozens of studies, both quantitative and qualitative in nature and focusing on such diverse topics as

- How much curriculum differentiation occurs in elementary classroom settings?
- How effective is ability grouping on high-ability students' mastery of content?
- How much grade-level curriculum content do gifted students know *before* they enter that particular grade level?
- What innovative practices are being used to identify gifted students?

The NRC/GT, re-funded in 1996 for another cycle of research, will continue to add to the knowledge base of how best to meet the needs of gifted children, as well as virtually all other areas of concern related to this special population.

THE CIRCLE GAME: REDEFINING—AGAIN— THE CONCEPT OF GIFTEDNESS

Under the auspices of the U.S. Office of Educational Research and Improvement (OERI), an advisory panel was convened in 1991 to write yet another "state of the art" report on how gifted children were faring in America's public schools. The resulting document, *National Excellence: A Case for Developing America's Talent* (1993), did not paint a pretty picture of what existed. Teachers lacked skills, classes lacked content, and every world nation with which we competed economically was beating us in the race toward academic excellence. A "quiet crisis" was in the process of developing in our country's schools. Still, the specifics of the detrimental findings could be argued as being overblown and one-sided, and Delisle (1994a) questioned whether the purpose of the document was more political than instructional.

EXCERPTS FROM "NATIONAL EXCELLENCE: A CASE FOR DEVELOPING AMERICA'S TALENT"

- The United States is squandering one of its most precious resources—the gifts, talents and high interests of many of its students. In a broad range of intellectual and artistic endeavors, these youngsters are not challenged to do their best work. This problem is especially severe among economically disadvantaged and minority students, who have access to fewer advanced educational opportunities and whose talents often go unnoticed. (p. 1)
- Students are not asked to work hard or master a body of challenging knowledge or skills. The message society often sends to students is to aim for academic *adequacy,* not academic *excellence.* (p. 1)
- Americans assume that our best students can compete with the best students anywhere. This is not true. International assessments have focused attention on the relatively poor standing of all American students. These tests also show that our top-performing students are undistinguished at best and poor at worst when compared with top students in other countries. (p. 8)
- Two beliefs—a distrust of the intellect and an assumption that people should be allowed to develop to their full potential—have clashed throughout American history and have muddied efforts to provide a quality education for the nation's most promising students. Today, exceptional talent is viewed as both a valuable human resource and a troublesome expression of eccentricity. (p. 13)
- The following national recommendations for action would provide pathways toward an education that allows American students to be as well prepared as those anywhere else in the world:
  - establish challenging curriculum standards
  - establish high-level learning opportunities
  - ensure access to early childhood education
  - expand opportunities for economically disadvantaged and minority children
  - encourage appropriate teacher training and technical assistance (pp. 27–28)

One section of the report that stirred up the cauldron of controversy was (yet) another new definition of giftedness that the *Excellence* report put forth. The reason for the controversy? In defining who a gifted child was, the committee decided consciously to omit one word: *gifted.* In its place, the terms *outstanding talent* and *exceptional talent* were substituted. The rationale for this was that "the term 'gifted' connotes a mature power rather than a developing ability and, therefore [was] antithetical to recent research findings about children" (p. 54).

Since then, whatever *could* hit the fan, has.

First, the definition of *giftedness* that was proposed:

Children and youth with outstanding talent perform or show the potential for performing at remarkably high levels of accomplishment when compared with others of their age, experience, or environment.

These children and youth exhibit high performance capability in intellectual, creative, and/or artistic areas, possess an unusual leadership capacity, or excel in specific academic fields. They require services or activities not ordinarily provided by the schools.

Outstanding talents are present in children and youth from all cultural groups, across all economic strata, and in all areas of human endeavor. (*National excellence,* 1993, p. 3)

The first thing noticed in this definition is the similarity that it has to previous federal definitions—the way that giftedness (sorry . . . "talents") are interspersed throughout society and are seen in varied motifs; the reality that some "talents" are obvious in children whereas some are more latent; the fact that special provisions will be required if these talents are to be brought into fullest bloom. What is different in this definition is the *de*emphasis on the personal. No longer is the phrase "realize their contribution to *self* and society" included as it was in the 1972 federal definition; the focus is on what this child will give back to the society that raises it. This represents a major shift in thinking *away* from individual benefit and *toward* a utilitarian agenda.

Actually, it should have come as little surprise that this definition emerged, because the movement to "demystify" giftedness and make it something visible for all to see began with Renzulli's 1978 definition of *giftedness* as a set of behaviors (see chapter 3) and continued to expand with Howard Gardner's work on multiple intelligences (MI). Since the 1983 publication of Gardner's best-selling *Frames of Mind: The Theory of Multiple Intelligences,* in which he asserted that there are at least seven distinct ways to be intelligent (expanded to eight in 1996; see Figure 2.4), including many of the ways put forth in the newest federal definition, educators nationwide were falling over each other beating a path to Gardner's office door at the hallowed halls of Harvard. Gardner's seven-category demarcation of intelligence had two qualities that made it acceptable to so many: It was *simple* to understand and it was *convenient,* as teachers could now plan their lessons and principals could restructure their schools around the various talents, making sure that sometime during each school week they offered lessons that

FIGURE 2.4

Howard Gardner's Multiple Intelligences

IDENTIFYING YOUR INTELLIGENCES

Which of Howard Gardner's eight intelligences do you have?

Linguistic Intelligence. You enjoy writing, reading, listening, and speaking, and you do them all with ease. You enjoy memorizing information and building your vocabulary, and you may be an excellent storyteller.

Musical Intelligence. You can detect rhythms, patterns, and tempos in things that seem to have none at all—like chirping birds, crickets, and even some of the music your parents listen to. You can "hear" tone and pitch, and you may be talented at playing one or more musical instruments, either by ear or with instructions. You may appreciate many kinds of music.

Logical-Mathematical Intelligence. You instinctively put things in order and comprehend quantities—often in your head. Numbers and math concepts come easily to you, and you love brain-teasers, logic puzzles, games, and computers.

Visual-Spatial Intelligence. You readily notice when a building (or painting, or person) is not quite symmetrical. If you're an athlete, you can judge almost perfectly the angle needed to score a goal in hockey or a basket in basketball. You can mentally rotate complex forms, and you can draw whatever you see. You're good at taking things apart and putting them back together, and you love games.

Bodily-Kinesthetic Intelligence. You are good at handling and manipulating objects, and you move your body with grace and ease. You enjoy training your body to do its physical best, and you may be a great mimic. You may be talented at one or more crafts—carving, sewing, making pots.

Interpersonal Intelligence. You easily understand other people, perceiving their moods and feelings. You're a natural leader and a skilled mediator; you can break up a fight between two of your friends and still remain on each person's good side.

Intrapersonal Intelligence. You understand yourself very well; you're profoundly aware of your feelings, dreams, and ideas, and you're true to your goals. People may say that you "march to the beat of a different drummer." You enjoy journaling. (Are you keeping a journal while reading this book?)

Naturalist Intelligence. You feel a deep connection to the natural world and its inhabitants—plants and animals. You enjoy experiencing and observing the out-of-doors, and you may be a talented gardener and/or cook.

—Excerpted from The Gifted Kids Survival Guide: A Teen Handbook *by Judy Galbraith, MA, & Jim Delisle, PhD, Copyright © 1996. Used with permission of Free Spirit Publishing, Minneapolis, MN.*

targeted musical and spatial intelligence, not just the typical areas of linguistic and mathematical abilities. Given this MI mind-set, it did not take long before the following sentiment began to become prominent: "Using Gardner's MI theory, *everyone* is gifted in some way!" Add to this Robert Sternberg's views on SI (successful intelligence), which combines analytical abilities, creative abilities, and practical intelligence ("street smarts"), and Daniel Goleman's ideas about EI, (emotional intelligence), and you have an alphabet soup of theories that caused many people to exhibit signs of DI—definitional impairment—as they tried to reconcile how so many good thinkers could have such diverse views on the subject of intelligence.

Among those in the gifted child education field who piggybacked on Gardner's ideas were John Feldhusen, Joyce Van Tassel-Baska, and Donald Treffinger. Indeed, all three were so strongly convinced that these ideas had merit that they proposed that the entire field of gifted child education change its name and its focus. As Feldhusen explained in introducing a series of articles in a special edition of the *Roeper Review* addressing this issue, "The articles . . . reflect the new orientation in the field that was called gifted education and is now rapidly becoming the field of talent development" (Feldhusen, 1995, p. 92).

Proposing a plan called "The Purdue Pyramid" (see Figure 2.5), Feldhusen stated that the overall goal of education (and life) is the commitment to the full development of one's ability and talent. To reach those heights, one must be surrounded by experiences and people that elevate you to an awareness of what those talents and abilities are. These experiences and people are the essence of what constitutes talent development and, in Feldhusen's mind, what the goal of what we now call "gifted education" should be.

Van Tassel-Baska (1995) elaborates on Feldhusen's conceptual model by filling in gaps related specifically to curriculum. Her plan, the Integrated Curriculum Model for Gifted Learners, provides advanced content, higher order thinking skill development, and instruction based around real-world themes, done in a climate of excellence in which trained teachers group students flexibly, depending on their learning needs and interests. An excellent plan; indeed, strong enough that some might argue that it would be beneficial for all students.

The Talent Development movement, according to Treffinger (1995), is a wholesale shift from "business as usual" in gifted child education. "Not merely a cosmetic change, nor merely an effort to employ more politically correct terminology . . . the trend towards a talent development approach represents a deep or fundamental new orientation concerning the nature, scope, and practice of our field" (p. 95).

Despite its allure, some have questioned whether the talent development idea is possible or beneficial in the field of gifted child education. François Gagne (1991), a critic of the casual interpretation of the terms *gifted* and *talented,* states that the term *gifted* is so entrenched in the psyches of laypersons and scholars that it "would require a monumental force to eradicate it from collective memory" (p. 104). Further, because the terms *gifted* and *talented* have often been used interchangeably over the years, many now regard them as synonyms, making

FIGURE 2.5

The Purdue Pyramid

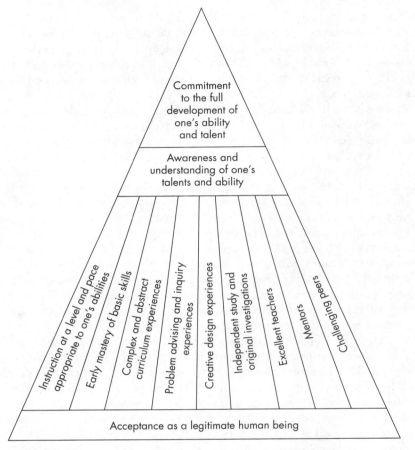

Commitment to the full development of one's ability and talent

Awareness and understanding of one's talents and ability

Instruction at a level and pace appropriate to one's abilities

Early mastery of basic skills

Complex and abstract curriculum experiences

Problem advising and inquiry experiences

Creative design experiences

Independent study and original investigations

Excellent teachers

Mentors

Challenging peers

Acceptance as a legitimate human being

—Reprinted with permission, Roeper Review, *P.O. Box 329, Bloomfield Hills, MI 48303.*

the *name* of what we do not so important as the actions that we undertake to enhance a child's gifts or talents. Lastly, in citing a study that showed that most people interpret "gifts" as something innate whereas "talents" are acquired (Gagne, Motard, & Belanger, 1991), Gagne asked whether talent *implies* the presence of well-above-average abilities and, if so, then mustn't one first be "gifted" (innately) to allow these talents to expand and develop?

Delisle (1996) was less concerned about the logistics of changing our terminology than he was about the personal loss that such a shift might entail. He argued that giftedness is something you *are* rather than something you *do,* and the talent development approach oversimplifies the very complex being that constitutes every gifted child. Further, the developmental nature of giftedness and the fact that some gifted children have varied rates of development—mental, emotional, physical—make the curriculum-driven focus of talent development short sighted and one-dimensional.

Perhaps one of the reasons for this increasingly heated debate goes back to the *National Excellence* report and a statement made there that too many gifted child educators may have taken to heart:

> How can we use what we have learned about gifted education in the last 20 years to improve education for all youngsters and provide the caliber of schools we need for the future? (p. 25)

The above quote raises two important distinctions between the gifted child education movement of today and that of previous generations. First, the focus has shifted from the gifted *child* to the *education* of that gifted child. What was historically a field with its roots firmly based in psychology now has been replanted into the field of education. In doing so, what has been gained? What has been lost? Second, researchers and practitioners who were once committed to locating the best ways to meet the unique and complex needs of gifted children are now seeking educational practices that will benefit *all* children. The gifted child of the past, once an entity unto him- or herself, now serves as a host, someone off of whom to feed for the betterment of others. Was this ever the intent of gifted child education? *Should* it be the intent?

The talent development movement, and the discussions and debates it will continue to spawn, give firm evidence that this field of gifted child education, whatever it is eventually called, will continue to intrigue, amuse, frustrate, puzzle, and challenge those individuals who choose to make it their career.

The history of gifted child education is, indeed, a complex interplay of education, psychology, politics, and economics.

GUIDING QUESTIONS FOR CHAPTER 2

1. How did America's need to reign supreme globally affect the education of gifted children?

2. What roles do politics and society play in the presence or absence of gifted programs?

3. Who were some of the emerging leaders in gifted child education, and what were their ideas?

4. What role has the federal government played in the education of gifted children?

5. What specific areas of focus captured the attention of gifted child educators and researchers from the 1950s through the 1990s?

CHAPTER 2 RESOURCES TO REMEMBER

Marland, Sidney P. (1971). *Education of the gifted and talented, Volume 1: Report to the Congress of the United States by the U.S. Commissioner of Education.* Washington, DC: U.S. Government Printing Office.

Despite its ominous and boring-sounding title, this publication—popularly known as "The Marland Report"—is a wealth of historical and statistical data, as well as some of the best hyperbole you are apt to find in gifted child education! People who provided testimony at the congressional hearings that preceded the publication of the report were *very* passionate about their beliefs, and these intense emotions come through strongly. Dig this gem up at the government document room at your nearest major library. It's a paperback litany of the status of our field at a point at which gifted child education began, once again, to blossom.

Newland, T. Ernest. (1976). *The gifted in socioeducational perspective.* Englewood Cliffs, NJ: Prentice Hall.

I never met T. Ernest Newland, but I wish I had. If he was as bluntly honest in person as he is in his writing, I would have been in for an intellectual adventure as we discussed the field that was the focus of his career: gifted child education. Reviewing everything from the political and philosophic bases of this field of study to instructional and administrative concerns of gifted education specialists, Newland lets readers know of his preferences and biases. As he states in his Preface, "This book has its share not only of the author's convictions and contentions but also of his overt professions of ignorance" (p. x). It's a wise man who knows what he does not know!

Roeper, Annemarie. (1990). *Educating children for life: The modern learning community.* Monroe, NY: Trillium Press.

In this small book, Annemarie describes her SAI Model, the "Self-Actualization Interdependence Model," which effectively allows children to grow intellectually and emotionally. Based on the curriculum design and teaching strategies of the school she began with her husband, George, this book gives educators both ideas and theoretical support for connecting together the world of the mind and the world of the heart. A sensitively written "keeper" of a book.

CHAPTER
3

IDENTIFICATION OF GIFTE
AND TALENTED CHILDREN
STATISTICS, OPINIONS, AND PRACTICES

Phrenology: The *American Heritage Dictionary* defines it as "the practice of study-ing character and mental capacity from the conformation of the human skull" (Davies, 1976, p. 534).

A common trade of traveling charlatans of the 19th century, phrenology was a form of palm reading with hair. Your future glory could be predicted based on how your skull was structured, its bones aligned, and its nooks and crannies configured. Even Lewis Terman himself, grandfather of the gifted child move-ment, was wowed by the possibilities of his head bumps, as a roadside phrenol-ogist informed an adolescent and impressionable Lewis that his skull forebode a successful life for him.

Today, of course, we look at phrenology as shameless exploitation of gullible people. Instead, when we look toward measuring people's mental capacity, we consider far more refined measures: their genetic makeup, their answers to ques-tions such as "What is the definition of uxoricide?" and their ability to complete a paper-and-pencil maze quickly and accurately. (How far we have progressed!)

In this chapter are descriptions of the many ways that educators and psycholo-gists have chosen to identify gifts and talents among children. Not surprisingly, there is a great variety of approaches and an even broader array of instruments, using tests with acronyms that could double as detergents (WISC and GAIN) or as insults (BITCH; Imagine the phone call: "Hello, Mrs. Jones, I'd like to re-view the results of the BITCH test that I performed on your daughter. Is now a good time?"). At chapter's end, a "clean and perfect way" to identify gifted and talented children is not presented. Indeed, if such perfection existed, if there were one fail-safe way to guarantee that all the abilities that exist in the chil-dren we serve were already uncovered, a chapter on this topic would be unnec-essary. However, there are some ways that appear better than others to tap into the obvious and latent talents present in young people. The best of many ideas are presented here.

Along the way, intermingled among the reviews of identification procedures and instruments, there will be reference to both conceptions of giftedness and methods of challenging the gifts and talents of young people. These digressions, when imposed, will be done to clarify the intimate link that does exist between all aspects of gifted child education. For as should be apparent by now, no one aspect of understanding gifted children takes place apart from all the others; how giftedness is defined affects how gifted children are identified and what is chosen to do for them in our schools and homes.

A LETTER FROM JACQUELINE

Kia Ora (that's Maori for "hello"). I am writing to you with many questions in hope of at least a few answers, although I'm not quite sure what you can tell me. I guess I should start with a brief family history. . . .

Throughout her schooling, my mother was labeled "gifted," although she was never given an IQ test. She was bored through most of her schooling, and she found that other children often used her and expected her to do their work for them. (Her teachers used to use her to help the other kids because she always finished her work so quickly.)

My father is very intelligent but left school as soon as he turned 16 to go to work. He is now a managing director of a prominent company here in New Zealand.

Here's my history:

- At 8 months, I was talking and out of diapers.
- At 9 months I walked, holding onto furniture. I opened the cookie cupboard and opened a cookie tin, taking a small bite out of each cookie, so as to claim them as my own.
- At 18 months, I accompanied my mother to the dentist. He asked me if I liked TV, and I told him I watched *Sesame Street*. He asked what that show was, and I told him it was "a production of the children's television workshop," just like they say at the end of the show. Needless to say, he was quite taken aback!
- In preschool, I asked questions about anything and everything; I understood "grown up" humor; I was highly sensitive to emotions and emotional issues, whether or not they affected me; I collected everything; I could talk my way out of trouble with anyone; I liked to be the boss—and I liked to be the best; I used great detail in describing imaginary friends; I invented words when I needed one and, when I was told that word didn't exist, I would tell people, "well, it should"; and I made up my own poems, clapped to the rhythms of songs I heard once, and performed them whenever I had the opportunity.

- When I began school at age 5, I was reading at a ninth-grade level. Two weeks later, I was moved up a grade, but was held back the next year because teachers said I was socially immature. In later grades, I was told I was "bright, but lazy" because although I wrote well, I wrote slowly. In high school, I was one of four students chosen for a special gifted program, but the program ended after one year and I languished once again. I continued to excel in classes that didn't require much writing, but failed in those that did.

- In eleventh grade, I dropped out of school. I got sick of feeling like a failure when I knew deep down I was much smarter than I seemed. Desperately, I searched for an answer at the local library and found a book about gifted kids who had learning disabilities. Sure enough, I found I fit into both categories. Today, I am enrolled in a school for dramatic arts and, with the help of a tutor I found, I am finally getting somewhere academically.

Still, something isn't right, and I need to put my mind to rest. So, please, answer me the following questions:

- Should I have an IQ test to see how smart I really am? (The only other one I have ever had was given to me while I had a migraine and a severe chest infection, and I was to testify against my ex-boyfriend in court the next day, so I'm not sure if its result was too low.)

- From what you've read, do you think I may be gifted, or do you think that I'm just smart enough to know that I'm capable of more, but stupid enough to think that I'm capable of more than I am?

Please write back soon. I am DESPERATE!

Sincerely,
Jacqueline

P.S. I just reopened this letter. My mother said I should tell you the fact that as a baby I never slept during the day. Right from Day One, I wanted to see what was going on in the world. Oh yes! One last thing! Although I have been playing the violin since I was four, I can't read music at all. Is this common?

Jacquie's letter points out just some of the difficulties in assessing the intelligence of children. For example,

- She appeared very smart as a preschooler, yet her social skills were at a level commensurate with her age. So . . . is it a wise idea to place her in an environment that is intellectually challenging but socially frustrating?

- Jacquie's parents both appear very talented themselves, yet their formal schooling was limited. Will genetics or environmental surroundings play a bigger role in their daughter's intellectual development?

Intelligence tests are most often criticized because of their *misuse,* not because the information they generate is invalid. It is good for parents and educators to keep in mind that IQ tests do not generate "false positives"; however, they can generate endless "false negatives." . . . If the IQ score is in the gifted range, the child is gifted. There is no way you can fake abstract reasoning or just guess correctly. But if the IQ score is not in the gifted range, the child could still be gifted, since all tests generate *underestimates* of people's abilities. So, the best way to think of an IQ test is as a minimal estimate of a child's abilities.

—*Linda Kreger Silverman is a psychologist who has passionately advocated for the gifted for more than 35 years.*

My child attends school in a district that is proud of the multiple methods it uses to identify its gifted children. They use test scores, observations and recommendations from teachers and, for young children, they even seek parent recommendations. Near the end of the identification process, my daughter was required to take an individual IQ test. Several weeks later, when I questioned why my daughter was not admitted to the gifted program even though her scores and ratings were far above average, I was told that her IQ score was three points shy of the cutoff.

"But I thought you looked at children from many perspectives, not just IQ," I stated.

"Oh, that's true," I was told, "but if a student doesn't have the minimum IQ cutoff, then we look no further."

I went home perplexed. Why did they bother gathering all this other information when all they really wanted was a high IQ? Is this what multiple methods of identification is all about?

—*Personal communication, Ohio parent, 1997*

- Jacquie was selected as intelligent by her behaviors, yet her test scores were never indicative of her advanced abilities. Which do we choose to believe, the actions or the numbers?
- The one time Jacquie *did* have an IQ test, she took it under adverse conditions—a physical illness and some emotional burdens. How accurate is her score?
- Jacquie was diagnosed as dyslexic, but not as gifted. How much did this learning difficulty affect her poor test performance?

As should be obvious by Jacquie's example, the route to take in identification of gifted children is filled with roadblocks and dead ends, for except in the cases in which children achieve in school, do well on standardized tests, are emotionally and physically healthy, and are mature enough to fit in with classmates who are as able as (or more so than) themselves, the process of identification becomes cloudy. In other words, the perfect child for being identified as gifted is one who fits the positive stereotype of the kid who "has it all"—brains, brawn, and sophistication! However, in our increasingly complex and diverse world, this stereotype becomes less common every year.

ONE POTATO, TWO POTATO . . .

To reiterate the obvious: The exact number of individuals who qualify as gifted is subject to one's definition of giftedness. Lewis Terman (1925) set the stage by making a cut-and-dry decision: Anyone who scored greater than 140 on the newly standardized Stanford-Binet Intelligence Test entered the wonderful world of giftedness. Statistically, this limited the number of children selected as gifted to about 1% of the school-age population—a number determined by applying the bell-shaped curve to the range of scores possible on the Stanford-Binet, with a score of 100 being average and a score of 140 being superior. Even today, school districts nationwide use Terman's conception of giftedness as an IQ number to determine who qualifies for gifted program services—although it is doubtful that many of these districts are even aware of who Terman was! They preselect a high number (usually 130 to 145 IQ) and make that point the beginning of giftedness. So, a 130 IQ may welcome you to the grand world of gifted whereas 128 IQs need not apply.

Of course, something odd can happen to a child whose family moves from one town (call it Springfield), where the IQ cutoff for giftedness is 130, to another (call it Estate Acres), where the prevailing IQ cutoff is 140. Somewhere, the child has lost his or her giftedness en route. Because, more often than not, a child included (and probably succeeding) in Springfield's gifted program will not be welcome in Estate Acres' gifted classes until the IQ bounces upward 10 points or more.

If this sounds confusing for the child and the parents, it is. However, that does not mean that the practice is uncommon.

Such silliness disguised as policy did not have too many practical implications in Terman's time, as the most common form of school accommodation for smart kids was grade skipping. Teachers merely took it on themselves to advance a child in school if that seemed to make sense.

Today, however, is a different story. In many a school district's search for precision, they have given up any element of subjectivity—a teacher's or parent's recommendation, for example—in deference to the almighty IQ number. Oddly, although today's prevailing notion is that gifted children are multidimensional beings, composed of a heart and body as well as a mind, their identification often is undeniably unidimensional: a magic, unalterable number achieved on a one-time IQ test. One has to wonder if Terman ever meant for his work to be abused in this cruel and crude fashion.

As mentioned in chapter 2, in the 1940s a renegade named Paul Witty suggested that a gifted child is one "whose performance is consistently remarkable in any potentially valuable area" (1940, p. 516).

You can imagine how the conservative number crunchers took to *this* interpretation! It took all of the fun out of qualifying

Laura (not her real name), age 4, was brought to my office by troubled parents at the advice of their only child's preschool teacher, who thought she might be autistic. Although these young parents saw quite different behavior at home, the teachers had good reason for their suspicions. Laura had spent the first day of preschool exploring materials and quietly observing her classmates, but since the second day, she had spoken only rarely and preferred to sit alone, doing over and over the same four-piece fruit puzzle. We discovered that Laura was not only very bright (Verbal IQ = 148; Performance IQ = 126) but seriously depressed, having concluded that her school years loomed interminably ahead as boring, boring, boring. Once we moved her into a preschool for gifted children, Laura brightened into a sociable little girl who entered enthusiastically into complex play, displayed passionate curiosity, and became her sunny self again.

—*Nancy Robinson is a professor, psychologist, parent, and grandparent of gifted children.*

someone as gifted and another as not, because giftedness was now to be seen as a trait that was as versatile as was human activity itself. Witty's rationale for this departure from logic was, ironically enough, based on his observations of children. Beginning in the 1920s, he began to study the play patterns of gifted children to see if their informal interactions could provide any clues to their intellectual prowess. Then, way before it was politically correct to do so (1930, to be exact), Witty began to investigate the presence of giftedness among disadvantaged and minority children. His findings were too bold to lead him in any direction but that of a very broad conception of giftedness.

Unfortunately, like many martyrs who have died at the hands of the mob he was trying to reform, Witty's work went largely unnoticed in any practical sense. The number crunchers remained in control, and giftedness continued to be identified by a culturally biased set of testing instruments that had been normed on a privileged group of 1,500 white children from California—Terman's "genius" subjects.

ENTER THE FEDS

The next major trend in identification took a long time in coming. Once the federal government wrote a definition of giftedness (see chapter 2), people began to see that it made sense to identify *differentially* those children who were intellectual powerhouses from those who were creative thinkers; children whose talents were found on the athletic fields from those whose talents were heard in concert halls. This was not to imply that a single gifted person could not occupy more than one category, but it gave permission for school personnel to look at giftedness as a set of behaviors, performances, or abilities. The first visible crack in the IQ eggshell had appeared.

The use of both new and already available alternatives to IQ tests began to explode on the scene like so many illegal Fourth of July fireworks. The Torrance Tests of Creative Thinking (TTCT; Torrance, 1966) looked at ways that children could produce innovative verbal and pictorial responses to questions or illustrations. Unlike so many similar tests, the TTCT carried with them the statistical reliability and validity that commanded respect among those who are concerned about such matters. Also, a new set of instruments came onto the market in response to J. P. Guilford's ideas about the multidimensional nature of giftedness and creativity. The SOI Learning Abilities Test (1975b) included 26 subtests that could be used to pinpoint high abilities in a number of dimensions related to learning and creative thinking. Of a more informal nature, The Scales for Rating the Behavioral Characteristics of Superior Students (Renzulli & Hartman, 1971) asked teachers (or others) to evaluate children for potential giftedness on 10 different and separate measures, including intellectual, creative, leadership, motivational, and various measures in the performing arts. Although never standardized with a precision that many statisticians would like, the scales provided an alternative method of seeking children's abilities. Equally as important, the scales finally gave teachers an instrument across which children could be compared based on their performance and abilities in a real-world setting of school or play.

This is not to say that IQ tests were no longer used—on the contrary, test developers themselves began producing *group* IQ tests that purported to measure a

---

AN INTERVIEW WITH DR. KAY BRUCH

On Testing Children Fairly and Honestly

Although I always followed the standardized directions given by the test developer, I relieved the anxiety of the kids while testing. For example, I would say, "This will not affect your grade. This is to understand you, the ways you perform and how I can help you." And I meant it! And they understood the test was not punitive and I was just looking to learn about their strengths and weaknesses.

On Creative Teaching versus Creative Teachers

When I was at UCLA, I did a study of the creative teacher as a person versus the creative teachers who brought out their students' own creativity. I found that the one who brought out creative qualities in kids was much more productive with children than a teacher who did all of the creativity him or herself—like writing the plays, writing the music, whatever. These teachers were dynamic and exciting in front of the class, but their own style and creativity often overwhelmed the kids' creativity.

On the Dangers of Making Assumptions

I had a kindergarten kid who tested out at 150 on the Stanford-Binet. But on the report form from his kindergarten teacher, it read that he couldn't handle himself in independent behavior. All the kids in kindergarten could tie his shoes except him. The need for a parent interview was evident.

In working with the parents, it was obvious that they knew they had a bright youngster. But they had catered to him a lot. Living in a rural area, his only companions were often adults, and they just gave him so much attention that he never had to do independent things—"grown up" things. So, when I did accelerate him to first grade (he was reading at a fourth grade level) I had to work with the parents and teacher on helping him get social skills and independent behavior skills so that he could function more independently. But his mind . . . it was fine!

On Abolishing Stereotypes

One good way to train people to change their cultural biases is to expose them to the reality of real persons who are not like the stereotypes you've made up and been brought up with. The most exciting thing I observed

continued on the following page

continued from the previous page

in my classes was in an early experimental program at the University of Georgia where we asked teachers to refer all kids with any signs of gifts or talents. One kid's name was Isaiah. He was chosen because he had creative strengths on the Torrance Tests of Creative Thinking. He perceived holistically and yet he couldn't read well. The learning for the teachers who were observing him was the reality that Isaiah could not get to school and would probably have had no breakfast even if he *could* get to school. So, the teachers decided to pick up Isaiah. Before they brought him to school, they took him for breakfast, and then watched as Isaiah blossomed for the rest of each morning. Without this personal contact with and commitment to him, Isaiah would never have been seen as the great kid he was.

On Lifelong Learning

What has kept me in this field for so long is the field's total openness for further inquiry in giftedness or creativity. It is a field that has constant potential for change even if some people go backwards. There is still a potential for new and improved inquiries into ways of working with what we learn. I crave openness—I don't like to be boxed in. Gifted education gives me that.

—Catherine (Kay) Bruch is a lifelong advocate and researcher for gifted and creative children, specializing in the identification of giftedness and creativity in disadvantaged children.

child's intellectual status *in only 50 minutes!* Yes, instant intellectual analysis was now possible by the introduction of school testing programs such as the Otis-Lennon School Ability Test (Otis & Lennon, 1977); the Test of Cognitive Skills (Keyser & Sweetland, 1985); and the Cognitive Abilities Test (Thorndike & Hagen, 1954). Proponents pointed out that classroom teachers could administer these tests (*monitor* would be a more precise term), saving time and money. Detractors, however, emphasized that the tests were too easy for many gifted children, so that the scores they received—even high scores—told you little about what a child knew and how high his or her abilities really were. Besides, a 50-minute, classroom-based test of an entity as complicated as intelligence just struck some folks as an overly simplistic solution to an issue that has no easy answers: the accurate measurement of a person's intellect.

Unfortunately, school districts nationwide did not debate the merits and flaws of these group intelligence measures to determine if they were appropriate for use with students. Instead, these tests became a staple, an annual October exercise that students completed along with the accompanying group achievement tests that determined how well a child could spell, write, or do math— again, in 50 minutes or less.

Defenders would say that group tests are mere starting points, gross measures of a child's abilities that can then be followed up with more intense, individual assessment. And in some school districts, that is true. The unfortunate reality, though, is that these measures may indeed be considered gross for an entirely different reason: They demean the integrity of an entity that is both multifaceted and complex—intelligence.

A NEW VIEW OF GIFTEDNESS; A NEW WAY TO LOOK FOR IT

In 1978, an article that shook the field of gifted child education right off its comfortable test-based perch hit the presses: "What Makes Giftedness?" by Joseph Renzulli. A major premise of the article was that giftedness had been seen historically, by educators and psychologists, as a trait within an individual—mental capacity, as measured by a standardized intelligence test. Renzulli argued, though, that the reasons that we notice people as gifted in the real world have little to do with their measured IQs and much more to do with their creative productivity—the patents they devise, the poems they write, the buildings and theories they construct. Stating that giftedness in our culture is less a trait than a set of behaviors *based on* traits, Renzulli urged his colleagues (and still does so today) to stop talking about gifted *children* and start talking about gifted *behaviors.*

To many, this sounded like a welcome alternative. After all, the identification of gifted children had become a difficult process and often a contentious one, especially among parents whose children missed an arbitrary cutoff by the slimmest of margins. Also, the prevailing methods of identification made it much easier to identify children as gifted from affluent suburbs than from poor rural or urban neighborhoods. Simply put, the suburban children were often more worldly, having been exposed to the kinds of experiences that the writers of many IQ tests covet.

Renzulli's conception of giftedness (see Figure 3.1) would put the emphasis in identification less on a set of testable preconditions (for example, high IQ or achievement test scores) and squarely on the shoulders of what children did with whatever abilities they had. He based his idea on this: In studying eminent people from both past centuries and today's headlines, it was obvious that it took more than brilliance for them to become notable. In fact, it took at least two characteristics other than intelligence: *task commitment* (sustained motivation in a specific field of study) and *creativity.* Renzulli believed that these factors were at least equally important in the fruition of talents as the typical benchmark of high intelligence. Taking this notion even further, he believed that the evidence from history suggested that people with above average, but not necessarily superior, intelligence were often credited with society's best thinking and creations. Thus, intelligence, when combined with the factors of task commitment and creativity that were brought to bear on a specific domain, was the

FIGURE 3.1

■

Graphic Representation of the Three-Ring Definition of Giftedness

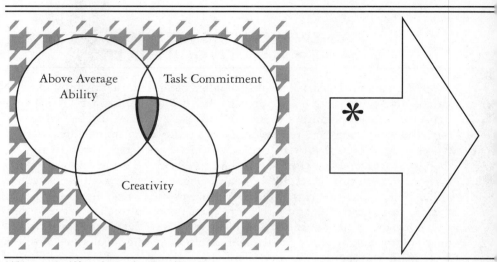

* This arrow should be read as ". . . brought to bear upon . . ."

real mark of genius; it was only when people "got their rings together" that true gifted behavior emerged. The eminent architect, cartoonist, ecologist, or educator is the one whose work stands out above the others. And once it does, no one bothers to ask what the person's IQ is.

This conception of gifted behaviors sent many heads spinning. Arguments waged at national gifted education conferences on the legitimacy of this three-ring definition, its usefulness, and its implications for a field of study just regaining a comfortable niche in American education and psychology. Naysayers postulated that Renzulli based his new conception of giftedness more on wishful thinking than any research-based evidence. Others contended that it "cheapened" giftedness, relegating it to a mere set of behaviors, with little regard given to the inner workings of the human mind and spirit. Also, by Renzulli's definition, there could be no such thing as a "gifted underachiever," as the term would now become an oxymoron.

Affecting the thinking and the practice of gifted child education, this three-ring conception of giftedness sent major ripples through an educational community that preferred the safety and ease of "135 IQ, you're gifted; 133 IQ need not apply."

General Performance Areas		
Mathematics	Visual Arts	Physical Sciences
Philosophy	Social Sciences	Law
Religion	Language Arts	Music
Life Sciences		Movement Arts

Specific Performance Areas		
Cartooning	Demography	Electronic Music
Astronomy	Microphotography	Child Care
Public Opinion Polling	City Planning	Consumer Protection
Jewelry Design	Pollution Control	Cooking
Map Making	Poetry	Orinthology
Choreography	Fashion Design	Furniture Design
Biography	Weaving	Navigation
Film Making	Play Writing	Genealogy
Statistics	Advertising	Sculpture
Local History	Costume Design	Wildlife Management
Electronics	Meteorology	Set Design
Musical Composition	Puppetry	Agricultural
Landscape	Marketing	Research
Architecture	Game Design	Animal Learning
Chemistry	Journalism	Film Criticism
Etc.	Etc.	Etc.

—*Reprinted from* Systems and Models for Developing Programs for the Gifted and Talented. © *1985, Creative Learning Press, Inc., Mansfield Center, CT.*

GIFTED IDENTIFICATION IN A DIVERSE CULTURE

Although the brouhaha over Renzulli's behavioristic view of giftedness was something new in the late 1970s, something *not* new continued to plague the field of gifted child education: the underrepresentation of minority and economically disadvantaged children from most forms of advanced school programming. Was it the limited intellects of these groups of individuals, or was it something else, such as inappropriate methods of locating gifts in children living outside the mainstream, middle-class culture, that limited the number of minority-culture children identified as gifted? Perhaps this example will help to clarify this issue.

Picture the setting: You are strolling through a crisp, clear northern forest enjoying all that nature provides. A far cry from your overcrowded and developed suburb, this place exudes clean, odorless air. Suddenly, a bull moose crosses your path—and stays there. He looks you in the eye and snorts so powerfully that puffs of air come out of his nostrils. What do you do?

a. run toward the moose
b. run away from the moose
c. drop to the ground and play dead
d. climb the nearest tree
e. other: _____

> IQ tests seem to have selected those who would be consummate adapters to the demands of society, but not those who would shape society—not those who would lead it into the future.
> —*Sternberg, 1997, p. 8*

Or how about this: "Explain the meaning of a 'joggling board' by writing a sentence and drawing a picture of how you would use one."

Still stumped? Perhaps this analogy might appeal to you: "Sungka is to _____ as Chevrolet is to car."

The point of these seemingly baffling questions is this: Much of what we know is based on the specific culture in which we were raised. Thus, if we are asked to answer questions that have little or no relationship to our everyday existence, it might appear that we are not as smart as we really are.

This issue takes on critical importance in the intellectual assessment of children whose backgrounds and experiences do not mesh with the types of questions or tasks that they are asked to complete on standardized IQ or achievement tests. For example, if we ask a child whose native language is not English to answer vocabulary questions that require familiarity *with* our language, then how can we be sure that we are getting an accurate assessment of that child's verbal ability? Or if we show four illustrations and ask two different children—one from a wealthy suburb and one from a crowded slum—to "point to the gazebo," which child is more likely to answer correctly? Obviously, the child whose background and experiences include familiarity with this middle-class backyard feature would have a distinct advantage in getting this question right—and would be much more likely to be seen as intelligent and selected for inclusion in a gifted program.

Several themes have emerged in the literature regarding the underrepresentation of African American students in gifted programs. These factors include:

1. *Inadequate identification practices:* a too-heavy reliance on standardized (and often culturally biased) testing instruments
2. *Too little attention to non-intellectual barriers to achievement:* racism, lower teacher expectations, poverty and cultural conflicts regarding values and priorities
3. *Too little attention to learning style preferences:* how students learn (i.e., visually rather than auditorily) may impact their identification as gifted
4. *Over reliance on quantitative definitions of underachievement:* the discrepancy between measured ability and daily performance may be less extreme, but underachievement may still exist
5. *Lack of family involvement in the educational process:* parents of African American children may be apprehensive about becoming involved in schools

—*Ford, 1994*

The cultural and linguistic biases in many of the tests used to measure intelligence and achievement in children are a well-researched problem (Richert, Alvino, & McDonnel, 1982; Moon, Feldhusen, & Kelly, 1991). The end result—more middle-class, white children getting selected for gifted programs with a disproportionate number of minorities chosen for special education classes—may lead to the incorrect conclusion that some races and cultures are, indeed, more intelligent than others. In fact, although gifted child educators are often embarrassed to admit it, some gifted programs in ethnically diverse areas of our country look like a *de facto* segregated school; a "whites only" club in the midst of a rainbow of cultures and colors. Gifted program planners may *say* that they are diverse and inclusive in their identification practices, but even a quick glance into that resource room for gifted students might lead observers to believe otherwise. Hence, the oft-heard complaint that gifted child education is an elite grouping of privileged kids whose parents want them to have a private school education in their neighborhood classroom is difficult to dismiss.

Even when researchers have tried to be more inclusive in their identification practices, many have been criticized for merely "watering down" the standards by which a child from a minority culture might qualify as gifted. The accusation of having a double standard—one set of criteria for whites and a lower one for minorities—has caused many a well-intentioned educator to admit defeat or frustration over this issue, for that was never their goal; instead, these individuals were simply looking for alternative assessments that could showcase the talents of children who, for whatever reasons, did not "show what they know" on the usual battery of IQ and achievement tests pervasive in our schools.

Still, some interesting attempts have been made, especially in the 1970s. Bruch (1971) isolated those elements of the Stanford-Binet Intelligence Test that were found to show high degrees of performance by blacks—problem-solving skills with visual or auditory content, memory questions, and questions that had only one right answer—and developed an abbreviated Binet test that would tap into these talents and not those areas in which blacks were shown, in her research, to be lower on performance (e.g., vocabulary).

I've been in gifted and talented programs all through school, beginning in about third grade. What I've experienced most in terms of discrimination has been in relationship to my peers within my own culture. Many black people would think I was trying to be white because I was in those programs and spoke differently, and that would really hurt. As a teenager, I was once confronted by a group of black girls who asked me, "What color do you think you are? What are you trying to be?" It was very tense—they literally blocked my path in the school hallway. I was scared, of course, especially since no one was around at the time. . . . I told them that they might think I was trying to be white, but it wasn't true, and that I didn't see myself as being any better than they were.

Even today, things aren't easy for me because I face the same problems. Sometimes I feel down and even cry. What helps me is to remember who I am inside and to keep building that up. People can make fun of you, but only you can decide if conforming is what you really want to do.

Danita Salone is a college senior, majoring in marketing and international business.
—*Excerpted from* The Gifted Kids Survival Guide: A Teen Handbook *by Judy Galbraith, MA, & Jim Delisle, PhD, Copyright © 1996. Used with permission of Free Spirit Publishing, Minneapolis, MN.*

Mercer (1977) chose to focus not on a single test but on an entire system to determine intelligence in minority children. In using the System of Multicultural Pluralistic Assessment (SOMPA), Mercer included not only objective test data but also subjective interview data, gathered from parents who took time to describe the various elements of family life that might help explain certain deficiencies in a child's test scores. So, if the SOMPA assessment determined that the social or economic conditions of a child's home precluded much interaction with books or conversations about complex ideas, that might help explain why a child's test score performance was weak. Another test, the culture-specific and oddly named BITCH test (*B*lack *I*ntelligence *T*est of *C*ultural *H*omogeneity) was yet one more entrant into the pool of assessments used to identify giftedness in more equitable ways.

FORGOTTEN PIONEERS: AFRICAN AMERICANS WHO STUDIED GIFTED CHILDREN AND THEIR EDUCATION

- **Horace Mann Bond:** Born in Nashville in 1904, Bond became a voracious reader at a very young age. At 15, he entered Lincoln University in Pennsylvania, a liberal arts college for African American men founded in 1854. In 1924, he became director of the School of Education at Oklahoma's Langston University, while simultaneously beginning his PhD at the University of Chicago. In an article published in 1927, "Some Exceptional Negro Children," he wrote about the appalling effects of using IQ tests on Negro children who had little background information that would allow them to excel. Using an African American examiner to test 30 black children, Bond found that 26% scored at least 130 IQ on the revised version of the Binet-Simon Scales. Bond's work is the first known published account of intellectually gifted African American children as a special population.

- **Lillian Steele Proctor:** Lillian grew up in Atlanta in the early 1900s, where there was no public high school for African American students. She paid tuition to attend a high school at Atlanta University, and eventually won scholarships to study social work in New York and Chicago Universities. In 1929, she completed her Master's thesis, "A case study of 30 superior colored children in Washington, DC," but had to convince her advisor to let her conduct the study at all. She compiled the 30 case studies, including developmental histories, personality traits and social adjustment, making this the first such study to appear in the literature. Eventually, Proctor returned to Chicago, where she became the city's first black supervisor of social work.

- **A. Janet Terwilliger:** Janet was born in 1903 and graduated from Southhampton High School in New York in 1921. Going to college in education, she eventually studied at Teachers College, Columbia University, completing her Master's thesis, "A study of Negro children of IQ above 125," under the guidance of Leta Hollingworth. Hoping to study Negro children in eight suburbs, Terwilliger received no responses to her inquiries, eventually selecting children from Harlem to study. She studied 10 children whose IQs ranged from 125–157. The 10 intensive case studies found that 90% of the gifted children came from superior homes. Her most outstanding result was that the consciousness of racial differences disappeared with the presence of superior intelligence.

- **Martin David Jenkins:** Born in Terre Haute, Indiana in 1904, Martin's father was a civil engineer, a position that placed the family as one of the few middle class African American families in the city at that time. He attended a segregated elementary school and a large, integrated high school, being one of the few African Americans to graduate. He went on to college, receiving a doctorate from Northwestern University under the direction of Paul Witty. Jenkins's study of Negro children of superior intelligence provided evidence that the emergence of giftedness was only likely if sufficient provision was made to "feed" the intellect. Jenkins also published a case study of "B," a 9-year-old African American girl with an IQ of 200. Later in his career, Jenkins became a professor at Howard University and president of Morgan State University. After serving as president for 22 years, he became director of the Office of Urban Affairs for the American Council on Education. Once asked why he studied gifted African American children, he stated simply: "I enjoy the topic."

—*Reprinted with permission,* Roeper Review, *P.O. Box 329, Bloomfield Hills, MI 48303.*

More recently, researchers have begun to reexamine the benefits of a cluster of standardized tests that have been around for some time: Raven's *Standard Progressive Matrices* (1980, 1990). These nonverbal tests of reasoning ability, developed in Great Britain in the 1950s, require that the child or adult (the tests can be used from early childhood through adulthood) complete a visual puzzle by selecting a piece that matches the pattern established within the pieces displayed. Because no verbal response is required, that possible contaminating factor has been eliminated in identifying these underlying elements of intelligence: recognizing patterns and deciphering logic.

In almost all cases, the advice is the same (Frasier, 1993): If you want to identify intellectual abilities in children from cultures or backgrounds that are different from the mainstream, you must look more at *qualitative* measures than *quantitative* ones. For example,

- Ask teachers to provide anecdotal examples—drawings, constructions, or other visible evidence—of a child's abilities, creativity, or complex thinking patterns.
- Include parents in the identification process, by asking them to contribute information on their child's early years and what the child does during spare time.
- Look for evidence of both general intellectual abilities and specific aptitudes in the child's daily work; document these examples in a journal or portfolio for later examination.

From the work done in Gary, Indiana (which, when I worked there, was 95% African American), I know that by identifying youngsters when they are in pre-kindergarten and/or kindergarten, I know that a diverse group of needs can be identified: students with potential talent, students with observable advanced skill development, as well as those students who score high on measured assessment instruments. It is important that once identified, the student and his/her parents become a part of the planning team for that student's educational career, that the student be given as many opportunities as possible to study with other students who have high intellectual potential. . . . Once parents are aware of the opportunities being made available to all students, they approach school personnel for additional information.

—Dorothy Lawshe is director of Gifted and Talented Programs at Michigan State University.

- Examine how a child uses creativity in solving a problem, in escaping a punishment, or in undertaking a task that is complex or made up of many parts. Observe the *process* of learning, not merely the end product done by the child.
- Interview the child whom you are concerned about. Better than anyone else, children can tell you what they enjoy doing both in and out of school, what they find easy, difficult, and challenging, and how they learn best—through reading, writing, acting, drawing, and so forth.

Such a comprehensive system of identification of gifts and talents would follow the advice given by authors of a most comprehensive report on identification (Richert et al., 1982), in which these elements were seen as essential:

1. **Advocacy:** Is the bottom line purpose of identification to *in*clude, rather than *ex*clude, children from the process of identification?
2. **Defensibility:** Do the identification measures "cover the bases" in the search for children's gifts and talents?
3. **Equity:** Are special considerations made to use instruments and assessments that are free of cultural or other biases?
4. **Pluralism:** Is the definition of giftedness comprehensive enough to include children from other than the majority culture?
5. **Comprehensiveness:** Do the identification instruments and assessments consider the child's abilities from a number of vantage points?
6. **Pragmatism:** Do the methods of identification, and the tools used to assess children, conform to local needs or special circumstances (e.g., economic poverty or a large percentage of non-English-speaking students)? If not, what adaptations can be made so that the instruments and assessments are more relevant and useful?

TEST SCORES OR OPINIONS: WHICH MATTER MORE?

Even those people who believe 100% in the infallibility of IQ tests to measure the intellect would probably not say this too loudly in public. The last time that was done, with the publication of the controversial volume *The Bell Curve*

(Hernstein & Murray, 1994), its authors were chastised as racist, sexist, and out of touch with contemporary thinking on the complex makeup of intelligence. In these politically correct times, it just doesn't sit too well to claim that IQ tests—or *any* standardized test, for that matter—carry the muscle they did in the early part of the 20th century.

Ironically, even though we are not comfortable with any single measure to determine one's intelligence, our schools and our society continue to be fascinated with the numbers that these tests provide. When the issue of identifying giftedness through multiple measures is brought up, everyone agrees in theory, but few are comfortable in practice. For instance, take this conversation:

> Enlightened teacher (ET): "You know, there are a couple of kids in my class who don't test very well, but whose daily work is very good. Also, they are constantly asking me questions about anything and everything. I'm thinking of nominating them for the gifted program."
>
> Bureaucratic Gatekeeper (BG): "But in order to qualify for our screening pool, there *are* certain minimum test scores that children to be identified as gifted must attain."

ET: "Wouldn't my observations over these last few months be enough to override any low test scores? I have kept portfolios of their work—I really do have evidence."

BG: "My dear, you don't understand. If we allowed these . . . opinions to be used as the basis for gifted program admission, the floodgates would open. *Everybody* would be nominating students!"

ET: ". . . And your point is?"

BG: "I'm not trying to be difficult, I'm just telling you the reality of the situation. However, let me double check these students' test scores. If the numbers are there, I'll contact you and you can show me their portfolios. It would be *wonderful* information to add to their file!"

ET: "But it helps them out only if my judgments agree with your test scores."

BG: "Yes, exactly! I'm *so* glad you understand!"

We asked several groups to listen to these descriptions of children and to predict the children's future development. In five years, we asked, would they be functioning as gifted, average-normal, psychotic, neurotic, delinquent, or mentally deficient persons?

Case 1: Girl, age 16, orphaned, willed to custody of grandmother by mother, who was separated from alcoholic husband, now deceased. Mother rejected the homely child, who has been proven to lie and to steal sweets. Swallowed penny to attract attention at five.

Case 2: Boy, senior year secondary school, has obtained certificate from physician stating that nervous breakdown makes it necessary for him to leave school for six months. Boy not a good all-around student; has no friends—teachers find him a problem—spoke late—father ashamed of son's lack of athletic ability—poor adjustment to school. Boy has odd mannerisms, makes up own religion, chants hymns to himself, parents regard him as "different."

Case #1 is Eleanor Roosevelt. Case #2 is Albert Einstein.

—*Goertzel & Goertzel, 1962, pp. xii–xiii*

It seems that in trying to find and use alternative means of assessment, it has been forgotten that not all the pieces need to fit together as neatly as a jigsaw puzzle. In fact, that is the main point of teacher, parent, or peer nominations: to find qualities, characteristics, or abilities in children that are not unearthed by the typical test-based measures used in schools. Unfortunately, as in the scenario above, the more subjective pieces of information provided by the teacher

In an investigation of promising practices used by schools to identify giftedness in children, Carolyn Callahan and her colleagues found some "clear directions...which merit attention (p. iv), including:

- *The acceptance of intelligence as multifaceted,* wherein children could show their intelligence in multiple ways
- *The recognition of multiple manifestations of giftedness,* in which the specific cultural context of children is taken into account during the identification process
- *The emphasis on authentic assessment,* in which the collection of observational data of students played as significant a role as did paper-and-pencil tasks
- *The expanded source of evidence of intelligence,* whereby information on children was sought from the home and other non-school sources
- *The development of inclusiveness rather than exclusiveness,* where the identification process sought to find "gifted non-conformers as well as performers" (p. vi), and to explore potential over demonstrated performance
- A strong *link between identification and instruction,* in which planned linkages between information obtained about individual children and the instructional services they were offered were meshed together
- *Collaborative efforts,* so that schools were linked with universities; classroom teachers were linked with gifted education specialists; and all staff members had a stake in a gifted child's success
- *An emphasis on staff development* to enhance the understanding of gifted students by the whole school community
- *Early and ongoing evaluation of the identification process,* to ensure that it met the needs of the children in the particular school or community
- *Relationships with ongoing school reform efforts,* so that gifted child education services were seen as a part of overall efforts to improve teaching and learning

—*Callahan, Tomlinson, & Pizzat, undated*

do not always carry the same degree of clout to gifted program planners as do "hard data." A frequently heard sobriquet is that "it would be hard to justify to a parent that *their* child, with an IQ of 137, is *not* in the gifted program whereas a child with an IQ of 'only' 129 *is* included due to the influence of a teacher's observation."

And there lies the problem: Until the field of gifted child education is willing to give as much credence to teacher and parent observations as it does to test scores, the assessment of giftedness in children will continue to be a process that is limited, unfair, and discourteous to those who know these children best, the teachers who educate them and the parents who live with them. The adage "put up or shut up" is most appropriate today, an era in which children whose giftedness is disguised by low test score performance are entering their third decade of being "underserved" by the field that, in theory, advocates for them.

IDENTIFICATION—FOR WHAT PURPOSE?

Consider this: To qualify for entrance into an Advanced Placement biology course, students must be able to run a mile in less than 8 minutes. Or, as a screening measure for inclusion into an accelerated reading program in kindergarten, students have to prove proficiency in multiplication and division. Last, to qualify for the middle school orchestra, the audition includes a reading test on which a score above the 95 percentile is needed. Sound absurd? Of course! Is it far from reality? Not by much.

The central purpose of identifying gifted children is to plan educational programs and options that challenge and develop their obvious or latent abilities. Yet in too many cases, not dissimilar to the exaggerated examples above, the overlapping issues of identification and program planning are not considered simultaneously but, rather, sequentially. Oddly, these perpendicular topics are often treated as parallel, without even a mathematical possibility of ever touching one another.

Gifted program planners and advocates need to ask this bottom-line question when the identification process begins: "For what purpose?" The vacuum created when an identification scheme is launched without consideration being given to the type of program(s) that the identified children will

> Many of the children of the past who were to become eminent . . . tended to possess superior ability in reasoning and in recognizing relationships. They showed intellectual curiosity, had a wide range of interests, did effective work independently. They showed their greatest superiority in treading ability; many read at the age of four. Almost all were early readers of good books. They were original thinkers and had scant patience with drill and routine. They were likely to be rejected by their playmates and had parents who valued learning. The majority of them came from middle-class business and professional homes. Their brothers and sisters were capable. Most of those children who became eminent would probably have tested high on today's intelligence tests.
>
> —*Goertzel and Goertzel commenting on the similarities of the eminent men whom they selected for inclusion in their book* Cradles of Eminence, *1962, p. x.*

be in remains one of our field's most frequent problems. Luckily, it is also one of our field's most *solvable* problems.

The common sense secret is this: If a gifted program is going to focus on language-based content or activities, then the use of mathematics test scores doesn't really apply. Conversely, in searching for students who will enroll in a sixth-grade prealgebra program, there is no need to spend a lot of time looking at the spelling and grammar portion of their Iowa Test of Basic Skills. (An aside: It is not recommended to use the spelling and grammar portion of *any* type of test for *any* type of gifted program!) Sounds simple, doesn't it? Yet this logical approach to linking identification and program options is sidestepped more often than not. As Piirto (1994) writes,

> Programming for talented children often has nothing to do with the strengths of the identified child. . . . Often, children who have been identified for different kinds of talents are put into the same class for special programming. One teacher told about three students in her accelerated junior high school mathematics class in the inner core of a major city. These children had been identified for creative thinking ability. Most of the class were eager for faster paced, in-depth mathematics, but the three students were lost. She had to decrease the pace and spend a lot of time explaining and repeating for these three students who were misplaced. Neither the mathematically talented nor the creatively talented were being served by this program. (pp. 94–95)

Now, as much as one might ask why the teacher above didn't individualize the instructional methods so that children could work at whatever pace was most comfortable for them, the deeper question is whether it makes sense to plan a program for one kind of talent and then include children in it whose abilities lie in other domains. The answer? No.

To prevent the problems that accompany this identification-programming mismatch, the following solutions are recommended:

A. **Establish a gifted education committee:** This committee, composed of classroom teachers, administrators, counselors, parents, gifted education specialists, and (perhaps) students, is assigned the task of looking at two related topics:

1. The existing options at each grade that already meet the needs of gifted or talented students; for example, Honors courses at the high school or an early admission policy for kindergarten. We call this compilation of options the "Inventory of Excellence."

2. The existing educational "gaps" perceived by various committee members, or policies that inhibit the fruition of gifts and talents. For example, if academically capable children are not allowed any grade level or content acceleration, this could be a problem. Additionally, a program that focuses on intellectual abilities may do so at the expense of the social and emotional needs of students. Each of these "weak

links" is a possible source of program growth or change for the committee to consider.

B. **Become familiar with multiple measures for identification of gifts and talents:** Invite someone who knows the field of gifted child education to make a presentation on different ways that gifted and talented students can be identified. Consider (and have on hand to examine) various formal and informal testing instruments (e.g., parent identification forms, teacher nomination forms). The purpose of this phase of the plan is merely to become familiar with methods of assessment that are varied and valuable. Can't find a gifted education expert around? Then assign "homework" to individual members to read particular textbook chapters on the identification of gifted children, and have each prepare a synopsis of ideas and useful materials.

> I don't believe in separate programs for minority students. I believe that if an educator is sincere about wanting to provide challenging educational opportunities and is sensitive to the needs of all students, then minority students will be included. In the Summer of 1997, we enrolled 90 students in our Mathematics-Science-Technology program. We had 1 American Indian, 13 Asian Americans, 12 African Americans, 1 Hispanic American, 56 Caucasian Americans, and 7 inter-racial children. The Program looked like the U.N. We are looking to increase the representation of Native American and Hispanic students, but in no case have standards been lowered in order to increase minority participation. Each student is in grade 7 or 8, and has standardized test scores at the 95 percentile or higher and an SAT Total Score of 1010 or better.
>
> —*Dorothy Lawshe, Michigan State University*

C. **Become familiar with different programming options and the benefits and drawbacks of each one:** There are many recognized ways to structure gifted program options for students, some of which work better than others at different grade levels and in different communities. *Resource rooms,* or "pull-out" programs, are very common in elementary schools and less so at higher grade levels, due mainly to problems with scheduling such classes. *Self-contained gifted classrooms* are just that, classrooms full of identified gifted students who remain as a separate group for an entire school year, or longer. *Inclusion-based programs* take on many formats but generally involve gifted children spending the majority of their time in their "regular" classrooms with the gifted education specialist serving their needs within that setting—instead of pulling students out, the gifted education teacher is "pulled in" to their classroom.

These and other options are discussed more fully in chapter 5; the purpose of mentioning them here is that the Gifted Education Committee must become knowledgeable of how these various programming options affect a gifted child's progress through school. There is no one best way to serve gifted students effectively, but decisions on which options *are* best for a particular school or district begin with understanding the pros and cons of each plan. Indeed, the Gifted Education Committee's "homework" can become extensive!

I have felt for a long time that if gifted education is to become legitimate and if gifted children are to be respected and liked, revered for what they can do to contribute to the quality of our lives, we have to sell their special needs and we have to ask the private sector to help us educate them. Because we have demonstrated time and time again that we can't do it ourselves and nobody else really cares, the best thing we can do is put together a private sector gifted education advisory council. The private sector can pull gifted education out of the fire because education as a whole is not doing that. Business and industry are more interested in gifted kids than in kids who still have to learn to read. I think it would be appropriate to look upon education and the private sector as equal partners.

—*Gina Ginsburg Riggs is the founder of the Gifted Child Society, a gifted advocacy group based in New Jersey.*

D. **Put the pieces together:** Once the preceding information-gathering stages are completed (although this task is never *really* done!), committee members need to sit down and evaluate all they have learned in the light of programs and identification measures that will best serve the children in their care. It is suggested that at least two, perhaps three, plans be compiled: (a) A pie-in-the-sky, K–12 plan that will probably cost more money than any one district is willing to spend; (b) A realistic but "meaty" plan that prioritizes the changes or growth in the gifted program that the committee feels should be accomplished over the next 3 to 5 years; (c) A bare-bones plan that, in effect, polishes up what already exists without adding many new dimensions or program features. Once compiled, these plans should be shared with decision makers whose role it is to spend the money and hire the appropriate personnel. With any luck and a lot of convincing, those who control the purse strings might see the benefit of "investing" (a better term than *spending*) in more than a bargain-basement approach to serving the needs of gifted students.

If these steps are taken, a 1-year time limit should be given for the committee's deliberations. Certainly, more time and energy *could* be devoted to such a large task, yet we have seen too many examples of endless committees in which interest begins to wane once the initial impetus (and, perhaps, goals) was lost.

By addressing the issues of programming and identification simultaneously, the full scope of the gifted program's aims and benefits can be better understood. Decisions regarding placement of children (which, again, should be a committee task, in which the most basic question is "What educational alternatives do we offer that best meet the needs of this child?") become purposeful, unbiased, and legitimate. And even though mistakes will occur and alterations in these best laid plans will need to be made, at least the full range of possibilities will have been considered in completing the ultimate task: the identification of gifts and talents to provide educational options that make sense for the individual children involved.

THESE ARE A FEW UNFAVORITE THINGS

Even with decades of experience in designing and implementing identification methods for gifted child education programs, program coordinators and others still make some obvious mistakes. When considered thoughtfully, these errors defy logic; still, they exist. In beginning or expanding options for gifted students, consider these unfavorite things and do whatever possible to ensure that they do not occur.

VEXING PROBLEM 1: ONCE IDENTIFIED, ALWAYS IDENTIFIED

There are times when children participating in gifted programs at the high school level may be doing so based on the results of standardized tests that they took years earlier. Once the label of "gifted" is attached, it, like a tattoo, remains permanent.

Now, that's not to say that children should be "retested" for giftedness annually, tossing them out like so many unsavory leftovers if they miss an IQ cutoff by three points. Instead, though, it is essential to conduct an occasional "checkup" to see if the gifted program, as it exists, is meeting the needs of individual gifted children, as *they* exist. Remember, the ultimate goal of gifted identification is to design an appropriate array of educational experiences and placements that benefit the child. Without an occasional glance at the child who exists *today,* gifted program services may be provided for the child who existed *yesterday.* Too many gifted children opt out of gifted programs at some time in their educational career. Perhaps this is appropriate, as long as their reasons for doing so make sense to them and the adults who care for them. Still, many gifted children become "g/t dropouts" because who they are and what they need are no longer what is offered by even well-intentioned school personnel. A scheduled reevaluation of the children involved in the gifted program, perhaps every 3 years, will be just one more quality control check that our goals and their needs are meshing.

VEXING PROBLEM 2: ONCE NOT IDENTIFIED, NEVER, EVER IDENTIFIED

Every issue has an opposite, and this one is the obverse of Vexing Problem #1. Indeed, it is even more serious; for rather than involving an error of *commission,* this problem generates an error of *omission.* If children are not identified as gifted at a grade level where such identification typically occurs in a school district (the end of third grade is a common time), they may never be considered again unless a very astute and/or persistent parent or educator makes a special case to nominate the child. The lesson to be learned by this is that identification is never fully "done," which leads to the next issue. . . .

VEXING PROBLEM 3: IDENTIFICATION IS A PROCESS, NOT AN EVENT

In many school districts there are not only cutoff points for who is considered gifted, there is also a cutoff date by which people can make their nominations. It is the Academy Award equivalent of "if you don't get your ballot in on time, then your vote doesn't count."

> Identification should begin as early as possible in the child's life and go on as long as possible, because there are always opportunities for discovering new insights and correcting old errors of judgment.
> —*Tannenbaum, 1983, p. 365*

> The search for students distinguished by new types of motivation, new or developed abilities, or potential enrollment in new curricula also implies continuous assessment, but using new procedures attuned to the new circumstances. It may be wise to risk error on the side of inclusion rather than exclusion, in order to assure the student of the most suitable education and to avoid litigation by disappointed parents who recognize the risk of error in decision based upon test scores.
> —*Shore, Cornell, Robinson, & Ward, 1991, p. 44*

I've never been in any special programs. Until this year, I had never even heard of being gifted. I'm not advanced in my classes, although they're never challenging.

As for school, it has always been boring, but I never rebelled. I do talk a lot in class, but no one sees me as a discipline problem.

They tell me I'm gifted, so I suppose I am. Until now I didn't care. Recently I've decided that if I'm so smart, maybe I should do something with my life.

—*A gifted teenager's comment, the American Association for Gifted Children, 1978, p. 8*

To be sure, there are times when deadlines and votes need to occur: presidential elections and the aforementioned Oscars being two cases in point. However, with something as fluid as human abilities, and children emerging as gifted or talented at different times and for different reasons (e.g., a teacher who finally sees a "spark" in a child that had not been noticed previously), the process of identification needs to be considered as ongoing, not static. To do otherwise downplays the reality of children's differing patterns and rates of development.

VEXING PROBLEM 4: NATIONAL NORMS ARE USED TO IDENTIFY LOCAL KIDS

This issue, particularly relevant in the case of standardized achievement tests, involves the mistake made by gifted program planners who use national norms instead of local norms when determining qualifications for a gifted program. For instance, take Scenario #1, the case of a gifted coordinator in a wealthy district where most students perform far above the 50th percentile—that is, when compared with other children nationally, they rank in the top half, perhaps even as high as the 85th to 95th percentile. *Someone* has to score that high, and it is often children from financially privileged school districts. If national norms are used for selecting children into the district's gifted program, more than 20 to 30% of the students can rank at the 90th to 99th percentile. Almost *everyone* qualifies for the gifted program!

Scenario #2: The town adjacent to the one above is a poor school district where many students struggle to learn and to achieve. When ranked against other, more academically successful school districts, these students (on the whole) have a very low level of performance. This may lead some persons to think that no gifted children at all exist in this town.

The problem in both of these districts, as different as their situations may seem, is identical: The use of national norms does not accommodate the reality of each student population; national norms are making the students appear as something they may not be.

However, if local norms were used instead of national ones, a much more accurate picture of the children in each district would emerge. In effect, when using local norms, students in one district are compared with other students in the same or similar districts, not some national standard that does not quite fit. Thus, the wealthy district, when considered by itself, will have its own set of percentile ranks, from the 1st to the 99th percentile. Percentiles being what they are, a gifted program coordinator will be able to determine which of the able students are, in fact, the *most* able, at least when compared with their classmates. This same principle applies in the low-performing district, except now, instead of finding *no* children who appear to be outstanding, those who are the highest achievers *when compared with their classmates locally, not others across the country,* will be found.

It seems puzzling that local norms are not considered more often in the selection of gifted children. For an academically struggling district, local norms will provide a more positive vision than the district may have seen before, and that is always good. In academically strong districts, though, local norms are seldom used because it might make parents, educators, and school board members think that their children are no longer as "successful" as the national norms made them appear to be. The numbers sent home that state the percentile rank of students will be lower when using local norms in above-average districts, and this may be perceived as a slap in the face to people who don't take the time to realize a simple truth: Children in our country are educated *locally,* not *nationally,* so a national barometer of academic success is an artificial yardstick that a town's schools can get no better.

Using local norms is a more honest approach to educating and understanding children who live in *your* town, not someone else's. It seems sensible to use these data instead of using nationally based statistics.

VEXING PROBLEM 5: A CHILD IS GIFTED IN ONE TOWN, BUT NOT ANOTHER

The above review of national/local norms may make it seem that this problem runs counter to the previous argument. In addressing this vexing problem, then, it is necessary to relent and say that this argument comes more from the heart than the head, more from an artist than a statistician.

In a nutshell, here is the dilemma: An intellectually capable child who lives in Springfield is included in its gifted program—and being successful. Mom or Dad gets transferred to Lancaster, and the whole family moves. Now, in this district's schools, the criteria for giftedness differ from Springfield's.

"Sorry," comes the letter or phone call, "Your child does not qualify for inclusion in our gifted program."

Curious, isn't it? Gifted in one town but not in another. This happens every day of every school year in this country.

" . . . and well it should!" some people may state. "For if you move from a 'weaker' school district to an academically healthier one, one might expect the level of classroom instruction to be higher in this new district, meaning that this displaced gifted child is actually being served just fine in a regular education program." And, perhaps this is so.

The emotional argument lies not in the numbers or in the level of education offered in different school districts, but rather, in the minds of the children who perceive themselves to be less capable than they thought they were. After all, if the child was *really* as smart as people said, wouldn't that be so in both Springfield *and* Lancaster? In a child's view, the answer is "yes."

One solution is this: If a child was receiving gifted program services in one town, then the town into which the child moves next should have a benevolent policy that admits this child to the gifted program on a trial basis. At the least,

If we are fishing for sizable intellectual talent, standardized testing will not single out the species or net the catch for us. But it will tell us which pools are likely to contain the "big ones." —*Chauncey, 1958, p. 30*

My family is in the military, so we move a lot. I was first identified as gifted in Germany, but when we moved back to the States I wasn't gifted anymore. Then, we moved again, to Missouri, and I *was* gifted again. When we got transferred back to Germany, I figured I'd just pick up where I left off, but I wasn't gifted there anymore. Now, I live in Texas, where I've been for the past five years. I've been gifted every year since we moved here.

It's a little hard for me to understand how these "gifted" decisions get made!

—*Tenth-grade girl, personal communication, 1997*

the child can be told that after a 4- to 6-week adjustment period to the school, a decision on gifted program placement can be made. Then, based more on observation than test scores, the child should be given the opportunity to experience what he or she had before, an education that matches his or her educational and intellectual needs, even if a particular cutoff score is not achieved.

There are other problems that surround the issue of gifted identification—in fact, there is probably no other area within this field that incites as much controversy and differences between what we *know* to be true and what we *show* to be true as identification. But by being alert to the traps into which one can fall, gifted education personnel will be able to mesh together identification and programming of gifted children in ways that will stand two arduous tests: the test of time, and the test of common sense.

GUIDING QUESTIONS FOR CHAPTER 3

1. What are the principal issues and problems in the identification of gifted children?

2. What roles do IQ tests play in the identification of giftedness? What role *should* they play?

3. How do more recent conceptions of giftedness affect the identification of children for gifted program services?

4. How does a school district establish procedures for identification of giftedness that are both equitable and sensible?

CHAPTER 3 RESOURCES TO REMEMBER

Eby, J. W., and Smutny, J. F. (1990). *A thoughtful overview of gifted education.* New York: Longman.

This textbook contains one of the best compilations of testing instruments for identifying gifted and talented students. In addition, a very insightful discussion of the issues involved in the identification of gifted students is offered. Other aspects of the book are also worthwhile, including a very comprehensive section on the practices and pitfalls of evaluating programs for gifted students.

Guilford, J. P. (1967). *The nature of human intelligence.* New York: McGraw-Hill.

There are several books that could be considered "classics" in the field of intelligence as it relates to gifted children, and this is one of them. Prior to the publication of this work, human intelligence was almost synonymous with IQ. Guilford dared to butcher that sacred cow and explore and expose the many facets of what it means to be intelligent. Either directly or indirectly, this book influenced all aspects of gifted program development: philosophy, definition, identification, and programming. A "must read" for the serious student of gifted child education.

Sternberg, R. J. (1988). *The triarchic mind: A new theory of human intelligence.* New York: Viking Press.

In this book, as well as several other subsequent publications on this same topic, Sternberg argues for the Triarchic Theory of Intelligence, which takes into account three (of course) aspects: analytical thinking, synthetic thinking, and practical thinking. These "intelligences," when combined with the wherewithal of which one to use when, make for a most intriguing, real-world approach to the study of giftedness as it exists in day-to-day living. Always a pleasure to read, Sternberg makes complex topics understandable through his many examples of his various intelligences as they can be seen in everyday occurrences.

CHAPTER
4

THE CREATIVE MIND
AND SPIRIT

It's the first week of school in a kindergarten class. It's your first year of teaching. It's the first time you sat all your students down in front of you and read them a story that had more than 10 pages. It's 1957.

Politically incorrect now but seemingly legitimate then, the story you read dealt with a stereotypic battle between cowboys and Indians. There were rifles and bows and arrows and covered wagons and horses—especially horses.

At the story's conclusion, the children have heard that the cowboys won the battle, and being the warm souls that they were, they invited the Indians to sit down and discuss peace. So, despite the recent bloodletting and scalpings (all sanitized, of course, to fit 1950s standards of good taste), everyone who survived did so happily ever after.

The children applaud as you give them their assignment: They are to return to their desks and draw a picture about the book's story. Crayons are encouraged.

Within 1 minute, the following drawing appears on your desk, given to you by a smiling young boy who awaits your reaction:

How *do* you react? Do you

a. Ask him to tell you what the picture represents so you can better understand it?

b. Send him a puzzled look and ask point blank, "What's *that* supposed to be?"

c. Take him by the hand to show him what the other children are drawing, in hopes that he will want to imitate their art?

d. Keep this first drawing for yourself, but encourage him to complete one that looks like everyone else's?

The right answer, of course, is "a," which presupposes nothing and asks merely for a first-person description of the child's creation. And if you did choose "a," as did the real teacher of this story, here's what you would have been told. The little boy explained that he knew that the cowboys had won the battle because they had fast horses, much faster than those of the Indians. However, he did not think that he could draw good horses, so instead of trying to do so, he drew only the parts that he knew he could draw—the tail and the hoof—and he represented the horse's speed by drawing it as if it were running off the page. The squiggly lines behind the hoof indicate the dust that flew up as a result of the steed's speed.

Did this child understand the story? Definitely. Did he present his understanding in a meaningful way? "Yes" to that one, too. Did his teacher hang this picture up alongside all the others that showed 2-inch horses and 10-inch cowboys? Of course she did!

HOW PARENTS CAN RECOGNIZE CREATIVE BEHAVIOR: INDICATORS AND EXAMPLES

- Intense absorption in listening, observing, or doing ("But I didn't hear you call me for dinner!")
- Taking a close look at things ("Hey, this centipede only has 99 legs!")
- Eagerness to tell others about discoveries ("Guess what, guess what, guess what!")
- Showing relationships among apparently unrelated ideas ("Hey, Mom, your new hat looks just like a flying saucer.")
- Various manifestations of curiosity and wanting to know ("I just wanted to see what the yard looked like from on top of the roof.")
- Honesty and intense search for truth ("Mom, I hope this doesn't upset you, but I've come to the conclusion that there is no Tooth Fairy.")
- Boldness of ideas ("But I think that children should be allowed to vote.")
- Penetrating observations and questions ("When the snow melts, where does the white go?")
- Willingness to consider or toy with strange ideas ("What if dogs were masters and people were pets?")

—Kaufmann, 1976; 1987, pp. 12–13

The human mind is prepared to wrap the whole planet in a shroud, and the exercise of all our best effort and ingenuity has produced no assurance whatever that it will be deterred from that end. The prolonged failure of traditional means in dealing with this problem does not prove those means useless. It does strongly suggest their inadequacy. For, as knowledge of the creative process drives us to conclude, although a problem which stubbornly resists solution by traditional means may perhaps be insoluble, the probability is rather that those means are themselves inadequate: the concepts, attitudes, and procedures employed are probably at fault and in need of being transcended in a fresh approach. The only reasonable step, at this point, then, is to act upon the supposition that our problems in world crisis, as at other times, may be soluble only creatively—that is, by a profound and thorough alteration of our inner life and of the outer forms in which life finds expression and support.

—*Ghiselin, 1954, p. 3*

It has always seemed to me that the ability to think critically and creatively is the prime cause for any important discovery that man has made.
—*Albert Einstein*

By legitimizing this youngster's work, she also validated his worth—as an artist and as a creative thinker. To have dismissed his drawing as silly, or to have admonished him because he DNFD (*d*id *n*ot *f*ollow *d*irections) would have sent a stifling message to this child: that his creativity was not welcomed in a place as serious as school. Instead, this teacher chose the kinder and more rational route of allowing this child's mind and spirit to progress on its own self-chosen path. In doing so, this teacher gave the child a precious, rare gift: the freedom to be an original.

The creative mind, the creative spirit: two halves that make up greater than a whole, and the two attributes that are the focus of this chapter.

WHAT IS CREATIVITY?

There is no way that a single chapter in a general textbook can do justice to the vast field of creativity. Books have been written on what creativity is and how it is attained, increased, recognized, rewarded, and stifled in a society that prefers conformity to individuality. Like two other concepts discussed elsewhere in this volume, giftedness and underachievement, the vision of creativity is often discernible only to the prepared mind, and the nuances of its complexity are evident only to the intellectually adventurous.

Still, there are some front-line thinkers who have taken on the task of trying to delimit this seemingly limitless topic. Some have looked at the concept of creativity with the precision of a mathematician, calculating the width and depth of creative ideas and products. Others have appeared more as gardeners, seeking nurturing ground that allows creativity to flourish. Still others have taken on the role of psychologist, wondering what conditions did (or did not) exist at home to force the emergence of creative thoughts and acts. Yet more have assumed the role of playmate, enjoying the presence of the creative thinker's mind and extolling the virtues to be found in letting go of the harness of reality. In this chapter, you meet these scientists, these psychologists, these playmates.

Whatever you think creativity is, you will probably find someone to agree with you. Whether you believe it should be channeled or allowed to roam freely, you will locate advocates of both approaches. Creativity is, simply, a human trait that defies precise definition. Oddly enough, though, people with different views on creativity often agree with each other on one thing: They know it when they see it.

An edited volume on creativity by Irving Taylor and Jacob Getzels (1975) presents many different and diverse views of the creative mind. They contend that the early days of creativity research (1900 to 1965) pigeonholed creativity as a unitary trait, one that was directed toward the creation of something new or original. It emanated, early researchers contended, from the conjuncture of mental states that seemed only remotely associated with each other (Ribot, 1900; Mednick, 1962). It was when these uniquely diverse views collided that something new—a creative act, idea, or object—was born.

For example, consider an invention that began as a failure. When the United States was involved in World War II, scientists were looking for ways to invent an artificial rubber that was both lightweight and durable enough to be made into boots for footsore GIs. Experimenting with all manner of concoctions using boric acid and silicon, the results were less than spectacular. Instead of hard-formed rubber, what they got was this too-soft compound that resembled day-old chewing gum. Samples of this goo were sent to scientists worldwide, but no one could think of a good use for it.

Several years later, Peter Hodgson thought again of this useless product and, with $147 of borrowed capital, began to encase this substance in plastic eggs. It stretched, bounced, and made Dagwood Bumstead take on added dimensions of weight and height when pressed onto his comic pages. Hodgson had created America's first toy fad: Silly Putty.

Years later, other creators found yet more uses for Silly Putty—as a tool to strengthen arm muscles, as a device to clean typewriter keys, as an effective lint remover, as an adhesive to keep tools from floating around in space on the Apollo 8 spacecraft, and as a mold from which to take handprints and footprints of gorillas at the zoo in Columbus, Ohio.

This invention of Silly Putty, and the ripples of applications it later had in many other dimensions of life, reveal many elements of the creative process: changing one's perspective, viewing with a new set of eyes, imagining the possible, being playful and asking "what if. . . ." These same qualities are prerequisites for the invention of ether, ice cream cones, glass, and Coca-Cola (which was first marketed as a headache and hangover remedy!), and they are the by-products of creative thoughts.

But where do these creative thoughts come from? Do they simply arise in the mind of someone who is prepared to notice them?

> Every new and good thing is liable to seem eccentric and perhaps dangerous at first glimpse, perhaps more than what is really eccentric, really irrelevant to life. And therefore we must always listen to the voice of eccentricity, within ourselves and in the world. . . . This does not mean we should surrender to whatever novelty is brought to attention. It does mean that we must practice to some extent an imaginative surrender to every novelty that has even the most tenuous credentials. . . . We must expect to live the orderly ways we have invented continually conscious of the imminence of change.
>
> —*Ghiselin, 1954. p. 21*

> The work in process becomes the poet's fate and determines his psychic development. It is not Goethe who creates *Faust,* but *Faust* which creates Goethe.
> —*Carl Jung*

Again, Taylor and Getzels have an answer; in fact, several answers. Finding no consensus on what fuels the creative thought machine, they categorized conceptions of creativity into four categories:

- **psychoanalytic views of creativity:** Clinicians such as Freud and Jung viewed creativity as an unconscious act brought forth by inner conflicts and tensions within the individual's psyche. After filtering one's creative thoughts through a sieve of socially acceptable alternatives (the ego and superego), creative behaviors were displayed for general consumption. Alfred Adler, also a psychoanalyst, agreed to a point but believed that creativity was a conscious act; a behavior whose owner sought positive inner growth by inventing something new.

- **humanistic views of creativity:** Believing that everyone possesses creative potential, humanistic psychologists such as Abraham Maslow and Carl Rogers saw creativity as a natural step toward the process of self-actualization. Creativity emerges when one is mature enough to desire something more than "the basics" of life and is (in the words of any good humanist) a transformational step in the journey of "becoming."

- **trait-factorial views of creativity:** Forget the feel-good-about-yourself gobbledygook put forth by the humanists! These researchers see creativity as separate, measurable aspects of the human intellect that are innate. The main proponent of this theory is J. P. Guilford, whose complex "Structure of the Intellect" in *The Nature of Human Intelligence* (1967) subdivides the intellect into 120 factors, all of which can be measured but few of which are by standard methods, such as IQ tests. The mind, then, is multidimensional, with creativity being a "subsection" of the intellect, which is itself multidimensional. Thus, creativity is both complex and widely distributed in people, although it is not always noted as such due to the simplistic methods used to determine whether someone is "smart."

- **associationistic view of creativity:** This view of creativity relates specif-

> The distinction between self-actualized and special talent creativity is an important one. Few of us can achieve recognition and riches for fantastic creative achievements. However, everyone can increase his or her self-actualized creativeness by becoming creatively conscious, by understanding creativity, by cultivating one's talents, and by working toward a more creative approach to living. Of course, one's professional success also will benefit from increased self-actualized creativeness.
>
> —*Davis, 1983, p. 6*

> When I am, as it were, completely myself, entirely alone, and of good cheer—say, traveling in a carriage, or walking after a good meal, or during the night when I cannot sleep; it is on such occasions that my ideas flow best and most abundantly. Whence and how they come I know not; nor can I force them. Those ideas that please me I retain in memory, and am accustomed, as I have been told, to hum them to myself. If I continue in this way, it soon occurs to me how I may turn this or that morsel to account, so as to make a good dish of it.
>
> —*Wolfgang Amadeus Mozart in Holmes, 1932*

cally to the earlier Silly Putty story. Associationists believe that creativity emerges when two or more disparate objects or ideas collide to create a new whole. The "AHA!" experience achieved by people who finally see a crystal-clear solution to a problem that once appeared fuzzy gives proof, advocates would say, that the associationistic view of creativity is the view most based in the real world.

Contemporary proponents of this idea include Sidney Parnes and Alex Osborn, whose work in the Creative Problem Solving process requires people to solve problems by removing the mental barriers and blinders that our more practical side erects.

Most of the myriad definitions of creativity would fall, at least somewhat cleanly, into one of the preceding categories. However, methods of enhancing creativity will differ depending on one's view of its origin. There are many beliefs about what works best to jump-start the creative mind.

THE CAR RADIO

When the car radio was first introduced in 1929, it was seen as an expensive and dangerous luxury. But William Lear, an eighth-grade dropout, thought of a way to marry these two new inventions—cars and radios— into what has become, today, an essential automobile option.

. . . But there were problems. The car's engine and spark plugs created static, and since the radio relied on the car's storage battery for power, the radio worked only when the car was turned off. Not a big incentive to buy it for the $150 it cost to install on a $300 Model T Ford!

Lear joined intellectual and creative forces with an engineer from Zenith, and together they designed a prototype radio that could be made from $22 worth of materials—cheap enough for mass production. Then, instead of running the radio off the storage battery, Lear concocted a way to run wires to the dashboard where they were linked to two knobs—one for volume and one for tuning. He even put in a small light so that the driver could monitor the frequency. He called his invention the "Motorola."

His new, inexpensive invention did not make many friends. Some cities banned them as a safety hazard, and one banker's radio shorted out, setting fire to his Packard. Still, with better refinements and increased usage by the public, Lear sold more than 780,000 car radios by 1934.

Taking his creative energies into new directions, Lear went on to design a radio for airplanes, later turning his attention to airplanes themselves: the first Lear jet rolled off the production line in 1963.

With William Lear, creativity took flight, in more ways than one.

—Reprinted with permission of US Airways Attaché *magazine*

CREATIVITY: HOW CAN IT BE TAUGHT?

Fish swim, birds sing, ducks waddle, people create: Each behavior is a natural part of being a specific species. The argument is no longer *can* a person be taught to be more creative, but *which techniques and environments* are the most conducive to doing so.

Perhaps the oldest and most well-respected model for teaching for creativity is represented in the work of Graham Wallas (Davis & Rimm, 1998). It was Wallas who, in 1926, identified four stages in the creative process; ever since then, practitioners of creativity have, in one way or other, massaged these four stages into their own thinking. The first of Wallas's stages is *preparation,* during which time you try to refine the problem that you are experiencing, isolating it from the scads of related issues that might cloud over the real problem. Unravelling the messy situation presented when a problem is not clear-cut requires analysis of all available information.

The *incubation* stage is explained well by creativity researcher James Adams (1974):

> Everyone has had the experience of having the answer to a problem suddenly occur in his mind. One maddeningly familiar phenomenon to many people is a late answer to an important problem. One may work for days or weeks on a problem, complete it, and go on to other activities. Then, at some seemingly random point in time, a better answer "appears." . . . This better answer came straight from the unconscious as a result of the "incubation" process it was going through. I have found in my own case that this "incubation" process works and is reliable. (pp. 57–58)

This is why people keep notepads at their bedside, or waterproof markers in the shower, or a pen in their glove compartment: to be able to write down their breakthrough when it appears unexpectedly.

The third step, *illumination,* is a descendent of incubation, for it is the more orderly follow-up to what you do with your once-incubated solution. This "AHA!" experience leads to the final stage, *verification,* during which time you evaluate the illuminated thought and check it out for feasibility and acceptability to the situation in question. A further step, not mentioned by Wallas but cited by Davis and Rimm (1998), is "implementation," for an idea is no good if it lies fallow in one's mind; but as they state, "perhaps this step was assumed" (p. 189) by Wallas.

Taking a different view of learning to become creative, Frank Barron and Donald MacKinnon were two researchers who thought that the best way to determine the roots of creativity was to look at the characteristics of people who *already are* creative. In separate studies (Barron, 1969; MacKinnon, 1978), these two men analyzed the lives of nationally recognized writers, architects, and mathematicians, seeking what it was that made them tick. They observed these creative individuals over a 3-day period and analyzing the results of various intelligence and personality tests (e.g., the Myers-Briggs Type Indicator and the Minnesota Multiphasic Personality Inventory [MMPI]); their findings were more confirming than surprising. They found that the traits of originality, flexibility, independence, nonconformity, energy, aesthetic appreciation, and unconventionality were common among these individuals. These positive traits led to new inventions or theorems, or variations on existing themes that caused new insights to be gleaned. However, some darker, more negative personality traits were also present among these creatives, including self-centeredness, rebelliousness, and moodiness. Likewise, the MMPI results showed a high tendency toward psychopathology, especially in creative writers, with high ratings of indices of depression, hysteria, paranoia, and schizophrenia. Still, a measure of positive mental health called "ego strength" was also among the most prevalent characteristics, causing Barron (1969) to assert that these creative individuals were both sicker and healthier psychologically than people in general, but their high levels of ego strength gave these individuals greater resources to deal with any troubles they might encounter.

Another interesting approach to studying creative individuals has been to study their lives and lifestyles, investigating their hobbies, interests, preferences, and life choices. Not surprisingly, a child with unusual hobbies (collecting buttons; coloring only *outside* of the lines) or who "adopted" an imaginary playmate often grew to be an adult who was creative. Other quirky findings (Schaefer, 1969) about creative people include that creative high school students were more likely to have friends who were younger than they and to have had more travel experiences as young people. Also, creative high school girls were found to own cats more frequently than would be expected by chance! Davis (1983) states that "in your author's personal experience, two biographical traits are virtually 100% accurate as predictors of creativeness: having had an imaginary playmate and/or participation in theatre activities. Persons who claim one or the other, or both, of these invariably show the typical creative personality traits . . . [and] also report a background of creative activities, such as in art, creative writing, photography, unusual hobbies or collections or inventing gadgets and games" (pp. 49–50).

Indeed, the creative personality does seem to live up to some of its stereotypic standards of nonconformity and originality. But it must be remembered that there is a difference between correlation and causation, meaning that just *because* a 15-year-old girl owns a cat we cannot conclude that she will be creative. Further, a 10-year-old boy with playmates who are all flesh-and-blood real rather than figments of some overactive imagination will not necessarily be relegated to an unoriginal life. Correlation—the statistical method that shows the degree in which things occur (or do not occur) in relationship to one another—does not imply a cause-effect relationship.

Still, keep those easels and brushes available, because there is *no* evidence that denying someone a creative outlet or two will force them to become more creative in the long run.

Schiller liked to have a smell of rotten apples, concealed beneath the lid of his desk, under his nose when he was creating poetry. Walter de la Mare has told me that he must smoke while writing. Auden drinks endless cups of tea. Coffee is my own addiction....For goodness sake, though, do not think that rotten apples or cigarettes or tea have anything to do with the quality of the work of a Schiller, a de la Mare, or an Auden. They are a part of a concentration which has already been attained rather than the causes of concentration.

—*Spender, 1954, p. 114*

THE CREATIVITY CONTINUUM

Rather than being something you either possess or do not own, creativity is generally seen as a trait that occurs in degrees. John Gowan was a developmentalist who believed that creativity, like human cognition or emotion, grew in a series of stages; unlike Carl Rogers and Abraham Maslow, two humanists who espoused the theory that creativity was a result of positive mental health, Gowan saw the reverse: that mental health was possible only through the fruition of one's creative talents. Also, Gowan et al. (1981) distinguished between two types of creativity: personal and cultural. Personal creativity, a teachable "skill" that can cause a person to act, react, or interpret things in new ways, was different from cultural creativity—the type that produces major discoveries and ideas that have the ability to change the future of humankind. Both were important to Gowan, and both were merely part and parcel of being human:

> Creativity is a characteristic not only of individual human behavior, but also of the species in general. What is true of the development of the superior individual is also true of the developing aspects of mankind. The emergence of creative abilities is a triumph not only of individual development, but...the harbinger of evolutionary progress for all men. (Gowan, 1972, p. 70)

Lev Vygotsky, a developmentalist whose work spanned from 1917 until his too-soon death in 1934, believed that the genesis of creative thought was observable in children's games. When a child takes a stick and makes it go "bang! bang! bang!" as a bulletless gun, or a broom handle, which becomes a horse on which to gallop from room to room, or a box, which becomes a fort used to protect him- or herself from huge monsters, played by stuffed animals or dolls, the child is engaging in symbolic play. This symbolic play contains two features of Vygotsky's view of creativity: *reproductive imagination,* in which the child acts from memory and past experiences, and *combinatory imagination,* in which previous knowledge or experiences combine with new situations or behaviors to create a new insight or direction. This imaginative spirit and ability, if brought to fruition in adulthood, allow for a conscious choice to seek creative solutions or options to life's smallest and biggest dilemmas. The creative life, as considered by Vygotsky, is, indeed, within reach of those who chose to play with ideas as children and adolescents.

Aligned with this creative process of imagining objects to be what they are not is what Vygotsky calls the "zone of proximal development," the distance between the developmental level of an independent problem solver and the level of *potential* development that is noted when the individual is working under adult guidance. This "zone" is the gray area that parents and other educators have to work with in getting their children to be more independent problem solvers, a matter of importance for both intellectual and creative endeavors.

The artist is not a person endowed with free will who seeks his own ends, but one who allows art to realize its purposes through him. As a human being he may have moods and a will and personal aims, but as an artist he is "man" in a higher sense—he is "collective man"— one who carries and shapes the unconscious, psychic life of mankind. To perform this difficult office it is sometimes necessary for him to sacrifice happiness and everything that makes life worth living for the ordinary human being. —*Jung, 1954, p. 229*

THE STRUCTURE OF THE INTELLECT: CREATIVITY AS COMPLEX THOUGHT

Leave it to J. P. Guilford, the man who tweaked the imaginations and minds of his fellow psychologists in 1950 (see chapter 2), to come up with a view of the intellect that depended very much on creative thinking as a primary component. His theoretical model, the Structure of the Intellect (SOI) (1959, 1975), represents a view of creativity that ties it directly to mental qualities. As Guilford (1975) wrote, "The aspect [of creativity] with which I have been most concerned is that of intellectual abilities or functions. This does not mean that I have not recognized the importance of other qualities, in the form of motivational and temperamental traits" (p. 37).

The SOI Model (see Figure 4.1), as its name implies, is not limited to a description of creativity. Rather, it is a theoretical depiction of intelligence, describing all mental functions that can be operated by one's brain. Subdividing the intellect into three major components—operations, contents, and products—Guilford postulated that there were 120 separate and unique cognitive abilities, each one represented by a "cell" in the SOI block shown in Figure 4.1. The *divergent production* operation section of the model is where Guilford's view of creativity is most apparent, and indeed, creativity tests have been designed to check the presence of "the divergent production of semantic units" or the "divergent production of figural relations," or any of the other 22 combinations of divergent production with Guilford's various other products and contents. A sample item for the "divergent production of figural transformations" might involve the manipulation and realignment of matchsticks to go from six squares to four by removing only two matches.

Mary Meeker was instrumental in gathering together into test form questions and puzzles that would measure talents *à la* SOI. By using a diagnostic/prescriptive approach, Meeker and her cadre of associates across the world have tested thousands of individuals for strengths and weaknesses of intellectual (and creative) functioning, even going so far as to have a bill passed in the Oregon state legislature in 1997 that established "a pilot program that shall use as its model the Structure of the Intellect Model School" (SOI Systems, 1997, p. 7), in which detailed intellectual assessments would be conducted, followed by a student-specific program driven by the assessment results. A total of $1.5 million was appropriated for this 3-year pilot program.

The direct application of practice from the complex SOI theory does have its detractors. Clark (1988, 1997) cautions that SOI focuses on intellectual functioning solely, to the exclusion of noncognitive factors such as motivation or affect. Further, the discrete nature of the 120 cells of the SOI model provides little room for overlap among these "pieces" of intellectual functioning; yet most people would agree that virtually every complex mental task requires a combination of factors to achieve success. Even Guilford himself (1975) raised the issues of motivation, temperament, and genetics as possible other factors in the

Creative abilities are a part of intelligence, not something apart from it. Most critically involved, particularly at the stage of generating ideas, are the divergent-production abilities or functions and those involving transformations of information. The former provide an abundance of alternative ideas; the latter a flexibility in the structuring of information so that alterations and adaptations can occur.
—*Guilford, 1975, p. 57*

FIGURE 4.1

Guilford's Structure of the Intellect

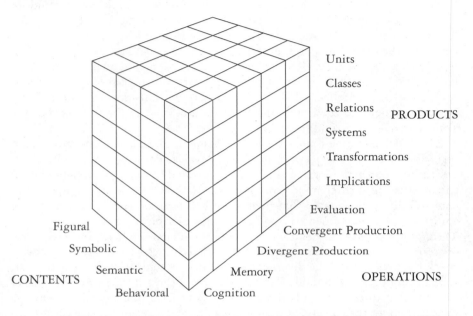

—*From* The Nature of Human Intelligence, *Copyright © 1967 by McGraw-Hill. Reproduced with permission of The McGraw-Hill Companies.*

Using the SOI Model as a frame of reference, I recommend that every student be given the chance to show what he can do with respect to all the intellectual functions. Each child is thus likely to find areas in which he can do relatively well, and in which learning can be more rapid and more rewarding. He is thus also likely to find areas of stronger interests. Assessments of the status of the student in various SOI abilities would also be informing for teachers and counselors.
—*Guilford, 1975, p. 54*

emergence of creative behaviors, while arguing that the teaching of creative thinking strategies has seldom been embraced by our nation. Too, he questioned whether creativity will continue to be a pronounced ingredient in our American culture if it is not rewarded:

America is recognized historically as leader in mechanical inventions, and the founding fathers of the United States were also innovative in bringing into the world new forms of government. But the innovations needed to make our social, economic and legal systems serve us better have been slower to come than those providing for a superb gadgetry. One reason is that while our patent system has richly rewarded the inventor, there has been no comparable system of rewards for innovative social ideas" (p. 49).

The SOI model has been noted for its complexity by some and reviled for its simplistic, "piecemeal" approach to intellectual functioning by others. Some stand by the multitudinous SOI tests as intricate ways to tease out talents in individuals, whereas others note their diagnostic/prescriptive design as averse to everything we know about the blending of intellectual abilities to achieve success. But whatever one's reactions to SOI (the most common one from graduate students being "Huh?"), there is no denying that Guilford's introduction of this model sparked as much interest in intellectual and creative functioning as did his 1950 speech to the APA on the lack of creativity research. Joy Paul Guilford etched his permanent mark on psychology and education by following through on his own dictum: to study creativity as an essential part of human existence.

FROM DEFINITION TO FRUITION: TRAINING FOR CREATIVITY

Facts which sank at intervals out of conscious recollection drew together beneath the surface through almost chemical affinities of common elements . . . there in the darkness moved phantasms of fishes and animiculae and serpentine forms of his vicarious voyages, thrusting out tentacles of association and interweaving beyond disengagement. (Lowes, cited in Davis, 1975, p. 18)

The above interpretation of creativity is proof positive that metaphorical thinking has its disadvantages. *No one* could possibly hope to implement a program of creative thinking that uses the above conception of colorful hyperbole! What is needed, instead, is a definition of creativity that is able to be translated from theory into practice; and no one has given a better one than the Master himself, E. Paul Torrance (1970), who defines creativity as

becoming sensitive to or aware of problems, deficiencies, gaps in knowledge, missing elements, disharmonies and so on; bringing together available information; defining the difficulty or identifying the missing element; searching for solutions, making guesses or formulating hypotheses about the deficiencies, testing and retesting these hypotheses and modifying and restating them; perfecting them and finally communicating the results. (p. 22)

The beauty of Torrance's depiction of creativity is that it has a beginning, middle, and end. It takes the creative person on a ride from the emergence of a problem, on through the journey, either focused or fuzzy, in search of resolution. Finally, the creative trek ends in a product or a hypothesis that satisfies the searcher (at least until the next problem appears). In this view, creativity is a *process* that is focused on any type of problem of interest to the person trying to solve it. When the issue is seen from this vantage, educators, parents, peers, colleagues, and counselors all have a stake in both problem seeking and problem solving. Given this universal nature of creative problem solving, it might be expected that researchers and practitioners would have devised ways to give this creative journey some structure. Indeed, that is so.

The ability to conceptualize productively and creatively is as important in painting the bathroom as in moving oil from Alaska, in taking family vacations as in designing spacecraft, and in spending a family income as in protecting the environment. Although my major interest is in the design of things, I am convinced that the conceptual process is a general one and that the same problems arise in thinking up a more nutritional diet as in thinking up a better way to image the heart ultrasonically.
—*Adams, 1974, p. 9*

#1 METHOD FOR TRAINING FOR CREATIVITY: CREATIVE PROBLEM SOLVING

Imagine your dilemma: You own a dog that you love with all your heart, yet your dog is destroying your everyday existence. He eats shoes, chews carpets, plants himself in your prized perennial garden, and interrupts your dinner by hopping up on the table and grabbing your steak. You try to put him in a closed-off room, but he cries a river of tears and wails like a siren. You try putting him on a leash and sending him outside to his doghouse, but the incessant barking makes the neighbors a tad upset. What *do* you do?

With creative problem solving (CPS), the first thing you have to do is figure out what the problem really is, because only then will workable solutions present themselves as rational. In effect, CPS is a *divergent* approach to arrive at a *convergent* solution to life's everyday dilemmas—such as misbehaving dogs. Here is its history, followed by its specific elements.

Like many good educational ideas, CPS began elsewhere; in this case, the world of business. In 1963, Alex Osborn, the originator of the "brainstorming" process and cofounder of a highly successful advertising agency in New York, was seeking a specific strategy or plan that would help advertising executives break their mental barriers and arrive at new ideas that were innovative and original. With the help of Sidney Parnes, a college professor with an interest in creativity, the CPS process crystalized (Osborn, 1963).

Evolving over 30 years, the CPS process now has six steps, as highlighted by Isaksen and Treffinger (1985):

1. **Mess finding:** determining the main problem that needs to be solved among myriad other, related problems vying for attention. With the dog story, is it most important to stop the barking, the food snatching, or another annoying habit?
2. **Data finding:** collecting facts and opinions about the mess that has been selected for study so that the mess can be seen from a variety of viewpoints. Back to the dog: When does he misbehave the most? When does he put his best paw forward and act like least like a cur? Are there certain times of day that he behaves better than at others?
3. **Problem finding:** constructing or selecting several specific problem statements that describe the job ahead, with the goal of selecting the one problem statement that you wish to solve first. Most of these statements begin with the words "In what ways might we" (IWWMW). So . . . IWWMW quiet his barking? IWWMW punish the dog for his bad behaviors? IWWMW show the dog that he is loved, especially when he behaves? IWWMW reward proper dog etiquette during mealtimes? IWWMW determine if the dog is lonely for another canine companion?
4. **Idea finding:** brainstorming in its purest form, as all manner of possible solutions are considered—both tame ones and wild and crazy ideas—that

could be used in solving the problem. For example, the dog could wear a muzzle at all times, the house could be soundproofed, that annoying dog-version of "Jingle Bells" could be played continuously so that even the dog gets tired of hearing his own voice, the dog could be given his own steak each day, or he could be lavished with praise every time he does something right. The solutions are endless! But . . . are they workable? That is step #5.

5. **Solution finding:** developing criteria for examining the merits of the potential solutions generated in idea finding. In the case of the dog dilemma, it might be asked whether the solutions are economical, efficient, ethical (it *would* be cruel to muzzle the dog at all times, wouldn't it?), or legal. Generally, each potential solution is then placed on a grid with each solution assigned a ranking, say, 1 to 5, to determine which ones are the most workable, based on the criteria established by the problem solver—you.

6. **Acceptance finding:** formulating a specific plan of action and implementing the choice(s) receiving the highest rankings that in solution finding show to be the best.

One last time, back to the dog: After considering all the ramifications of the possible solutions, a course of action is determined; another dog will be purchased so that Fido can have a playmate, thereby occupying his attention and (it is hoped) cutting off his need to chew the house to bits. Also, Fido's owner will buy a book on positive reinforcement, rewarding the dog's good behaviors while punishing any continued bad behaviors with a loud cry of "bad dog."

And, if all else fails, and the solution finding proves to be erroneous, the CPS process can begin again, examining other workable solutions for dealing with the messes that these *two* dogs now present.

The CPS model is used in Future Problem Solving and can be used in virtually any life dilemma. Whether in the field of business, education, or human relations, CPS is a model that works because it examines the context of a problem

> I once heard a professor of medicine say to his students at the conclusion of a course: "Within five years, about one-half of what I have told you will either be untrue or not worth a darn. This doesn't really bother me; but what *does* irritate me is that I can't even tell you which half is which!" After all, the atom was taught as being irreducible—until World War II.
> —*Parnes, 1981, p. 21*

THINGS TO IMPROVE BY THINKING CREATIVELY

- corks that break off in wine bottles
- hard drives that crash
- wallpaper that doesn't stick and bumper stickers that stick too well
- people who don't use turn signals
- artificial flowers that look it
- voice mail that doesn't allow you to connect to a real person
- movies that look good in reviews but are lousy in person
- $8 million dollar athletes who pout
- spouses who snore
- little balls of fuzz on expensive sweaters
- incompatible computers

Now . . . use some creative energies and fix these things!

before one rushes headlong into selecting a solution. Instead of reacting in the mode of "ready-fire-aim," CPSers choose the more logical sequence of "ready-aim-fire."

#2 METHOD FOR CREATIVITY: THE AUTA MODEL

Some methods of becoming more creative are kinder than others, and the AUTA model (Davis & O'Sullivan, 1980) ranks right up there with warm fuzzies and group hugs. Based on a humanistic model of creativity, AUTA, which stands for *a*wareness, *u*nderstanding, *t*echniques, and *a*ctualization, makes the *person* the central figure in the creative process.

At the *awareness* level of AUTA is the seed of the idea that everyone can be more creative than they now are. As stated by Davis (1986), the learner must appreciate the importance of creativity to one's personal growth—"for developing one's talents, for self-actualization, for mental health, and simply for getting more out of life" (p. 30). With this consciousness, combined with the knowledge of how creative actions have spurred imagination and inventions throughout the centuries, the individual is aware of how creativity can affect a person's life.

The second step, *understanding,* focuses on the building blocks of creativity: understanding the characteristics of gifted people, the ways that creativity is attained and enhanced, and measurement instruments and techniques used to assess creativity. Learned through listening or reading, this element of creativity offers an academic component often lacking in other models. (There is, by the way, a "threshold theory" of creativity, which postulates that one must have a certain IQ, approximately 120, to be creative [Barron, 1969; Starko, 1995]. So much for the idea that creativity is a domain separate from intellectual giftedness!)

After understanding comes *technique,* the "T" of the AUTA model. Each person will have his or her own preferred style and set of methods for becoming creative; each will find a different set of circumstances that enhance the "AHA!" experience of finding a solution to a mind-boggling problem. For instance, "some writers take ideas from political or other news events, developing them into good- or best-sellers. Hollywood script writers often use ideas from books or news items. Clothes designers may visit museums to borrow ideas from ancient Egypt, the Civil War period, China, the Aztecs, and so on" (Davis, 1986, pp. 31–32). Learning what works for the individual (which makes the "understanding" component of this model so vital) is one of the keys to creative accomplishment. Figure 4.2 presents some of the more popular creative thinking techniques that have withstood the ultimate test: the test of time.

The fourth and final step of the AUTA model is *actualization.* It is here that the difference between special-talent creativity and self-actualized creativity becomes obvious. Although not everyone will grow up to be as fluent as Shakespeare, as dramatic as Lillian Gish, as entrepreneurial as Bill Gates, or as comical

Once we learn that everything can be viewed in many different ways, we may discover more of the positives inherent in any situation that we face. Furthermore, we may come to realize that the "impossible" is no longer absolute. Failures previously viewed as discouragements can become stepping stones to success.

—Parnes, 1981, p. 51

FIGURE 4.2

Strategies for Enhancing Creative Thinking

1. *Brainstorming:* Based on Osborn's (1953) view of the benefits of deferred judgment, brainstorming is a nonjudgmental listing of possible answers to a particular question or problem. Likening the common practice of evaluating ideas as they are generated to driving a car while pushing down simultaneously on the gas and the brake pedals, brainstorming encourages wild and crazy ideas and the "piggybacking" of one idea onto another. Example brainstorming questions might be to ask people for all the uses of a discarded auto tire or encouraging children to list all the ways that things would be different if they were in charge of their school. The goal of brainstorming is to eventually come up with workable solutions from what might appear, initially, to be "dumb ideas."

2. *Attribute Listing:* Developed by Robert Crawford (1978), attribute listing takes ideas and objects that already exist, dissects them into their component parts, and modifies those parts to make improvements. For example, if a company is trying to design a new snack food, it should examine some of the elements of *existing* snack foods—color, taste, sound, nutritional value, shape, targeted audience, and the toy surprise that comes inside each box. The goal would be to examine these attributes and see how changing some of them might make the food more interesting to a consumer. The classic example of attribute listing appears in the children's book *Charlie and the Chocolate Factory* by Roald Dahl, in which an eccentric, billionaire candy maker—Willy Wonka—makes intriguing inventions such as "Everlasting Gobstoppers," an eternal candy that changes flavors as you think of them, or "Lickable Wallpaper," which comes in a variety of sweet flavors, aromas, and colors. By listing the attributes that exist and by modifying even one or two to make something new and appealing about the product, creative invention can occur. Tied in with brainstorming, teachers could ask children to figure out ways to make their playground more fun or their cafeteria food more palatable. Who knows what good ideas lurk in the minds of creative kids?

3. *Morphologic Synthesis:* An extension of attribute listing, morphologic synthesis does exactly what its fancy words imply: puts words (and the ideas behind them) together in new and interesting ways. Davis (1986) gives an example of sixth graders who tried to design a better sandwich (see Figure 4.3) by combining ingredients that may or may not go together in an appealing fashion. By using morphologic synthesis, products emerge that would probably remain hidden if using logic alone. Some combinations could revolt or repel their designers, but within their disgust might come a new way to look at a problem, issue, or product.

continued on the following page

continued from the previous page

4. *Synectics:* The word *synectics* comes from two Greek words meaning the joining together of different and apparently irrelevant elements. Designed by William Gordon in 1961 as a tool for business management, synectics seeks to do the opposite of the preceding techniques: It urges the *dissociation* between things rather than their commonalities (Dacey, 1989). By performing one of four types of analogy (direct, personal, fantasy, or symbolic analogies), participants are asked to do two things: (a) make the strange familiar, and then (b) make the familiar strange. An example of a symbolic analogy is a "life-giving killer" (chemotherapy, perhaps). Another example is a "rude compliment" ("You don't sweat much for a fat person"). For a direct analogy, children might be asked to consider ways that plants and animals protect themselves from harm. Their answers might lead to their understanding of ways to protect their own personal safety. In a fantasy analogy, children might be asked to explain which weighs more, a brick or a frown, or which is tastier, a book or an escalator. By examining ideas from these seemingly disparate angles, new ideas might emerge as to how to approach problems whose solutions are "blocked" by logic.

—Delisle

as Whoopi Goldberg, each person has it within him- or herself to be more flexible in thinking. It is from this personal vantage of creativity that the child within each individual can flourish.

#3 METHOD FOR CREATIVITY: LATERAL THINKING

Edward de Bono, a prolific writer who has earned millions of fans (and dollars) by systematizing a way to think more creatively, is another of creativity's most innovative thinkers. Underlying the themes of his many books and curriculum materials is his concept of lateral thinking, as opposed to vertical thinking. In his book *New Think* (1971), de Bono refines the difference: "Vertical thinking digs the same hole deeper; lateral thinking is concerned with digging a hole in a new place" (p. 15). Thus, in getting people to see that the source of their problem-solving frustration may be that they are examining the wrong circumstances, de Bono offers a specific and practical alternative. But first, the elements of lateral thinking:

- *It is generative, rather than selective.* Concerned more with "richness than rightness" (Dacey, 1989, p. 120), lateral thinking opens up new pathways of thought.

FIGURE 4.3

A Morphologic Sandwich

A sixth-grade Milwaukee class used the morphological synthesis method to generate 121 zany ideas for creative sandwiches. Can you find a tasty combination? a revolting one?

New Companions to Add Zest

	Celery	Applesauce	Cucumbers	Peppers	Tomatoes	Raisins	Nuts	Dates	Bananas	Cottage Cheese	Cranberry Sauce
Liversausage											
Egg Salad											
Chicken											
Tuna Fish											
Peanut Butter											
Jelly											
Sardines											
Deviled Ham											
Corned Beef											
Salmon											
Cheese											

Standard Sandwich Favorites

Ratings of Various Spreads

			Choices		
Flavor	1st	2nd	3rd	4th	5th
Super Goober (Peanut Butter/Cranberry)	17	2	1	0	4
Charlie's Aunt (Tuna and Applesauce)	3	16	2	2	1
Irish Eyes are Smiling (Corned Beef and Cottage Cheese)	0	0	16	2	6
Cackleberry Whiz (Hard-Boiled Eggs/Cheese Whiz)	1	3	2	14	4
Hawaiian Eye (Cream Cheese and Pineapple)	3	3	3	6	9

(Six girls had squeamish stomachs and did not participate.)

—Davis, 1986

With respect to conformity, it is well to consider the difference between (1) the nonconformist who honestly attempts to behave more effectively, and (2) the nonconformist who simply wishes to show people that he/she is different. The latter individual may be better described as a *counterconformist*—or one who almost automatically does the opposite of what others do, right or wrong. There is also the pseudo-nonconformist who suddenly desires to be a nonconformist like everyone else!
—*Parnes, 1981, p. 75*

- *It is provocative, not analytical.* The lateral thinker seeks information for its ability to provoke emotion. Even if erroneous, the information may help in solving a dilemma.
- *It welcomes irrelevant information and intrusions.* The more seemingly irrelevant information is, according to de Bono, the greater the chance that it will provoke new thinking.
- *It welcomes intuitive leaps.* Jumping from one thought to the next, without regard to logical reasoning, is welcomed. Refining and reorganizing ideas can always happen later.
- *It favors quality over quantity.* Although vertical thinking will give many satisfactory answers, but few superlative ones, lateral thinking does the reverse: It provides fewer solutions but a higher likelihood that one of them will be a great solution.

Some techniques are prized under de Bono's plan. One is called "the creative pause," an intentional break from one's stream of thought to examine if the direction in which the thinker is going is a good one. Whether the pause takes place in writing assignments, art projects, or Superpower summit meetings, it can become, like a popular soft drink, "the pause that refreshes." It is de Bono's belief that looking at one's mental and creative landscape from a slightly removed distance can jar one's thinking in worthwhile ways.

Another of de Bono's strategies is the inclusion of "po" into one's creative psyche (1970). Po is a deliberate provocation of thought in which the thinker asks "I wonder what would happen if . . . ?" to question the current reality. One type of po is the reversal, in which you think of things as they might have been. In a social studies class, for example, the teacher could ask, "How would your life be different if Germany had won World War II?" Responses to this type of question could cause students to reexamine their own thoughts and prejudices. Another type of po is the exaggeration, as epitomized by the question, "If everyone had to eat 10,000 calories a day, how could they do so and stay healthy?" New ideas about diet and exercise might emerge from thinking about this situation from a grossly exaggerated context. Still another po is based on the distortion of time sequences in events. He gives the example of "What happens if you died before you died?" which, although distorted in thought, may have been the provocation for developing life insurance policies that pay terminally ill people their benefits in their time of greatest need (de Bono, 1992).

The po technique, a sophisticated version of a childhood game of make-believe, can get real complex real fast, causing you to think in a new direction—lateral, not literal. Like all complex thought processes, it takes time to develop and maturity to appreciate.

Perhaps de Bono's most well-known aspect of lateral thinking is his idea of the Six Thinking Hats (1986). He uses these colorful hats to explain different ways of investigating a problem. The hat colors, and their meanings, are as follows:

The *red* hat seeks information about feelings, emotion, or intuition.
The *white* hat seeks general information, looking for gaps that might be helpful to know about as one goes about solving a problem.
The *green* hat looks for evidence of creative efforts.
The *yellow* hat looks for benefits and possibilities within ideas.
The *black* hat considers thinking that requires critical judgment.
The *blue* hat is the "sentry" who monitors the other types of thinking being used.

This approach to thinking could be used by both children and adults. For example, if a family is trying to decide what kind of car to buy, they would wear their collective white hats when seeking information on a car's warranty, while donning their red hats to say how much they loved the idea of a sporty convertible. The yellow hats are put on when the benefits and drawbacks of the turbocharged convertible are aligned with the fact that the car's drivers would include two teenagers, and the black hat concerns would be whether the monthly car payments will fit the family budget and whether the small confines of a sport coupe would serve well a family of four. The blue hat time would come into play when someone asked the question, "Have we considered this purchase from all different angles?" The purpose of these hats, of course, is to show the benefits of considering problems, issues, or situations from many angles. By introducing students to this technique, they are able to self-monitor their own hats as they encounter situations in life that require careful and diverse considerations.

Another of de Bono's contributions to the creative thinking movement—I told you he was prolific—is his introduction of the Cognitive Research Trust (CoRT) thinking strategies (1983,1986) workbooks and related materials. CoRT is designed to teach thinking as a skill, and students complete all manner of exercises, some more exciting than others, to test out the agility of their ambidextrous thinking. Using the three-letter acronym PMI, students are taught to look at any situation, activity, or event from three vantages: its pluses (P), its minuses (M), and things that are neither good nor bad but, rather, interesting (I). By using the PMI technique, students learn to defer judgment, to explore the possibilities of an idea that looks lousy on initial view, and to tease out the possible negative effects of an idea that looks great on first view.

In all, de Bono has made a major contribution to the field of creative thinking by giving teachers tools to use with students in their collective quest for quality in thinking.

#4 METHOD FOR CREATIVITY: THE BIG FOUR

As alluded to in chapters 1 and 2, there is one view of creativity that has been made popular thanks to the Torrance Tests of Creative Thinking. Those tests, both the figural and verbal forms, are scored on the basis of four criteria that

Since a person can behave creatively in an almost infinite number of ways . . . it would be ridiculous even to try to develop a comprehensive battery of tests of creative thinking that would sample any kind of universe of creative thinking abilities. The author does not believe that anyone can now specify the number and range of test tasks necessary to give a complete or even an adequate assessment of a person's potentialities for creative behavior. He does believe that the sets of test tasks assembled in the Torrance Tests of Creative Thinking sample a rather wide range of the abilities in such a universe.

—*Torrance, 1974, p. 21*

have become as familiar to students of creativity as are Catechism responses from altar boys: fluency, flexibility, originality, and elaboration. Each category is analyzed below, and a specific example of each is given.

Fluency is easy to define: It is the number of responses given to a problem. So, if the question is the ever-popular creativity mantra, "How many uses can you find for a red brick?" fluency would just be how many different ways are named.

Flexibility is being able to respond to a question or issue from various vantages. Take the red brick: It can be built on; it can be used to knock out one's younger brother; it can be used to prop open a door; or it can be used as a pendulum in a physics experiment. With this variety of responses, the flexible thinker shows how to use an object in ways other than the original intent of a red brick, which was probably as a building block in construction. The more categories considered (e.g., building block, tool, weapon, prop), the more flexible is the thinking.

Originality is related to both fluency and flexibility, but it refers specifically to the statistical rarity or uniqueness of responses. Thus, if the suggestion was made to take this red brick and use it as sidewalk chalk, that would probably not be seen as an unusual use. But, if the red brick was hollowed out and its size increased 20-fold (no one said that this *couldn't* be done), it could then be used as a raft supported by big balloons in a tranquil sea. Now *that's* original!

The final step, *elaboration,* deals with the embellishments made to the red brick. So, not only could it be used as a raft, but when the person inside the raft was finished sunning, the red brick could be taken onshore, combined with other red bricks and transformed into a barbecue pit.

There is a strong positive correlation between fluency and originality, meaning that the *more* ideas a person has, the more likely it is that one will be original. Also, there is an inverse relationship between fluency and elaboration, which makes sense; for if creative thinkers are so busy designing major Rube Goldberg-type contraptions, they may not have as much time for coming up with dozens of fluent uses for the brick.

A good example of how children can impart flexibility, originality, and elaboration into their drawings is shown in Figure 4.4, which shows responses given by 5-year-old children when asked to "draw a family and tell me when you're done." Notice that some children chose families that may have represented their own, whereas others took a more original route, selecting a cluster of Picasso-like cats or (my personal favorite) the Banana Family, which has to make one wonder what kind of family this child *really* lives in!

FIGURE 4.4

Draw a Family Test Responses

—*Delisle*

Which is the most important of these Big Four? That's hard to say. Perhaps at the beginning stages of training for creative thinking, fluency should be valued, especially because its close links to originality are evident. Later, with students who are comfortable thinking in innovative ways, elaboration may be more desirable, because that is the stage where most plans go from blueprint to construction. Or, perhaps it doesn't matter much at all which segment of creative thinking is the most vital, for the world is not so rich a place that it can afford to repress or denigrate *any* of these elements of creative thinking. Just choose your poison (or your brick) and just start creating!

ANOTHER TYPE OF BRICK: THE MENTAL BRICK WALL

Everyone knows them—the naysayers whose favorite expression is "Where did you ever get *that* stupid idea?" If only they knew that they are chipping away at an individual's self-worth while also denying the world some important and necessary gray areas whenever they utter a killer statement; a "psychic put-down" that makes every original idea suspect.

Psychic put-downs are just one of the many hindrances erected by the self and others to limit the presence and effectiveness of creativity. Although the externally imposed put-downs are painful, annoying, and potentially stifling, they can be tuned out or ignored if other people are present who cherish creative thinking. It is the internally imposed barriers, those imposed by our own limited vision, that *really* tend to slow down the imagination express. James Adams, in his classic book *Conceptual Blockbusting: A Guide to Better Ideas* (1974), discusses the omnipresence of certain attitudes and beliefs that stall creative thinking. Adams calls these "conceptual blocks," and he defines them as "mental walls which block the problem solver from correctly perceiving a problem or conceiving its solution" (p. 11). *Perceptual blocks* are obstacles that prevent the individual from perceiving clearly either the problem itself or the information necessary to solve it. This situation could arise if a person cannot isolate the problem because it is wrapped up in too many other

> Some types of creativity tests are fakable, if a [creativity] test-wise person is so inclined. For example, when so instructed, college students can deliberately score high on an inventory assessing creative personality characteristics . . . students also can inflate originality scores on divergent thinking tests by deliberately listing "wild" ideas.
> —*Davis, 1998, p. 271*

SOME TIME-TESTED PSYCHIC PUT-DOWNS

"We've never done it that way before."
"That idea will never work."
"The boss/principal/parents won't like it."
"You're new here, aren't you?"
"The Union won't allow it."
"It's not in the curriculum."
"Because I'm the teacher, that's why!"
"It'll be too expensive."
"It wouldn't work with *my* students!"
"Get real!"
"You must have picked *that* idea up in college! This is the *real* world!"
"What you just said proves that not every idea is a *good* idea."
"Wait'll you're here a few years—you'll change."
"I have too many students in my class to try anything new."
"We tried that 10 years ago and it didn't work then."

extraneous issues (in CPS, the "messy situation") or, conversely, that someone perceives the problem from so limited a range that he or she cuts off possibilities that might work. A classic example is this: "Prove that half of 8 is 6." To the straight-line thinker, half of 8 is 4—always and forever. But if you write "eight" in Roman numerals (VIII) and then cut it in half (VI–II), then half of 8 is, indeed, 6 (VI). Or, half of 8 could even be 2 (II). By limiting the vision of "eight" to Arabic numeration, the range of possible options is also limited.

Cultural and environmental blocks are acquired by living in the time, space, and circumstances that we do. For example, if you live in a school climate in which every teacher hoards materials and expertise, there is little chance that cooperative team planning will be effective. Or if you are ruled by a school principal who talks incessantly about "the good old days," when desks were bolted to the floor, in rows, and children had respect and wore uniforms, there is little chance that teachers will feel free to propose a "dress-down day" or cluster their desks together to encourage student-to-student dialogue. These cultural and environmental blocks, often external to the person living within the situation, can still cause disharmony in the mind of those creative souls who wish to push the envelope of reality. If so, creativity goes "underground," disguised or hidden from full view for fear that it be "discovered" as sabotaging the status quo.

Emotional blocks are fueled by the fear that a particular creative action will be perceived as wrong or silly. As Adams (1974) writes, "The expression of a new idea, and especially the process of trying to convince someone else it has value, sometimes makes you feel like an ass, since you are doing something that possibly exposes your imperfections. In order to avoid this feeling, people will often avoid conceptualization, or at least avoid publicizing the output" (p. 50). Perfectionists are especially vulnerable to emotional blocks, because they often fear mistakes so radically that they refuse to participate in any activity or endeavor in which their own success is not guaranteed. A low tolerance for ambiguity and open-endedness is also a characteristic of this block, as is a desire for quick closure on issues and an unwillingness or inability to let ideas incubate. Strong doses of looking silly in a safe environment, free from the criticism and surrounded by the support of others, are an antidote to this block. Another solution, often far simpler, is for people to surround themselves with small children, who think that silly behavior is the finest form of adult expression and that armpit noises rival symphonic melodies in their beauty.

The last category of conceptual blocks mentioned by Adams is the *intellectual and expressive blocks*. Intellectual blocks often

> I believe that it is possible to be an expert and still view the world in new ways. One does not need someone who grew up alone on a desert island to invent a better can opener. One can use people who not only are quite knowledgeable about electrical, mechanical, physical, chemical, and whatever other phenomena, but who also have been closely associated with presently existing can openers. It is only necessary that these people be able to view the world in new ways in spite of all of their prior knowledge. If they can do this they should do better than someone from a desert island.
>
> —*Adams, 1974, p. 71*

You may have read about the American prisoner-of-war who maintained his sanity during years of captivity and torture by deliberately exercising his imagination. He pictured himself building the dream house he wanted—room-by-room, brick-by-brick, nail-by-nail—until he had designed and built every square inch of the house in his mind. If, when being tortured, he lost the mental vision, he would begin all over again. His mind prevailed, and on his return to the United States, he built the dream house he had conceived.

Our mind can be our most powerful possession. It can discover our most exciting challenges, solve our toughest problems, and serve us when all else may seem to have failed. Don't ever lose sight of the "magic of your mind!"

—Parnes, 1981, p. 231

emerge when an individual tries to solve every problem by using the same "language." Whereas some problems require visual or mathematical "languages" to solve them, some people may be comfortable only with the verbal language. This is equivalent to using a hammer for every household fix-it job—hanging pictures (appropriate), inserting screws (effective, but messy), or unclogging the toilet (geyser! geyser!). Obviously, when only one tool is used—a hammer or a problem-solving "language"—results are often less than satisfactory.

Expressive blocks are well described in beach-music performer Jimmy Buffett's lyrics. In one song, he warns people not to describe things to people if they have never seen them—his examples include the ocean and a Kiss concert. By being unable to communicate what *we* know well to people who have little or no direct knowledge about what we are describing, everyone gets frustrated. Expressive blocks are overcome by people willing to share their preferred languages of thought in ways that allow for *other* languages to be heard respectfully and meaningfully.

Actually, many of the solutions to these conceptual blocks were highlighted earlier in this chapter. By practicing a little CPS, while wearing each of de Bono's six thinking hats, and simultaneously remembering that the intellect is structured in at least 120 unique configurations that allow everyone to use their various "intellectual languages," the big conceptual blocks can be split asunder into littler bricks—red ones—from which we can build castles, be they real or imaginary.

Happy dreaming. . . .

GUIDING QUESTIONS FOR CHAPTER 4

1. What models of creative thinking have been developed, and which are the most useful?

2. Can creativity be taught, or is it an innate trait?

3. What are some typical "blocks" to creative thinking in children and adults?

CHAPTER 4 RESOURCES TO REMEMBER

Davis, G. A. (1992). *Creativity is forever.* Dubuque, IA: Kendall-Hunt.

Who says a book on creativity can't also be great fun to read? This volume contains all the requisite information for understanding the theory and practice of creativity but is done in such a humorous way that you won't even realize that you're learning something. A great beginner's resource, or one to which you can refer if you need a refresher course on any aspect of creativity's definitions, assessments, or practices.

Torrance, E. P. (1962). *Guiding creative talent.* Englewood Cliffs, NJ: Prentice Hall.

Almost anything Paul Torrance writes is "verbal gold," but this volume, one of his earliest on the subject of creativity, clearly stands out as among his best. In a very sensitive manner and incorporating sensible suggestions, Torrance advises educators and parents to look out for those children who are capable of being so inconvenient in the classroom: creatively talented students. Readers who take the time to listen to the proddings within this heartfelt volume will find many good methods for helping to keep a child's creativity intact amidst many societal obstacles—and the suggestions are as valid today as they were in 1962.

Torrance, E. P. (1979). *The search for Satori and creativity.* Buffalo: Creative Education Foundation.

When Paul Torrance visited Japan to determine the correlates of creativity in a culture that has often been distinguished by how well its people refine the original thoughts of others, he learned some important aspects about how to initiate and maintain creativity in both children and adults. Let's just say that Japan has as much to learn from us as we have to learn from them. This volume, noted for its personal anecdotes of culture meeting culture, serves as a perfect backdrop to understanding the importance of creativity in the production of worthwhile ideas and products.

CURRICULUM, INSTRUCTION,
AND PROGRAM PLANNING
FOR GIFTED STUDENTS

INTRODUCTION: THE EDUCATIONAL
TOWER OF BABEL

If it is a mark of intelligence to disagree on matters of critical importance, then the field of gifted child education is wise, indeed. For just as there are many ways to define and identify giftedness in children, there are an equally vast number of ways offered to serve their intellectual needs. Some believe that "quicker is better," as they seek to accelerate children's learning by providing advanced material and content as early as possible. Others espouse "broader is better," as they seek to enrich a child's repertoire of experiences by providing an array of parallel educational events that allow gifted children to extend their learning into new areas. Still others counter that "two are better than one," stating that a coordinated teacher can juggle higher-level content and enrichment opportunities simultaneously.

Not only what teachers do but the ways that they do it also invite many and varied opinions. Whether you prefer independent study, teacher-directed instruction, teaching through creative problem solving, or providing intensive, in-depth exposure to difficult subjects, you are bound to find some gifted child educator who agrees with you on the benefits of this strategy. And if you want these experiences to take place in a regular classroom, a resource room "pull-out" class, a self-contained classroom of identified gifted students, or an honors section of high school physics, you will, likewise, find advocates for each approach.

In this chapter, you are introduced to the cogs that drive the machine—the multiple and varied ways that educators (and others) challenge the intellectual and academic needs of gifted students. As with many other issues in this book, you discover more grays than blacks or whites; more ifs than absolutes. Whether this lack of agreement about how to serve our most able children is good or bad is a judgment call that you alone can make. One thing *is* certain: If you are easily frustrated when confronted with diverse possibilities of "what works best," now would be a good time to reach for the aspirin. However, if you enjoy the challenge of form-fitting educational options to the specific needs of each child, then welcome to the glorious world of teaching gifted children.

DEFINING THE TERMS

Surely, this part should be easy—and if using strict dictionary definitions, it would be so. However, the definition of some of our field's most common terminology defies what Webster's unabridged might make them out to be. For example, "acceleration" tends to get interpreted as moving students through the curriculum content at a faster pace than would be expected for a child of a certain age or in a certain grade. However,

> There are three traditions in American politics that have filtered into American education. The first, *Hamiltonian* tradition, is essentially elitist and is based on the idea that there is an upper cognitive or other class that is intrinsically superior to other groups. The second, *Jacksonian* tradition, is essentially egalitarian and is based on the idea that everyone is equal to everyone else in every way that matters. These two traditions have battled for dominance in American society, as the polar right and polar left, and have largely crowded out a third. *Jeffersonian* tradition is neither elitist nor egalitarian. Those following this tradition believe in equality of opportunity but not necessarily of outcome. People are given equal chances to produce but are rewarded for what they actually do produce. Gifted education is best served allied with the Jeffersonian tradition.
> —*Sternberg, 1996a, p. 263*

a look at the definitions provided by some of our field's leading authorities shows that this view of acceleration is only one interpretation. For example, Davis and Rimm (1994) view acceleration as "offering standard curriculum to students at a younger-than-usual or lower-than-usual grade level" (p. 105). Fox (1979), however, is stingier in her view of acceleration as being any strategy that results in advanced placement or academic credit. Van Tassel-Baska (1994) is concerned less about the credit and more about the content. Her view of acceleration provides that "more complex information is presented, the material is denser or more information is covered, the material is presented more rapidly than in typical classroom instruction, and students are confronted by a greater challenge than is customary with regular on-grade level material" (p. 24). Last, David Elkind, a firm believer that too many children are pushed ahead too quickly for their own good, in school and in society, actually calls the term *acceleration*, as applied in the above definitions, a misnomer, because gifted children doing advanced work are not really being *accelerated* ahead of their developmental level; rather, Elkind (1988) believes that they are being served with curriculum and instruction that is *at* their intellectual level.

Even though the term *acceleration* brings on a variety of definitions, they do have the common thread (except for Elkind's view) of higher level content or a more rapid pace of instruction. Such is not the case for acceleration's counterpart, "enrichment." Whereas Piirto (1994) views enrichment as "adding more to the traditional curriculum" (p. 65), Cutts and Moseley (1957) combine various interpretations of enrichment to arrive at their own: "the substitution of beneficial learning for needless repetition or harmful idleness" (p. 37). Their definition of enrichment goes on to elaborate on the goals for enrichment, yet clearly, Cutts and Moseley advocate that enrichment be purposeful and directed towards addressing individual student needs. Newland (1976), in his typically acerbic way, reminds readers that "enrichment is relative, not absolute. . . . Whether an activity is enriching must be determined in the light of the learner's psychological and educational characteristics and of his cultural and social milieu" (p. 282). (Indeed, Newland goes on to state that one person's "enrichment" is another person's "diversion," with the bottom line being that an activity is enriching only if it contributes to a child's conceptual growth.) Perhaps most biting in her review of enrichment's definition is Burroughs (1979), who wrote that

> The word "enrichment" is worthy of Madison Avenue at its best. "Rich" has traditionally been a prestige word. Add a scholarly prefix and suffix to give it a profound academic aura, and the result is nicely calculated to sell the product without leading too many buyers to ask what, specifically, the product is. . . . "Enrichment" is as vague as word as "something." It is vague as to what is offered; that much is obvious at the most casual glance. It is vague, also, less obviously and more seriously, in how it is managed. (p. 14)

As can be noted in the above comments, there is considerable disagreement over the terms *acceleration* and *enrichment*. Likewise, there is considerable disagreement about which plan works best, why, and under what conditions. These issues are addressed (somewhat) in a forthcoming section but now, look . . . up in the sky . . . it's a bird . . . it's a plane . . . it's. . . .

WHAT JIMMY OLSEN KNOWS

Superman buffs recognize Jimmy Olsen as the naive and ambitious cub reporter who learned early on that a reporter's main job is to answer several basic questions about any story: Who? What? When? Where? and How? As gifted child educators, it is our job to ask those same questions. Before suggestions for change can be implemented, the educator must have a good idea about the issue—the story—that is taking place.

Perhaps it is wise to begin with the question of *who*: Who should teach gifted children? And what better way to decide than to let a student do the talking:

> [With Mrs. Draper] I am treated not as a void to fill with useless trivia, but as a living, breathing being possessing the will to learn, the need to learn, and the sincere love of learning.

High school student Leila Sinclaire wrote this tribute to her English teacher, Sharon Draper, the 1997 National Teacher of the Year. What Mrs. Draper offers is a challenge to herself as well as her students: to tweak out every drop of learning from whatever situation that they confront. Few would argue that Mrs. Draper is a superior teacher for gifted students.

Here is another example, one that displays the collective merit of excellence in teaching:

Starting with second grade and on through high school, there have been nine teachers I've admired. I admired them because their own strength and natural rapport with students in turn demanded our respect. Kindness, sensitivity and intelligence were among their many qualities and

In her undergraduate thesis completed in the Honors College of Kent State University, Julie K. Verholt (1993) reported that intellectually gifted undergraduates ($N = 131$) selected the following characteristics as being most important for effective college instructors. The characteristics are ranked from most to least important:

1. knowledge of subject matter
2. exhibits enthusiasm for the subject being taught
3. treats students fairly
4. is open to new ideas
5. challenges students to think at higher levels
6. teaches in an organized manner
7. shares a love of learning
8. exhibits personal concern for the students
9. is a good listener
10. respects creativity
11. allows open class discussions
12. has a sense of humor
13. encourages students to be imaginative
14. is self-confident
15. is sensitive to students' feelings
16. is comfortable with students of high intelligence
17. offers flexible opportunities for self-directed learning
18. is of above average intelligence
19. supports the provision of honors-level classes
20. acts authentically
21. has diverse interests
22. uses different strategies in teaching class
23. is experienced in teaching
24. requires more work than non-honors classes of a comparable level
25. dresses in a professional manner

—*Verholt, 1993*

virtues. Most importantly, they made each student feel significant, as if each of us had a part of them in reserve. (American Association for Gifted Children, 1978, p. 54)

The trio of characteristics possessed by these nine teachers—kindness, sensitivity, and intelligence—are of obvious benefit to gifted students seeking a teacher who imparts much more than knowledge.

The question begging to be answered is fairly obvious: Aren't these the type of teachers that *all* students should experience, not just gifted students? If the answer is "Yes" (which it is), then how can it be said that teachers of gifted students should have certain characteristics, while those working with other students need not be endowed so richly? Thus, the initial question: *Who* should teach gifted students?

PERSONAL TRAITS AND PROFESSIONAL CREDENTIALS: WHAT MATTERS MOST?

Matt loved school. He did beautifully academically, but socially, he was a disaster. So, Matt had a difficult time for a few years. He started to retreat into himself. Then, he discovered computers and started getting involved with them instead of developing a social life.

Matt had a wonderful math teacher who took him by the shoulders one Friday and said, "Matt, you've got to think about life. You can either do your computer thing or you can join the human race. If you want to join the human race, you're going to need a little help. I'm willing to help you. You have until Monday to tell me."

So Matt, in true research fashion, came home on Friday and tried being a computer. He actually became a computer for 24 hours. He would lie in bed and when it was time to get up, he would say, "Do I want to get up? Yes/no." He went through the whole day using the binary method. And apparently, that did not satisfy him. So, he went out on the street and tried to play with other kids. He wasn't very good at it. So he went back to his room and thought.

On Monday, he went to his teacher and said, "I think I need your help." And if Matt is a successful person today, I think he owes a lot to that teacher.

—*Gina Ginsberg Riggs is founder of New Jersey's Gifted Child Society.*

All parents want their children to have teachers who are creative, knowledgeable about their subject matter, actively supportive of their students, and able to teach in a variety of ways. To arrive at an agreed-on list of personality traits or teacher behaviors that are prerequisites *only* for teachers of gifted education seems both ludicrous and a tad elitist. As Gallagher and Gallagher (1994) state, "There is probably more nonsense and less evidence dispensed about the needed characteristics of the teacher of the gifted than almost any other single issue in this field of gifted education" (p. 383).

Then, what *does* distinguish a teacher of the gifted from others? In about half of the individual 50 states, the answer is a "credential," a specific teaching certificate or "endorsement" that verifies that a teacher has had coursework and experiences related to understanding and teaching gifted children. States vary in their requirements for what constitutes an endorsement. For example, Texas requires that teachers receive 30 *classroom* hours of instruction on the intellectual and psychological needs of gifted children before they receive their endorsement, whereas Ohio requires that teachers take 20 *semester* hours of advanced coursework (usually as part of a Master's degree program) and practical experiences with gifted students prior to receiving their credential. In New Hampshire, no certificate or coursework is required at all. Generally, what you will find is this: In states that have made gifted education a relatively big-ticket item in their state budget (at least $5 to $10 million a year), more credentialing will be required. In states with small or no state budget for gifted education (again, New Hampshire, whose state allocation for gifted education is nonexistent), there are few if any requirements other than those normally required to become certified as an elementary or secondary teacher.

However, for a state or province wishing to adopt standards for these credentials, several guideposts have been erected. Feldhusen (1985) and Parke (1989) have suggested that such certification programs include information on the following:

1. coursework and experiences that allow teachers to become knowledgeable about the intellectual and emotional characteristics of gifted children and youth
2. coursework and experiences that introduce teachers to various methods of instruction that capitalize on students' independence and advanced thought processes
3. teacher possesses in-depth knowledge of one or more content areas and is an enthusiastic lifelong learner, always seeking to absorb more knowledge
4. teacher possesses a firm understanding of human psychology and learning so that he or she is able to individualize instruction for especially able children

To this list of super-traits, perhaps several others should be added, based on my personal experiences of being a teacher and administrator of gifted programs:

1. *The ability to talk:* There should be a willingness and aptitude to stand up in front of a not-always-friendly crowd and defend the rights of gifted children to have an education commensurate with their abilities.
2. *The ability to listen:* Almost everyone has an opinion about the benefits (or lack thereof) of providing for gifted students in public schools. A talent for hearing these persons' opinions with respect is essential to the success of a teacher and a gifted program.
3. *The ability to defer judgment:* Because so many people have opinions about gifted children and programs (see #2), it is essential that the effective gifted child educator be willing and able to withhold judgment about the people *making* these statements. An "attack dog" personal style surely makes more enemies than friends, which, ultimately, detracts from a gifted education program and the children whom it serves.

STATE PROVISIONS FOR GIFTED AND TALENTED EDUCATION PROGRAMS

Coleman and Gallagher (1992), in an exhaustive study of each state's legislative provision for gifted child education, found that two-thirds of the states "have some type of mandate regarding attention to gifted students, which is supported, to some degree, with state funding; 14 had no state mandates and two states had 'no mention' of the gifted" (pp. 7–8). When it came to defining who gifted and talented children were, 49 states included intelligence and achievement in their definitions and identification procedures; 40 states incorporated creativity, 34 states cited artistic ability, 28 states named leadership abilities, 15 states included critical thinking, and in 10 states, psychomotor abilities were mentioned.

A related study by the Council of State Directors of Programs for the Gifted (1994) found that "thirty-seven states reported an estimated $394,874,326 in state funding being distributed between local education agencies and intermediate agencies for gifted/talented programs" (p. 23). The individual state dollars spent in these states ranged from $100,000 to more than $88 million. To be sure, where one lives in this country makes a big difference when it comes to local and state support of gifted child education programs!

Passow and Rudnitski (1993), having reviewed the varying policies regarding gifted child education in 49 states and finding so many different approaches being used, suggested strengthening the foundation of gifted child education nationally by adopting particular policies and attitudes. Several of their suggestions are

1. State policies should state unequivocally the support for gifted programming. Local education agencies often seek such support prior to spending local dollars on gifted child programming.
2. States must create and communicate sounder rationales and philosophies for the existence of gifted programming options, integrating them into the overall goals of American education.
3. Definitions of giftedness in state documents should reflect current thinking about the nature and diversity of human talents, as most states now rely too heavily on IQ and academic aptitude. In turn, these definitions should then direct broader efforts to identify gifted children in a variety of areas, by using a variety of methods.
4. State policies regarding curriculum and instruction need to be based more on students' individual needs than on the mere provision of a resource room program or an Advanced Placement course.
5. States need to consider the specific counseling and guidance needs gifted students may have and incorporate policies and procedures that will address these needs.

4. *The ability to deflect arrows:* Sometimes, it is the messenger who is killed because the message itself is one that teachers or administrators do not want to hear. The mentally healthy gifted child educator must know or learn that criticisms and loudly voiced concerns are seldom the personal slams that they appear to be. Developing a thick skin is key to one's success in this controversial field.

5. *The ability to juggle:* Most teachers of gifted students also play a part in identifying gifted students, providing in-service workshops to colleagues, administering the program's paperwork, and communicating with anxious and often-vocal parents. A third hand and a spare brain come in very handy.

6. *An appreciation for public relations:* Educators of gifted children must often speak to the media and other outside audiences about the philosophy and logistics of gifted program operation. An ability to speak in 30-second sound bites comes in very handy, indeed.

By now you might have realized that the opening analogy to Jimmy Olsen and *Superman* seems especially appropriate in the light of the characteristics that gifted education specialists seem to need. A closer look reveals another obvious truth: that the characteristics required for teachers of gifted children often parallel the learning styles and traits of gifted children themselves; or as stated eloquently by Virgil Ward (1961), a gifted child education philosopher, teachers of the gifted "should be deviant with respect to those qualities common to the gifted group" (p. 115).

DOROTHY SISK: EXPERT EDUCATOR

On Serendipity and Expert Guidance

I guess I was very fortunate because I went to California as a classroom teacher in 1958 and began teaching in a district that already had a supervisor of the gifted—a woman named Jeanne Delp. Jeanne was revered by people from California! At the time, she was working on some of Torrance's ideas about creativity, and had her students writing stories like "The monkey who didn't like bananas" and "The elephant who was fearful." Jeanne had been very struck by the fact that many gifted children who wrote these stories had the animals give up their discrepancy to be like the other animals. She was fearful that if school and society didn't help these kids, they would give up their giftedness.

On Her First Teaching Experiences with Gifted Children

I began teaching a "cluster group" of gifted youngsters and when I look back on it, those gifted children taught me. Many of the strategies I have

continued on the following page

continued from the previous page

used over the years I used because of their needs. A story that comes to-mind: in those days, we had playground duty and I remember standing out on the field and Dale—who was probably my highest gifted kid; a brilliant, brilliant child—was way off by himself by the fence. So, I asked Ralph to go see what was wrong with Dale. As I watched him run over to Dale, and then return quickly, saying, "Dale's OK—he's just thinking." From that encounter I internalized the idea that gifted kids sometimes need to be alone. Sometimes they just need to think. Nobody taught me that—or, I guess Dale did.

On the Need to Adjust Curriculum

. . . Another Ralph story. I was teaching math and assigned the students to do page 341. Ralph raised his hand and said, "I've been noticing that this whole page is the same type of problem." I answered by saying, "Yes, you're right." (By now, of course, all the other students were listening!) Ralph asked, "If I get the first one right, do I have to do the rest of the page?" I responded by telling him to do the first row, which he did, and he got them all right. "Go on to the next page!" I told him. Then, Ralph asked again, "If I do the first row right, do I have to do the rest of the problems?" My fear was that he would complete the entire book that morning!

Then, of course, Cynthia raises her hand and says, "If Ralph is doing this, can I do it, too?" It was then I said, "Hold on! I think something's happening here!"

That was how the atmosphere was. We discovered as we went along, and I still hear the echo every now and then of one of the teachers saying, "The more I give them, the more they can do, and the more I give them to do, the more they *can* do!"

It's interesting that one of the things that educators are now championing is called "vertical curriculum," and I'm saying, "Gee...we were doing that in the '50s!

—*Dorothy Sisk, former director of the U.S. Office of Gifted and Talented, is a professor at Lamar University in Texas.*

So, if "deviance" is a strong point, then the job of teaching gifted students who, truth be told, are very much like their most effective teachers, might be a good career choice. One thing for sure: It will be memorable. The ultimate question of what it takes to be an effective teacher of gifted children is one that will never be answered fully by any list of personal qualities or professional credentials. The bottom-line answer lies elsewhere, in a person's heart, as indicated by a final but vital quality, perhaps, in fact, the one that is the most important quality of all: To be effective educators of gifted students, teachers must *like*

WHICH OF THE MANY TEACHERS YOU'VE KNOWN DO YOU REMEMBER THE MOST?

The teacher I have in mind is your "typical" classroom virtuoso: a scholar and pedagogue who loved, respected, and understood her students while teaching them with near-missionary zeal. She taught in Jefferson County, Colorado, and was regarded there as a jewel in its crown. She had devised and taught a memorable enrichment course that synthesized history and literature at the high school for gifted students.

I happened to interview a student who had just finished this course. In the course of my interview, I asked the student to talk about her work habits in getting the most out of this aforementioned course. She described her unique experience in taking the final exam. As usual, she had read her notes, reread her texts, memorized facts, and analyzed the course content critically in anticipation of the "thought questions" that were sure to be on the exam.

On the "day of reckoning," the virtuoso teacher came into the examination room, distributed the usual blank booklets on which the essays were to be written. But something was missing. The teacher had no sheets with exam questions on them. Instead, she strode to the front of the room, announced that the exam would consist of two words to which the students were to respond. She turned to the blackboard, and wrote the words in big, block letters: IMPRESS ME! The student I interviewed, though extremely bright, articulate and poised, was still shaking from the experience, while emphasizing that her admiration for this teacher will know no bounds for the rest of her life.

—*Abraham Tannenbaum, professor emeritus, Teachers College, Columbia University*

gifted students. They must enjoy their company, their challenges, their impositions and inconveniences, their humor, and their need for respect and challenge. If teachers have outstanding paper credentials but lack this genuine fondness for children who many occasionally "show them up" intellectually, they will be less successful than teachers who like gifted students, even if they have never taken a course about how to teach gifted students effectively.

"WHAT" DO WE TEACH GIFTED STUDENTS?

A typical reporter's question, be it from Jimmy Olsen or Larry King, is "What do you *mean* when you say 'gifted education'?" This is an easy question to ask and a most difficult one to answer, for the reason alluded to in the previous section on acceleration and enrichment: One person's gifted program is another person's pabulum; an accelerated class may hold little allure for a child curious about everything he or she touches, and an enrichment program could frustrate a third-grade mathematician ready and eager for quadratic equations.

It is for this reason that I have chosen consciously to refer in this book to "gifted *child* education" rather than "gifted education." Because I am a firm believer that the main emphasis of our teaching is on the individual children in front of me rather than the content that I am assigned to teach them, this person-focused word choice is intended to deflect questions about what *is* "gifted education" and what *is not*. Frankly, I do not know the answer to the "is/is not" question. Perhaps you do:

- Is allowing a child interested in dinosaurs to pursue an independent study project on the topic and to talk via the Internet with a paleontologist about the latest "dino-discoveries" a "gifted" assignment, or does it merely represent good, solid flexibility in teaching?
- Does permitting a seventh-grade student to take an advanced science course at the local high school qualify as a "gifted education" option, or does it simply imply that a district is committed to allowing its students to progress on individual paces?
- When a child enters kindergarten at the age of 4, because everyone who knows her agrees that she is intellectually, socially, and emotionally ready for this early leap into academia, is she receiving a "gifted" education, or is this just common sense being applied by astute adults?

Gifted education, if such a thing does exist, appears to be very much in the eyes of the beholder. However, gifted *child* education seeks the best fit between an individual youngster's learning needs, styles, and preferences and construct options that make sense from intellectual and psychosocial vantages. This distinction is an important one; indeed, it undergirds both the way to think about and deliver quality educational services to help gifted children use and appreciate their abilities.

So . . . back to the question that has dogged the field of gifted child education

---

Some of the very best gifted programs exist in urban areas, not affluent suburbs. I fell in love in 1961 with the High School of the Performing Arts in New York City. The National Association for Gifted Children was holding its convention there and I wanted to go to an elementary school to see an enrichment program. But, I got in the wrong taxi with several others and ended up at this high school on West 46th Street. It was the old school that was later used as the model for that television series, *Fame.* I walked into this crummy old school in the middle of downtown New York. The floors were rickety and it was dirty, but everybody there was exuberant. The freshmen and sophomores would take their academics in the afternoon and their arts area in the morning. I went to an English class that had 41 students in it. The teacher was relating English literature and language to the arts. I sat there in utter awe. I watched kids pass cigarettes and the teacher wasn't getting upset by it. One kid said, "I forgot to do homework last night—I had a rehearsal." The teacher said, "Fine. You know what time—4:30—I'll see you then; you can make it up before you go home." That was it; no questions asked.

—*Bill Vassar, former director of gifted education for the State of Connecticut and past president of the Association for the Gifted and the National Association for Gifted Children*

for generations: Which is better, acceleration or enrichment? The answer is "yes." There is no way that such a complex question can be answered without first taking into account the individual child, the peaks and valleys of his or her previous academic experiences, and the present state of individual intellectual, social, and emotional needs. Only then can educators design educational options that make sense for gifted children, be they accelerated, enriched, or a combination of the two.

The above statement neither downplays nor discards the decades of research and clinical studies that others have conducted about the relative benefits and drawbacks of particular acceleration options or enrichment experiences. Indeed, most other textbooks in gifted child education devote page after page to such findings. However, it is questionable whether the results of one specific enrichment program or acceleration strategy will achieve similar results in another place, at another time, with other students. The following questions and answers provide a summary of many research studies on enrichment and acceleration:

- Do specific interventions with gifted children show any long-term evidence of academic success? Yes, especially in studies that deal with acceleration, which is usually a more "cut and dry" option than enrichment, with its fuzzy definitions and myriad operational procedures.
- Does accelerated content give students a greater understanding of their field of study? Yes.
- Do experiences with using creative problem solving help students to seek alternative solutions to problems that they face every day? Yes.
- Is early entrance to college or kindergarten a beneficial strategy? It depends on the child and the individual circumstances surrounding this placement.
- Do gifted children prefer independent study options and hands-on learning experiences to reading from texts and answering questions at the end of chapters? Of course!

All the research on gifted children and the curricular and instructional options that

My major concerns about curricula for the gifted and talented remain two-fold: (a) the continuing fragmentation of the K–12 curriculum and (b) the lack of the empowerment of classroom teachers to alter this situation. The first step toward improvement is for school administrators to clarify 3–5 non-negotiable, K–12, district-wide goals which are differentiated for the gifted and talented and which are not among the general education goals for all students. When these *non-negotiable* outcomes have been clearly formulated, all teachers must become committed through training to insure that all their classroom objectives for gifted learners further either these goals or the school's general educational goals. In this way, non-negotiable learning can replace the negotiable and "nice-to-do" learning prevalent in many classrooms.

The curriculum carrying out these goals and objectives, which teachers should be trained to adapt or develop, must become interdisciplinary, thematic, concept-based, and open-ended, reflecting multiple viewpoints. To effect these dramatic changes district-wide, administrators must give priority to continuing staff development to empower classroom teachers.

—*Irving S. Sato has been a teacher, elementary through college, and has directed statewide gifted/talented programs and a national outreach project for the gifted/talented.*

they experience—the "what" of gifted education—can be summarized in this seemingly overly simplistic statement: When a gifted *child's* individual rate of development is taken into account, and the appropriate options applied, these educational experiences are successful in at least one area of development—social, emotional, or intellectual.

The "what" of gifted child education is not half as important as is the "who" to which they are being applied. Gifted child education is a series of stories and the people who made them; the same is true for the gifted children who are, themselves, very important players in this continuing saga.

A RETURN TO THE PYRAMIDS

When June Cox and her colleagues released the results of their survey of the nation's gifted child education programs (Cox, Daniel, & Boston, 1985), they said something that most thoughtful educators already knew: that very few comprehensive *programs* for gifted children were available in America's schools; rather, there existed in school districts a variety of *provisions,* many of them singular in design and not connected to anything in higher or lower grade levels.

What is the difference between a program and a provision? It's the difference between a Burger King Whopper and a gourmet feast; a Cliff's Notes version of *Anna Karenina* and the full text of the novel. The difference is bulk and quality.

Cox et al. did propose a "Pyramid Plan" (see chapter 2, Figure 2.5) that took into account the various educational services that could be offered from grades K–12, including everything from "enrichment in the regular classroom"—the base of the pyramid—to a special school designed for children with extraordinary talents in academic subjects or creative endeavors. In between these two extremes was a vast array of other options—competitions such as the Academic Decathlon or Future Problem Solving; "pull-out" programs and special classes or courses in which enrollment was based on ability and/or achievement; concurrent enrollment in high school and college; distance learning or correspondence courses, in which the learning took place locally but the teacher could be hundreds of miles away. The common denominators for all these provisions were three:

> *Ongoing assessment:* Children were not given a life sentence in (or *not* in) a particular option. Their progress was to be monitored frequently, with adjustments made to their placement based on their success and emerging new needs.
> *Appropriate pacing:* Even an accelerated math class can be paced too quickly for students to understand the concepts being presented or, conversely, the same class could trudge along too slowly, failing to keep pace with students' minds and interests. Appropriate pacing implies that different children will have varied speeds of learning, even within the same "gifted class."

Counseling: Whether it is academic counseling ("I think this is the appropriate course for you. Here's why."), personal counseling ("How can I help you do better?"), or career counseling ("It's not easy to decide what you want to be when so many careers sound interesting."), the presence of a counseling component was seen as a vital ingredient in the overall Pyramid Plan.

Unfortunately for everyone concerned about the appropriate education and care of gifted children, the Pyramid Plan, as well-thought out and designed a model as has ever been presented in gifted child education, did not get implemented in many locations. The simple reason was finances, as it would be expensive, in terms of dollars and personnel, to implement its many provisions. A more complicated reason is that the Pyramid Plan required a commitment of philosophy as well as dollars, as school districts would have been required to "take inventory" of how invested they were in arranging options that would benefit its gifted students—as well as many *other* students. Sadly, this did not occur with any great frequency.

Still, good ideas have no statute of limitations, and if a school district is seeking an educational utopia for its students, it need look no further than the Pyramid Plan as a source for excellence in gifted child education program planning.

ALSO-RAN PROVISION #1: THE RESOURCE ROOM

In the absence of a cohesive outline of action such as the Pyramid Plan, many districts choose one or more options that fit their budgets and their school schedules. As noted by Cox et al. (1985), the most frequently visible provision is the resource room.

Essentially, the resource room is a place gifted children go for the equivalent of up to one school day per week. They leave their regular classrooms and trot off down the hall to meet with another teacher, usually someone with at least a passing familiarity with gifted children and their needs—at times, the teacher may possess a certificate in gifted child education. What they do in the resource room depends very much on the interests and proclivities of the teacher, as *very few* resource rooms have explicit curriculum standards or a rationale behind what the children do there. So, if a resource teacher happens to be a camera buff, you can be sure there'll be a unit called "Photography in Nature." Or if science and math are the teacher's strengths, you're bound to see some dissecting and bisecting going on. Although capitalizing on a teacher's strength areas can be among the resource room's greatest assets, it can also be one of its biggest flaws. Indeed, too often, the teacher *becomes* the program, and its success rises and falls on how well he or she can attract the kids' attention.

Belcastro (1987) highlighted some strengths of the resource room approach, including the fact that it gives gifted children a chance to learn alongside a group of intellectual equivalents—other gifted kids who might be spread out throughout the school's other classes and with whom they might otherwise have little or no contact. Also, for students who have always wanted to explore a topic in depth, most resource room teachers will allow (even encourage or require!) that students attempt a self-selected independent study project. And students themselves speak highly of their resource room opportunities:

> I think gifted classes are a good idea because kids get bored in school and might start getting bad grades.—Boy, 9, New York

> I like to be around children who are as intelligent as I am.—Boy, 11, North Carolina

> . . . without the gifted program, I would have no reason to go to school.— Girl, 12, New York

> *—Delisle, 1984, pp. 18–19*

Ironically, the strengths of the resource room model—the lack of a set curriculum, the separateness of these children from their classmates—are cited by critics as reasons that they should *not* exist. Eby and Smutny (1990) speak of several issues that make the resource room model less than ideal, including

- It may cause resentment on the part of students not involved in it.
- When students are away from their regular class, they may be missing some valuable instructional time, or they could even miss a class party or special event (an even *more* heinous crime, in the eyes of a child!).
- Students may "brag" about their fun activities in the resource room, bringing on the resentment of classmates and the teacher.
- The resource room schedule can be disruptive to the flow of a regular day's classroom schedule.

Add to these concerns the fact that there is seldom a connection between what happens in the resource room and what content is being taught in the regular classroom, that children must frequently make up the classroom work missed for the time they were in the resource room, that the resource room program may give the classroom teacher the idea that "I don't have to modify my curriculum" because the gifted children's needs are being met elsewhere, and that the "pull-out" schedule is seldom convenient and certainly does not fit a school structure in which students are responsible to more than one classroom teacher, and you have the makings for a patchwork program that offers little more than window dressing: the illusion that gifted children's needs are being met fully by a small-scale program that is often isolated from the mainstream of the school's curriculum.

Of course, there are those who believe that these issues can be overcome by careful program planning and extensive staff development. Renzulli and Reis (1985) suggest the Schoolwide Enrichment Model, which gives a comprehensive set of guidelines for using the resource room as the star around which all other educational planets will revolve. They include up to 20% of all children in a "talent pool," and the children circulate throughout the school year into and out of the resource room, depending if they are showing "gifted behaviors" that require intervention by the gifted child specialist. The schoolwide aspect of this plan, elegant in theory yet messy in practice, is both its greatest strength and its most obvious weakness; for just as an assembly line works flawlessly when everyone is tuned in to the job, it takes but one foul operator to gum up the entire operation. Also, Reis (1983) suggests that teachers in resource room programs be very aware of the negative dynamics that can be created if classroom teachers do not feel a part of the resource room model. She suggests such simple solutions as calling the program a "send-out" rather than a "pull-out" program; distributing a newsletter to staff highlighting activities and projects that their children are pursuing; sharing instructional resources; and tapping into the talents of staff members by inviting them into the resource room to share their expertise and interests while the gifted education teacher takes over their classrooms. Such focused activities and strategies help, Reis contends, to build "ownership" of the resource room program by the entire school staff.

> ## MILLICENT BORGES DESCRIBES HER EDUCATION IN GIFTED PROGRAMS
>
> Being in gifted programs helped me immensely. These programs provided me with the freedom to work ahead, at my own speed, and to explore creative avenues that were initially out of my realm of thought. I was able to break away from the "wrong side of the tracks" stigma. I was able to make friends with other gifted children—which helped my self esteem. I was given so many wonderful opportunities that I have nothing bad to say about the three gifted programs that I had the luck and good fortune to have participated in. I am thankful for the early encouragement. You see, I was the first person in my family to graduate from a four year college! Without gifted programs, I seriously doubt that I would have made it through high school—much less graduate school!
>
> —*Borges, 1997, p. 12*

Despite its problems, and notwithstanding the call from Cox et al. for a more comprehensive system of programming for gifted children, the resource room continues today as the most popular (in terms of number) design for serving gifted children in the elementary school years.

. . . Which some find hard to believe, given the early 1990s emphasis on a word that sent gifted educators everywhere scrambling: *inclusion.*

ALSO-RAN PROVISION #2: THE INCLUSIVE CLASSROOM

Actually, educators should have seen it coming. Jeanie Oakes, an articulate and respected opponent of academic tracking, called the presence of homogeneously grouped students in classes—smart kids in one class; not-so-smart kids in other ones—ineffective, discriminatory, and unfair in principle to students who *might* do better in school if they had some academic challenges to get excited about (Oakes, 1985).

She spoke, and gifted child educators didn't respond.

Then, Paul George, an equally articulate and respected leader of the newly dubbed "middle school movement," spoke eloquently of the need for belonging that young adolescents share, a need that could best be addressed if middle schools created small "families" of about 100 students and four teachers who, together, would learn to appreciate each other's strengths and weaknesses. (George, 1988). Certainly, separating students out by ability would be injurious to this familial concept.

He spoke, and gifted child educators didn't respond.

Simultaneously, Robert Slavin (1988) and David and Roger Johnson (1987), vocal critics of ability grouping, had evidence to bolster their claims that cooperative learning—the mixing of students of all abilities to work together to solve a common problem—had cognitive, social, achievement, and motivational benefits for all students.

. . . And gifted child educators? Like Nero, they fiddled while their Rome burned.

When a heterogenously grouped classroom of sixth grade students were asked to comment on an extended cooperative learning project on which they worked, here were their comments:

- I learned that I can be creative in anything I study.
- I learned that I should pick more hard working people for my project.
- I found that whenever I work with others I come up with more ideas and better ones than when I work alone.
- I found out that when I want to I can really get a lot done. When I do not want to exert much effort, I am nonproductive.
- I learned that I am very hard to work with and I usually end up doing the entire project by myself!
- I learned that sometimes I can be a jerk but at other times I can work really hard and get a lot accomplished.
- I learned that I can get along with other people and follow what they say and it still comes out great.
- I learned never to wait until the last second.

—Comments from sixth-grade students at
Brady Middle School, Pepper Pike, Ohio

As a field, gifted child education seemed to sit on its collective haunches, hoping that these trends in general education would slide off of us as if we were made of Teflon. "Certainly," gifted child experts and educators seemed to assume, "parents and school boards wouldn't buy into the arguments of these 'outsiders.' *Of course* our gifted programs (or provisions) would remain intact."

Let's just say that the competition was underestimated.

Almost overnight (or so it seemed), the movement away from separate classes or provisions based on perceived student abilities began to go from the impossible to the probable. A new term emerged—*inclusion*—which was supposed to limit the movement of students out of their regularly assigned classes and give teachers the wherewithal and resources to instruct students of all abilities. No longer would "gifted specialists" have that little resource room at the end of the corridor. No more would learning disabled students have to pack up and take off to have individual attention in that small cubby to the left of the computer room. Instead, the teachers who previously taught these special classes would become partners with classroom teachers, working alongside them and focusing attention on the students who, heretofore, had been pulled out for special services. The "pull-out" programs changed their focus, as teachers were now being "pulled in" to offer on-site classroom assistance.

It was a marvelous provision, except for one thing. As with so many good ideas that came before it, inclusion was interpreted one way in theory and managed another way in practice. Becoming the rationale for eliminating positions for special teachers (especially gifted child specialists, whose salaries, unlike those of special education personnel, were seldom tied into federal or state funds), inclusion became a way for school boards nationwide to say they were both cutting budgets and implementing the latest educational research simultaneously. Everyone was a winner.

. . . With two exceptions: students and the teachers who cared for them. In a study of 871 academically gifted students of elementary through high school age, Gallagher, Harradine, and Coleman (1997) found that these students

---

Mary Ruth Coleman and James J. Gallagher investigated how gifted education strategies blended with two other issues: the middle school movement and cooperative learning. They studied ten school sites selected specifically for their excellence in achieving notoriety for meeting the needs of gifted students within the context of school reform. These attributes were noted as being of particular importance:

- *Administrative leadership must be strong at the school level:* Principals must be instructional leaders and have the autonomy to plan programs that fit the needs of the student population.
- *Educational objectives were made explicit:* Teachers, parents, and students knew what standards each was expected to meet. Specific, detailed plans that differentiated educational objectives for gifted students were clearly delineated.
- *Some form of ability or performance grouping was found in each school:* This grouping was not done for philosophical reasons but, rather, because it seemed to be the most effective and efficient way to meet the varied instructional needs of all students.
- *Ongoing staff development opportunities were available:* Cooperative learning and the middle school movement, as well as gifted education, each have specific agendas and strategies of approach to achieve success. The availability of school personnel to discuss and work through these issues was vital in each program's success.
- *Each school emphasized high standards for ALL students:* Even though high expectations were in place, this did not imply that the *same* level of standard applied for all students.

—*Coleman & Gallagher, 1995, pp. 362–384*

reported being academically challenged the most in their gifted programs, with mathematics and science classes following closely behind. The least challenging class was health. The language arts classes varied considerably, with 70% of high school gifted students finding them challenging compared with only 40% of elementary students. Overall, the students who found school least challenging were middle school students, which could be interpreted in at least two ways—either the content was weaker than the students desired, or the students were doing what middle school students are *supposed* to do: complain about school.

Delisle (1994b) addressed ways that inclusion for gifted students can be managed successfully, including extensive *staff development* focused on methods of differentiating instruction, with gifted child educators working alongside their classroom colleagues; *continuous progress options,* in which students' strengths and skills are monitored by gifted child educators and classroom teachers, allowing gifted students (and others) to progress to classes or content based on individual needs and interests; and *new views of intelligence* that incorporate varied learning styles and approaches to teaching. Some students learn better visually whereas others succeed with hands-on materials. By "buying into" the view that intelligences (or talents) can show themselves in multiple ways, all educators can see the benefits of diverse instructional methods and settings.

Mara Sapon-Shevin (1994), a former promoter of gifted program development, wrote a blistering attack on the elitist nature of gifted child education. In *Playing Favorites: Gifted Education and the Disruption of Community,* she contends that a more egalitarian (i.e., inclusive) approach to serving gifted youngsters would benefit all students. In response to criticism of her work, Sapon-Shevin (1995) commented that

> There are millions of brilliant, creative, innovative and flexible ways to provide exciting educational opportunities for students. I am always heartened to visit schools and classrooms in which children of many levels and interests are all productively engaged in learning tasks appropriate to their needs. I am not convinced, however, that these opportunities can only be provided in segregated, pull-out, exclusive (members-only) settings. (p. 10)

"Them's fightin' words," of course, to many advocates of special programming options for gifted students. Still, because pendulums swing vastly (if slowly) in intellectual circles, it is difficult to predict whether the term *inclusion* will still be in our educational vernacular 10 years from now. Educational trends come and go (remember outcome-based learning? constructivist teaching?) as quickly as frost on a sunny Georgia morning, so the fate of inclusion is definitely not a secure one. However, the side effects of inclusive practices deserve a place in an educational hall of fame, for if gifted child educators and classroom teachers can remember for millennia that *all* children learn better when educators work as teams; that *every* teacher is a teacher of gifted children the minute that such children cross the threshold into any classroom; and that the high level content possessed by most teachers, when combined with a focus of higher level thinking espoused by gifted child specialists, creates a powerful formula for exceptional learning opportunities; then the benefits of inclusive practices will ripple throughout our schools long after another educational term and trend has become the newest panacea for "fixing" education.

ALSO-RAN PROVISION #3: THE SELF-CONTAINED GIFTED CLASSROOM

How *dare* the self-contained classroom for gifted children be called an "Also Ran" provision! Often seen as the ultimate in special programming for gifted children—the instructional Nirvana sought by bored students and their parents, the pot of gold at the end of a seldom-seen rainbow—it would seem ideal to identify gifted children and then place them with a trained teacher all day, every day. Isn't this the best of all possible options?

. . . Well, not exactly.

Certainly, there are those who do think that self-contained classes are the best alternative for gifted students in terms of cost-effectiveness (Piirto, 1994) and academic achievement of the selected students (Kolloff, 1989). And indeed, these advocates do have some good points to make. As Piirto points out, a self-contained class of gifted students eliminates the need to hire another staff member to serve gifted children—after all, the 20 to 30 students identified as gifted would have to be housed in a classroom *anyway,* so keeping them all together with a trained teacher of gifted students costs no more than would hiring a teacher *not* so trained. Too, the achievement level gains made by students in self-contained gifted classroom, as Kolloff points out, do tend to be higher than for gifted children in other options, such as resource rooms. This is to be expected, of course, as the overall academic abilities of these specially selected children tend to be significantly higher than in a heterogeneously grouped classroom.

So, if the benefits are so good, than what's the problem? Actually, there are several. First, as pointed out in the Richardson Study, even the best self-contained class represents merely

> If students have experienced poorly implemented heterogeneous classrooms in which their own education has been damaged by the presence of disruptive students, and the curriculum has been boring, and inflexibly unmotivating, this is indeed problematic. It says much about the need to support teachers far more extensively as they move away from tracking and towards heterogeneous teaching. And it speaks volumes about the ways in which teachers are prepared in colleges and universities and about their need for expensive preparation for heterogeneous teaching and community building. It says little, however, about how we should organize our schools so that students get to know and value a wide range of fellow students.
>
> — *Sapon-Shevin, 1995, p. 10*

> I still advocate for full time classes for gifted students because in them you can identify individual strengths. I am not an inclusionist with respect to gifted and talented kids. It's just that they need to be in pressure cooker environments that are high-powered and challenging if they are going to go on to high level achievement.
>
> —*John Feldhusen has been a professor of gifted child education for over 30 years.*

a *provision,* not a full program. Case in point: If the self-contained class has room for 26 students, what is to become of students #27 and #28? Can it be assumed that these two students' educational needs are of a lesser concern than those of student #26, who *is* placed in this self-contained class? Unless other provisions are in place, these "almost enrolled" students could easily fall through some pretty major cracks in the educational system. The second issue relates specifically to the first: In schools in which self-contained classes are in place, there is often a mind-set that *all* the gifted kids have been identified and, therefore, the regular classroom can go on with business as usual, with little differentiation for students who may be in dire need of it. Self-contained classes give the impression—even to students—that there is a definite, intimidating line between "gifted" and "not gifted."

A third concern with self-contained classes is what goes on within the classes themselves. On too many occasions, self-contained classes operate where every gifted student is reading from or completing the same activity from the same page of the same workbook at the same time. How ironic: Students are identified on the basis of their individual needs and abilities and are then given an identical curriculum! Managing a self-contained class is (or should be) as difficult as trying to juggle a classroom full of mixed-ability children because that is exactly what it is! The children in self-contained classes for gifted children are as different from one another in temperament, ability, interests, and motivation as anywhere else in a school. If this is not taken into account in curricular and instructional planning, the self-contained gifted classroom can become just one more way to purport to meet individual learning needs when, in truth, this may not be so.

AN INTERVIEW WITH JAMES J. GALLAGHER

On Growing Up Gifted

When I was about six, I went to a special school for gifted kids run by the University of Pittsburgh. I didn't realize it at the time (but I realized it afterwards) that these were all really bright kids. I was tested by some of the psychologists at the University and they recommended that I go to this school. My mother, a teacher, was delighted. I actually scared people, though, because to get to the school, I had to take the streetcar from one end of Pittsburgh to the other. I had to change streetcars downtown (not a desirable event for a young child) to get to this school, but my mother was so crazy for me to attend this school that she said "ok"—we didn't have a car.

We did fascinating things at this school. I remember arguing the Neutrality Act, when Roosevelt gave 50 destroyers to England. We had a debate about this in sixth grade. We had a very open, exciting kind of education where there were 15 kids in the class and the teachers were really good teachers. It was an outstanding education. I didn't appreciate it at the time, of course, but afterwards, and after thinking about it, I realized that I had had a really wonderful opportunity. I suppose I carried that over to my life now.

On the Social Stigma of Being Gifted

I didn't feel strange about going to a special school because all the kids there were the same. The issue of being away from the neighborhood school *was* a problem, though. I didn't have as easy a social life as I might have because I was traveling on the streetcar all the time. But I was always interested in athletics. I played baseball, softball and football as often as I could, and sports gave me an entree into a social world.

On Choosing a Career . . . or Two

My mother taught mentally retarded kids so I didn't have any fear of mentally retarded kids or feeling strange about them. I knew these kids and I knew what my mother was able to do with them, and so I became interested in that, too. I figured that if I had a chance to look at both sides of intelligence—youngsters who were developing slowest and youngsters who were developing fastest—that it would be interesting from a child development point of view. My experiences with both of these areas were such that I didn't want to give up one for the other.

On the Societal and Personal Impact of Sputnik

When Sputnik came, Illinois (where I was living) got excited about the area of the gifted and passed some legislation which opened the door for a lot of special kinds of activities. At the University of Illinois there was a special high school called the University High School—which still exists, by the way—which went through a very elaborate selection process, essentially taking the brightest kids that they could find. I started a research project with some money I got from the Office of Education, which I would not have been able to get had there not been a Sputnik. I just hit the right seam in history.

We started studying the interactions of teachers and students in gifted classrooms. We set up microphones and audiotapes and taped 200 classroom sessions and coded the thinking of students and teachers as it was revealed by tape recordings. Out of those 200 sessions, I came away with an understanding about instructional strategies and how people really were trying to work with these students. My book, *Teaching the Gifted Child,* really came largely out of that experience and all of that rich set of data that I was able to collect. But again, there was no way the Office of Education would have supported that research without Sputnik.

—James J. Gallagher is Kenan Professor of Education at the University of North Carolina and past president of the National Association for Gifted Children.

Children [move] from grade to grade through a preplanned sequence of standard subjects, as if on factory conveyor belts. At each stage, certain facts are poured into their heads. Children with the greatest capacity to absorb the facts, and with the most submissive demeanor, [are] placed on the rapid track through the sequence; those with the least capacity for fact retention and self-discipline, on the slowest. Most children end up on a conveyor belt of medium speed. Standardized tests [are] routinely administered at certain checkpoints in order to measure how many of the facts [have] stuck in the small heads, and "product defects" are taken off the line and returned for retooling.
—Reich, 1992, p. 229

Certainly, the ability to offer advanced content or accelerated learning options does exist within the structure of a self-contained class for gifted children. A self-contained class is only *one* provision among many that must be offered by a school system if it truly cares about meeting the needs of *all* its gifted children, not just the *crème de la crème* selected for the self-contained class.

ALSO-RAN PROVISION #4: ACADEMIC AND CREATIVE COMPETITIONS

Academic Decathlon, Future Problem Solving, Odyssey of the Mind, Quiz Bowl, Power of the Pen, Model United Nations, Science Olympiad, Invention Convention, Mock Trial, History Day: With all these options abounding in schools, it's surprising that there is any time to teach "the basics" to students. Or, perhaps, the above options could be used to teach the basics in a far, far different way.

Academic competitions, or their equivalent creative options, are a popular adjunct to many schools' menu of options for students to explore. The above programs (and others) all have a few points in common: Students choose them on the basis of interest, there is (usually) no set criteria to prove you are gifted before you can participate in them, and skills that many teachers try to drill into students are learned in interesting and cooperative ways.

Take, for example, Odyssey of the Mind (OM). This provision, founded in 1978 as Olympics of the Mind (a title found to have infringed on the copyrighted term *Olympics*), allows students from across the globe to compete with each other in teams of five to seven students. Similar to athletic competitions, there are different age divisions (e.g., primary and high school) and different levels of competition (local, state, international).

Each year, students are given some intriguing puzzles or projects to complete, such as constructing a car that gets its motion only from springs, or designing and building a structure made from balsa wood that will withstand hundreds of pounds of weight. In addition, students are asked to complete more verbally oriented projects, such as writing a new last chapter for a famous novel such as *Moby Dick* and then enacting the chapter complete with script, props, and stage directions. These "odysseys" are planned by students well in advance of the competition, and there are strict guidelines regarding the types of materials that can be used, the amount of money spent on props and equipment, and the time limit for demonstrating your answers.

Another aspect to OM, and one for which no specific preplanning is possible, is the "Spontaneous Problem," a kind of verbal joust that includes questions even more trivial than those on *Jeopardy!* For example, students might be asked to brainstorm the names of any food that is green or to come up with different ways to cross a street. In roundtable fashion, students must think spontaneously about their answers, piggybacking on teammates' responses to increase their point totals. The goal of the Spontaneous Problem is to think on your feet, as a team, the way that many businesses and corporations have found is essential to productive management.

It is easy to see the many basic skills, creative, academic, and otherwise, that are built into OM and competitions like it. There is great opportunity for open-ended thinking that eventually gets transformed into well-reasoned responses to problems; there is learning through varied learning styles—building, writing, acting; there is the challenge of working toward a group goal, with each member of the team responsible for the project's ultimate success; and there is the joy of discovering that learning can be fun. Further, a big component of OM (and several other competitions) is parent involvement, for just as Little League teams have volunteer coaches and community sponsors, so does OM. In fact, many schools could not (or *would* not) sponsor OM teams if parent involvement were not a primary component of its operation.

Unfortunately, *also* like Little League, there is the danger of attracting over-zealous parents and participants who take the competitive aspect so seriously that the allure of learning for learning's sake is lost. When this occurs, the Nike T-shirt slogan that reads "Second place is the first loser" can dominate, limiting the positive impact for children who want to participate, first and foremost, for the sheer pleasure of intellectual stimulation. As Kohn (1996) states, "Academic competitions are a seductive way to manipulate students into pursuing some subject matter, but they turn learning into a quest for triumph." In deference to those who believe that the competitive edge is just a bit too sharp, the National Association of Secondary School Principals publishes annually a list of contests that meet the following criteria: They do not encourage competition at the national level, and they do not require more than 2 days of school absence to participate.

Last, a final word of warning: Limiting "admission" to competitive teams such as OM or Future Problem Solving to students identified as gifted is shortsighted and wrong, yet it is sometimes done. This is a silly requirement for several reasons, the biggest of which is that some of the most creative and innovative thinkers may have been "missed" in gifted program identification because their abilities are in domains other than those being tested by IQ or achievement tests. Also, it sets a dangerous misperception in the minds of students and parents that the only students capable of solving problems are those who have been preselected as gifted. But, as far as we know, the front offices of IBM, Kodak, and government agencies (*especially* government agencies!) are filled with people who were never identified as gifted during their school years. Still, they are making decisions based on team consensus, brainstorming, and many other skills that are fostered through OM and its myriad counterparts. It makes more sense to even the playing field when children are children, so that the problem-solving practices that they use there can be applied later when these children, as adults, are making important decisions about our pensions, our health care systems, and the style of toaster Americans really want to buy.

Academic and creative competitions are hotbeds of learning opportunities for all interested children. They should be a part of any complete program that

Many students do take AP courses but *don't take the tests!* This seems absurd, for omitting that last step negates some of the main purposes of the program—to provide some continuity between high school and college; to avoid repetition of course work already covered; and to allow for more flexibility in choosing college courses. In effect, advanced placement courses become honors courses, no more.
—*American Association for Gifted Children, 1978, p. 86*

is meant to challenge and stimulate the minds of its young participants. Just be mindful that learning, not competition, remains the paramount goal.

WHAT'S A HIGH SCHOOL TO DO?

Most of the school provisions suggested for use with gifted students better fit the structure of elementary schools than they do secondary schools. It would be rare (and silly) to find a "pull-out" resource program in grade 10 or 11, as students have responsibilities to so many teachers that to pull them from one to be taught by another just would not make sense. Also, the self-contained classroom would not be practical, as it would require that one teacher be expert in all content areas—highly unlikely unless your last name was daVinci. Also, it would probably take just a few nanoseconds for such a class to become known as "Dweebville," a place in which no teenager would choose to reside.

That is not to say, though, that gifted child education experiences cannot exist in a secondary school setting. Indeed, in a good, comprehensive high school, most of the provisions for an exemplary gifted child education program already exist and, with today's technology, excuses such as "my high school is too small" or "we live in too rural an area" just don't apply as they did even a decade ago.

Cases in point: Here are some options that frequently exist *inside* the walls of a secondary school:

- *Advanced Placement* courses allow students to take high school classes and (possibly) earn college credit.
- *Honors classes* provide advanced or accelerated content in a classroom where students are (generally) grouped for their high abilities.
- *Independent study* options can be taken (often) for elective credit toward graduation, allowing students to pursue topics of specific, individual interest.
- *Block scheduling of classes,* whereby students focus for concentrated periods of time daily or weekly on specific subject matter. Thus, students may have fewer courses to take each semester, but the classes that they do take are (theoretically) more intensive and in-depth.
- *Accelerated options:* Once in high school, students can enroll in classes that match their ability rather than their assigned grade level, releasing them from courses whose content they have already mastered.
- *Extensive experiences in arts and athletics* tap into talents that are often not met through the above academically focused options.
- *Service learning opportunities* allow students to serve as volunteers in community-based programs. At times, course credit is involved; otherwise, the service is done as part of an organized extracurricular school group.

- *Distance learning options* allow students to take classes for credit by computer, and use interactive technology to link them to other students and professionals worldwide.
- *Clubs focused on particular interests* range from chess clubs, to stock market clubs, to opportunities in journalism, to the aforementioned options such as OM or Future Problem Solving.

. . . And here are some options that often exist *outside* the school walls:

- *Mentorships or internships* provide opportunities to work in a career-oriented setting or with individuals who share a particular passion area of a student.
- *CLEP opportunities:* The College Level Examination Program (CLEP) tests student competencies in particular subjects even if the student has acquired the needed content outside of regular high school courses.
- *Exchange programs* permit students to take extended visits to other schools or places, including exchange programs with other countries.
- *Summer enrichment programs* are often sponsored by universities eager to matriculate high-ability students; these programs offer experiences in the arts and academics, often at a very low cost.

REFUSING TO TAKE "NO" FOR AN ANSWER

In October, 1993, the high school counselor in my small, rural Oregon school district told me that my 12-year-old son, who had been grade and subject accelerated, would graduate at age 14 because there would be no classes left for him to take. Jack didn't want to graduate that early. . . . Dual high school and community college enrollment wasn't an option, the counselor told me, because of the college's minimum age requirement.

I started researching. The community college catalogue stated they required a minimum age of 16 for dual enrollment, yet they also claimed they didn't age discriminate. I continued my research at the University of Oregon Law Library. . . .

[Eventually we] received front-page coverage in every major Oregon newspaper. . . . The State Board of Education chairperson was quoted as stating this problem had to be addressed. . . . The district added more advanced classes as well as distance learning options, and I had discovered the power of the press and public opinion. . . .

Jack just turned 15 and is completing the last available high school classes, along with foreign languages through the district's satellite dish program and AP calculus through Stanford University. . . . He will add community college classes in chemistry, physics, computer programming and literature as a dual-enrolled high school senior next year.

—*Lloyd, 1997, p. 13*

What should be obvious from this list of options is that most high schools actually have a limitless supply of opportunities to enrich and accelerate the learning abilities of its students. Although the provisions may not be "packaged" as neatly as those of an elementary school—that is, few of these options are for the exclusive use of gifted students—they do, nonetheless, serve the same purpose: to balance a teenager's life with exemplary academic, artistic, and life experiences that put them into contact with fascinating aspects of their world and its people.

A worthwhile exercise for secondary school personnel is to conduct an "Inventory on Excellence," a no-holds-barred examination of the many good opportunities available in their local secondary school(s). Using the preceding list as a base, secondary educators could compile for students these and other options that can both broaden their intellectual horizons and deepen their aesthetic appreciation for the world in which they will soon become full-fledged, adult members.

THANKS, COACH!

Stretching the athletic analogy just one last pull, a comprehensive array of services at a secondary school would offer the same degree of flexibility and "give" offered by coaches. That is, students with natural abilities and talents, combined with an intense drive to succeed in a chosen endeavor and the willingness to learn even more, could join the "varsity gifted program," taking on the most challenging and intensive of the options the high school (or community) has to offer. Students whose gifts and talents are strong but whose commitment or time is stretched a bit thinner would entertain some "junior varsity" options—an honors course or two, combined with an extracurricular that was enjoyable but not necessarily straining. Students with a modicum of interest or the desire to merely "play around" with some new experiences could opt for an "intramural" section of the Chess Club and one course that offers advanced or enriched content.

Different teams, similar goals: to take from school what is meaningful, and to enjoy the experience as one or more of life's many adventures. Perhaps students could even spring for trophies for those varsity scholars who hurdle over the intellectual or creative highbar with grace, style, and a lot of hard work.

Coaches have long realized the importance of having multiple options for athletes with diverse levels of talent and drive. All educators interested in unleashing the scholastic, artistic, and altruistic abilities of their students will follow the lead of the trendsetters, the jocks and jockettes who envision the possible within themselves and strive to do the best that they can in fields of personal dreams.

SO . . . WHAT IS CURRICULUM FOR THE GIFTED?

The answer to this question remains elusive, and try as they might, no two authors seem to agree on the correct response. Perhaps it would help to consider curriculum from a totally different angle: your next vacation.

If you are the outdoor type, you probably can't wait to lace up those hiking boots, pack up your tent, and head into the woods for a 5-day trek across virgin turf. Your efforts will be rewarded with sore feet, but with a cool stream to soak them in at night and views of violet-tinged mountains as your backdrop, you realize that life doesn't get any better than this.

. . . But then, there is your companion, who grumbles that a vacation should be relaxing, not strenuous, and whose personal definition of "roughing it" is having to stay in a Marriott hotel that does not have an indoor pool or 24-hour room service.

What is enjoyable—enriching—for one is tedious for another. What qualifies as merely a challenge to the hiker is a burden for the resort buff. And vice versa.

The key distinction drizzles down to a single word: *preference.*

The same is true in trying to define or describe "curriculum for the gifted." If a sales representative from a publishing company offers prepackaged curriculum materials guaranteed to challenge and enthrall every gifted student, it is likely that some students would excel while others would languish. "But these ideas are *stimulating,*" the publishing representative says, "gifted students will *love* this stuff!" Maybe yes, maybe no, for stimulation and challenge must be personally defined, not shrink-wrapped in arrays of color-coded activities segmented by subject matter or advanced thinking skill operation.

Therefore, you can no more look in a publisher's catalog and buy a one-size-fits-most "gifted curriculum" than you can look in a travel brochure without pictures and determine whether a place you've never heard of would be worth a visit. "Challenge," "enrichment," and "enjoyment" are not just nouns you can purchase; they are concepts to be experienced, and they will be experienced differentially by every student.

Still, even if it is agreed that no curriculum materials exist that are good *only* for gifted students, aren't there some aspects of available curriculum materials and instructional strategies that are, in fact, better than others? To this question the answer is a qualified "yes"; qualified because most any of the ideas that follow make perfect sense to use with *any* student who is ready to receive them, whether or not the student has been identified as gifted.

Perhaps better than anyone, A. Harry Passow put the idea of curriculum for the gifted into a realistic perspective. As the editor of the 78th Yearbook of the National Society for the Study of Education, which was devoted entirely to gifted children and their education, Passow (1979) pointed out that curriculum can be adapted in three ways:

1. *In breadth or depth:* For example, students would not just study about the dates and players of the Iraqi invasion of Kuwait; they would also analyze the surrounding political climate and the cultural, economic, and religious factors that played into this global scenario.
2. *In tempo and pace:* For example, through either grade skipping or a form of content acceleration within the student's classroom, the gifted student would explore geometry in seventh grade, or chapter books in

My faith has become very strong that if children have an opportunity—a challenging opportunity—in a focused kind of learning experience—a class in math, in computers, a class in nursing, a class in working with small animals, a class in astronomy—if they have a chance to work in such a climate and think "maybe I've got something going here," and if they have a teacher who is attuned to recognizing these developing talents, then something very worthwhile, both in the way of identifying and nurturing talents, will happen.
—*John Feldhusen has been a professor of gifted child education for over 30 years.*

kindergarten, or French III as a freshman. If students were ready to learn, the curriculum would be there for them; the pace and tempo of either or both the student and the class would be quickened.

ISSUES AND TRENDS IN CURRICULUM FOR THE GIFTED

In his 1986 keynote address to the National Association for Gifted Children, A. Harry Passow offered a series of specific suggestions, hopes, and dreams of what curriculum for the gifted would look like in the decade ahead. How well have we done?

- I would like to think that there is a trend toward more comprehensive curriculum planning for the gifted than the unarticulated, isolated, fragmentary provisions we have found too often in the past.
- I would like to think that there is a trend toward total curriculum planning and not just planning for that portion of the student's experience that we call "gifted education."
- I would like to think that we have come to understand the multiple dimensions of cognitive and affective growth so that our goals for the gifted go beyond high academic achievement and include creative, productive behaviors of many kinds.
- I would like to think that we have discarded the perennial argument of acceleration versus enrichment and have focused instead on deepening our understandings of what constitutes an adequate and appropriate learning experience for a particular individual.
- I would like to think that we are developing educational programs that are based upon the needs of individual learners rather than upon making up for program deficiencies in a curriculum for the non gifted.
- I would like to think that we have come to understand the importance of the climate and the environment in implementing challenging learning experiences for the gifted.
- I would like to think that we have come to understand that every teacher must be a teacher of the gifted, and not just those individuals who have a special responsibility for teaching the gifted.
- I would like to think that we have come to understand that the curriculum for the gifted extends beyond the confines of the classroom and the school into the rich resources of the many non-school agencies, educative agencies—the family, the community, the media, museums and libraries, religious institutions, laboratories, and studios, to name a few.

3. *In kind:* For example, students would be exposed to courses or experiences that do not ordinarily occur in the context of K–12 education, such as starting a day care center at the high school, or studying comparative religions while in middle school, or assisting a paleontologist on an archeological dig.

By adapting curriculum in these ways, individual needs can get addressed to make for personally meaningful school experiences. Further, Passow (1979) states that the strategies used in implementing the breadth/pace/kind combination should include the following:

1. helping students learn how to learn—to investigate problems sufficiently that they no longer need the total guidance of a teacher
2. ensuring that the educational activities are appropriate for the intellectual and social development of the child
3. allowing students to progress from relatively low levels of complexity and abstraction to increasingly higher levels of these cognitive operations

—*p. 448*

Sandra Kaplan (1979), an expert on curriculum development, used Passow's ideas (and her own) to develop elaborate plans for modifying what she called the *process, product,* and *content* changes that needed to take place with curriculum for gifted students. Joyce Van Tassel-Baska and colleagues have edited several books (1988, 1996) with similar themes: designing challenging and enriching instructional units within content areas. And, to be sure, countless teachers have taken courses and curriculum workshops on differentiating subject matter and its delivery to gifted students.

But truth be told, teachers who work with "regular" students, as well as those who work with "at risk" children, would benefit from reading these books and designing instructional strategies and materials that put some rigor into the pabulum that many school children have been served in the name of curriculum. Indeed, Henry Levin, leader of the accelerated schools movement, has taken the idea of focusing on a child's strengths and structuring curricular experiences that are meaningful and interesting and adapted them successfully with remedial students who had generally received rote "drill and kill" as their basic educational diet. His accelerated schools idea (1992), a mirror image of what gifted child educators have espoused for generations, has proved successful with those who had heretofore been called "reluctant learners." Wouldn't any student be reluctant if what he or she was expected to learn bore no resemblance to the questions that he or she had and the ideas that he or she pondered about life and learning?

THE MORE THINGS CHANGE . . .

The biggest question and the most difficult solution (in educating gifted students) is undoubtedly recognized as this: "How shall their superior powers be challenged, and how shall curriculum and schoolroom procedure be modified to meet more fully the rightful demands of superior endowments?"

—*National Society for the Study of Education Yearbook, 1924, pp. 63–64*

A TRIBUTE TO A. HARRY PASSOW

By Abraham Tannenbaum

Harry Passow was keenly attuned to changing educational and cultural conditions that could affect the development of giftedness in young people. Recognizing how fragmentary, faddish and vulnerable to extinction enrichment programs could be, he spent the better part of his career supporting quality programs for the gifted, which might otherwise collapse under the weight of criticism and the pressures of modern cultural and social life. He did it for the sake of these extraordinary children and for the world they will hopefully serve with distinction some day. We must therefore do no less than perpetuate our commitment to the goals that he cherished and bequeathed to us.

—*Presented at the 12th World Council for the Gifted Conference, Seattle, Washington, July 30, 1997*

So . . . is there such a thing as *a* curriculum for the gifted? The evidence points to "no." Are there some *strategies* and *approaches to instruction* and *content* and *pace* that make good sense to use with gifted students? Of course there are! However, these identical approaches, or their slightly less arduous first cousins, are also appropriate for *any* learner who is to enter and exist in the 21st century as the complex thinker that our time now demands—indeed, that *all* times before us have also demanded.

In conclusion, as instructional planning for gifted learners is considered, it is probably purposeless to ask the question "Is this good *only* for gifted students?" Such a general question can never be answered accurately, and it only shows professional naivete as regards the relationship that is established between any learner's personal need to know and a school's ability to offer a satisfying menu of appropriate learning experiences.

Go read books on curriculum for the gifted. Purchase materials from "gifted catalogs" to use in the classroom. Pore over the enrichment sections of the teacher's editions of school textbooks. And then realize one thing: The minute a curriculum strategy is offered for a select few students, not only are the "nongifted" students' educational horizons being limited, but also, the depth and breadth of a teacher's own vision of what is possible by *all* students become myopic.

GUIDING QUESTIONS FOR CHAPTER 5

1. What are the essential traits for effective teachers of gifted students?

2. Is there "one best way" to teach gifted students? If not, what ways seem better than others, and why?

3. In what ways are acceleration and enrichment defined, and how is each beneficial to gifted students' learning?

4. What provisions work best with gifted students: self-contained classes, resource rooms or "pull-out" programs, or inclusion-based strategies within the regular classroom?

CHAPTER 5 RESOURCES TO REMEMBER

Brown, R. G., Cole, D. B., and Cornell, R. H. (Eds.) (1981). *Respecting the pupil: Essays on teaching able students.* New York: Dell.

This book is a wonderful array of appealing essays on how teachers at one of the world's most preeminent schools gear their curriculum and instruction to gifted learners and/or academic achievers. Focusing not only on the typical academic subjects, this book also includes essays on teaching drama, religion, physical education, and moral education to students whose capacity for knowledge is very high. Hard to find but well worth the search!

Shore, B. M., Cornell, D. G., Robinson, A. W., and Ward, V. S. (1991). *Recommended practices in gifted education.* New York: Teachers College Press.

After reviewing 100 textbooks on gifted child education, the authors arrived at practices that either were or were not supported by research or theory. Is acceleration a worthwhile option? Is career counseling for gifted students different than for other students? Which type of program format is "best" for serving gifted children in our schools? By distilling generations of research into this one volume, the authors have drawn some conclusions about the benefits (or lack thereof) of the day-to-day thinking and practices of educating gifted students.

Tannenbaum, A. J. (1983). *Gifted children: Psychological and educational perspectives.* New York: Macmillan.

I cited this book many times while writing my own book. There is a good reason for that: It is the most valuable general text ever written in the field of gifted child education. Words such as *profound* and *erudite* come to mind; the book is thick with description and complexity. For the serious student, this book is unrivaled in its quality and breadth of coverage on topics related to understanding and educating gifted children.

CHAPTER
6

INSTRUCTIONAL STYLES
AND STRATEGIES

Let's begin with a story: A tenth-grade geometry class is being introduced to the world of angles, sides, and theorems. Because geometry differs from students' previous experiences in mathematics, in that there are no arithmetic problems to complete nor algebraic expressions that can be underlined and labeled "answer," students are often taken aback by the abstract and proof-driven nature of this branch of mathematics.

When given a problem such as the following:

Given: $\angle 1 = \angle 2$
$\angle 3 = \angle 4$

Prove: $\angle 7 = \angle 8$

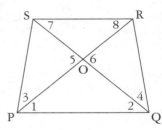

students proceed in lockstep fashion, hoping to arrive at the correct "proof" through a variety of step-by-step logical reasoning (which, of course, they had memorized previously).

Enter a creative teacher who provides the same problem with only one small change: He erases "Prove Angle 7 equals Angle 8," inserting in its place an alternative assignment: "With the above information, see what you can prove."

As the teacher in question reports:

The whole exercise would change from the teacher's problem or the book's problem to the students' problem. The second process is far more fun than the first, and even slower students can enjoy success because they can generally prove *something.* . . . As the students quickly learn the deductive process of building on the deductions of others, the class discussion is likely to become animated."

—*Brown et al., 1981, p. 64*

ව

In the last chapter, the point was made (again and again!) that although some curricula are more appropriate than others, there is really no such thing as a gifted curriculum. How odd, then, that the focus of this chapter is a review of instructional methods and strategies that should be used in teaching gifted students. Isn't this talking out of both sides of our mouths? For if there is no such thing as a gifted curriculum, then how can there possibly be "gifted teaching strategies"?

. . . A good question, which deserves a direct answer: There is no such entity as a teaching method or instructional style or strategy that is the exclusive property of gifted students and those who teach them. However, for many years, the leaders in the field of gifted child education acted as though this were the case, siphoning off the best approaches to teaching "higher level thinking skills" or offering "in-depth explorations" or "independent study" only to those chosen few students who qualified as academically capable or intellectually gifted. This stance, which was naive, paternalistic, and elitist, certainly bothered and bewildered many educators not involved with gifted students, and it provided a foundation of sand on which to build theories of instruction for gifted students.

So, as you read in this chapter about the various methods of teaching that benefit gifted students, please insert in your mind the idea that these approaches *can* and *do* work effectively with any student who has a desire to learn. Indeed, the strategies in this chapter have been used by many educators who work with wide ranges of children, including those identified as learning disabled or developmentally delayed and children of poverty and/or neglect. In some cases, the reason the following strategies *did* work with disengaged learners was because the students' minds had been numbed for years by the dull and tedious drill of "lecture-read-test." But once introduced to higher levels of thinking or problem-solving strategies that involved hands-on experiences, success was reached and self-esteem was raised.

This chapter contains information and ideas that are covered more in depth in textbooks that focus specifically on differentiating classroom instruction. The intent here is not to give so full an explanation of each strategy or model that they can be implemented tomorrow; rather, the purpose is to "scratch the surface" of curriculum differentiation, with hopes that the curious reader will seek a more complete explanation of implementation strategies in other resources. The ideas in this chapter are aimed at providing some directions as to how the refinement of instruction and teaching style can make a difference in the lives of children, gifted or not.

. . . Back to the creative geometry teacher. In discussing further the benefits of providing his students with a more open-ended assignment than that provided by the text, he stated that most students ended up "discovering" a theorem that had been around for centuries. This was perfect, for the students were

Fulfilling standard requirements for graduation in standard courses is just where a lot of gifted kids bog down. We can go through the motions easily enough, but there often isn't enough there to stretch the imagination or to stimulate creativity. *If* we don't tune out altogether at this point, a lot of us knock off the requirements as fast as we can and then fill up on elective courses, *if* we can manage to squeeze enough time in to do so, and *if* there are a variety of interesting electives offered at our school. Three big "ifs."

—*American Association for Gifted Children, 1978, pp. 68–69*

Children should learn how to obtain information and put it into a form in which it may later be retrieved. This implies that they must have a full understanding of the material as well as the higher-level abilities to synthesize from it, and to follow through to novel understandings. Problem-solving skills should be built in to teaching in many subject areas, so that pupils are obliged to think for themselves. The skills of communicating what they have found are as important as the discoveries themselves, and should be taught and practiced in schools.
—*Freeman, 1985, p. 17*

realizing an educational dream of every educator: They were discovering and then learning, rather than the artificial reverse:

> Their discovery is often exciting enough to warrant naming the theorem for the student discoverer. In my class last year, for example, the Baley-Siegal Theorem (which states that a quadrilateral is a parallelogram if its diagonals bisect each other) was named for the girl who conjectured the result and for the boy who proved it. Next year the same result will probably be named for someone else. (Brown et al., 1981, p. 66)

It is often said that the best teacher you ever have will be the one whom you never need again. In this chapter, some methods for making this transition from dependent to independent learner are reviewed, in the hope that it will be useful for *all* students.

PROBLEM-BASED LEARNING: A NEW NAME FOR A TIME-TESTED APPROACH

Every decade or so, often sooner, some new jargon enters our educational vocabulary. Teachers seek to learn more about exotic-sounding and innovative topics such as integrated thematic instruction, or double-block scheduling, or "looping," or a particularly hot newcomer, problem-based learning (PBL). Interested educators clamor to understand its intricacies, attending workshops on how to implement these new strategies usually begun by some university researcher or in some affluent school district that prides itself on constant innovation and has the funds to attempt whatever it pleases. And then, after exposure to the "new" idea, we learn the inevitable: This latest trend may actually be decades old but packaged with a new acronym and professional videos that extol its merits. Such is the case with PBL, a "new" idea as old as apprenticeships—but just as valuable.

PBL, in its latest iteration, began at McMaster University in Ontario, Canada, in the early 1970s. Under the leadership of Howard Barrows, PBL became the method of choice used at McMaster's Medical College, as an alternative to the textbook-driven memorization approach that made so many students despise their time in medical school because it was not "real" enough (Checkley & Willis, 1996). The most basic component of PBL is its focus on the ill-structured problem, a loosely phrased scenario (in this case, a patient's complaints about pain or illness) that does not give enough information from which to make a positive diagnosis. Rather, what the ill-structured problem *does* provide is a vehicle from which medical students can ask questions and pose hypotheses regarding possible reasons behind a patient's affliction.

The benefit to the PBL approach is obvious: Seldom in a real hospital will a patient's case history provide a clear-cut, positive diagnosis and prescription on initial examination. Why, then, should medical school training do anything less? Better to let these students, through hypothetical case studies, follow some blind alleys and ask some questions that may or may not be helpful with an eventual diagnosis. This exposure to the real world of medical emergencies will prepare them to handle complex cases that defy easy classification.

One of the main components of PBL and a recurring question regarding its merits involve the role of the teacher. No more is the instructor the "sage on the stage," pontificating about the facts and figures and theories and body parts that generally constitute one's medical training. Rather, the instructor becomes the "guide on the side," coaching students' thinking, answering questions with more questions, and helping students to analyze both the data given and their own interpretations of it. As the coordinator of medical curriculum and admissions at Southern Illinois University (the first U.S.-based PBL site) stated, "I was skeptical at first. . . . Although I saw that there would be real advantages to the PBL approach, especially the value of early clinical experiences, I was uncertain that students would be able to take the responsibility to learn what they needed to" (Checkley & Willis, 1996, p. 2).

Ah, yes, the inevitable anxiety: "Would the students be learning enough *facts* to be able to make reasoned judgments from the data presented?" According to the 60 medical schools now using the PBL approach nationwide, the answer is "yes."

As might be expected, the education community outside of medical school has grasped onto PBL as an approach that might be beneficial in use with school-age populations. Advocates believe the PBL approach works most effectively in areas in which problems have multiple *resolutions* rather than singular *solutions* (Gallagher & Gallagher, 1994), which is often in the realm of science or social studies. For example, when an archeologist unearths an artifact in a previously unknown field site; when an astrophysicist discovers a pulsating object in a previously black sector of the night sky; when a historian finds a heretofore hidden set of letters between Thomas Jefferson and his daughters; or when an architect is hired to erect a unique structure on a parcel of land that others have declared unbuildable, each is presented with a real-world dilemma, a problem that can be interpreted in several ways, but one in which a firm understanding of the problem's context helps arrive at a legitimate resolution, effectively reviving the "romance" involved in real-world exploration of one's area of passion.

Problem-based learning allows students to become better problem solvers because

When gifted high school students in Arkansas were asked to brainstorm ways to get more out of school, here were their suggestions:

. . . go into greater depth . . . skip a grade level . . . be able to ask more questions without being ridiculed . . . have a positive outlook . . . participate in extracurricular activities . . . work ahead . . . be able to talk more with teachers . . . have more time to read . . . develop our emotional selves . . . meditate . . . learn to think more creatively . . . have time to draw . . . be able to change teachers when we don't "click" with someone . . . take extra classes . . . take college-level classes . . . be able to ask teachers for alternatives to regular assignments, such as writing papers . . . do independent studies . . . have more time to sleep . . . be able to play music, listen to music, write music . . . help others.

—*Excerpted from* The Gifted Kids Survival Guide: A Teen Handbook *by Judy Galbraith, MA, & Jim Delisle, PhD, Copyright © 1996. Used with permission of Free Spirit Publishing, Minneapolis, MN.*

they are able to practice and hone the skills of reasoning within a cooperative setting. The other students involved in the same exploration become collaborators rather than competitors, and teachers are often seen as co-learners in the quest for solutions.

. . . But how new is this idea of PBL? Didn't E. Paul Torrance use this same idea in his call for students to be involved in Future Problem Solving, substituting the phrase *messy situation* for *ill-structured problem*? Hasn't Harvard Law School made a name for itself for decades by focusing on real cases that have perplexed the courts and using this method in its introductory law classes? Indeed, didn't John Dewey and the others involved in the Progressive Education movement of the early 20th century propose that learning by discovery was the most potent form of all and that all learning is a process of continuous reconstruction, based on our experiences and the result of the implementation of one or more solutions that made sense at the time that we made them? Didn't Leta Hollingworth make such methods of education the basis for her "Evolution of Common Things" curriculum? Didn't Joseph Renzulli propose his Enrichment Triad Model so that students could act like "practicing professionals" in the projects that they complete (more on Triad later in this chapter)? These questions are raised not to downplay the current emphasis on PBL and its potential good effects on gifted learners and others; indeed, there are many benefits. Rather, the questions are posed so that observant readers will see how connected and reconstructed are many of our newest "theories" of instruction.

Underpinning PBL and its historical corollaries is an approach to the structure of knowledge and learning that has been embraced by virtually all who have come into contact with it. Indeed, if the field of gifted child education has a "pre-primer level," an essential beginner's guide to the understanding of *why* we do *what* we do, then our field's equivalent of Dick and Jane is a man with an engrossing name: Benjamin Bloom.

BLOOM'S IDEAS BUD

In 1948, a group of college-level instructors and administrators got together at the annual convention of the American Psychological Association (APA) to discuss a common problem: There were as many interpretations of what constituted solid instructional objectives as there were people who practiced education. Now, for those teachers working in the classroom trenches, such high-minded issues were probably of less concern than how to handle the arrival of millions of postwar babies into the nation's classrooms. Still, someone has to address the lofty aspirations of educational theory, and who better than conventioneers looking for a legitimate reason to meet annually at a nice hotel?

For several years thereafter, a core group of these educators met, with the task of assigning its 30 committee members the responsibility of compiling as many educational objectives as they could envision. Both simple and complex

> One of the first problems raised in our discussions was whether or not educational objectives could be classified. It was pointed out that we were attempting to classify phenomena which could not be observed or manipulated in the same concrete form as the phenomena of such fields as the physical and biological sciences, where taxonomies of a very high order have already been developed. Nevertheless, it was the view of the group that educational objectives stated in behavioral form have their counterparts in the behavior of individuals.
> —*Benjamin S. Bloom on the initial thoughts on the cognitive taxonomy of educational objectives.*

objectives were solicited, as the main outcome of the group's deliberations was to be a common core of educational objectives that all could agree constituted the full range of human learning, in the cognitive, affective, and physical (psychomotor) dimensions. Their hope was to "facilitate communication between psychologists and educators in such areas as test construction, research and curriculum development" (Maker & Nielson, 1995, pp. 53–54).

Because the cognitive area was considered the most critical, this area was tackled first by the whole committee. Once ready for review, the compilation was sent to more than 1,000 college and secondary educators for evaluative feedback. The resulting publication, *The Taxonomy of Educational Objectives—the Classification of Educational Goals Handbook I: Cognitive Domain* (Bloom, 1956), had an impact on curriculum design and instructional planning that even its designers could not have anticipated. Several years later, with interest waning and the original committee no longer intact, the *Taxonomy of Educational Objectives—the Classification of Educational Goals Handbook II: Affective Domain* (Krathwohl, Bloom, & Masia, 1964) was completed by a subcommittee and distributed with less fanfare and (sad to say) little direct impact on classroom practice. The psychomotor taxonomy was never completed but seems to me like good fodder for a doctoral dissertation for an ambitious student.

So . . . what is the big deal about the taxonomies, and why have gifted child educators wrapped themselves in their virtues for two generations? Perhaps a review of Bloom's cognitive taxonomy, which even today affects classroom practice, will answer these questions.

Split into six main sections with substantial subgroupings within each, the cognitive taxonomy is composed of these hierarchal components (from simple to complex):

Level 1: **Knowledge:** behaviors that emphasize recall or memory ("What is the capital of Idaho?")

Level 2: **Comprehension:** behaviors that indicate a literal understanding ("Explain how Boise got its name.")

Level 3: **Application:** behaviors that require students to use what they have learned in a new way ("Produce a diorama displaying the city of Boise and its suburbs.")

Level 4: **Analysis:** behaviors that break down knowledge into its component parts ("What do you believe is the reasoning behind locating Boise as Idaho's capital city?)

Level 5: **Synthesis:** behaviors that combine elements of learning into a new whole ("Select a specific location in Idaho and write a rationale as to why this site would make a better state capital.")

Level 6: **Evaluation:** behaviors aimed at assessing the value of particular ideas or solutions ("Considering all the possible new capital sites you and your classmates have proposed, justify which one you believe is the best choice.")

Some teachers believe their students should "really understand," others desire their students to "internalize knowledge," still others want their students to "grasp the core or essence" or "comprehend." Do they all mean the same thing? Specifically, what does a student do who "really understands" which he does not do when he does not understand? Through reference to the (cognitive) taxonomy as a set of standard classifications, teachers should be able to define such nebulous terms as those given above.
—*Bloom, 1956, p. 1*

As is evident, each level of Bloom's cognitive taxonomy requires a little more thought, a little more information, and increasing levels of sophisticated thinking or judgment. For example, to justify why a specific site in Idaho would be a better location for the state capital (synthesis), one must first know (among other things) that Boise *is* the capital (knowledge) and that state capitals are generally located near major rivers or transportation hubs or in a locale central within the state (comprehension and/or analysis).

To many educators, the taxonomy has certain distinct advantages and uses. First, it breaks the realm of knowledge down into its component parts, allowing teachers and students to see clearly how and why some learning is easier than others while some is more complex. (It is often suggested, in fact, that educators teach their students about Bloom's levels.) Also, it gives teachers a clear-cut roadmap as to how they can write educational objectives, test questions, and independent assignments that are designed to elicit higher levels of thinking. Too, the structure of the taxonomy is readily understood, and its hierarchal nature has been shown in research to be accurate, with the possible exception that evaluation may not, indeed, be the highest level of thinking (Maker & Nielson, 1995).

The main reason that educators of gifted children seem to have latched on to Bloom's taxonomy is their collective concern that too much classroom instruction and time are spent on the lowest two levels, knowledge and comprehension (Feldhusen, 1998), skills that many highly able students seem to have mastered already, leading them to say all manner of impolite things such as "This is boring" or "Didn't we already learn this stuff last year?" By emphasizing the higher levels of the taxonomy, it is assumed that learning will become more vibrant and interesting, even if the subject matter is as mundane as understanding state capitals and why they are where they are.

A main argument against using Bloom's taxonomy exclusively with gifted students is one cited previously: If much of our classroom time in general is spent on the lowest levels of learning, isn't this boring and educationally detrimental to *many more* students than just the few identified as gifted? Or as stated by Maker and Nielson (1995), "The Taxonomies of Educational Objectives can-

What bothers me in gifted education today is that we are still doing it *to* children rather than *with* them. And true motivation is when I am involved in the process. For example, there are wonderful curriculum units that are written on different topics, but do they ever get to the point of discovering the passions that a child has? Kids can sit down and learn all about Bloom's Taxonomy or other models of teaching and learning, but they need to have a chance to design their own curriculum—to explore their own passions. I'm not saying to throw out the content, but let students choose what they will learn sometimes.

What I have learned is that a lot of times disenchanted kids don't have a passion related to school, but they do have one out of school. Maybe it's a passion for rock and roll. If so, we should start out at the exploration level and investigate what they can learn about that passion that applies to school.

I believe that gifted kids of 4, 5 or 6 years of age live their passions but that we mess them up or take them away from them. For passion learning, I think one of the most important things a teacher can do is just get out of the way.

—*George Betts is the designer of the Autonomous Learner Model for the Gifted and Talented.*

not be defended as a total approach to curriculum development for gifted learners and are sometimes difficult to justify at all due to their widespread use in regular education" (p. 90). Although it could be argued that Maker and Nielson seem to be seeing the educational glass as half-empty rather than half-full (just because *other* kids benefit from certain instructional methods, does that disqualify them as being appropriate for gifted learners?), it makes sense to state that Bloom's taxonomy is only one piece in a big puzzle that can make curriculum and instruction more intriguing for both the educators and the students whom they teach.

In addition to the cognitive taxonomy, there is the affective taxonomy, that also-ran stepcousin to Bloom's original, which asks educators to remember that every lesson taught contains an affective component, as students either respond to it well or with distaste (the *receiving, responding,* and *valuing* levels); that every time a lesson is taught, students have a choice to integrate it with what they already know or discard it mentally (the *organization* level); and that every time a lesson is taught, students will either change their behaviors as a result of what they have learned or dismiss it as not being important enough to guide their future actions (the *characterization by a value or a value complex* level). The affective taxonomy adds a valuable and necessary component to all cognitive learning: the importance that a child places in learning something new that may cause him or her to think or act differently as a result of new knowledge gained.

> We found the affective domain much more difficult to structure, and we are much less satisfied with the result. . . . Several difficulties beset this work. First, there was a lack of clarity in the statements of affective objectives that we found in the literature. Second, it was difficult to find an ordering principle as simple and persuasive as that of complexity, which worked so satisfactorily in the cognitive domain. Third, few of the examiners at the college level were convinced that the development of the affective domain would make much difference in their work or that they would find great use for it, when completed. There was no doubt that the affective domain represented a more difficult classification problem than the cognitive domain.
>
> However . . . our pessimism about the possibility of completing it satisfactorily was more than offset by the many letters we received from teachers, specialists in measurement and evaluation, and educational research workers asking when the second Handbook would be published. It was evident that we had dropped one shoe and that the tenants in the room below were waiting for the second shoe to fall.
>
> —*Krathwohl et al., 1964, pp. v, 13*

STANDING ON YOUR OWN TWO FEET: INDEPENDENT STUDY AND SELF-DIRECTED LEARNING

What Nestle is to chocolate chips and Kellogg's is to cereal, self-directed learning is to independent study. Long considered one of the most defensible and least controversial ways of modifying curriculum and instruction for gifted learners, independent study options often fell short of their goals, and the students

THE TAXONOMY OF EDUCATIONAL OBJECTIVES, HANDBOOK II: AFFECTIVE DOMAIN

Level 1: *Receiving:* The student is in a cognitive and psychological position to learn. ("OK, it's time for social studies. Time to tune out my Walkman and tune in to the teacher.")

Level 2: *Responding:* The student is willing to volunteer answers or choose to attend to activities related to the subject. ("Even though I think social geography is pretty boring, it is interesting to hear Ms. Johnson describe how people migrated from one place to another in similar ways that other animals do. It kind of makes us more like them.")

Level 3: *Valuing:* The student takes a stand on an emotional issue raised by the content being studied. ("Do I think there is ever a valid reason for forcing people to move from their homes to another part of the country or world? Hmmm . . . interesting question! Here are my initial thoughts. . . .")

Level 4: *Organization:* The student chooses between solutions when issues of cognitive and affective dissonance arise. ("If the government says that a certain region is too hazardous to live in, but I have a home and am willing to take the risk, should I be forced to move? What if my decision endangers the lives of others, not just me? Would my decision then be different?")

Level 5: *Characterization by a value or a value complex:* The student has analyzed all sides of an issue and is now ready to take a stand that encompasses both pertinent data and personal beliefs. ("Even though the issues are complex, I believe the central focus is individual rights versus governmental responsibility. Having considered everything I've read and heard, here's where I stand and here's why I believe I am right.")

—Delisle

fell short of their own learning desires, due to a lack of understanding that independent study does not mean that a student is left on his or her own, marooned on an island of data without a map that shows how to dig for treasure. Independent study does not imply that teachers are removed from the learning equation; rather, it is just a different role that they get to play.

The Self-Directed Learning (SDL) Model, initially proposed by Donald Treffinger in 1975, provides a clear structure for developing the research and organizational skills required to complete an independent project. Realizing that even gifted students have vastly different levels of independent skill development, Treffinger discusses three tiers to SDL. Within these tiers, teachers can adapt a student's independent study project so that the skills they have and the skills they need can be combined to make a successful experience with independent learning.

A review of three students who are operating at different levels of the SDL Model is provided below. Assume that all these students are in sixth grade:

Sara, a bright girl who is interested in everything but has trouble focusing for an extended period of time on any one idea. Also, Sara tends to collect more information than she needs to finish a project and has some trouble sifting through what is important and what is extraneous.

Julio, a boy who is able to move along quite efficiently and successfully after he has a good grasp on the topic of study and his approaches to learning about it.

Ernestine, a girl whose independent learning skills are refined enough that teachers feel comfortable that she need only give them an indication where she is headed. From past experience, it is clear that Ernestine will deliver on the project she promised to complete.

Although these students' teacher may wish for all of them to pursue an independent learning project, the teacher will soon realize that preparing each student to do so successfully will require some differentiated experiences and expectations. Sara, for example, will probably need both help and direction in targeting a specific topic to study. To do so, the teacher may provide Sara with a list of three to five options, asking her to select the one that interests her the most. Then, together, they will refine the chosen topic into its component parts, so that Sara may work on them one at a time. With Julio, the teacher may ask him to think about several options from which, after brief discussion with the teacher, one is chosen. Julio is then given some suggestions for starting points, with knowledge that he can come to the teacher when he is stuck or needs a new direction. Ernestine, more often than not, will know what she wants to study when she first comes to the teacher; the teacher's role with her is to provide resources and materials that will guide Ernestine on her independent path. In a sense, Sara could be considered a "chooser," Julio a "developer," and Ernestine a "director" as regards their levels of independence in SDL.

As these students progress with their projects, they will each need continued support but of different types and intensity. For example, whereas Sara (and to a lesser degree, Julio) may be required to fill out a contract, specifying deadline dates and specific projects that need to be completed within this timeline, Ernestine may not need such external structure. Instead, she can check in with the teacher informally, mentioning the progress to date that has been made. In terms of evaluation, Sara may turn in her project to the teacher for final review, whereas Ernestine completes a self-evaluation, telling the teacher in a narrative what she has learned during this SDL process. Julio might use either of these methods, or he might share his project with classmates to get their evaluation to add to the ones given by himself and his teacher.

A one-on-one learning experience is a really beautiful thing, because, for one thing, you cannot put each other on; there is a direct interaction of minds and there is no place for shoddy efforts on either part. There is especially no place for "mechanical" teaching or rote learning.

—American Association for Gifted Children, 1978, p. 72

My senior year (of high school) I set up a conference course with an artist who had many talents and interests. Even though I was employed in a totally different field, he took me—my experience, my ideas and my work—seriously. With no prior experience in studio art beyond grade school construction paper and crayons, I did three things: I worked in various media, I kept a journal, and I talked frequently with this teacher about both my artwork and my journal. From this experience I learned (1) a concept of processes I had articulated through the art work but found much wider use for, (2) the conviction that exploration and a sense of play are legitimate parts of learning, and (3) the sense that my own experience is important and a valid source of learning.
—*Simpson & Kaufmann, 1981, p. 43*

Whatever the level of SDL being enjoyed by a student, Treffinger suggests weekly "seminars" be held with the teacher and all students who are conducting independent projects. During these seminars, students discuss their project's progress to date, but just as important, they review the processes that they used in discovering new information and any problems or dead ends that they may have encountered. The goal is for the students to see *each other* as potential resources, so that they may use one another's skills to help them get beyond any snags that their research might have hit.

It is hoped, of course, that the more opportunities students have to participate in SDL, the more independent they will become as learners, and the better able they will be to pursue personal learning interests without the direct guidance or instruction of a teacher. The adage "give me a fish, I eat for a day; show me how to fish, I eat for a lifetime" certainly seems to apply to SDL and its underlying purpose: allowing gifted students (and others) to undertake independent learning experiences with the knowledge that they develop the skills to have the reality match their dream.

Another form of independent study for students, and one that fits into a greater whole, has been proposed by Joseph Renzulli. Based on his conception of giftedness being one of "gifted behaviors"—above average abilities, creativity, and task commitment—Renzulli put forth his plan for student involvement in their own educations: The Enrichment Triad Model (1977). The Triad Model involves students in three types of activities:

Type I: general exploratory activities that introduce *all* children to interesting ideas, events, and people that they may wish to learn more about at a later time. Examples of type I activities include guest speakers on archeology, a field trip to a local dig, or a learning center established by the teacher that includes hands-on materials, resource books, puzzles, or games.

Type II: "learning how to learn" skills, such as creative thinking strategies, time management, outlining, and other research skills, and self-knowledge discussions on affective issues such as perfectionism. Type II activities are good for *all* students, as everyone needs to know how to find the resources required to complete research papers or projects and everybody could stand to be just a little more creative.

Type III: independent or small-group projects with real audiences—publishers, galleries, school boards—that serve the dual purpose of displaying a child's gifted behaviors while generating new information that is shared beyond the classroom teacher. An example of a type III activity is students petitioning for a change in a local law regarding curfews. They would need to learn about why the law was enacted (type I), while simultaneously learning how to make an effective presentation to city council (type II) before presenting their petition and their arguments in a public forum (type III).

In the years that followed the release of the Triad Model, Renzulli and his colleagues expanded further the ideas presented by the Triad Model's approach. Their Schoolwide Enrichment Model (SEM) (Renzulli & Reis, 1985) is "designed to provide advanced-level learning and creative productivity to a broad spectrum of the school population by making various types and levels of enrichment available" (Clark, 1997, p. 451). In presenting SEM as an option for total school improvement, Renzulli and Reis have tried to do what many others have proposed: take the general principles of curriculum and instruction underlying the education of gifted children and make it available to anyone with the potential for "gifted behaviors."

More of a "package deal" than a single solution to school efforts to improve student learning, SEM weaves together a behavioristic view of giftedness with strategies of approach to reach the educational goals of both students and their teachers.

> The development of persons who may become producers of and contributors to existing knowledge must begin with at least some experience in an instructional model that provides young people with an opportunity to experience the *modus operandi* of the first-hand inquirer.
> —*Renzulli & Reis, 1985, p. 7*

WORDS OF WARNING ABOUT INDEPENDENT STUDY

Not every teacher will want to take the time to implement SDL when using independent study. Some prefer more informality, finding it somewhat oxymoronic to establish a set of precise guidelines for something as individualistic as independent study projects. To a point they *have* a point, but any independent study project is done best if certain procedures are followed. For instance:

1. *Make sure the topic idea is the student's, not yours.* Many teachers themselves are lifelong learners with passions that run the gamut from guitars to gourmet cooking. As your students are deciding to look into a new area of interest, make sure they are doing so because of *their own* area of personal interest rather than one they have adopted because it was of interest to you or another individual. Questions such as "Why are you interested in this topic?" and "For how long have you been curious about this?" will be good indicators as to how invested the student is in this supposedly self-selected project. (By the way, this advice is as good for doctoral students pursuing a dissertation topic as it is an eighth grader looking for an independent project that can last 6 weeks.)

2. *Not every independent study needs to end with a visible project.* In our product-driven world, and living as we are in an era of accountability that demands that every precious moment in school have evidence that it was time well spent, there is a tendency to believe that nothing good is learned unless you've got something to show for it. The old phrase "the proof is in the pudding" has a newer corollary: "The proof is in the product."

   To many scholars and philosophers, this view seems to be a myopic view of the world of learning. Everyone, at times, gets intrigued about something that seems new and interesting—modern art, mountain

INDEPENDENT STUDY, INDEPENDENT SPIRIT

I spent two weeks assisting a medical brigade in Honduras. I belonged to a wonderful group of people including doctors, nurses, electricians and translators who were willing to give of their time and money to help others.

The town we went to, Santa Lucia, is located six hours from the closest paved road and ten hours away from the closest city by bus. The travel is a treacherous wind through mountains and rainforest, preventing most inhabitants from ever being treated by doctors.

We treated many cases of infections, broken bones and asthma. I was even able to assist in a delivery! But the medical experience pales in comparison to what I learned through the people. Their simple farming lifestyle and sense of community are refreshing. They are very poor and live under conditions that people in the United States have only read about. Most sleep on mud floors and wear the same clothes for weeks at a time. The kids craved attention because there are so many of them in their homes. Yet the people are accepting and I never heard a complaint. Once I asked a young woman, "Are you happy here?" She smiled and replied, "This is what I have, and who I am. Why shouldn't I be happy?" I made no answer to the reversed question because I knew she was right.

—Vanessa Madrigal completed this project as a part of her
Honors College experience at Kent State University.

climbing, 19th-century British literature—only to find that once the initial curiosity has been satisfied, it is time to move on to something new, something more emotionally or intellectually attractive. When this happens to adults, they simply glide from one interest to the next, realizing that the world is a big enough place that it can accommodate many interests, however brief or prolonged they may be.

Essentially, this same logic holds true for children, many of whom have this same proclivity toward wanting to dabble in this and that and something else for short, but intense, periods of time. If always required to show evidence of learning in some dramatic way—an independent study or enrichment triad type III project, for example—they may begin to resent the proddings to produce observable documentation of their learning. In extreme cases, students will learn to keep their interests to themselves, closeted away in the privacy of their own free time, for fear that well-intentioned adults will want them to make a big production out of a kernel of interest.

The benefits of "learning for learning's sake" must be revisited, understanding that nothing absorbed by our minds is wasted. Indeed, it may become fodder for some future exploration of yet another topic.

Projects are fine for students to complete. But it must be remembered that learning can be either a visible entity or an invisible feeling of satisfaction.

3. *It is better to succeed at something small than to fail at something big.* One of the most common problems with independent study learning experiences is the overwhelming nature of the topic being studied. Every teacher has run across students who are intrigued by dinosaurs, or are history buffs absorbed with World War II, or are junior scientists worried about the ecologic health of our planet.

But to tell a student, "OK, go ahead and do a project on World War II" is like giving a chocoholic the opportunity to buy only one item from the world's largest Godiva Chocolate Shop: The choice is just too overwhelming, the options too many. Besides, they all look good.

Teachers do favors for their students by asking some probing questions about their proposed study: "What is it about WWII that interests you? Are you intrigued more by the European Theatre or the Pacific Theatre? weapons or generals? battle plans or naval blockades? the Marshall Plan or D-Day?" The more specific and small scale students can get as they plan independent projects, the more likely it is that they will find success in their quest for information and learning. If, later, they choose to expand their topic to other aspects, that's fine. But by starting small and

> I was studying psychology independently as an adolescent in the days when almost no junior or senior high school offered psychology. My teachers were vaguely aware of what I was doing, but not terribly interested in it. I turned this interest into an adult career and a lifelong quest.
>
> —*Robert Sternberg, IBM Professor of Psychology and Education, Yale University*

Hunter Scott, a Florida sixth grader, knows just how far an independent study project can go. He began a school history project about the *USS Indianapolis,* a World War II ship that was sunk by enemy fire, killing 880 of its crew members. The captain of the ship, Charles McVay III, was court-martialed for not taking appropriate evasive action. He committed suicide in 1968.

Scott decided to contact the remaining survivors of the *USS Indianapolis,* many of whom spent four days and nights in shark-invested waters waiting to be rescued. He e-mailed or called each of the 153 survivors, wanting to learn more about the ordeal they suffered and gain their perspectives on the court martial of their captain. Scott received 80 responses from the crew.

Since then, Scott has learned that many of the crew saw their captain as a scapegoat. In response, Scott has written to the president and senior military officials trying to earn a pardon for the now-deceased captain.

Even if Hunter Scott doesn't gain this pardon, he has gained the respect of the survivors of the *USS Indianapolis:* they invited him to display his independent study project on this incident at the reunion of the *USS Indianapolis* survivors, held, appropriately, in Indiana.

—*Excerpted from "Project Now Crusade Against Court-Martial," 1997, p. 6A*

being successful, students will more likely say "I learned a lot" rather than ask "Am I done yet?"

CUTTING THE CURRICULUM DOWN TO SIZE

Most teachers would lament that as school boards and state education agencies place additional topics into the K–12 curriculum, nothing seems to be discarded. Few would argue that AIDS education, technology training, service learning projects, and nutrition in a fast-food world are irrelevant for today's students, but where does one squeeze these topics amidst the readin', 'ritin', and 'rithmetic that parents demand and standardized achievement tests target?

At least one answer that is available and is especially useful for high-achieving students, gifted or not, is a process that has come to be called *curriculum compacting* (Renzulli, Reis, & Smith, 1982), a plan wherein students who are able to show competency in basic skills can move on more quickly to new areas of academic challenge.

As an example of curriculum compacting, recall the following from your own days in school. It's Friday morning, and one of your teacher's usual sobriquets can be heard: "Take out a piece of paper for your spelling test." Dutifully, you do so, and because you are a good speller, you wait without anxiety for each word to be read. Exchanging papers with the kid to your right, you get back a corrected paper with it expected result—100%, the grade you've been earning in spelling since first grade. You feel proud. But in a way, you might also feel cheated: 100%s should not come this easily.

The following Monday you get a list of this week's spelling words. You write them out five times each. On Tuesday, you place each word in a sentence and on Wednesday, it's alphabetical order. Thursday is a word search puzzle or some other "enrichment" activity, all in preparation for what is to come: another spelling test on Friday, another 100%. A 100% that you could have attained on Monday, if only the teacher had given you the chance to show it.

In its most basic form, curriculum compacting would allow you this chance to "show what you know" *when you knew it,* rather than at some artificially imposed time like a Friday morning, just before recess. If you also happened to be good in math and were able to prove to your teacher that you could multiply "456 × 7,398" (and its myriad cousins) accurately and repeatedly, think of the time you would save by showing him or her once and then moving on to more advanced curriculum. And if those language papers that ask you to "change the 'y' to 'i' and add 'es'" could be given to you, a great writer, *before* the teacher taught a lesson on this skill to the class, imagine all the hours that you could have explored the more intriguing intricacies of language.

Curriculum compacting removes the grade-level or content-imposed barriers that many gifted students feel victimized by within their class placement; for just because some textbook publisher thinks that all fourth graders need to practice their multiplication tables daily, *you* may not have to if you've known them since second grade. What Renzulli, Reis, and Smith do is provide step-by-step instructions for both compacting the basic skills curriculum and adding in some more energizing options of acceleration or enrichment.

Few educators disagree with curriculum compacting in theory, but as the saying goes, the devil is in the details. For one, the term itself is off-putting, for "compacting" is something that is generally done to . . . trash! Few teachers regard the meat and potatoes of their classrooms as trash, and this insensitive term does little to endear the process of compacting curriculum to classroom teachers. Instead, try calling it *curriculum telescoping,* a less offensive and more satisfying alternative.

Second, the management system that Renzulli et al. propose includes all manner of large, color-coded forms that look ominous and time-consuming to even the most enthusiastic teacher. And, frankly, they *are* ominous and time-consuming! Better, instead, for teachers to look over the materials available on curriculum compacting and then devise their own methods for systematizing the process. Susan Winebrenner's book, *Teaching Gifted Kids in the Regular Classroom* (1992), has many such options that are very teacher-friendly.

Third, many teachers have been doing curriculum compacting for decades, but they have done it under the moniker of "common sense." If teachers *know* the skill level of their students and they have enrichment and acceleration options available within the classroom for students to explore as an *alternative* to what they already know how to do, they may not need all the forms and the paperwork that can often accompany this "telescoping" process. If this is the case, these teachers should continue to benefit their high achieving students by doing what they have done for years.

Curriculum compacting is a valuable addition to any teacher's bag of tricks in the continuing quest to make education relevant to children. Just call it something else.

> Effective teachers at all grade levels have found that students differ in the ways they learn best and therefore learn better when teachers vary approaches to learning. Compacting and contracts make it possible for teachers to present alternative activities to highly capable learners that are challenging, promote cognitive growth, and are based on student interests. Regular use of compacting and contracts will benefit not only gifted students, but also provide interesting educational opportunities for the entire class.
>
> —*Winebrenner & Berger, 1993, p. 2*

> In my opinion, (curriculum compacting) is much more appropriate than the practice of "extra credit." It doesn't take long for gifted kids to figure out that they'd better slow down or face having to do more than the regular amount of work. There are also students so driven to accomplish all the extra credit activities that they feel they've failed if they are not able to complete everything.
>
> The "Most Difficult First" strategy is used when teachers assign a certain amount of practice work to the whole class. Students who can demonstrate their concept competency by doing the most difficult part of the assignment *first* are excused from the balance of the practice assignment to work on their differentiated activities.
>
> —*Winebrenner, 1997, pp. 30–31*

CHARACTER EDUCATION AND LEADERSHIP DEVELOPMENT

> Goodness without knowledge is weak and feeble, yet knowledge without goodness is dangerous. Both united form the noblest character, and lay the surest foundation of usefulness to mankind.
>
> —*John Phillips, 1781*

It would probably be a consensus that our schools do a better job at transmitting knowledge than engendering goodness. After all, the calling of schools has been to equip the next generation with the skills and abilities to solve problems that could only get worse if left unattended. Thus, students are taught to write clearly, to compute accurately, and to approach difficult situations with an eye toward solutions.

Gifted students, in particular, have been touted as being our greatest hope for global redemption. As Gallagher and Gallagher (1994) state, "Failure to help gifted children reach their potential is a societal tragedy, the extent of which is difficult to measure but which is surely great. How can we measure the loss of the sonata unwritten, the curative drug undiscovered, or the absence of political insight? These gifted students are a substantial part of the difference between what we are and what we could be as a society" (p. 4). This attitude that gifted children are our future leaders precedes the work of Lewis Terman and is based in the centuries-old fascination with intelligent people. Great things are expected from those with fine minds, and this message is transmitted to gifted children in both obvious and subtle ways.

But how do educators supplement the acquisition of knowledge with the inculcation of values? Which values should be targeted, and how are the various beliefs held by people and cultures respected? These are the challenges—some would say the "land mines"—of bringing a moral dimension to the work done in schools.

A movement that was reintroduced to public schools in the 1980s, the character education movement, attempts to tread the choppy waters of blending knowledge with goodness. One of its strongest proponents, Amitai Etzioni, from George Washington University, advocates teaching character from a conceptual framework that includes two skills that are prerequisite to the development of character: *empathy* and *self-discipline.* Only when students can appreciate another's perspectives, prejudices, and feelings (empathy) and when they can choose a course of action that is consistent with their own establishing values (self-discipline) does character develop. To realize these goals, schools must provide opportunities for student discussion and decision making within a thoughtful "community" setting, in which each person's view is as valued as the rest. This democratic view of education will not be found in a school with rigid rule structures or guiding principles that rely more on coercion and punishment

The educational community frequently thinks about strategies for making the child adjust to our expectations rather than understanding, supporting and developing the child's enormously rich inner life. . . . Education tries to reach its goals by creating *strategies of approach* rather than by building *channels of relationship.* The inner agenda, the Soul or the Self, are intangibles which are not as amenable to research as they are to observation and empathy.
—*Roeper, 1996, p. 18*

than cooperation and logical consequences. In other words, these schools are more the exception than the rule.

In gifted child education, one of the strongest advocates for character education is Annemarie Roeper. Believing that gifted children are possessed of an enormous sense of justice, Roeper (1995) writes that "gifted children are questioners, keen observers, logical thinkers. They notice inequities, unfairness, and double standards and question them with passion" (p. 169). From this perspective, Roeper believes that character education is not a curriculum that can be taught between 10:30 and 11:15 a.m. every other Tuesday; rather, it is an attitude and set of actions that pervade a school's climate. The way that rules are established, the consequences for actions that could harm the community, the decision-making procedures regarding curriculum—all are necessary facets to a school that doesn't just educate children for the next grade level, but rather, educates them for life.

Another advocate of leadership opportunities that enhance gifted students' knowledge about and appreciation of their world is Frances Karnes. In her study of the personal and social correlates of leadership, she found that the factors of emotional maturity, conscientiousness, persistence, low levels of inhibition and anxiety, and the ability to control one's own behaviors (akin to Etzioni's "self-discipline") were among the traits and behaviors that helped students to become leaders in the minds of their peers. The use of her Leadership Skills Inventory (Karnes & Chauvin, 1985) helps others to pinpoint specific skills, attitudes, and values that are qualities in many young leaders.

Still, the development of leadership, as perceived by Karnes, and the development of character, as proposed by Roeper, appear more parallel than perpendicular. The former view implies that certain individuals have more of "something" that will eventually distinguish them as leaders, whereas the latter view is more inclusive, asserting that every person has a stake in the continuation of the planet and is, therefore, a part of the global equation. Schools have been much more comfortable in establishing leadership programs based on Karnes's view of leadership than they have in embracing the schoolwide commitment to character of which Roeper writes. For evidence of this, consider the popularity of student council and "Student of the Month" programs to see how easy it is to reward leadership, as it is typically perceived. Both views are good, but they approach the issues of leadership and character from vastly different perspectives.

Also, with leadership programs that are more discrete entities rather than pervasive attitudes, there is a danger that students who talk the talk may not choose to walk the walk. So, even if a student can extol the virtue's of Shakespeare's *King Lear,* discovering charity and compassion, he might still belittle a disabled student on the bus ride home. As stated by Knowles and Weber (1978),

All of us have known students who graduated from our schools with highly distinguished academic records but with minimal interest in other

> We seem to cut everything into smaller and smaller pieces. We never look at the whole, the soul, the mystery of the individual. We try to understand the child with the intellect, not with our empathy, our own emotion. We judge, we evaluate. Feeling has a low priority. We have lost the vision. I feel we must reinstate the psyche to its proper place.
> —*Roeper, 1997, p. 1*

> One of the reasons ethical education does not play a role in the daily programs of schools is because it does not play a significant role in the daily lives of the adults. We are so concerned with living that we often do not think about *how* to live.
> —*Roeper, 1995, p. 171*

> Character is not what you do, it's the way you do it. . . . For character we look as much to the soldier's letter on the eve of battle and the families at home away from the action as to the plans laid out in the general's tent.
> —*James Hillman, 1996, pp. 252, 254*

people, with imperceptible commitments to compassion or service. But most or all of us want to work in schools that try to nourish and that *tend* to nourish a less selfish orientation toward life; we want to create environments which encourage generosity of spirit and principled decision-making, not sophisticated selfishness, in our students and ourselves. (p. 15)

The word itself, *character,* comes from the Latin and originally meant a marking instrument that cut indelible lines, leaving observable traces. Certainly, this etymologic dissection of character is broad enough to incorporate the varied views of leadership development espoused by those who, after all, are seeking the same Nirvana: a world for our children that is better for *their* children, and even better still for the next generation.

INVITING SCHOOL SUCCESS

When was the last time you, as a teacher, unwittingly played a "dirty trick" on your students? You know, a "zinger" of a comment or practice that caught someone off guard and let him or her shine in the worst possible light?

Teacher Jim Nixon (1993) highlights 17 of these dirty tricks, including

- *The Silent Treatment:* not responding at all to students' work or returning it without any comments other than the grade
- *The Lockout:* offering no opportunity for students to correct their answers to earn a higher grade on an assignment
- *Try a Little Sarcasm:* writing on a student's paper: "A+ . . . excellent work! Too bad no name . . . F"
- *Catch 'Em with Their Pants Down:* displaying student papers for public view without first asking the students' permission to do so
- *True Confessions:* having students grade each other's assignment or test and then calling out the grades aloud as you record them into your gradebook

Each of these dirty tricks, in and of themselves, is little more than an educational misdemeanor, a small crime against kindness worthy of a small-scale punishment. But if you find yourself (or your school as a whole) guilty of most of these classroom infractions, you might be charged with Murder 1: the death of a student's self-concept at the hands of a disinviting teacher.

One of the most important features in the success of a classroom or school is the same feature that needs to be present in a successful family, house of worship, or personal relationship: a sense of community. Activities or practices such as Nixon's dirty tricks (Jim's, not Richard's) do much to erase any feeling of cooperation and group spirit, as the top-down style of management or discipline assumes that children do not deserve a basic commodity adults demand from their colleagues: respect.

Many authors have addressed the need to combine the heart and the head in the design of classrooms, but few have focused specifically on gifted students. The reason for this is obvious: Gifted or not, students realize which school personnel are there to earn a paycheck and which ones are there for something more. However, many authors in gifted child education *have* focused on gifted students' abilities to perceive deeper or earlier the intricacies of adult interactions with children (Hollingworth, 1942; Whitmore, 1980), making the classroom climate issue an important one for gifted child advocates to address.

James Comer, a professor of child psychiatry at Yale University and the director of the School Development Program, a consortium of more than 650 schools committed to developing a sense of community, addresses the need to reestablish trust and caring within test-driven, performance-oriented schools:

> In the past, we tended to overlook how important community is. It provided social and emotional support for children, but we didn't see how that related to academic learning. This is still not widely understood. Now we're experiencing a breakdown in our communities, and we still need to help students attain high levels of academic achievement. The solution is to restore a sense of community . . . within the school. (O'Neil, 1997, p. 10)

Comer and his associates suggest readily replicable ways to foster this sense of cohesiveness between home and school communities. For example, Back To School potluck suppers can be held to establish relationships among the adults and to show students that there are people available to them to provide both academic help and emotional support. Another example is the establishment of a school support team, which, among other tasks, can set up a welcome program for students who transferred into the school, instead of just depositing them in new classrooms with the hope that they will acclimate well to them. A third example is the implementation of a social skills curriculum, which is begun only after parents are consulted regarding the interpersonal skills that they believe their children need to succeed as adults.

Another person whose career has focused on the important links between academic achievement and classroom climate is William Purkey, whose idea of *Invitational Education* (Purkey & Novak, 1984) relies on four basic principles:

1. People are able, valuable, and responsible and should be treated accordingly.

> My younger son, who attends preschool, recently asked me, "Why is it when kids do things that aren't really good (like drawing a picture that's messy), parents and teachers tell them it's good, when it really isn't?" He isn't fooled—nor are most other youngsters when their evaluations are sugarcoated. Making shortcomings sound good is a disservice. . . . When we give our children a false sense of success, we ultimately deny them genuine self-esteem. As hard as we may try, self-esteem can't be given—it must be *achieved*. When children don't overcome the "valleys" of experience, they cannot truly understand or appreciate the thrill of reaching the "mountaintops."
>
> —*Friede, 1997, p. 41*

The term "invitational education" was chosen because the two words have special meaning. The English word *invite* is probably a derivative of the Latin word *invitare,* which means "to offer something beneficial for consideration." Translated literally, *invitare* means "to summon cordially, not to shun." The word *education* comes from the Latin word *educare,* which means "to call forth something potential or latent." Literally, invitational education is the process by which people realize their relatively boundless potential in all areas of worthwhile human endeavor.

—*Purkey & Stanley, 1994, p. xiv*

2. Teaching should be a cooperative venture.
3. People possess untapped potential.
4. This potential can become realized in an environment that respects individual differences and preferences.

Given these guidelines, Purkey and Novak place their collective trust in educators, assuming that most do not generally wake up each morning and utter: "I wonder whose life I can ruin today." However, being the realists that they are, Purkey and Novak also understand that some educators *unintentionally* set up students for failure or embarrassment. They categorize teachers (and others, by implication) into one of four groupings:

1. **Intentional Inviters:** These are the teachers who are remembered for all the right reasons. They know theory and content, and they apply the spirit of community to their classrooms. They focus on the positive and on alternative behaviors that are acceptable rather than wrong. The intentionally inviting teacher's classroom rules might look like those in Figure 6.1.

2. **Intentional Disinviters:** These individuals make observers wonder why they ever chose a human service profession as person-centered as teaching for their careers. They seem to enjoy digging out the worst in children and never letting them forget when they have found it. These teachers mean it when they say the best three things about teaching are June, July, and August, and their inflexible teaching motto reads, "It's my way or the highway." For their own and their students' good, these individuals should never again work with anything organic.

3. **Unintentional Inviters:** These teachers do not give themselves enough credit for the good that they do. They spend hours writing comments on student essays; they keep an extra few dollars in their desks in case hungry but forgetful students leave their lunch money at home; they allow students to select from an array of assignment options rather than just giving everyone the same task. When reminded of the benefit, emotionally and otherwise, such behaviors have on students, their usual comment is "It's no big deal." But to the students positively affected by them, indeed it is!

4. **Unintentional Disinviters:** Thinking that it is a good idea to pass back student tests in descending order of grade, they do so, believing that it will reward high achievers and encourage low achievers to do better next time. Of the opinion that tedium teaches lessons, these teachers punish students by having them write 100 times, "I will respect other people's

FIGURE 6.1

Classroom Rules

1. Walking in the halls prevents accidents.
2. Be mature and serious during fire drills.
3. Enjoy chewing your gum at home.
4. When in groups, talk in 6-inch voices.
5. Ask before you use.
6. People can be hurt by words and actions, so use both carefully.

Please remember: kindness is contagious!

—Delisle & Delisle, 1996

property," not realizing the stifling effect it can have on a student's desire to write anything else. Thinking it appropriate to do so, these teachers routinely have students write their names on the board when they misbehave—open for all to see how bad they are, including strangers. Honestly believing in the truth of their own convictions, unintentional disinviters would be appalled that someone saw them as anything but a student ally. Their actions may be unintentional, but they still cause students to say "ouch."

In their book, Purkey and Novak provide hundreds of ways to reach the educational higher ground of intentional invitations. Through humor and examples that make most educators see themselves in less-than-perfect conditions, they do, nonetheless, provide both hope and suggestions for developing a sense of community within a school setting.

A SUMMARY OF STRATEGIES

The issues and ideas presented in this chapter fall under the collective umbrella of educational interventions that can benefit gifted students' intellectual learning or emotional growth. Whether it be setting up a classroom climate that invites learning and comfort, designing independent learning opportunities with the end goal of personal growth, or designing curriculum units that stretch students' minds through the use of higher level thinking, each intervention has a similar foundation: a belief that children are capable of much more than adults sometimes think they are.

But it would be wrong to understate the advantages of these options for *every* student. When *every* teacher is of the belief that "I can" is more important than "IQ" and when *every* parent buys into the idea that it is more important to ask their children "what did you *learn?*" rather than "What did you *earn?*" only then will the ripest seeds in our students' minds bear fruit. And as Purkey and

In my early years as a mathematics teacher, I often said to my students, "Now watch, it's easy!" Purkey and Novak are surely correct when they warn us that such a remark—intended as friendly and reassuring—is in fact disinviting. Students who find a procedure hard, when the teacher has proclaimed it is easy, feel like idiots. I learned to say, "This is hard, but you can do it. It takes practice, but don't worry—I'm here and I'll help." "This is hard" turns out to be far more inviting than "this is easy." It invites students to try something worthy of their efforts, and it cushions them against the hard blows of occasional failure.

—Purkey & Novak, 1996, p. xii

Novak state, it is sometimes the smallest courtesies that indicate the deepest beliefs in the possibilities of childhood. An example, perhaps, can help illustrate the pervasiveness of a kind gesture and a bit of trust on a student's willingness to learn:

> It was the first day of school. . . . A boy came up to me and said, "I'm John. I can't read. I'm special ed." I extended my hand and said, "Glad to meet you, John. I'm Mrs. Foley and I can't fly. I'm a mammal. You are luckier than I am. No matter how hard I try, I will never be able to fly. All *you* have to do is just keep practicing and eventually you will be a good reader. If you had a weak arm, you wouldn't put it in a sling, it would just continue to get weaker. Instead, you would exercise that arm, and eventually it would be as strong as the other arm."
>
> When I distributed report cards nine weeks later, John proudly displayed his A. I overheard one student say to John, "She just gave you an A because she felt sorry for you. You're special ed." John looked at me with a flicker of doubt in his eyes, and I winked. A big smile crossed his face as he flexed his right arm and pointed to his muscle.
>
> —*Fahey, 1996, p. 4*

How high students fly is up to them and their own ambitions. How willing they are to attempt to soar at all is the job of each individual who calls him- or herself an educator. It takes more than strength to stretch one's wings; it also takes an emotional updraft given by someone—a mammal such as Mrs. Fahey—who believes in the power of dreams.

SO . . . HOW'RE WE DOIN'? EVALUATING GIFTED PROGRAMS AND THE STUDENTS IN THEM

The race is about to begin. The runners are in their starting positions awaiting the crack of the starting pistol. As soon as it sounds, they're off, and true to form, the race leader strides around the oval like a leopard. He arrives in less than 4 minutes, to the cheers of an appreciative crowd.

"How'd I do, coach?" asks the anxious sprinter.

"Same as usual—3:58::47. Within half a second of your best time ever."

"Damn! Why can't I break that 3:58 mark?" asks the disappointed victor.

Meanwhile, a teammate reaches the finish line in 4:10::31. He jumps up and down, accepting hugs and congratulations from everyone he sees. It was his best time yet!

There it is, in a nutshell: the problem of evaluating gifted programs and the students whom they serve. For when students are already performing at the top of their academic game, how do they show that they have improved or learned anything? Similarly, how do gifted program evaluators show others that the gifted program services make a difference in the lives of the children involved in them, and how do they counter critics who contend that "these smart kids would've done fine even *without* that g/t program"? How does anyone get any better, as an individual, when they are already the best? How can growth be shown, in a program, when the students involved in them are also involved in so many other activities that could have affected their positive performance?

These are just some of the difficulties that keep gifted program coordinators awake at night, causing many to forgo the evaluation process altogether. For unlike other educational interventions (e.g., remedial reading programs) where growth can be measured because the children being taught there have so much room to grow, evaluating gifted students and specialized programs runs into a problem that other fields of study might envy: There is very little room to grow, at least numerically, which is how virtually all other educational interventions are evaluated. In the section that follows, issues and problems related to evaluating gifted programs are reviewed, in the hope of clarifying this always murky aspect of gifted child education.

ANSWERING UNFAIR ACCUSATIONS

Choose one of the following to discuss in a small group:

A. Evaluation is the weakest area of most educational programs. . . . It is sometimes hastily planned at the end of the program, and is seen by the program staff as a necessary evil. (Eby & Smutny, 1990, p. 188)
B. We currently do not have many good ideas about how to evaluate programs for the gifted and . . . those who operate too many programs do not even bother to try. (Borland, 1989, p. 196)
C. Suppose you teach children Sanskrit in your program for the talented. No one else in the district is learning Sanskrit. After you teach them Sanskrit, you check to see whether they've learned any Sanskrit. They have. You call the program successful, even though no one else has had a chance to study Sanskrit. (Piirto, 1994, p. 80)

No matter which one of these statements you chose, you probably came to a similar conclusion: Evaluation is as welcomed by gifted child educators as is a rainy wedding day to a bride and groom. But why should gifted child educators, who are seldom an obstinate lot and frequently deal with issues that are "messy" or volatile, shy away from proving the worth of what they do? Because . . . they are asked to do the impossible or the unimportant: to provide numerical proof of their worth. This does not work for a variety of number-based reasons, the most important of which is a statistical artifact called *regression to the mean*.

The regression problem is defined, loosely, as the tendency for a group of persons who do extremely well on a pretest to move more toward (regress) the average (mean) during a follow-up testing session. This regression tends to occur even if there were actual changes in students' behavior or knowledge base; it just would not be picked up by this follow-up testing. Regression, then, brings on depression for the gifted program coordinators who have to try to answer someone who asks, "You mean we spent all this time and money on these smart kids and they actually are *worse off* than before?"

There are other numerical problems with this type of program evaluation, including "ceiling effect," which implies that the initial test was oh-so easy for the children and, subsequently, they all scored at its highest levels, making it impossible for them to show any growth—when you're already at the 99th percentile, the best you can do is the same, which, of course, you won't because of regression to the mean. This circular logic continues when one considers that most tests, when they were developed, did not contain a lot of high-achieving students in their samples, so very few of the subjects who took the test initially scored at its highest levels. This means that when high-achieving students *are* tested, anyone considerably above average may appear to be extremely smart, whether they missed 1 test item or 12 test items. This makes these norms *unreliable* for use with gifted students because, in a sense, the ceiling effect once again came into play.

There are other numerical minefields that a gifted child educator would want to avoid, and they are described in ascerbically humorous detail by Borland (1989). But rather than spend any more time focusing on the problems, here are some solutions.

FORMATIVE VERSUS SUMMATIVE EVALUATION AND THE UNDERLYING ZEITGEIST

Assume that you have been on a diet for 2 weeks. After the initial ecstasy of losing 5 pounds, you hit that inevitable plateau where nothing drops off except your confidence. After one-too-many friends has asked you, "So . . . how's the diet going?" you decide to evaluate your progress to date. You can do this through either formative or summative evaluation. For example, a summative evaluation would allow you to tell your friend, "So far, I've lost 5 pounds." Clean, simple, and to the point, you've been specific, basing your conclusion on actual data provided by your bathroom scale. Or using a formative evaluation, you could say, "The data show that I have lost 5 pounds; however, I have reconsidered my approach to dieting and I've decided to add an exercise regimen and lower my caloric intake by 30% more." Here, you are using the data collected— a 5-pound weight loss—and using it as diagnostic evidence that, perhaps, something else needs to occur if you are to reach your goal.

Evaluating gifted child education services is something like dieting: If you're not careful, all the good you did for yourself will leave you back where you started, or worse. Thus, before beginning any type of evaluation, the following two questions should be asked:

1. *What are the up-front purposes for conducting this evaluation?* Is this evaluation being conducted because of the need to find out others' perceptions of the strengths and weaknesses of the gifted child education program, with the ultimate goal of improving services to gifted students? If so, this is formative evaluation: a diagnostic analysis designed to give direction for future improvements. Conversely, data might be gathered so that the information can be summarized for a school board presentation—for example, how many students are involved in the gifted program, or what do teachers and parents say are its greatest strengths and weaknesses? This is summative evaluation, which, oftentimes, is a preliminary step to a more comprehensive formative evaluation.

2. *What "hidden agendas" are causing this evaluation to be done now?* This is the part in which the "Underlying Zeitgeist" comes into play. Perhaps a school board member is a particular fan (or foe) of the gifted child education program and wants to expand (or disband) the services offered. Or perhaps the superintendent is being pressured to prove that the school district is better than the test-score averages published in the local newspaper indicate. Or maybe a vocal group of parents is complaining that "nothing is being done for the gifted students in our schools." All these reasons and innumerable other political agendas could prime the initial push toward conducting a gifted child education program evaluation. It is a wise gifted teacher or coordinator who realizes the underlying Zeitgeist that is prompting calls for a program's status.

Once these questions are answered, the next step is relatively easy: You must conduct the evaluation. Indeed, compared with the political maneuverings that precipitated it, the evaluation itself *may* seem less arduous.

EVALUATION METHODS AND PROCEDURES

In the previous section, mention was made that standard evaluation methods like test-score gains are inappropriate for evaluating children's progress in gifted programs. That being the case, most evaluators will implement "soft-data evaluations," including questionnaires that are completed by anyone involved in the gifted child education program. This could include the parents of the enrolled students, the teachers who work with the students, the students themselves, and any mentors who may have been involved with students. Some of these people—even some teachers—will claim little knowledge of or interest in the gifted child education program, which, of course, is an interesting finding in itself. Others will ramble on about a specific aspect that they either loathe or love, letting this grandstand be their podium for pounding or praising the program.

Some individuals in gifted child education scoff at the use of questionnaire data as being too unscientific a base from which to make decisions. But if the

I was labeled the hope of the future; included among the famous people honoring me at that Presidential Scholar ritual were the first man to fly in space and the man who invented a polio vaccine. I felt whatever I did with my life should be as BIG, as socially visible, as John Glenn or Dr. Salk. That's a burden bigger than I want to carry now.
—*A Presidential Scholar writing to Felice Kaufmann, 1979*

goal of an evaluation is to improve program services to gifted children, then the best way to learn how to do that is pretty straightforward and simple: Ask what is good and bad about the program, and request specific suggestions for improvements. The data may not be as scientifically precise as a statistically significant increase in gain scores or a test of divergent thinking, but which better serves the purposes of teachers, parents, or administrators?

This final issue is, perhaps, the most important one of all, for if the evaluator does not know how to take the accumulated data and do something with them to alter, expand, or limit the program offerings, then evaluation becomes little more than an exercise. To be sure, there will be critics who poo-poo the data collection efforts and wish to read more general information about the benefits and drawbacks of gifted child education programs. Satisfy these individuals by steering them toward the work of Kulik and Kulik (1982, 1991), who discovered that there are no adverse effects—academic or social—when gifted students are grouped together for instruction and, indeed, that other groups of less academically oriented students find no ill effects to their own educations when the highest ability students are removed from their classes. These findings, based on an analysis of more than 50 statistical studies of ability grouping conducted over several decades, should do much to dispel some fears and tirades from individuals who believe that "separating the chaff from the wheat" gives everyone a blight.

A FEW WORDS ABOUT EVALUATING INDIVIDUAL GIFTED CHILDREN'S PROGRESS

A colleague of mine related the story of his teenage daughter, an intellectually gifted girl who excelled academically. While attending a summer program in mathematics, this girl received a B+ for her final grade for a course in calculus—the first grade below an A that she had received in memory.

On the long car ride home at the course's conclusion, the girl's father tried to console his daughter, whose tears expressed her personal dissatisfaction with her class performance. Dad tried to remind his daughter that the knowledge gained was more important than the grade itself and that the content was harder than she'd ever dealt with before. It didn't work; the tears still flowed.

Finally, Dad reminded her that when she received straight-As the previous school year, she didn't seem overly pleased with herself. "So," he reasoned, "if As don't make you happy, yet a B+ makes you miserable, don't you think that is odd, since the grades are so close?"

"You don't understand!" daughter reacted, "this time the grade *mattered,* because I was actually learning something!"

The conclusion that can be drawn from this is that if students are not invested in the work they are performing, then the grades that they receive are meaningless. People esteem what is of value to them, and if an "Easy A" was attained when not even cracking open a book, it can be as meaning*less* as a grade of B+ or C- is meaning*ful* if the content required a student to stretch his or her mind.

Evaluating gifted students' progress can be a difficult process, when the benchmarks of typical academic success—high grades—don't always apply or matter. Instead, researchers and practitioners have tried to locate other methods of student evaluation that are more legitimate barometers for measuring success in students who are already successful by expected standards.

Many of these ideas can be grouped under two related terms that have become *de rigueur* in today's educational communities: *alternative assessment* and *holistic evaluation*. Alternative assessment, the broader of these two ideas, refers to methods of student evaluation that are both more comprehensive and more informative than any letter or numerical grade or ranking could ever be. For example, students might design a learning contract that pinpoints specific content or strategies with which they want to become more familiar. If they succeed by some predetermined standards, *that* is the truest measure of their learning, and should a grade need to be assigned for administrative reasons, the student and teacher can decide together what that grade will be. Another example of alternative assessment might involve a student's completion of a community service project, where letters from people or agencies involved in the project attest to its merits. Still another form of alternative assessment could be a student teaching what she has learned about dinosaurs to a class of younger children, with the videotaped lesson counting as a logical and visible form of assessing both one's knowledge and the ability to transmit it to others.

Many states and locales have embraced this form of student measurement, especially in the lower grades. Vermont, one of our smallest and most homogeneous states, has adopted such measures in a big way, with mixed reviews of its success. But as Piirto (1994) reminds us, "Enthusiasm for the new means of assessment has outpaced research on their effectiveness. It seems that the political agendas of school reformers have harnessed their hopes to alternative assessment and the research is burdened to catch up" (p. 383).

Holistic evaluation asks teachers (and others) to see all student work as tentative, in terms of completion. Delisle and Delisle (1996) state what holistic evaluation is and is not according to these specifics:

What It Is	What It Isn't
Comments that:	Letter/number grades that:
• give second chances to improve	• say "one strike, you're out!"
• consider the paper or product as a whole	• dissect individual segments
• offer constructive ideas for growth and improvement	• provide little, if any, constructive feedback
• ask the student, "What did you learn?"	• ask the student, "What did you earn?"

Distinctions between perfection and excellence are so important in order for kids to feel good about their accomplishments. Otherwise they get burned out . . . even just having permission to try new things without having to worry about "success" or "failure" and external pressure to perform. I also think it's important to develop other interests and enjoyable activities as a part of discovering who you are. So often, gifted kids are defined by their smartness, which is not the only aspect of your personality.

Paulita, 18 years old —Excerpted from The Gifted Kids Survival Guide: A Teen Handbook *by Judy Galbraith, MA, & Jim Delisle, PhD, Copyright © 1996. Used with permission of Free Spirit Publishing, Minneapolis, MN.*

Of course, both alternative assessment and holistic evaluation run counter to the now-popular movement of using competency tests *en masse* to tell us how schools, school districts, and individual children are faring, *in comparison with others*. Such a wholesale shift away from individual attainment of educational objectives that are meaningful to the child and toward a group ethos that is based on numbers and statistics is a dangerous precedent based much more on political maneuverings than educational realities of the nation's schools.

In trying to marry the good ideas of alternative assessment with the practical realities of report card grades, Winebrenner and Berger (1993) offer several suggestions, some of which are

1. If the work to be done by a student is an extension of the regular curriculum, projects done with this content should earn at least a grade of B, because the students are going beyond what is required.
2. All criteria for evaluation should be presented and understood before students begin an extension assignment.
3. Students earn a grade of B if the completed work represents typical research that merely reports secondary sources and if the presentation is properly made to appropriate audiences.
4. Student earn a grade of A if the completed work represents unique or creative research, provides evidence of primary sources, and provides a synthesis of available data. (p. 2)

However individual gifted students' work is evaluated, it is important to remember (and to tell students) that the truest standard of success is their own level of fulfillment that they have, indeed, learned something. The grade and comments they receive will pale in comparison to the inner satisfaction of having been someplace exciting and new: inside the world of knowledge.

THAT'S ALL, FOLKS!

One thing about curriculum: There will always be more of it than there is time to teach it to students. New fads and ideas—some good, some not—enter our schools and our psyches on a regular basis, causing educators to wonder if this elusive panacea that educational reformers always seem to seek does, indeed, exist.

The schools of the new millennium will require students to be technologically proficient. They will require that students learn all sorts of scary medical acronyms—STDs, HIV, PCP, LSD—to protect their bodies and minds from infection. They will require the skills of problem *finding* as well as problem *solving*. They will require that education be considered a year-round enterprise, with some of our best classrooms and teachers being far removed from any school building. In other words, education will continue to be what it has always been:

a hodgepodge of conflicting theories, goals, and activities whose ultimate *raison d'être* is the continuation and improvement of the prevailing culture.

To be sure, gifted students have a major role to play in this enterprise. So does every other student, for in a diverse society, the suggestion of dismissing even one member as unimportant cannot be granted. Each individual exists in a space and time in which humanity supersedes one's talents and gifts, however extensive or limited these may be; and differences aside, the common denominators that unite all people are both more present and more powerful than any division imposed by intellect, income, or geography. If the collective energy of our inherent possibilities could ever be harnessed, we would create a force stronger than any army and kinder than any saint.

So, in conclusion, as the very big questions of "What curriculum matters most?" and "What instructional strategies and styles are best for my students?" are considered, it is important never to lose sight of the biggest reality of all: that unless all students believe in the possibilities within their own potentials, education will be merely a 12-year course to be run, rather than a lifelong adventure in learning and self-understanding.

GUIDING QUESTIONS FOR CHAPTER 6

1. What is "differentiated curriculum," and how does it apply to gifted learners?

2. In what ways can "Invitational Education" enhance a school's academic climate and curriculum?

3. What program models do gifted child educators use to organize learning experiences for gifted students?

CHAPTER 6 RESOURCES TO REMEMBER

Smutny, J. F., Walker, S. Y, and Meckstroth, E. A. (1997). *Teaching young gifted children in the regular classroom: Identifying, nurturing and challenging ages 4–9.* Minneapolis, MN: Free Spirit.

As commonly practiced, gifted child education programs seem to begin at the third or fourth grade level. However, there is no denying that many gifted children are identified at much younger ages. What are parents and teachers supposed to do until the schools catch up and provide programs for young gifted children? A good suggestion would be to pick up this supremely practical book, which is filled with charts, forms, and teaching resources that will benefit gifted young children. This book will fly off your office shelf by eager teachers as soon as they see it.

Stone, E. (1992). *The Hunter College campus schools for the gifted.* New York: Teachers College Press.

What happens when you interview more than 200 past and present teachers, administrators, students, and parents about their experiences with one of the nation's best known schools for gifted children? What you get is a broad spectrum of possibilities to help educators achieve that elusive middle ground between the pursuit of excellence and the practice of equity. Part history and part research, this book offers perspectives that provide insights and suggestions that reach far beyond the Hunter Schools' campuses.

Ward, V. S. (1961). *Educating the gifted: An axiomatic approach.* Columbus, OH: Merrill.

The book title alone tells you that you are in for quite a heady read! Virgil Ward is our field's most philosophically based scholar, and his goals for what is possible in educating gifted children have yet to be achieved. Later reissued under a slightly more subtle title (*Differential education for the gifted*), this book remains as the paragon of possibilities for those interested in and intrigued by designing curriculum and instruction that are advanced in content and intense in presentation.

CHAPTER
7

THE SOCIAL AND EMOTIONAL
NEEDS OF GIFTED INDIVIDUALS

Giftedness is not something you do. Giftedness is something you are.

If I had wanted to write the world's shortest book chapter on the social and emotional needs of gifted persons, the above line would have sufficed. It would get across the point that the essence of giftedness lies in the emotional equipment and supersensitivity that are inherent in every gifted individual. Indeed, this emotional component overrides the intellectual aspects that first come to mind when one hears the word *gifted,* superseding even the most precise definition that has anything to do with academic prowess or intellectual agility.

More than being a way of thinking, giftedness is a way of living. It is seen in the 10-year-old who cries when he hears of a battle being waged in a far off land. It is heard in the plaintive desire of a 7-year-old who wants more than anything else to find a friend who understands her vocabulary. It is noted in the gifted adolescent who refuses to participate in any activity that does not guarantee perfection as the end result. It is present in the gifted adult seeking a soulmate and a relationship based on more than the physical trappings of love. It is observable in the 4-year-old who asks about death's permanency and life's purpose.

If this view of the inner world of the gifted individual seems extreme, you are asked to speak with several parents and educators of gifted children, asking them to describe the gifted person whom they know best. Your informal poll's results will certainly be instructive. Most likely, people will mention personality factors more often than they do academic ones. Too, the one descriptor that will probably be mentioned more than any other will be one overarching noun: *intensity.*

- *Intensity of thought:* "Her mind is always whirring."
- *Intensity of purpose:* "Once he makes up his mind to do something, he's not satisfied until it's accomplished."
- *Intensity of emotion:* "She internalizes everything anyone says about her."
- *Intensity of spirit:* "He's always looking out for someone less fortunate than he who needs help."
- *Intensity of soul:* "She asks questions that philosophers have asked for centuries and gets upset when I can't give her a definitive answer."

A GIFTED TEENAGER SPEAKS OUT

"Gifted and talented" is not something you can take up lightly on free weekends. It's something that's going to affect everything about your life, twenty-four hours a day, 365 days a year. It's something that can force you into being more mature before you might be ready; it's something that can go all wrong on you and leave you torn apart.

But there are peaceful uses for atomic energy. There are good deeds to be done. There *are* opportunities waiting for you. "Gifted and talented" can be, basically, what you make it. But you can't just *sit* there. If you're willing to accept the responsibility, which is the prerequisite course around here, you can take off from there and really have a good time. Why not now?

—*American Association for Gifted Children, 1978, p. 141*

THE HERMIT

> *I am a hermit. Let the sad world*
> *roll*
> *On with its burdens and its pain and strife.*
> *I look to a better and higher life,*
> *For I shall chasten and preserve my*
> *soul.*
> *From all the world's wild cares I*
> *make me free,*
> *And naught have I to do with human pain,*
> *Nor have I fear of loss nor greed of*
> *gain,—*
> *And yet I heard them say they*
> *pitied me.*

—*Reprinted with permission,* Roeper Review,
P.O. Box 329, Bloomfield Hills, MI 48303

Although the field of gifted child education was founded by people who were interested in the intellectual aspects of brilliance, even they succumbed to the allure of the obvious, that a capable mind is but one facet of a gifted person's existence. In this chapter, you meet leaders in the field of social and emotional aspects of giftedness. Some you have read about in previous chapters, such as Annemarie and George Roeper and Joanne Whitmore. But new names will also emerge: George Betts, Michael Piechowski, and Linda Silverman, among others. Contemporary thinkers all, they present an emerging vision of what growing up gifted truly means to the children and adults who wear that label.

Having said this, please indulge me and do me a favor: Find a comfortable chair, grab a favorite beverage, and settle in for a love story between two people who never met. It may not qualify as a blockbuster movie, but the plot is just as rich. The title of this poignant script: *Leta and Me.*

A RETURN TO OUR ROOTS

Although she and her work were highlighted in an earlier chapter, Leta Hollingworth deserves extended mention here, for it is her monumental work, neglected for far too long, that serves as the bedrock of gifted child education's emphasis on the social and emotional needs of gifted children.

It is hard to describe fully the scope of Leta Hollingworth's work. First and foremost, she was a teacher of children, her work in the classroom serving as the dais from which she lectured about the neglected inner needs of highly able children. Also, she was a professor, one of the few females of her time who held her own with her male counterparts at Teachers College, Columbia University. Without grant money to underwrite her research efforts or secretarial staff to assist her, Hollingworth managed, nonetheless, to write two landmark books, *Gifted Children: Their Nature and Nurture* (1926) and *Children Above 180 IQ Stanford Binet* (completed posthumously by her husband, Harry, in 1942), and dozens of articles and book chapters.

But Leta Hollingworth's legacy—and, indeed, that is what it is—was one born in crisis and discomfort, forcing her to transcend both her environment and a culture far more sexist than today's to achieve recognition for her brilliance.

LITTLE DUGOUT ON THE PRAIRIE

Even today, the northwestern plains of Nebraska are isolated from the mainstream of American culture. The largest town, Chadron, is smaller than a midsize college, surrounded by the Oglala National Grasslands and the Nebraska National Forest; and the local landmark, the Museum of the Fur Trade, reminds visitors of the heritage days when the Oregon Trail was a lifeline between East and West.

It was here that Leta Stetter began her life in 1886. Born in her grandparents' earthen dugout home, Leta spent her earliest days amidst poverty and domestic turmoil. The oldest of three sisters, Leta and her siblings were sent to live with her maternal grandparents when Leta's mother, Margaret, died in childbirth. These people, the Danleys, cared for the Stetter girls as best they could, giving them a much-needed segment of stability in their lives, as evidenced by Leta's dedication of her first book to them.

But once Leta's father, Johnny, remarried, the children were brought back to live in Valentine, Nebraska, site of the Palace Saloon and Pool Hall, co-owned by her father and her Uncle Henry. The presence of the children seemed an unwelcome one to her new stepmother, Fanny, who "was demanding and would yell violently at the Stetter girls for even minor misbehavior. Life with Fanny was cruel" (Roweton, 1990, p. 140).

For 3 years, Leta existed in this home, her single bright spot in Valentine being the high school she attended and the attention she received from her first mentor, Professor Watson, who served as school superintendent and one of Leta's teachers. "That good, good man," Leta wrote many years later, "who by the spirit in his face kept alive for me faith in high things." (Hollingworth, 1943, p. 51). Graduating with six girls and one boy from Valentine High School in 1902, at the age of 15, Leta was even then showing the spunk riven through her later writings. Specifically, in her response to an ancient quote with which she disagreed, Hollingworth wrote about both a fellow student's and society's bias against women: "Mr. Growden contends that there is a certain statement in Caesar which includes the expression 'Women, children and other household utensils'. If such is the case Caesar has lowered himself in the H.S. girls' estimation" (Roweton, 1990, p. 140).

Years before the Suffragettes call was heeded, 14-year-old Leta Stetter was raising a feminist voice of her own.

Leaving Valentine to attend the University of Nebraska in Lincoln, Leta seemed to know even then that the train out of Valentine, in a very large way, was a one-way ride toward greatness and personal fulfillment:

> I shall never forget a certain "immediate" moment which touched the consciousness as the train took me to Lincoln for the first time. The journey had made me dead tired, and I laid my head down on the window-sill and felt the grind and the movement of the whole thundering train. An "emotion" of the irresistible swept over me, an "impression" of inevitable moment and destination. . . . And the thought flashed through my mind that my life must always be like that, and the thought bound itself with the visual memory of a red sun setting across farms." (Hollingworth, 1943, p. 60)

Still, on graduation, Leta returned to her roots, entering the teaching profession in Nebraska so that she could support her two younger sisters. As principal of School District Number 6 in Saline, Nebraska, Leta also taught seven different subjects and served as the school's janitor. For obvious reasons, Leta left that job the next year, moving to McCook High School, where she taught English and German.

But she did not stay long, for her fiance, Harry, whom she had met in a psychology class at the University of Nebraska, was moving to New York to enroll as a graduate student at Columbia University. With great reluctance, she gave up a life that she knew well to one that was a mystery.

OF COCA-COLA AND CHILD E

One can only imagine Leta's first thoughts as this girl from the rural Midwest first saw the New York skyline! Reality hit twice, and soon: First, the wide expanse of the Plains was given up for a small, one-room apartment, and second, Leta's goal of continuing to teach was thwarted by New York's rule against married women being allowed to do so. She settled in to a life of housework and dressmaking, trying all the while to enter the same university where her husband was now a student. Again, though, she hit a dead end: Women were not eligible for the financial aid that her husband was receiving.

But then, thanks to Coca-Cola, her life began to change. Her husband, Harry, had received a grant from the soft drink giant to study the effects of one of its ingredients—caffeine—on people's behavior. The federal government had charged that this ingredient was harmful, and Coca-Cola was anxious to prove the safety of its increasingly popular product. Harry hired Leta to be his research assistant, enabling her to pay her tuition at Columbia. Also, this first glimpse at the wheels of research methodology gave Leta some skills that were helpful in completing her own dissertation. Leta completed both her Master's degree and, at age 30, her PhD at Columbia University. The topic of her dissertation? To investigate (and, she hoped, disprove) the then-popular dogma that

"Staying at home eating a lone pork chop" was the way (Leta) sometimes facetiously described her experience in those days. There were occasional periods of discouragement. . . . These slips from her customary determined and courageous procedure—she could hardly explain them, even to herself. Later she was able to make it clear that it was because she could hardly bear, with her own good mind and professional training and experience, not to be able to contribute to the joint welfare more than the simple manual activities that occupied her.
—*Hollingworth, 1943, p. 99*

women are "incapacitated" each month due to their menstrual cycles, making them inferior to men in their physical makeup. Indeed, she found no correlation between motor control and "functional periodicity," causing her to pen this thought:

> Thus, in time, may be written a psychology of women based on truth, not on opinion; on precise, not on anecdotal evidence; on accurate data rather than on remnants of magic. (Hollingworth, 1914, p. 115)

The little girl from the earthen dugout had, indeed, arrived. And, thanks to her energy, so had the field of female psychology.

Immediately on receipt of her doctorate, Leta was named as an instructor of educational psychology at Columbia. Still, she wanted to maintain the other jobs that she held at the time: a clinical psychologist at the city-owned Bellevue Hospital, and a consulting psychologist to the New York City Police Department. In typical Leta fashion, she did them all. As Leta wrote about her own styles of learning and daily living:

> I was intellectually curious, I worked hard, was honest except for those minor benign chicaneries which are occasionally necessary when authority is stupid, disliked waste, and was never afraid to undertake an experiment or to change my mind. (Hollingworth, 1943, p. 107)

It was during these formative years that Leta Hollingworth first came into contact with the subject that would, eventually, be the focus of her life: gifted children. As a psychologist for the city of New York, Leta had the opportunity to test many people with the recently designed mental tests developed by Binet and Goddard, two prominent psychologists, as well as the Stanford Binet, which debuted the same year that Leta was appointed to her position at Columbia, 1916. Generally, the tests she administered were given to children who, at the time, were labeled "mentally defective." Indeed, she often gave these tests in the presence of her own Columbia students, so they could see firsthand how such tests were administered correctly.

Then, in her attempt to show her students the variability in human abilities, she tested a very able young boy—"Child E"—from the nearby Horace Mann School. His score of 187 IQ, at the age of 8, was among the highest ever recorded on these newly available tests. This one demonstration changed Hollingworth's life forever:

> I did not at that time have any expert knowledge of highly intelligent children. I had been working for some years in the hospitals of New York City with persons presented for commitment to reformatories, prisons, and institutions for mental defectives. I had tested thousands of incompetent persons, with Goddard's Revision of the Binet-Simon Scale, scarcely ever finding anyone with an IQ rating as high as 100. This throughgoing experience of the negative aspects of intelligence rendered the performance

of E even more impressive to me than it would otherwise have been. I perceived the clear and flawless working of his mind against a contrasting background of thousands of dull and foolish minds. It was an unforgettable experience. (Hollingworth, 1942, p. x)

Shortly thereafter, Hollingworth began her search for other children of exceptionally high abilities, locating about 1 per year for the next 5 years, eventually finding 12 and highlighting their lives in her book *Children Above 180 I.Q. Stanford Binet* (1942). Like a doting grandmother, Hollingworth followed the lives of these 12 children until their own deaths (two died during Leta's lifetime) or her own, taking a personal interest in them, advising them in matters educational and personal, and testing them frequently. A generation later, in two follow-up studies of Hollingworth's students (Harris, 1990; White, 1990), these "children" still remembered her fondly. Child J, with an IQ of 197 at the age of 7, remembered her experiences with Leta Hollingworth. In speaking to an interviewer, Child J, now divorced and the mother of three adult children, said:

When you showed me her picture today, I just felt warm. I recall two or three meetings with Dr. Hollingworth, but I don't recall what they were about. I do remember that she never talked down to us. She seemed wise and comforting—always a nice person. (White, 1990, p. 224)

These children, Hollingworth's lifelong subjects, were lucky enough to be a part of a great experiment in education that took place beginning in 1922 in two New York City public schools. It was in these two environments that Hollingworth's focus on gifted children's social and emotional development blossomed into beauty.

HOLLINGWORTH'S THOUGHTS ON THE SPECIFIC NEEDS OF GIFTED CHILDREN AND THE IMPORTANCE OF EDUCATING THEM

On Identifying Gifted Children

When we hear repeatedly, from various people, that a given child is "old for his age," "so reliable," "very old-fashioned," "quick to see a joke," "youngest in his class," or that he has "an old head on young shoulders" or "such a long memory," we usually find him to be highly intelligent, by test. (p. 281)

Teachers may judge as "most intelligent" very dull, over-age children, doing good work in lower grades. Thus, for instance, they may not realize that being "youngest in the class" is an important symptom of superior ability. (p. 282)

Teachers rate bright children higher in all respects so far reported than their parents do. This is because teachers know a great variety of children, including the incompetent; whereas parents know well only their own children and those of their own friends, constituting usually a very restricted range of competency. (p. 284)

On "The Illusion of Decreasing Brightness"
In the primary grades the whole range of school children of an age is present, and the bright seem very bright in contrast. As children go on up through the grades, however, the dullest are constantly "left back"; so that by the time high school is reached all of the extremely dull children have been eliminated from the comparison. A child of 130 IQ is a very bright member of his group in kindergarten; a rather bright member of his group in high school; and but an average member of his group in a first-rate college. His intellectual quality does not change, but his group of competitors becomes more and more highly selected, creating the illusion of retrogression on his part. (p. 289)

On Societal Expectations for the Gifted
Should all children who test very high, as regards intellect, be educated for science, for the professions, and for the direction of industry? Should society induce some of them to join the manual trades, as hand workers? Should unskilled labor be drained by educational policy more thoroughly than it now is drained by competition, of all first-rate intelligence? These are disturbing questions of consequence, which affect the educator.

On Genetics and Environment
The very intelligent are those who rise in the world by competition, and who are also able to produce children like themselves . . . it remains to be added that the parents of superior children produce very small families. Apparently the extremely able will not choose the biological and economic burdens of repeated reproduction. This is a psychological fact which is interesting for the national future.

It has been stated that the census of the gifted has so far been confined largely to centers of population. We do not know to what extent children in the top quarter of intellect are to be found on farms in this generation. We do know, however, that where rural children have been tested at random, in this country, they yield a somewhat lower average intelligence than city children yield. (pp. 291–293)

—Excerpts from "Provisions for Intellectually Superior Children" in The Child, His Nature and His Needs, Hollingworth, 1922

P. S. 165 AND THE SPEYER SCHOOL EXPERIMENT: THE GOLDEN AGE OF THE INTELLECT

In 1922, thanks to a grant that Teachers College received from the Carnegie Corporation, special classes for gifted children were begun in P. S. 165 under the direction of Dr. Hollingworth. Two classes were designed for children from ages 7.5 through 9.5, one for those with IQs of 134 to 154 and another for those above 150 IQ. Some years later, similar classes were established at Teachers College's laboratory school, the Speyer School, P. S. 500, and in the then-rural area of Brooklyn, in P. S. 208.

Realizing that gifted children could learn the required curriculum in about half the time generally given to its instruction, Hollingworth covered "the basics" and then moved on to something more vital: the essentials. Hollingworth believed in an approach that focused more on enrichment and affective education than it did on learning more, faster. It was her desire to "fit the school to the child rather than the child to the school" (Passow, 1990, p. 135), and she did this through her instructional units, "The Evolution of Common Things," which used foreign language, art, music, history, and nutrition as the main components of her curriculum. In essence, Hollingworth was not trying to turn out masters of trivia, but rather, problem-solving experts who had fun as they discovered the possibilities that lay within one another and the world they shared. Children were evaluated in comparison with themselves, rather than against each other, and independent study in areas of personal interest was common, as were field trips.

The classes at Speyer School lasted only 5 years, but in that time, 90 highly intelligent children, grades 3 through 6, benefited from both the instruction that they received and the climate of intelligence that surrounded them. Comments from some of the children, more than 30 years after their participation in these classes, attest to their meaningfulness:

> I loved the atmosphere that was palpable in the air of that school and which I can summon in my mind, fresh as ever, 30-odd years after the fact . . . the atmosphere said "everything smart and good and worthwhile in education is possible if you go halfway to achieve it with us." (Harris, 1990, p. 217)
>
> I completed my PhD in 1972, and I enjoy art and music. I attribute Speyer with "nourishing" these areas that are very much a part of my family background. (White, 1990, p. 223)
>
> Speyer was a relief and a challenge . . . a much freer place; far less regimentation . . . it was a group of kids I could feel comfortable with. It was a marvelously diverse group . . . the general educational approach has left an impact. (White, 1990, pp. 225–226)

The elements of an exceptional education—challenge, fun, enthusiasm, and new adventures—were present in these classes for the gifted that, even today, stand as exemplars of the best that schools can do to accommodate the needs of gifted learners. As Hollingworth herself wrote prior to the onset of these special classes:

> Schools cannot equalize children; schools can only equalize opportunity. It may well be thought to be highly undemocratic to provide full opportunity for the exercise of their capacities to some, while to others the same offering means only partial exercise of their powers. It is hard for a psychologist to define democracy, but perhaps one acceptable definition might be that it is a condition of affairs, in which every human being has opportunity to live and work in accordance with inborn capacity for achievement. (Hollingworth, 1922, p. 298)

SOMETHING YOU ARE: THE ESSENCE OF GIFTEDNESS

> Society studies that which is socially annoying. The school attends to those who give it trouble. (Hollingworth, 1931, p. 1)

Leta Hollingworth had such a profound effect on so many diverse areas of education and psychology that it can be difficult to select her paramount area of study; the "quintessential Leta." From my point of view, though, the greatest of her achievements lies in her explication of the social and emotional needs of gifted children, which she learned about through the best ways possible: by listening to, talking with, observing, and teaching highly intelligent children.

Some of the issues that gifted children contended with daily involved school, the primary problem there related to the ease of the work required by teachers who did not understand that "children of 140 IQ waste half their time. Those above 170 IQ waste practically all of their time in school" (Hollingworth, 1939, p. 586). Using all manner of techniques to stimulate their vibrant, young minds, these highly able children will, at times, adopt behaviors that are socially annoying—speaking out, wandering off, interrupting, and so forth. It was Hollingworth's contention (and that of many who followed her) that these behaviors indicate the child's search for something to do that is more stimulating than listening to or studying concepts already mastered.

In her comprehensive review of Leta Hollingworth's articles and books devoted to the "emotional education" of gifted children, Linda Silverman extracted eleven key concerns:

1. finding enough hard and interesting work at school
2. adjusting to classmates
3. being able to play with other children
4. not becoming hermits
5. developing leadership abilities
6. not becoming negativistic towards authority
7. learning to "suffer fools gladly"
8. avoiding the formation of habits of extreme chicanery
9. conforming to rules and expectations
10. understanding their origin and destiny from an early age
11. dealing with the special problems of being a gifted girl

—*Silverman, 1990, p. 172*

Another school problem, and one that relates also to the social arena, is the difficulty encountered when gifted children are placed in grades inhabited by children 3 to 5 years older than they. As summarized by Silverman (1990), "They were too small for their seats, could not write rapidly enough, were unable to participate with their classmates in athletic activities, were out of their depth socially and emotionally, and were likely to be treated as babies" (p. 173). Although this type of radical acceleration is not as widely practiced today as it was in Hollingworth's era, children now and children then are similar: They want to be accepted not only for their brains but also for their being.

Yet another related area, although it sounds so inconsequential, is the problem of play. Hollingworth found that many gifted children chose solitary play, not as a first option, but because their efforts to socialize were met with either reluctance or animosity. Take this situation: A gifted 6-year-old, one who is verbally fluent and able to juggle multiple complex ideas simultaneously, wants to play a game that includes some rather specific and complicated rules and roles. Other 6-year-olds, not so intellectually endowed, just want to knock around and have fun until the recess bell rings. The goals are similar, to have fun; it's just that the gifted child's interpretation of "fun" is more multifaceted than is that of most first graders. According to Hollingworth, the typical gifted child's reaction could take one of two avenues: forgoing group play altogether and selecting more solitary pursuits, or seeking out older children whose idea of "fun" approximates their own.

But then . . . what 10-year-old wants a 6-year-old as a buddy? It just isn't cool. What Hollingworth found as a distinct benefit to the classes she established in the New York City schools was that gifted children could find agemates who were also soulmates: chronological peers who were also intellectual equals. This discovery, among the most important when seen through the eyes of children who want to be accepted, continues to be one of the greatest benefits of linking together gifted children with each other. Like minds, like bodies, like fun.

The next category of emotional need that Hollingworth explained can be categorized under one of these T-shirt slogans: "Who died and made you boss?" ". . . And your point is?" or "What part of 'no' don't you understand?" Indeed, it is the problem of negative attitudes toward authority figures who may expect conformity in a world filled with gray areas that seems to give gifted people the stereotype of being socially awkward or manipulative. In fact, they often are neither—they just want to be understood.

Hollingworth recorded, in 1939, a conversation between herself and a gifted child who was admonished for correcting his teacher:

> LSH: "What seems to be the main problem with you at school?"
> Child: "The teacher can't pronounce."
> LSH: "Can't pronounce what?"
> Child: "Oh, lots of things. The teacher said 'Magdalen College—at Oxford, you know. I said, 'In England, they call it Modlin College.' The teacher wrote a note home to say I am rude and disorderly."

As an effective line of defense for outspoken gifted children who get into trouble because they overzealously correct adults or agemates, to the intellectual embarrassment of the recipient and the social chastisement of the "corrector," Hollingworth offers a solution: Gifted people, including children, need to learn how to "suffer fools gladly." In essence, Hollingworth is not in favor of gifted children lording it over others by reminding them of how smart/not smart they are; rather, as part of their emotional education, Hollingworth believed that gifted children must learn tolerance and patience with those who might not be as adept with ideas as they. As she wrote, "It is more necessary that this be learned than that any school subject be mastered" (1942, p. 260). Realizing that all of us live in a world with social rules, Hollingworth wanted nothing more than to give her students the tools to accept individuals as people, irrespective of their intellectual capacities.

She even took this social grace into the classroom when she realized that trying to have a reasonable discussion on any topic with five or more highly gifted children is as difficult as putting toothpaste back into its tube. *Everyone* has an opinion, and *everyone* feels compelled to share it simultaneously, to attack the smallest inconsistency in one's logic, and to vocalize disapproval of tasks that they deem routine or boring. (And she found a correlation: The more intelligent, the more the compelling urge to correct!). By teaching her students the elements of debate and discussion used in forensics, Hollingworth provided her students with yet another valuable lesson in the vagaries of social etiquette—a life lesson that is yet one more piece in the puzzle of emotional education.

Last, but very important, Hollingworth found that gifted children question "the big issues" much earlier than parents or teachers are equipped or willing to address them: questions of life, death, sex, religion, and human origin. Too, not only do these children want to know the facts, they want to understand the reasons *behind* the facts—those sometimes annoying "Why?" questions that just will not be satisfied with a "Because I said so" response. As Hollingworth said, "To have the intelligence of an adult and the emotions of a child combined in a childish body is to encounter certain difficulties" (1942, p. 182).

Specific advice in addressing this complex issue is difficult to find, in Hollingworth's writing or elsewhere. In effect, how *does* one convince a child that the questions he or she is asking are wise, even if the answers are not always understandable? Some (Kearney, 1990; Silverman, 1990) have suggested discussing the idea of *asynchronous development* with gifted children, to let them know that it is expected that their minds, bodies, and emotions may all be growing at vastly different rates. Further, gifted children need to know that it is all right (although frustrating) to ask philosophical or ethical questions that have abstract or value-based answers rather than concrete explanations. It is vital to remind children that these same questions have been asked for centuries, and let them explore, as they are intellectually and emotionally ready to do so, the works of others in literature and philosophy who wondered why with an equal degree of ardor.

Hollingworth went on to explore other related areas of emotional growth and development, especially in adolescence. Curious readers are directed to study her work more, exploring firsthand the vast wealth of knowledge that existed untouched for many years and that has resurfaced at a time when we need it the most: the life and the work of Leta Hollingworth.

It seems appropriate to close this section with a quote from the young Leta, a 19-year-old preparing to graduate from college, who wrote about her life's longing to make a difference:

> I am possessed of a kind of curiosity to discover where (my own) boundaries are placed. . . . Someday perhaps I shall tell the old world what it looks like to me, after I get through taking a look. Then perhaps I never shall. (Hollingworth, 1943, p. 72)

EMOTIONAL GIFTEDNESS: THE NEXT CHAPTER

Disintegration

Have you ever noticed that all things seem to disintegrate piece by piece? McDonald's restaurants are disintegrating. They have taken all the slides out of our McDonald's because someone got burned on one. My class is disintegrating, too. Not everybody will be back next year. Sometimes I feel like I'm disintegrating when I have to do worksheets and worksheets at school and when I have to answer silly questions. I feel very frustrated and like I'm going to explode into 2,615,160 minuscule pieces. When I have to sit there and do what I already learned instead of something new and interesting, I feel like I'm in a battle and being torn apart bit by bit. The battle of work. Sometimes I feel like I'm disintegrating and leaving parts of myself in the past. I'll never be small enough for Daddy to carry me up the stairs again and I am too big to be on Mommy's lap while she rocks. DISINTEGRATION!

—*Jason Crowe, age 7*

When discussing the idea of emotional giftedness, it is best to relate to the concept through the eyes of a child. The above essay on disintegration, and how it impacts many aspects of this one person's life, is noteworthy in its vivid description of a reality that everyone experiences: change. Generalizing from slides at McDonald's to inappropriate schoolwork, or how one's body size changes family customs, this young author expresses at both intellectual and emotional levels the angst involved with growing up gifted. That the writer was only 7 years old when he penned "Disintegration" gives firsthand proof that not all minds (or hearts) are created equal. Some just have more of "something" than others, and in this case, that something is emotional giftedness.

The term *emotional giftedness* is difficult to pin down as to its origin. Certainly, Hollingworth implied such a concept existed as she stressed affective education for her gifted students. And Annemarie Roeper, in her writing (1995), describes the emotional lives of gifted children whom she has taught or counseled. More recently, Daniel Goleman, in his best-selling book *Emotional Intelligence* (1995), stresses that the "EQ" (emotional quotient) is more important than IQ in determining one's ultimate success in life, and James Hillman, in *The Soul's Code* (1996), says it is one's "daimon" (or heart) that is the guiding force in directing one's life. Hillman's "Acorn Theory" proposes that each life is formed by a particular image of what should be, and it is each person's destiny to aim toward that fulfillment, just as an oak tree's destiny is forged by a tiny acorn.

In reviewing the research on emotional giftedness and its implications for children, the cluster of individuals who come to mind are three: Kazimierz Dabrowski, Michael Piechowski, and Linda Silverman. Together, they have forged theories and practices related to emotional giftedness that are among the most exciting and far-reaching ideas that the field of gifted child education has embraced since the time of Terman and Hollingworth.

. . . Which is only appropriate, because Dabrowski was a contemporary of both Terman and Hollingworth.

Born in 1902, in Poland, Kazimierz Dabrowski survived both world wars, yet was tortured internally by some of the horrors of war that he experienced. In his youth, he saw all around him the cruelty, superficiality, and crass egotism of power gone awry. By contrast, he also saw how innocents became victims at the hands of those with low regard for human life. Imprisoned by the Nazis for giving asylum to Jews and, later, by the Communists, Dabrowski himself was tortured and forbidden to practice his dual specialties: medicine and psychology.

As both a psychiatrist and a neurologist, Dabrowski was able to link together the worlds of these related disciplines. Also, as a student of education, he interpreted children's "acting out" behaviors in ways that were far different from the typical, postulating that certain actions were the result of a central nervous system that was under tension. Thus, when children were told to "sit up straight and pay attention," some children reacted by doing so, others by squirming, and still others with an obedient but distant acceptance. Dabrowski interpreted these actions thusly:

> The imposition of restraint provokes emotional tension. This tension finds expression in several different modalities. Children who squirm in their seats release tension psycho-motorically; the daydreamers escape tension into the world of fantasy or spontaneously create pictures and scenes as images of the sources of tension; the upright, tense children feel the tension emotionally; the alert ones get their mind going and are ready to put their wits to use. (Piechowski, 1979, p. 28)

Yet some children, just as some inmates in concentration camps or other physically, intellectually, and emotionally torturous conditions, seemed able to transcend the absurdity of these daily life circumstances. They not only survived, but also helped others to do so. What was it that allowed such self-sacrifice and the ability to reach for something inside themselves to a storehouse of moral courage that allowed growth to occur? What was it about the psychological makeup of these individuals that caused them to seek higher ground, philosophically speaking? The answers, in part, came from Dabrowski's study of eminent artists, dancers, and actors and his interviews and experiences with gifted children and adolescents, some of whom had been referred to him because of their psychoneurotic tendencies of anxiety, perfection, and inferiority.

"Psychoneurotic? I don't think so!" might be Dabrowski's words if he were alive today, for he saw in these individuals some human qualities to be nurtured, rather than some psychological disturbances to be cured. Rather than being quick to accuse his clients of being overly concerned with problems (their own and others), Dabrowski saw in them a quest for a higher ideal, an inner need to understand and improve a world that was filled with inexplicable harshness and cruelty—he had seen much of it himself—coupled with elements of uncompromising beauty and hope. What others saw as psychoneurosis, Dabrowski interpreted as a search for clarity; and this quest would result in higher level development of both the intellect and the emotions. Dabrowski termed this sensitivity to analyzing and conquering problems *nadpobudliwsc,* or *overexcitability.*

THE OE PHENOMENON

Living and working in Canada, Dabrowski continued to explore and refine his work, demarcating the overexcitabilities (OE) into several categories:

- **Psychomotor:** expressed through an abundance of physical energy
- **Sensual:** heightened acuity through the senses
- **Intellectual:** a curiosity and drive for understanding complex ideas
- **Imaginational:** vivid creativity and inventiveness
- **Emotional:** a deep capacity to care

Although everyone possessed these abilities to some degree, the greater the strength of the OEs, the greater was the potential for taking this "developmental potential" and using it to live an ethical, compassionate life in adulthood. Thus, even though the actualization of the OEs was generally noted in adulthood, careful observation of children—such as the boy who wrote "Disintegration"—provided indicators, or "markers," of the latent developmental potential that existed within. According to Dabrowski (1979), overexcitable people are "delicate, gentle, empathic, nonaggressive, industrious, wise though unsophisticated, never brutal, often inhibited, likely to withdraw into themselves rather than retaliate, have deep feelings, [and be] idealistic" (p. 87). Dabrowski believed that with these qualities OE individuals were capable of elevating the world to a higher plane. Likewise, they were prime targets of ridicule and could be destroyed by others who interpreted this moral strength as weakness. Inner strength could, thus, become an outer vulnerability. Specifically, if an OE individual—child or adult—is surrounded by others who make him or her feel embarrassed or odd for being "different," the person may choose to disguise these essential personality elements. As stated by Piechowski (1995):

Criticized and teased for what they cannot help, they begin to believe there is something wrong with them. Sometimes they learn to disguise their intensity, sometimes they seek refuge in fantastic worlds of their own creation, sometimes they try to "normalize" it and as a result suffer depression or ill-defined anxiety. These reactions are the consequences of being forced to deny their own potential. (p. 367)

OK . . . so who is this "Piechowski" guy, and how does he fit into the OE equation? Very simply, Michael Piechowski is the individual who was able to take Dabrowski's ideas and ideals and make them understandable (literally, as he helped to translate them into English from the original Polish) to people who need stories and historical referents to put theory into a practical context.

Michael's story, like Kazimierz's, began in Poland. But as an adult, Michael moved to the United States to pursue a PhD in science—specifically, molecular biology. On completion of that degree, Michael entered another doctoral program, this one in counseling, and eventually took a faculty position in Canada, at the same university where Dabrowski was employed. The two became valuable colleagues, with Michael eventually translating some of Dabrowski's works.

MICHAEL PIECHOWSKI MEETS KAZIMIERZ DABROWSKI

In 1966, an Italian friend of mine told me about a Polish psychologist who had a new theory that psychoneurosis was a good thing, not a miserable condition but a process of inner growth and transformation. It didn't mean much to me then as I just finished my degree in molecular biology. Little did I know that soon after I was going to meet Dr. Kazimierz Dabrowski in Edmonton, Alberta, where I had my first faculty appointment.

His cordiality and graciousness were characteristic of a European gentleman of the older generation. He always met others with a big smile and a firm handshake. In discussion—and we always had discussions—he became very animated. He liked to question uncritically accepted notions, for instance, adjustment. He would ask with his characteristic accent, "What means this, adjustment to what?" Then he would elaborate on the difference between adjustment to everyday reality, to narrow horizons of survival and material comfort, and adjustment to higher values and ideals. His voice was strong and resonant, with a great range of expression from warm, quietly intense, and caring to tinging with indignation at the unjust treatment of the beautiful and often delicate flowers of giftedness being overwhelmed by the insensitivity of those who do not understand nor appreciate them but who took it as their task to shape the flowers to be like everybody else.

continued on the following page

continued from the previous page

What Drove Dabrowski to Care About Gifted People?

Because countless gifted people were suffering and many were perishing, Dabrowski felt a great urgency to help and save those who are sensitive, vulnerable, empathetic, and creative but who are not well adapted to the world where aggressive competition pushes people to get ahead with little consideration for their fellow humans. He had a vision of places where psychoneurotics could stay, be understood, be nurtured and assisted in their inner growth by a qualified staff—others, like themselves, who had gone through this process earlier. He had such a place near Warsaw, but World War II and the Nazis interrupted his work. He made every effort to get it going again after the war, but soon the Communists would not allow it. He was put in prison. After two years he was released and allowed to work, but not to teach. Eventually, things changed and he was told to seek his luck abroad, and thus came to Canada.

What Did Dabrowski Teach You?

From Dabrowski I learned the Theory of Positive Disintegration. He was always looking for people he could draw into his work. We had weekly meetings to transform his writings into readable English. I had to forever ask him what he meant and he always patiently explained it to me. Later, when he got a research grant, I analyzed the autobiographical material that was collected. From then on, most of my research, and that of some of my graduate students, was devoted to the application of the theory and to testing its concepts. Dabrowski's theory, like no other, describes the intensified and vivid way of experiencing that many gifted people recognize as their own. His theory also made it uniquely possible to study systematically self-actualizing people and even more advanced levels of human development.

—*Michael M. Piechowski is a professor, teacher, and a lover of*
Scarletti, Mozart, Chopin, Prokofiev, and Lutoslawski.

Then, with elaboration and his own brand of realism, Michael expanded the OE idea as a useful way to define, identify, and appreciate giftedness—emotional giftedness. Figure 7.1 shows one of the ways that Piechowski has taken each of the OEs and expanded on them by specific, visible behaviors that can be noted by parents, teachers, and friends, and Figure 7.2 provides excerpts from the Overexcitability Questionnaire developed by Piechowski and his colleagues to explore the range of OEs existing in individuals.

FIGURE 7.1

Forms and Expressions of Psychic Overexcitability

Psychomotor
Surplus of energy
> rapid speech, marked excitation, intense physical activity (e.g., fast games and sports) pressure for action (e.g., organizing), marked competitiveness

Psychomotor expression of emotional tension
> compulsive talking and chattering, impulsive actions, nervous habits (tics, nail biting), workaholism, acting out

Sensual
Enhanced sensory and aesthetic pleasure
> seeing, smelling, tasting, touching, hearing, and sex; delight in beautiful objects, sounds of words, music, form, color, balance

Sensual expression of emotional tension
> overeating, sexual overindulgence, buying sprees, wanting to be in the limelight

Intellectual
Intensified activity of the mind
> curiosity, concentration, capacity for sustained intellectual effort, avid reading; keen observation, detailed visual recall, detailed planning

Penchant for probing questions and problem solving
> search for truth and understanding; forming new concepts; tenacity in problem-solving

Reflective thought
> thinking about thinking, love of theory and analysis, preoccupation with logic, moral thinking, introspection (but without self-judgment), conceptual and intuitive integration; independence of thought (sometimes very critical)

Imagination
Free play of the imagination
> frequent use of image and metaphor, facility for invention and fantasy, facility for detailed visualization, poetic and dramatic perception, animistic and magical thinking

Capacity for living in a world of fantasy
> predilection for magic and fairy tales, creation of private worlds, imaginary companions, dramatization

Spontaneous imagery as an expression of emotional tension
> animistic imagery, mixing truth and fiction, elaborate dreams, illusions

Low tolerance of boredom

continued on the following page

continued from the previous page

Emotional

Feelings and emotions intensified

positive feelings, negative feelings, extremes of emotion, complex emotions and feelings, identification with others' feelings, awareness of a whole range of feelings

Strong somatic expressions

tense stomach, sinking heart, blushing, flushing, pounding heart, sweaty palms

Strong affective expressions

inhibition (timidity, shyness); enthusiasm, ecstasy, euphoria, pride; strong affective memory; shame; feelings of unreality, fears and anxieties, feelings of guilt, concern with death, depressive and suicidal moods

Capacity for strong attachments, deep relationships

strong emotional ties and attachments to persons, living things, places; attachments to animals; difficulty adjusting to new environments; compassion, responsiveness to others, sensitivity in relationships; loneliness

Well differentiated feelings toward self

inner dialogue and self-judgment

—*Falk, Piechowski, & Lind, 1994; revised from Piechowski, 1979*

Each of these OEs can be experienced by watching the child or by examining the products or words that individuals produce. And although there may be some degree of overlap among the OEs, each is unique unto itself. Let us examine each OE in a bit more detail.

PSYCHOMOTOR OE

The psychomotor OE, in and of itself, does not differentiate between gifted and average development but does so when it is integrated with other OEs (Piechowski & Cunningham, 1985). Individuals with psychomotor OE are always moving and highly energetic, very physical in their expressions of joy, anger, or sorrow, and often forgo sleep, even in infancy (Munger, 1990), to be more a part of the active world in which they live. Often misdiagnosed as hyperactive or as having attention deficit hyperactivity disorder (ADHD), they distinguish themselves from those who have ADHD by being able to focus and concentrate for extended periods, getting physically agitated most often as an expression of either their joy of learning or their frustration with intellectual boredom. They seem to have stamina way beyond that of their parents or colleagues; an unending supply of physical energy that is also marked by intellectual exploration. In response to the OE Questionnaire item, "Describe what you do when you feel full of energy," a 15-year-old boy wrote: "I feel the most en-

FIGURE 7.2

Overexcitability Questionnaire

1. Describe how you feel when you feel extremely joyous, ecstatic, or incredibly happy.
2. What kinds of things get your mind going?
3. Describe what you do when you feel full of energy.
4. What attracts you in people you like, and what in those you become close to?
5. What do you like to concentrate on the most?
6. Do you sometimes catch yourself seeing, hearing, or imagining things that aren't really there? Give examples.
7. How do you think about your own thinking? Describe.
8. Does it sometimes appear to you that things around you have a life of their own, and that animals, plants, and all things in nature have their own feelings? Give examples.
9. When you are faced with a difficult idea or concept, what must happen, or what do you do so that it becomes clear to you?
10. How often do you carry on arguments in your head? What sorts of things are they about?
11. When you ask yourself, "Who am I?" what is the answer?
12. When you were young, did you have an imaginary playmate? One, or several? Please, describe.

—*Developed by Michael M. Piechowski, Northland College, Ashland, Wisconsin*

ergy when it is a sunny afternoon and I'm in school. I can't get up and walk around freely and exert this energy so I have to suppress it until after class when I can get up and walk around, or sometimes, I will tap my fingers or my pen or else wiggle my legs." Notice the very deliberate plan and rationale this young man has for expressing his psychomotor OE.

SENSUAL OE

Did you ever pull your car over to the side of a highway to stop and appreciate a sunset? When the dessert cart comes by at your favorite restaurant, do you often have your waiter describe each option—sometimes twice—even if you don't intend to order

Learning about Dabrowski's work changed my life in so many ways. I learned that as an overexcitable person I was not broken or abnormal. Instead, my sensitivities are just part of my birthright. I also found a framework to explain why some people are interested in and pursue their personal development and others do not. The Theory of Positive Disintegration gave me a framework to view myself and others and to be more accepting of those who differ from me.

—*Sharon Lind is an educational consultant, teacher, and member of a gifted family.*

any of them? Can you listen to beautiful music and cry, or stroke a tree's rough bark to examine each ripple of its skin? Can you read an especially erotic or exotic slice of literature over and over, savoring each word and the pictures that it represents? If so, welcome to the world of sensual OE, a world in which you are bombarded by stimuli, each attractive or repulsive in its own unique way.

Sensual OE may be the most elusive of the OEs to measure or understand (Silverman, 1993), but you definitely know it when you see it (or feel it . . . or smell it . . .). Often criticized for being "too dramatic" or "overly concerned with details," sensually OE people merely experience the natural world in a higher key, absorbing what the Earth offers with a deeper personal meaning. One gifted adult, a physician, described a new calligraphic font that he had created on his computer; in describing his font, he was also describing himself as a sensually overexcitable individual:

> The calligraphy is something that I made up myself, and have been doing for a long time. It looks romantic because it is an expression of me, and how I am in the deepest part of myself. Romanticism is the source of my idealism, and thus, the birthplace of my dreams for a joyous, beautiful world with more carnivals than wars, more dancehalls than prisons, more gardens than parking lots. My romantic self is one which loves human beings, but is not so fond of the things which they do to each other and to the world which is their home. The blindness of this love enables me to see beyond the accepted limitations of people unto their great and attainable potential, and set my sights upon that greater existence.

Sensual OE may be something that every middle school teacher thinks his or her students have in abundance, yet when one digs beneath the veneer of hormones, the *real* sensual OE appears as a part of one's being, not merely an aspect of one's emerging libido.

INTELLECTUAL OE

The Intellectual OE is obvious in the continual request by Schroeder, the piano-playing *Peanuts* character, for something more stimulating than what is offered by school or friends. It is obvious, too, in a student's response to another OE Questionnaire item, "How do you think about your own thinking?": "I think about my thinking. Like what makes my mind work. Sometimes I think why I am here. Why do I think the way I do? How is my mind gathering this information and storing it so that someday I can remember it." (15-year-old boy)

The Intellectually OE person is a minefield of exploding thoughts. It is someone who is curious, mentally alert even while relaxing, driven to absorb and understand any new idea, and someone who likes any type of intellectual challenge, be they word games, three-dimensional puzzles, or the College Championship segments of *Jeopardy!* The intellectually OE child will be in bed at the appropriate bedtime but will more likely than not be reading under the covers with a flashlight. (Or as one mother of a 14-year-old college freshman in Texas told a news reporter, "When he was younger, I used to take his books away from him as punishment.") In young children with intellectual OEs, there is a constant barrage of "why?" questions; these children are frequently described by teachers and parents as "sponges," able and wanting to absorb as much as they can from the environment and the people around them. They are interested in learning for the sake of learning, not necessarily for the utilitarian purpose of acquiring information to spit it back on a test or during a college interview.

It would seem that Intellectual OE is synonymous with general intelligence, but Piechowski (1979) warns that not all high-IQ people are intellectually curious enough to be rated high on the intellectual OE index. If they show little interest in pure learning, theories, and expanding their knowledge base across many disciplines, it is likely that these "book smart" people would not qualify as intellectually overexcitable.

IMAGINATIONAL OE

The Imaginational OE is, simultaneously, the most fun and the most painful of the OEs; it is the domicile of the obscure and the curious, the abode of the possible. It is the wellspring where creativity and "what if . . ." are born, and it is the haven for thoughts that border on the absurd. Creative universes are manufactured here, as are the imaginary friends who inhabit them. Imaginational OE is the home of the spirit, where cabbages become kings, forgotten languages regain fluency, and nothing is bizarre except the ordinary.

The painful part of Imaginational OE is the reaction to it that one gets from others. Calls to "be realistic" or taunts such as "where did you ever get *that* idea?" are the barriers imposed by a society that prefers structure over chaos, straight-line thinking over imaginative play. Consider the odd looks this 15-year-old girl would get from others when she answered OE Questionnaire item #19, "Does it sometimes appear to you that things around you have a life of their own?"

> Of course they do! I used to think that my Barbies came alive in the night and played with each other. I was sure that they acted out this whole story that I had thought of. And I could never throw any of them out because they had feelings. That would be awful. They were a part of a whole fantasy world I created for myself because I didn't have that many playmates. And my Barbies and I would talk. They looked up to me because I would help them out. If one Barbie was mean to another, they would get me to mediate.

More than anything else, the child with a heightened Imaginational OE needs a compatriot, someone who shares either a similar predilection toward fantasy and wonder, or an advocate who will serve to protect this fragile, yet cherished

I've found that one part of my personal myth is the belief in myself, my abilities, and my thought processes. I am a spiritual being, capable of great wisdom, deep thought and personal happiness. I look into myself for answers, and often find pieces of myself I never realized existed. I put them into the puzzle of my life, and hope that one day the masterpiece will be complete.

—Senior project excerpt, 17-year-old boy

Whenever I talk about Dabrowski's theories to parents at conferences, they have lit up with recognition of themselves and their children. The overexcitabilities (OEs) are what strike parents the most. So many parents have come up to me afterwards or written to me thanking me for talking about the OEs. They have often shared that their children fit *all* of the OEs, and that this really worried them until they found out that OEs are normal in gifted children and adults. . . . I think it helps parents to know that there is a theoretical framework for understanding the enhanced moral sensitivity of their children. It is important for parents to know that this sensitivity can be squelched or nurtured so that their children can become moral leaders.

—*Linda Kreger Silverman is a psychologist who has passionately advocated for the gifted for more than 35 years.*

gift. In research (Piechowski & Colangelo, 1984; Gallagher, 1985), gifted adolescents were seen to have consistently higher Imaginational OEs than average adolescents, but oftentimes, it is questionable whether adults really want their children to be creative beyond a certain point. As Barry Grant stated in 1992, "As much as the movement for gifted education argues that gifted students deserve special education because of their differences, we don't want gifted students to be too different, too eccentric, and to pursue paths in lives that are too nontraditional. Parents are proud of their gifted children, proud of what makes them different, but they want them to turn out pretty much like they are" (pp. 3–4).

Imaginational OEs, untidy and inconvenient as they are to a world used to well-defined limits, are the essence of what makes us human. Imaginational OEs cause people to question the world of today and enter the world of tomorrow with fresh ideas and innovative spirits. If progress is to be made as individuals and as a species, Imaginational OEs must be cherished, not channeled. Even the corporate world seems to agree, as exemplified in the tribute to imaginative souls produced by Apple Computer (see Figure 7.3).

EMOTIONAL OE

On May 27, 1997, in a small town in Indiana, a memorial service was held. Titled "Harmony in the Park," it was to serve as a remembrance of 22 men, women, and children who were killed in Bosnia exactly 5 years earlier. The invitation read: "One man saw it happen and fought back. His weapon was his cello. Come celebrate the courage of Vedran Smailovic, the cellist of Sarajevo, who played his cello under fire for 22 days on the spot where the 22 people were massacred."

Musicians were asked to bring their instruments and share their harmony; vocalists, to bring their voice and share their songs. Artists could bring their easels, sharing their beauty, and writers could bring their words and share their imaginations. Last, humanitarians were asked to attend, bringing their hearts and sharing their love.

And come they did! Celebrating the life and spirit that can arise even from pain, dozens of people descended on the park, including two special people: a 16-year-old girl who was an exchange student from Bosnia and 10-year-old

FIGURE 7.3

To The Crazy Ones

Here's to the crazy ones.
The misfits.
The rebels.
The troublemakers.
The round pegs in the square holes.
The ones who see things differently.
They're not fond of rules.
And they have no respect for the status quo.
You can praise them, disagree with them, quote them,
disbelieve them, glorify them or vilify them.
About the only thing you can't do is ignore them.
Because they change things. They invent. They imagine. They heal.
They explore. They create. They inspire.
They push the human race forward.
Maybe they have to be crazy.
How else can you stare at an empty canvas and see a work of art?
Or sit in silence and hear a song that's never been written?
Or gaze at a red planet and see a laboratory on wheels?
We make tools for these kinds of people.
Because while some see them as the crazy ones, we see genius.
And it's people who are crazy enough to think they can
change the world,
who actually do.
Think different.

—Courtesy of Apple Computer, Inc.

Jason, the organizer of the event (and the author of the "Disintegration" essay that opens this section of the chapter) and the owner of an amazingly strong Emotional OE that allowed him to envision what too many adults bypass: the beauty of hope during a time of war.

Emotional OEs are the bedrock underlying the entire theory of overexcitabilities. With it, children and adults can see a world beyond themselves, and they can form attachments to people and ideas that integrate the emotions, intellect, and creativity. Likewise, they can be self-critical and perfectionistic, feeling that no matter what they do to help, it is still not enough, triggering the additional feelings of guilt and anxiety. Emotionally OE individuals may not be able to fathom how someone could squash a bug rather than just shoo it away or ridicule a new

Excluding emotional giftedness from our definitions of giftedness creates a huge void. Emotional giftedness is the passionate underpinning or core of many highly intellectually and creatively gifted individuals. To exclude it from our consideration is to look at an incomplete, monochromatic picture of the individual. Additionally, we lose a framework for understanding the compassion, empathy, drive, intensity, and morality of many gifted individuals . . . and perhaps most importantly, we would neglect looking at each individual as a total entity.

—*Sharon Lind is an educational consultant, teacher, and member of a gifted family.*

kid in school because of his or her haircut or looks or language. Emotionally OE individuals are seldom egocentric, doing their acts of kindness and charity for the altruistic purpose of helping others, not for self-aggrandizement or fame or attention. Call them "emotional patriots," if you will, for they act in accordance with a set of beliefs that some would call conscience and others might label charity. They see the "big picture" over the details, wanting to act on solutions without regard for monetary or political cost. Right is right, and, therefore, to emotionally OE people, the solution is obvious: empathetic action.

Annemarie Roeper (1982), in one of our field's classic articles, "How Gifted Children Cope with Their Emotions," relates this story about the obvious emergence of Emotional OEs in childhood:

> During a chess tournament, John, the obvious winner, began to make careless mistakes and lost the game. When asked what happened, he replied, "I noticed my opponent had tears in his eyes. I could not concentrate and lost my desire to win." John's empathy was greater than his ambition. Many adults, especially those who supported John, were disappointed. Yet, one could argue that his reaction was a more mature one than theirs, for his self esteem did not depend on winning the competition. (p. 82)

. . . which is exactly the point. For more than anything else—any*one* else—what the emotionally OE person needs is someone to believe in their values, to share their pipe dreams, and to allow that sometimes battling windmills is worth the effort. Without such support, people (especially children) who share this optimistic view of the world and their place in it may begin to feel abnormal or weird; altruistic outcasts in a cruel world based more on winning than cooperating, gaining power over sharing it. To accept that this view of the world is legitimate is the second greatest gift that one can give. The greatest gift of all is a helping hand in fulfilling these important dreams that are based in the internal world of the gifted child: emotional overexcitabilities.

Given the choice between a student who grows up to be a decent, loving person, at peace with himself and others, who makes a modest living in some form of service or pursuing some eccentric occupation, and one that later aggressively and coldly rises to the top of her profession, and makes great contributions, most of us would choose the former. Most of us, I think, see generosity, kindness, truthfulness, and self-realization as more important than money or status. I can say more confidently that we wouldn't want the latter without some of the former.

—*Grant, 1992, p. 3*

AND THE NEXT STEP IS

Losing the chess match even though you could easily have won it; talking to your Barbie dolls because they were the friends whom you didn't have in the neighborhood; choosing Anna Karenina over *Dick and Jane;* creating calligraphy, even when you are a physician; walking around in class and gazing out a window at a world of wonder: All are reactions that are perfectly legitimate even though, to some, they differ in their degree of social acceptability. Dabrowski saw these as survival techniques, of a sort, and labeled them with an oxymoronic term: *positive maladjustment,* the result of morally right actions that conflict with social expectations and pressures.

Someone who has seen this positive maladjustment in full bloom is the third person in our overexcitable triumvirate: Linda Silverman.

THE CONSUMMATE TEACHER

It is hard to tell if Dr. Linda Silverman's work is derived from the work of Dabrowski or an antecedent to it; for even though her professional experiences with gifted children took place only after Dabrowski had already done much of his research, her own work both parallels and builds on his own with uncanny similarity. Too, Linda Silverman's personal and professional attachment to the work of Leta Hollingworth—she edited a special issue of the *Roeper Review* devoted to Hollingworth and dedicated her 1993 text, *Counseling the Gifted and Talented,* to her—has been one of the primary reasons that Hollingworth's important work resurfaced after too many decades of neglect.

Linda Silverman is a clinical psychologist who directs the Gifted Development Center in Denver, Colorado, where she has both tested and counseled thousands of gifted children and adults. She is the editor of *Advanced Development: A Journal on Adult Giftedness* and also served as founding editor of *Understanding Our Gifted,* a magazine for parents of gifted children. A former primary school teacher and a prolific author, Silverman has been a guiding light in ensuring that the field of gifted child education does not stray too far from its roots in psychology. A vocal fan of the now politically incorrect individual IQ tests, especially use of the Stanford-Binet L-M to identify highly gifted children, Silverman (1994) insists that they are helpful for several reasons:

1. Individual IQ tests give at least one indicator of ways that cognitive development eclipses one's chronological age and physical development.
2. When individual IQ tests are administered to young gifted children, an equal number of boys and girls are selected as gifted, as opposed to achievement tests, which tend to discriminate against females.
3. Individual IQ tests do a better job of locating gifted students from minority cultures than virtually any other measure.

When gifted people, and those who live and work with them, are introduced to these (OE) concepts, there is often an instant recognition and a sense of relief. It helps to find out that there is a theoretical model that makes sense out of a manner of feeling and acting that is so often at odds with normal behavior and expectations of happy—or grim, as the case may be—adjustment. It helps for once to feel legitimate in one's "abnormal" reactions and what one cannot help experiencing and wanting to express.
—*Piechowski, 1991, p. 287*

In addition to these contributions, Silverman has also been one of our strongest advocates for highly gifted children, recognizing that their emotional and intellectual needs are seldom met even within many gifted programs. And not incidentally, she has been a reasoned critic of the recent movement away from giftedness and toward "talent development," stating that in moving this direction "we have lost the entire moral dimension of giftedness" (Silverman, 1994, p. 113). Further, she believes that the broader the net is cast to "catch" gifted children, the less differentiated will our programs become, lessening the distinctiveness of gifted programs, thereby leaving them open for elimination. As Silverman (1993) argues, "An enrichment program that serves the top 10% 45-minutes a week is likely to be attacked as an unnecessary frill because 'all students' could benefit from such enrichment" (p. 10).

Perhaps the contribution that Silverman made to the field of gifted child education that will have the most profound long-term effects is the definition of giftedness that emerged when she and a group of colleagues—practitioners, parents, and theorists—began to see the definition of giftedness being linked so closely with accomplishment and achievement. Instead, the Columbus Group (so named because this definition was forged during a marathon series of meetings in Columbus, Ohio) composed a conception of giftedness that reintroduced the idea of "self" into the consideration of giftedness. The Columbus Group's (1991) definition is

> Giftedness is *asynchronous development* in which advanced cognitive abilities and heightened intensity combine to create inner experiences and awareness that are qualitatively different from the norm. This asynchrony increases with higher intellectual capacity. The uniqueness of the gifted renders them particularly vulnerable and requires modification in parenting, teaching and counseling in order for them to develop optimally. (p. 1)

Unlike many other conceptions of giftedness, this definition touches on many aspects that are ignored in the more utilitarian definitions presented by the federal government, Renzulli, and others highlighted in chapter 2. Here, with this new definition, the focus is on *heightened intensity and awareness,* and it *requires* changes in the way that adults conduct themselves at home, in school, and in the counselor's office. The Columbus Group's definition gives back to gifted child education something that it has been lacking: a developmental view of intelligence that recognizes the fact that gifted people not only *think* differently, they also *feel* differently. As Silverman (1993) states, "This definition may be the first to acknowledge the emotional vulnerability of the gifted child and the importance of the counselor's role in the child's emotional development" (p. 7). In the generation ahead, it will be interesting to see whether the Columbus Group's definition of giftedness continues to gather momentum among educators and psychologists, adding depth and dimension to the conceptions of giftedness already put forth by Terman, Witty, and Hollingworth.

It does a person no good to be incredibly bright if at the same time she is also incredibly miserable or has such emotional impairment that she functions destructively. History has demonstrated many cases of persons who were highly gifted intellectually, but whose self-concept and emotions were so disturbed that entire countries, and even the world, have suffered as a result of their misguided intelligence.
—*Webb, Meckstroth, & Tolan, 1982, p. 26*

Another aspect of Silverman's work and guiding philosophy is her adherence to gifted child education as a part of the special education movement. Others in the gifted child education "business"—"talent developers," in particular—are loathe to make this comparison, suggesting that gifted child educators' work is more oriented to curriculum and instruction than it is to the tenets of special education. Silverman believes that exceptional children of all persuasions,

> We recognize the inherent difficulties of having a 17-year-old body with a 9-year-old mind. However, we still do not understand that it is equally problematic to have a 17-year-old mind trapped in the body of a 9-year-old. This type of asynchrony doesn't get much sympathy in our society.
>
> —*Silverman, 1994, p. 114*

FIGURE 7.4

Did They Fail School, or Did School Fail Them?

1. "School days were the most miserable years of my life. . . . I might have done better if I had never been to school."
2. This person so feared school that at age 11, he tried to throw himself down stairs to break a leg rather than attend class.
3. Expelled from Los Angeles High School.
4. Rejected from the School of Fine Arts because his work was "too disorganized."
5. Expelled from kindergarten.
6. "I preferred to endure all sorts of punishments rather than to learn gabble by rote," this person wrote about school.
7. "Teachers always used to think I was smart and it would torment me because I knew that I was really terribly dumb."
8. Refused to take a final exam in a class at Harvard, fearing failure.
9. He could never remember the sequence of the alphabet, and as a math student was so inept that even his private tutor quit.
10. Entered West Point near the bottom of his class.
11. Failed Speech 101 in college, and earned only a grade of D upon retaking the course.
12. Placed in an accelerated class due to IQ, but refused to do work and became a troublemaker, earning low grades.
13. Had two report cards: one from school, and one in which he put his own grades for his parents' signature.

•Mohandas Gandhi (1) •Actor Kenneth Branagh (2) •Artist Jackson Pollock (3) •Artist Paul Cezanne (4) •Singer John Lennon (5) •Albert Einstein (6) •Photographer Diane Arbus (7) •Author Gertrude Stein (8) •Pablo Picasso (9) •General Omar Bradley (10) •Rush Limbaugh (11) •Actor/Director Woody Allen (12) •Fidel Castro (13)

—*Excerpted from Hillman, 1996*

whether they be gifted or have extreme difficulty learning, require significant modifications in their environments to be most successful and personally fulfilled. However, she states that this assumption has been embraced by all except those interested in gifted children—a big mistake, she feels, from both a theoretical and a pragmatic perspective. "Without the shield of special education," Silverman (1993) writes, "it is difficult to justify why gifted children should have differentiated programming" (p. 7).

Linda Silverman is a counselor and a storyteller, a pragmatist and a philosopher, a parent advocate and a gifted student's best friend. Her writing and ideas have forced those content with the status quo to blink and to think. As a consummate teacher, she leads both adult and child alike down a path toward intellectual and personal fulfillment. Along with Dabrowski, Piechowski, and Hollingworth, Silverman has influenced our understanding of the social and emotional development of giftedness in the most profound ways possible: one child, one parent, at a time.

NEXT STEPS: PUTTING THE THEORIES INTO PRACTICE

The theories are all in place and the justification for addressing the social and emotional needs of gifted students have been eloquently championed by both educational pioneers and their contemporary counterparts. Now what? What do educators, parents, and counselors do to address these needs in legitimate ways, ensuring that gifted students see themselves in a mentally healthy context?

Actually, the methods found most useful are not much different from techniques that have been used successfully in other dimensions of counseling. For example, in the book *A Practical Guide to Counseling the Gifted in a School Setting* (Van Tassel-Baska, 1983), a quick glance at the guiding principles underlying a quality counseling program for gifted students includes these reminders:

> #4: Counselors should act as advocates for the gifted, assisting with their individual progress through appropriate school experiences.
>
> #8: Counselors should develop procedures for evaluating the strengths and weaknesses of gifted students, and help students develop plans around them.
>
> #12: Counselors must communicate with other school staff regarding problems and needs of individual gifted students.

The alert reader will realize that if the word *gifted* is taken out of the above statements, the sentence is true for *all* students in counseling situations! Thus, the advice offered in the Van Tassel-Baska book gives few examples of how counseling, like curriculum, is actually *differentiated* based on the specific needs of the population being served. And generic solutions seldom solve specific problems.

However, the work of Virgil Ward gets right to the heart of the issues involved in counseling and guiding gifted students. In his classic text, *Educating the Gifted: An Axiomatic Approach* (1961), Ward proposed that differential education of the gifted must focus on the unique social and emotional needs touched on by Hollingworth, because "it is perhaps truer in the area of character development than in any other significant undertaking by the school that the theoretical bases are not understood, the goals are not clarified, and the methodology is not explicitly developed" (p. 194). By using the time-tested methods of classical instruction—exposure, repetition, understanding, conviction, and application—Ward advised teachers and counselors to remember that the cognitive and emotional aspects of learning are intimately linked. Therefore, in discussing the gifted child's views of self-expectations, or society's views of how intelligent people must be willing to "give back" to the world that has given them so much, Ward espoused viewing these issues within the larger context of literature and civilization. Ward believes that reading and discussing how fictional or historical characters have addressed these same issues will accomplish at least two goals: First, the children (or adolescents, for whom Ward's work is particularly beneficial) will see that they are not the first individuals ever having faced a particular question or crisis; and second, they will be exposed to literature that has been noted over centuries for its wisdom and insight.

In addressing counseling issues from this curricular vantage, Ward believes that adults must take full advantage of the intellectual agility of gifted students—no fun-n-games "if you were an animal, which one would you be?" types of activities here! Such "instruction in the theoretical base of ideal moral behavior and of personal and social adjustments should be an integral part of the education of the gifted" (p. 201), and it will give gifted students the inner strength and skills to address these life issues on their own, once their formal schooling has ended. A concept-based advocate long before the idea of thematic or cross-disciplinary instruction became trendy, Ward believed that the *Synopticon,* a collection of essays, novels, and historical writings that emphasize the universal themes of life, is the most logical base from which to extend a student's learning about both personal and intellectual development. A listing of the *Synopticon*'s concepts is found in Figure 7.5.

I was working with a boy and his family. He was in sixth grade and as brilliant a kid as I have ever known. He was taking AP Calculus class at the high school and then he returned to his regular sixth-grade class. The seniors in the AP Calculus class liked him and respected his ability. He got along well with the seniors. He really liked the extra attention two of the senior girls were giving him and he decided that they were going to be his really good friends. He wanted them to come over to his house after school and play video games and watch TV. It took all of my counseling skills to work with his parents to help him understand that, yes, they were friends, but that they needed to do things with other friends who were their own age. I got through, but it wasn't easy.

—*Nicholas Colangelo is the director of the Connie Belin Center at the University of Iowa where he is the Myron and Jacqueline Blank Professor of Gifted Education.*

FIGURE 7.5

Concepts Found in the *Synopticon*

Aristocracy	Honor	Progress
Astronomy	Immortality	Reasoning
Beauty	Infinity	Religion
Being	Judgment	Revolution
Cause	Justice	Rhetoric
Chance	Knowledge	Science
Change	Labor	Sense
Citizen	Language	Signs & Symbols
Courage	Law	Sin
Custom & Convention	Liberty	Soul
Democracy	Life & Death	Space
Desire	Logic	State
Dialectic	Love	Temperance
Duty	Matter	Theology
Emotion	Metaphysics	Time
Eternity	Mind	Truth
Evolution	Monarchy	Tyranny
Family	Nature	Virtue & Vice
Fate	Necessity & Contingency	Wealth
Form	Oligarchy	Will
Good & Evil	One & Many	Wisdom
Happiness	Pleasure & Pain	World

—*From Joyce Van Tassel-Baska,* Comprehensive Curriculum for Gifted Learners,
2/e. Copyright © 1994 by Allyn & Bacon. Reprinted/adapted by permission.

For some reason, much of Ward's work has been either dismissed or ignored; yet, it is powerful in its intensity. Unfortunately, it is also lofty in its delivery, as Ward writes in philosophic discourse, using terms and sentence structures that leave many readers more perplexed than empowered. Still, it would be worthwhile to locate Ward's book on the back shelf of a research library (or its 1980 edition, *Differential Education for the Gifted,* a virtual copy of the original) and read it . . . slowly. Savor its richness and wallow in its wisdom. Then, do what few others have done: Implement it with the highly capable children who will appreciate both its depth and its power.

A MODEL FOR COUNSELING GIFTED STUDENTS

Using some of Ward's principles, but approaching them in a much more reader-friendly way, is George Betts (1985), whose Autonomous Learner Model (ALM) has been the nation's most widely accepted structure in planning a comprehensive, school-based program that addresses both gifted students' cognitive and affective needs, with an emphasis on the latter. The ALM was designed by Betts while he was a counselor at Arvada West High School in Colorado. Many of his gifted students were going through the motions of taking the "right" courses that would get them into the "right" colleges, but this lockstep movement toward academic success did little to soothe their hearts. More than anything else, these smart students' exemplary actions lacked one vital element: passion. Perhaps it was a passion for singing, or architecture, or rock climbing, or collecting Star Wars action figures—whatever the passion, it was seldom addressed in school. What you had, then, was a large group of accomplished students who led lives *outside* of school that had little direct connection to their lives *in* school. Noticing this oversight, George Betts (and his colleague at Arvada, Jolene Kercher) decided to include the pursuit of passions as a vital piece of the ALM.

In addition to having this passion for some activity or area of interest, something else was lacking from the high school students' daily routine that had been there in the elementary years: the opportunity to discuss the high points and hassles of growing up gifted with teachers who understood who you were and students who shared similar concerns to your own. Through their elementary school years, Betts's students had had both ample time and a safe place to share their feelings, dreams, and pangs. Now, though, high school provided less and less structured time to talk about anything other than academics. Spirits withered.

It was then that George Betts began to formulate his ideas for the ALM. By offering an elective class, for credit, that addressed issues such as *understanding giftedness, career counseling, interpersonal skills,* and *the discussion of controversial topics,* Betts was able to rekindle in his students the sense of family and community that they had enjoyed in earlier grades. And with his inclusion of many opportunities for independent study and individual exploration of areas of interest, he made certain that "pursuing your passion" was a part of each student's school regimen.

As the ALM expanded in scope and popularity, it added additional program components, and it also was made usable for middle school students. The model itself, represented in Figure 7.6, offers students many chances to experience enrichment and acceleration activities, while also offering the camaraderie of friends whose questions about life might be similar to their own.

Among the most valued of the experiences of the ALM is the "adventure trip," a multiday experience in which students might explore the geology of the Grand Canyon or visit a major city where life is far different from the one that the students experience in SmallTown USA. Each adventure offers both experiential learning and interpersonal revelations, a feast for the mind and a retreat for the soul.

The ALM, eminently flexible in its methods of operation, is a fine and specific model that addresses many of the blended issues of intellectual and emotional

I have in my own life five priorities—life, love, choice, balance and laughter. And these are not trite words. I think that if we were to look at the work we do in gifted education along those lines and with those priorities, we cannot go far wrong.

—*Gina Ginsberg Riggs founded the Gifted Child Society in New Jersey.*

FIGURE 7.6

Autonomous Learner Model

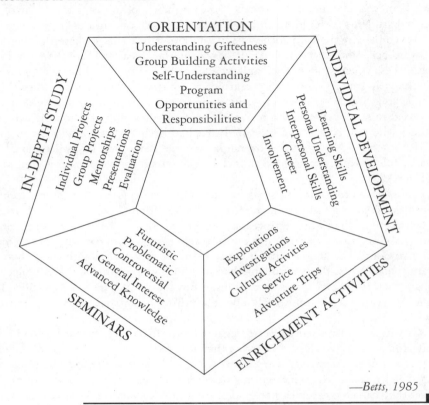

—*Betts, 1985*

growth of gifted students. If the founders of the gifted child education field could experience an ALM seminar or adventure trip, they would undoubtedly enjoy seeing just how richly their hopes for gifted children have been realized.

AND NOW, TO PARENTS

Much of this book has focused on the ways that educators can enhance the lives of the gifted children in their midst, but little emphasis has been placed on the parents' role. Yet, there is almost unanimous agreement that these home-based folks have at least as much influence on the lives that gifted children eventually grow up to lead as the impact of a well-placed teacher—most likely, even more

AN INTERVIEW WITH GEORGE BETTS

On Constructing a Definition of Giftedness

One of the things we do unconsciously is that we design our definitions so that they fit us. If we are intellectually gifted ourselves, then our definition of giftedness fits in that way. If you are a scientist, then giftedness exists for you in that realm. With me, it's from the affective dimension that I define giftedness. If you have never had a true sense of self, where you never looked deeply into yourself, then you won't really value that ability.

On the Role of Teachers

We must realize that we are facilitators in learning, but that the true answers to life really come from inside the child—if we allow those answers to emerge. I always quote the '70s group, *America,* who sing that "Oz didn't give anything to the Tinman that he didn't already have." What we are there to do with children is to help bring out their abilities. We don't develop these abilities in the child; we give the child the opportunities and the child develops them.

On Passions and Learning and Life

The autonomous learner is very close to Carl Rogers's concept of the fully functioning person or Maslow's self-actualizing person. To prepare children, we should develop their five selves. In the middle is the foundation: the emotional self. The next one is the physical self, Then there is the social self and the critical self, which is the combination of thinking skills that relate to problem solving and questioning. And the highest self is the passionate self, which is often the place that gifted programs fail, when they have too much prescribed content and direct instruction. Without this passionate self, children will never be fully functioning.

When you see an adult with a passionate self, they are fully functioning. If we don't cherish that passion that we are dedicated to, we are not going to meet our needs as adults. But it starts with kids. Gifted kids have more passions when they are younger, and we must nurture them then. Otherwise, by the time they get to high school, they are losing those passions and, by adulthood, the passions are gone.

—George Betts is a professor at the University of Northern Colorado,
an author, a parent, and a poet.

influence. So, when it comes to the parents' responsibilities in guiding their children's social and emotional development, what *are* their roles?

Jim Webb, Betty Meckstroth, and Stephanie Tolan provide much guidance and many answers. In their classic best-seller, *Guiding the Gifted Child* (1982), these authors—all parents of gifted children as well as serving the *gifted child education* field in professional capacities—collected information that assisted parents as they dealt with common childhood issues such as sibling rivalry and communication of feelings, as well as the more volatile topics of motivation and depression. For those who do not think that parenting a gifted child is any more difficult than parenting a less able youngster, consider these situations:

> When I discipline my child, she becomes a "Philadelphia lawyer" who argues about every loophole that I neglected to specify. Is this typical of gifted kids? How do I handle it? (p. 104)

> How do you channel motivation? My child wants to focus only on astronomy—morning, noon, and night. (p. 81)

> Are gifted children particularly likely to overschedule themselves? She tries to belong to every club in school, play all the sports, take every regular and optional class, and maintain a social life that would put Washington, D.C., to shame. I'm afraid she is going to burn herself out. (p. 124)

> My daughter talks about committing suicide, and I have heard that gifted children are extremely likely to kill themselves. How do I know whether she is just trying to get attention or whether she is serious? (p. 203)

The complexities of parenting, combined with the extraordinary intricacies of gifted children's minds, often create scenarios that are challenging to address in ways that are satisfactory to all parties. As one parent wrote to Jim Webb, "Gifted children really don't change your lifestyle; they destroy it." This book allays parents' fears and serves as a jumping-off point for discussion of parenting issues with other parents of gifted children.

. . . Which, in fact, is the story *behind* the story of *Guiding the Gifted Child.* Jim Webb was a clinical psychologist in the School of Professional Psychology at Wright State University in Dayton, Ohio. One day in 1980, he received a phone call from a set of parents who were looking for some help: Their son, a brilliant 17-year-old college student, had recently committed suicide, and they were looking for some group or organization that could help them to understand why someone so smart would choose to end his own life. What the Egbert family found was that even though there existed associations for educators of gifted children—the National Association for Gifted Children and The Association for the Gifted—there was nowhere to turn to get information helpful to *parents* whose gifted children were experiencing a social or emotional crisis.

Prompted by the Egberts' quest and questions, and his own inability to give them a resource group to soothe their souls, Jim Webb devised his own solution: He and a colleague (Betty Meckstroth, a graduate student and counselor)

Little by little I became interested in gifted education—and that's really all I did for a very long time. I was too shy to do anything. I read what I could find—it wasn't much, maybe an article in *Woman's Day* or something like that. I did not even join the PTA because I was afraid I would have to make a report and I was just too shy to speak up. I was cooking, baking, ironing and being enthusiastic about my kids' projects and homework. I was always there for my kids, but I didn't do their work for them. I expected A's, and when they didn't get A's when they should have, there were consequences. I think I ran, in my own shy, ignorant way, a pretty good environment for gifted kids—not for all gifted kids, but for *my* gifted kids.
—*Gina Ginsberg Riggs overcame her shyness and began the Gifted Child Society.*

would provide guided parent discussion groups for local parents who wanted to discuss their own concerns about raising gifted children. Topics were open to anything that was of concern to parents, although the 10-week sessions did address a set of concerns that seemed universal among parents of gifted children, including understanding what giftedness is (and is not), dealing effectively with schools that do not cater to the needs of gifted children, and parenting strategies that are effective even with nimble young minds. Further, Webb's university would provide formal intellectual and personality assessments, as well as follow-up treatment for families who needed it. Workshops for educators and school counselors, to help them to better understand the needs of gifted children, were also provided.

But this all took place in Dayton, Ohio—a nice city but hardly the hub of the universe. Were services such as these needed elsewhere, or was Dayton just an anomaly? That question was answered when Jim Webb, the Egberts, and then-director of The National Association for Gifted Children (NAGC), Joyce Juntune, appeared on a segment of the Phil Donahue Show in 1981 to discuss the suicide of Dallas Egbert, the 17-year-old genius, and to review the emotional needs of gifted children. Responses to that show were extraordinary: More than 20,000 people contacted NAGC asking for help, resources, and shoulders on which to cry. Indeed, the need to understand and help their gifted children was great; parents wanted answers and guidance, as did their children.

The capstones to all this interest were two: publication of *Guiding the Gifted Child,* and the formation of a group called Supporting the Emotional Needs of the Gifted (SENG), both in 1982. SENG continues to operate now, with its base at Kent State University in Ohio, just an interstate ride away from where it began in Dayton. Now retired from Wright State University, Jim Webb continues to work in support of SENG. Now a membership organization with members from virtually every state and several foreign nations, and an international conference that attracts hundreds of parents, educators, and gifted children every summer, SENG is a vital force for parents of gifted children. SENG's roots may be entrenched in tragedy, but its branches are clearly tentacles of hope.

> In the parents' group meetings, we have probably learned as much from them as they learned from us. We are deeply indebted to them for their sharing, courage and support. We all are learning to flow with, rather than fight against, a child's special abilities.
>
> —*Webb et al., 1982, p. iii*

> The Belin-Blank Center at the University of Iowa is important because of the traditional things it does, i.e., research, training and service. The Center is perhaps the most comprehensive of its kind since it also includes conferences, family counseling, and provides a practicum/internship site for graduate students. The Center serves students and educators not only nationally, but internationally. Again, a unique feature.
>
> But I feel another reason the Belin-Blank Center is important is the confidence that it instills in families and in professionals. Parents and families look to the Center for advice, understanding, and advocacy. I think a number of families feel that the Center understands their concerns and represents them well in consultations and discussions with their schools.
>
> Educators and researchers feel confident that the Center provides quality research, conferences, teacher training and professional service. There is a confidence that the Center staff is thorough and competent.
>
> —*Nicholas Colangelo directs the Belin-Blank Center.*

A PLETHORA OF STRATEGIES: ISSUE-DRIVEN GUIDANCE FOR GIFTED CHILDREN

It was mentioned previously that some of the techniques and strategies used in counseling people of high abilities are little more than general psychological principles applied to a different population, in this case gifted children. But what *are* some of these strategies, and how are they used most effectively? Although it is not the intent of this book to be a "how to" publication, several samples are definitely in order.

First, though, a distinction must be made between two related terms that are often used interchangeably but shouldn't be: *guidance* and *counseling.* Guidance is a preventive measure that provides information to children (or adults) that helps them to better understand who they are. As a *preventive* measure, guidance answers questions before they are asked. For example, by talking about how the issue of perfectionism often affects the lives of gifted people, gifted individuals can come to understand that they are not the first people to ever deal with this issue. Using a different example, when gifted high school students are allowed to interview college admission officials to discover what they look for in prospective students, they are provided with a source of in-depth knowledge that they can use to focus certain aspects of their future. Guidance does not assume problems exist; rather, guidance *presumes* that many people have similar questions about growing up and living a meaningful life.

Counseling, however, is a more direct and intrusive measure in which an individual—teacher, psychologist, therapist—targets a specific behavior, belief, or attitude that is intruding on a person's mental health. For example, a child with a measured IQ of 145 who is earning D's and F's in school is perceived by others as a failure; therefore, individual or group counseling to get to the reasons behind these low grades might be suggested. Or a teenager who drops consistent hints about his unhappiness with the world—"No one would notice if I'm gone" "The world is a stupid place and everyone dies anyway"—is probably seen as candidate for depression or suicide, and intensive counseling might be recommended. Unlike guidance, counseling targets specific areas of concern with the express purpose of changing one's behaviors or perceptions. If guidance is a searchlight that scans the horizon of developmental issues, counseling is a laser that pinpoints specific areas of perceived need.

Notice all the previous caveats: "perceived need," "intrusive measure," "probably seen as a candidate for depression." For whenever issues of guidance and counseling are addressed, there is an inherent bias on the part of the person doing the intervention that something needs to be "fixed" or "changed" for the client to enjoy a richer life. This attitude, of course, may run counter to what the gifted individual might perceive to be true, making the guidance and counseling process a difficult one to establish. Rebellion to the guidance or counseling process is a common reaction.

These issues notwithstanding, most experts and parents would agree that the social and emotional aspects of giftedness are well worth addressing with gifted children. And, once again, it is Linda Silverman who gives some of the best and most concrete advice as to how this can be done.

Silverman (1993, p. 73) divides the guidance and counseling interventions into several categories:

- Grouping with peers
- Restructuring systems
- Networking
- Group counseling/discussion
- Bibliotherapy
- Moral exemplars
- Mentors
- Internships
- Peer counseling
- Family counseling
- Individual counseling
- Support groups

Although lack of space here prevents a full discussion of each of these components of effective social/emotional interventions, a few examples are highlighted here.

1. **Grouping with peers:** Sometimes, the best strategy is one that is indirect, as is often the case with grouping gifted students with their intellectual peers. At that time, issues that affect their relationships with classmates, parents, and teachers can be discussed. Galbraith and Delisle's (1996) book, *The Gifted Kids' Survival Guide: A Teen Handbook,* offers advice and comments from both gifted teens and adults about ways to understand and appreciate giftedness within oneself. By having students read particular sections of this book, with follow-up discussion (and, probably, disagreements), a fuller understanding of giftedness might result. Further, Delisle (1987) compiled a collection of hundreds of comments from gifted young children about growing up gifted, categorizing them into sections such as *friends, expectations, parents,* and *future ambitions.* Allowing students to read and review these comments with others of "like minds" might ensure a fuller understanding and appreciation of their personal giftedness.
2. **Bibliotherapy:** The use of reading material to help solve emotional problems and to promote mental health, bibliotherapy is a time-tested technique that benefits many children, including gifted children. By associating with fictional characters who share concerns or attributes similar to their own, gifted individuals come to see the commonalities of the human condition.

This is what it means to be a gifted person:

A Afraid that at some point in time I'll slip and do something wrong and everyone will notice.

G Guilty, when pressured into *not* doing my best.

I Isolated, when others make me feel left out of "the group."

F Frustrated, when I do something great and everyone laughs.

T Terrified, when I don't know the answer and everyone stares at me.

E Excited, when I create something that everyone appreciates.

D Disgusted, when my special needs are neglected.

P Privileged, when I get extra time during school to do something for myself.

E Embarrassed, when the teacher announces my grades.

R Relieved, when people don't laugh at me for getting less than 100%.

S Satisfied, when I am able to help someone else with something they don't understand.

O On top of the world, when somebody says they enjoyed my work.

N Nervous, when pressured to always be the best.

Girl, 12, Pennsylvania
—Delisle, 1984, pp. 113–114

Each generation of young adult literature seems to have its own set of characters who spawn thoughts of similarity with gifted children. A currently popular book, *The Giver* by Lois Lowry (1993), details the life of a brilliant young boy who lives in a utopian world that he is selected to lead into the next generation—at a substantial loss to his personal identity. *Orange Cheeks* by Jay O'Callahan (1993) is a picture book about a 7-year-old, Willie, whose creativity always seems to get him into trouble. Before another visit to grandma's, Willie's mother admonishes her son to behave, warning him that if he doesn't, he won't return to his grandmother's house for a year. Of course, Willie gets into creative trouble once again (this time involving pencils and white-painted walls), resulting in a hilarious and poignant conclusion that many imaginative children will appreciate. Kurt Vonnegut's short story *Harrison Bergeron* (1950) shows what life is like in a future world where persons who are more intelligent than average must wear mental handicap radios in their ears to prevent them from taking unfair advantage of their brains.

Classic books such as *Wind in the Willows* by E. B. White, *A Wrinkle in Time* by Madeleine L'Engle (1962), *The Catcher in the Rye* by J. D. Salinger (1951), and *Bridge to Terabithia* by Katherine Paterson (1977), all help children and teens understand that their own uniqueness is actually shared by many who have come before them, both in history and in fiction.

For a detailed listing of books with gifted children as main characters, refer to Jane Piirto's book *Talented Children and Adults* (1994, pp. 416–418) or Judy Halsted's 1994 publication, *Some of My Best Friends Are Books: Guiding Gifted Readers From Preschool to High School.* Both resources share a wealth of titles that parents and educators can use with gifted children, or that they can use themselves, to comprehend their sometimes bewildering selves.

3. **Moral exemplars:** Another category of intervention mentioned by Silverman, the use of moral exemplars is similar in both intent and design to bibliotherapy. However, the distinction here is that instead of using fiction, gifted children are introduced, through biographies or autobiographies, to the lives of gifted individuals who maintained their integrity during difficult or torturous times. Well-known persons such as Eleanor Roosevelt, or lesser known individuals such as Etty Hillesum (1996), whose diary of her life in a concentration camp, *An Interrupted Life,* chronicles a life of pain and a refusal to relinquish her self worth, are useful, especially with introspective adolescents. Too, Anthony Godby Johnson's best selling *A Rock and a Hard Place* (1993), the diary of a teenager afflicted by AIDS after his parents sold him into child prostitution, also revels in the triumph of what can happen when a caring, compassionate outsider enters your life. Often more intense than fictional accounts, these true life stories carry life lessons that able students will understand and appreciate.

4. **Mentors:** As defined by Hillman (1996), mentors are individuals who have only one task: "to recognize the invisible load you carry and to have a fantasy about it that corresponds with the image in the heart" (p. 162). Mentors can be any age, but most tend to be at least a decade older than the "apprentice" (or "protégé"). What they share with each other is a common passion for an activity or area of study, but even deeper, they share a mutual respect that it is *important* to be enthused about whatever it is that excites them. Generally, mentors are in the enviable position of being able to correct and educate without the need to punish or discipline—similar to a doting grandparent who sends the kids home with mom and dad once they get cranky or tired.

The mentor/apprentice relationship goes through a predictable evolution, starting with the honeymoon period in which the mentor can do no wrong and the apprentice is as absorbent as angel food cake sitting in the high noon sun. Then, a comfortable pattern of learning takes place, with the apprentice generally receiving more responsibilities as his or her expertise begins to

---

THE FOUR MOST IMPORTANT FUNCTIONS OF A MENTOR

1. To serve as a role model in an area of mutual interest
2. To support and encourage the efforts of the apprentice
3. To provide support in the area of professional expertise
4. To provide opportunities for professional socializing and "networking"

He had an absolute passion for teaching! Nothing seemed to excite him like having a student suddenly grasp something. It is that excitement, rather than the specific subjects he taught, that has stayed with me and emerged as the most significant contribution of his mentorship.

—*Kaufmann, Harrel, Milam, Woolverton, & Miller, 1986, p. 577*

I participated in three semesters of a mentorship program. In one placement, I worked with a physician who does research at the university. In a second setting I worked with an attorney, and in a third a computer expert. I had great experiences in all three settings and felt like I could be successful in any of those professions. I guess I'm not any closer to knowing what I want to do in the future. Maybe I'll have to figure out a way to combine all three of those areas into a "custom designed" job.

Mike, age 17

—Excerpted from The Gifted Kids Survival Guide: A Teen Handbook *by Judy Galbraith, MA, & Jim Delisle, PhD, Copyright © 1996. Used with permission of Free Spirit Publishing, Minneapolis, MN.*

grow. Complaints of "this isn't fun anymore" tend to be heard now, as the apprentice realizes that any worthwhile endeavor requires more than a little effort to accomplish anything noteworthy. If the mentor begins to perceive that the apprentice is not receptive to the extra commitment it takes to be excellent, some resentment may begin to ooze into the relationship. Usually, an honest discussion of expectations is enough to reenergize the situation, and the working relationship continues to flourish.

More than occasionally, after an extended period of time together (longer than 1 year), the apprentice begins to want more challenge or to move in a direction that is different from the one being taken by the mentor. At this crucial point, one of two things generally occurs: The relationship evolves into one of shared equality, in which each member of the duo pursues independent work in the same general area; or the relationship begins to unravel, as neither party is comfortable with the new role that the other is assuming. That is, the mentor still expects the apprentice to follow his or her lead, whereas the apprentice is carving out new directions that seem unnecessary or in opposition to those of the mentor.

Mentor relationships tend to be especially effective with young gifted women seeking same-sex role models to emulate in career direction and selection (Kaufmann et al., 1986), as well as for economically disadvantaged gifted youth, who may need the opportunity to see possibilities that exist outside of the limited domain of their neighborhoods (Olszewski-Kubilius & Scott, 1992). Also, though, mentorships are purposeful for gifted youth in general, many of whom "suffer" from the dilemma of *multipotentiality,* the curiosity about many and varied fields of interest, and the ability to perform well in virtually any area that they choose. A mentorship gives gifted students with multipotential the opportunity to give their strong interest a "test run," to see if they truly understand and enjoy the many hidden facets of a career that may look great from a distance but a little less rosy up close (Sanborn, 1979; Delisle, 1992).

The best candidates for mentorship relationships appear to be students who are,

A weekly newspaper editor recently said that the only worthwhile thing he learned in college was how to use rubber cement. Unfortunately, he found his true interest too late. If he had known at the time of his high school graduation (or before) what field he would have liked to enter, he could have picked a college or university better suited to these interests and could have taken journalism, graphic arts, and communication courses that would have been beneficial. There are a lot of students now—including the gifted—in his shoes.

—American Association for Gifted Children, 1978, pp. 93–94

themselves, highly motivated, but they can also be extremely beneficial for students who have "turned off" to the constraints of formal education. This latter category of student will enter a mentor relationship with different attitudes and expectations than the more motivated student, but the results might be life changing.

Unfortunately, parents are not regarded as good mentors for their own children, for the obvious difficulties that ensue when one is playing the two sometimes conflicting roles of parent and teacher (Hillman, 1996). However, if parents do have specific, refined skills or talents that their child actively wishes to pursue with them, it would be best to follow the advice of Van Cliburn's mother, who taught him piano for years. "When I'm teaching you, I'm not your mother" was her admonition to him.

Mentor relationships are complex, living structures that can benefit all members involved, especially if both parties know in advance the different routes and junctions that this intimate relationship may take.

A CONCLUSION, OF SORTS

The Greeks had a word for the journey people take in their lives: *telos,* which translates into "that for the sake of which." Telos assumes that although each person has the choice to make decisions that affect his or her life, each decision is made with a general sense of purpose that it is a good choice in his or her overall growth. On an always rising trajectory, people strive to become better than they were the day before, more complete and satisfied than the selves they had been just hours earlier. It is those who understand and appreciate this telos the most who lead lives that are focused more on promise than plight, who transcend the day's shortcomings by realizing a bigger picture awaits those whose sense of vision is farsighted.

Gifted individuals, imbued with "a greater awareness, a greater sensitivity, and a greater ability to transform perceptions into intellectual and emotional experiences" (Roeper, 1982, p. 21), live their lives in a higher key. They know pain and elation as intimately as a mother knows her child, a fisherman his nets, a child his or her favorite blanket. They wonder why others do not sense what they sense or wonder what they wonder. They ask in subtle or overt ways to be understood as less of an exception and more of a rule, continually seeking reassurance that the person they are is perfectly acceptable, without modifications.

This chapter began with the statement that giftedness is something you are, not something you do. This one sentence, encapsulating the hopes, ambitions, and personal satisfactions that compose a satisfying life, was elaborated on eloquently by people named Leta and Linda, Michael and Kazimierz. In the end, understanding gifted children, and the adults who are a part of their lives, involves a commitment of the heart, a well-entrenched willingness to bypass stereotypes and expectations imposed by others, to reach a common hope stated

I was sure from the day I started high school that I wanted to be an English teacher. All the way through college, I took as many English courses as I could and the bare minimum in all other subject areas. The summer before I was supposed to go to graduate school, I got a part-time job at a bank. I liked it so much that I never left. Now, five years later, I wish I knew more about math and economics.

Andrew, age 26
—Excerpted from The Gifted Kids Survival Guide: A Teen Handbook *by Judy Galbraith, MA, & Jim Delisle, PhD, Copyright © 1996. Used with permission of Free Spirit Publishing, Minneapolis, MN.*

When I was growing up, I always wanted to be somebody, but I see now I should've been more specific.
—Lily Tomlin

long ago by someone who knew intimately the depth of the well from which sprang her soul:

> Sometimes I almost shake with the joy of thinking that I live in this day in the world, and that before I die I shall see the coming of a new religion, which is to touch the hearts of all. (Hollingworth, 1943, p. 116)

If one's reach must exceed his grasp, it seems that today is a good day to begin striving to do so.

GUIDING QUESTIONS FOR CHAPTER 7

1. Who are the principal leaders in research on social and emotional needs of gifted students, and what is the focus of their work?

2. What are the major issues in social and emotional development that affect gifted children?

3. What are "psychic overexcitabilities," and why is it essential for educators and parents of gifted children to understand them?

CHAPTER 7 RESOURCES TO REMEMBER

Mee, C. S. (1997). *2,000 voices: Young adolescents' perceptions and curriculum implications.* Columbus, OH: National Middle Schools Association.

This book is a compilation of 2,000 surveys and interviews with young adolescents talking about the lives that they lead—in school, at home, and with friends. Although this book is not targeted specifically for gifted students, all teachers and parents would benefit from hearing from the "consumers" of education: the students whom we teach. Many insights come from the mouths of babes, and we can learn much by listening to their concerns.

Rubin, N. (1994). *Ask me if I care.* Berkeley, CA: Ten Speed Press.

When a health teacher at a diverse, urban high school collects journals from her students for 16 years, you have to imagine that much wisdom can be found within these pages. *Ask me if I care* is an in-your-face portrayal of the angst suffered by many adolescents in this awkward age between childhood and adulthood. Many direct journal excerpts from students are included, on topics such as depression, teachers, and expectations. An especially valuable section that includes letters that students wrote to their parents but never sent offers poignant reminders of both the passion and sincerity possessed by high school students. Lots of strong language, but well worth it for the honesty portrayed.

Whitmore, J. R. (1980). *Giftedness, conflict and underachievement.* Boston: Allyn & Bacon.

If there is only one book that you read to understand the complex issue of under-achievement, this is the one to get—in fact, on this topic, it is the only resource that you'll need. Filled with a brief but thorough history of gifted child education, this book is a story of one teacher's attempt to change the behaviors and improve the self-concepts of young children diagnosed as severe underachievers. This complete volume is filled with so many personal and professional insights that it is no wonder that it began a whole new movement toward understanding gifted children who do not succeed in school.

CHAPTER
8

. . . AND ANOTHER THING

ADDITIONAL TOPICS OF INTEREST
IN GIFTED CHILD EDUCATION

Writing a book like this, one that purports to "cover the waterfront" with reviews of a multitude of topics, events, and people related to gifted children and their well-being, involves making many biased decisions. Which topics are important enough to devote page after page of text to them? Which individuals have had such a profound effect on future thinking and practice that they deserve their own biographic sketch or sidebar? What events in education and society have been transformational in relation to the ways that people think about and teach gifted children? Each of these decisions is based on the author's views and experiences within the field; and rightly or wrongly, this book is no exception to that formula. To the reader who believes, "I think more time should have been spent on _____ and less time on _____," all an author can do is say "You're probably right," because there is no way to argue logically a central point when it is being approached from different directions. To speak personally, how I teach, whom I have taught, and why I chose to be the kind of parent that I am all contribute to the selection (and omission) of content for this book. The same would be true if your name were on this book's cover.

Within this context, let me mention why this final chapter of the book is as vital as the previous ones, even if the topics themselves seem as diverse as the items on a buffet table at a United Nations luncheon. First, the researchers whose work is highlighted here have chosen to specialize in a field-within-a-field. Thus, the topic of perfectionism, a subsection within the broader topic of societal expectations of gifted individuals, has a small (but growing) base of theory and research that guides its practitioners. An entire chapter on perfectionism would be overkill, but its importance as a topic to someone living with a perfectionistic child or spouse might cause him or her to turn first to this section of the book. To this person, 2 pages on perfectionism are worth more than 20 pages on history.

A reader who enjoys a book—be it a textbook or a seedy novel—does so because he or she develops a personal relationship with its content. Similarly, an author writes best when he or she is committed to the book's purpose and style. The underlying message here is that one person's periphery is another person's core. With a little luck, this final chapter includes enough diversity of topic to give avid readers a launching pad from which to explore interesting ideas in greater depth.

The second reason for a final chapter that opens more doors than it closes is that the field of gifted child education was developmental in its origins, and it remains so today. It is ever-changing and growing, undergoing a metamorphosis as new research becomes available and the benefits of unearthing "old" knowledge become apparent. Indeed, from the time this book was first published until today, some aspects will already be incomplete or outdated. As an example, a current controversy involves the seeming "overabundance" of gifted children who are also labeled attention deficit disorder (ADD) or ADD with hyperactivity (ADHD). Ten years from now, that condition might no longer be used or its diagnosis popular, causing readers to question why the topic was broached at all. A similar case might be made for the popularity of the talent development approach to identifying giftedness. This idea came on us like a tsunami in the late 1980s and might just as easily return quietly to sea by the next decade. This final chapter, which takes into account the transient nature of some of gifted child education's "causes," gives readers of both today and tomorrow a glimpse into the dynamic nature of change.

Third, and most practically, not everything can fit into the previous chapters of this book without diminishing the importance of some of the subtopics covered here in more depth. Thus, a discussion on the effects of labeling gifted children, or of the legal issues that have arisen regarding the education of gifted children, might get lost in a gargantuan chapter on identification or curriculum. But in this chapter, where seemingly unrelated topics get to shine in their own lights rather than in the reflected shadows of others, more emphasis can be given where it is due.

In essence, please do not perceive this chapter as the "gifted attic," the place where dusty old ideas are stored because they have no direct use. Indeed, the topics herein may be as vital as any others in this book—who can refute that adolescent suicide among the gifted is important to address?—and by placing them together, as a collection, it is hoped that they will find a home in your head and in your heart.

PART A: ISSUES REGARDING THE EMOTIONAL HEALTH AND WELL-BEING OF GIFTED STUDENTS

Although it could be argued convincingly that virtually every topic in this book has some direct applicability on the lives of gifted individuals, there are certain issues that appear more connected to the real world of gifted children (and adults) than others. Among those are perfectionism, depression and suicide, underachievement, and the presence of giftedness with handicapping conditions such as learning disabilities or ADD. Each of these topics may be independent of the others, but some might appear linked together within the same individual.

It is important to note that perfectionism, depression, and other life circumstances are not present in every gifted individual, and even if these conditions are in evidence, they are not necessarily lifelong in duration. Like a summer cold or a winter fever, which can be suppressed by hot tea or antibiotics, these mental states can be overcome with "psychic balms"—an understanding counselor, a cherished confidant, a self-realization through reading biographies that your life, although unique, parallels those of countless others. Giftedness is a state of mind, literally and figuratively, and although research and clinical experiences forebode the likelihood of certain predispositions within gifted individuals, there is no universal correlation between the presence of high intelligence and that of particular mental or psychological traits or "flaws." The individual spirit or soul will always transcend any generalizations made about it, asserting its independence from a world of foregone conclusions.

Thus, as you read the following descriptions, keep in mind that not every gifted child or adult will contend with these issues in his or her life, and even for those who do, their personal end result may be more positive than the terms *depression* or *ADHD* imply.

ISSUE #1: PERFECTIONISM

Living a successful life is a lot like balancing a checkbook: Despite one's most careful calculations, there will occasionally be an unexpected bounce.

Perfectionism, a trait defined by Kerr (1991) as "a complex of characteristics and behaviors including compulsiveness with regard to work habits, overconcern for details, unrealistically high standards for self and others, indiscriminate acquiescence to external evaluation, and rigid routines" (p. 407), has been noted as being among the most pervasive and noticeable characteristics of giftedness (Whitmore, 1980; Silverman, 1993). Often involving all aspects of one's life—academic, social, physical—perfectionism has been seen by most as a tiger to tame, rather than a passion to be pursued. Perfectionism has been linked to anorexia and bulimia, especially in gifted teenage

Here are some of my concerns as a "gifted student." I hate it when adults are condescending to me simply because of my age (if it's because I've done something stupid, it's my fault). . . . I also hate it when my parents (usually my dad) show me off to friends and acquaintances. I talked to him about it and he does it less and less, but he still does it.

I hate it when I have so many thoughts that I lose one (which has happened to me at least a dozen times while writing this). I also hate it when I cannot think of anything, and when I have a really neat thought that I can't investigate more deeply because I just don't have the educational background.

I worry too much. I worry about "losing my talents." I worry about becoming average. I worry about my "lost childhood" and the opportunities I've missed because of my advancement. I worry I will burn out or overspecialize. I worry about how successful I will be in my career and whether my colleagues will accept me (and whether they do now).

Vamir wrote this when he was a 15-year-old college sophomore.

—*Excerpted from* The Gifted Kids Survival Guide: A Teen Handbook *by Judy Galbraith, MA, & Jim Delisle, PhD, Copyright © 1996. Used with permission of Free Spirit Publishing, Minneapolis, MN.*

girls, and also as a detractor to social relationships, in which someone's search for the ideal date or mate prevents him or her from associating with anyone who does not match the fairy-tale counterpart to Sleeping Beauty or Prince Charming (Adderholdt-Elliott, 1987). In a school setting, perfectionism in completing one's daily work was one of the prime reasons for underachievement in the highly gifted population of primary age children studied and taught by Whitmore (1980). The children *believed* they could not perform perfectly in academics; they would choose either to disrupt the class (. . . and do so perfectly!) or to ignore the work that they might succeed at if they gave it an honest attempt. They sought the status of "first worst" instead of "first best."

The pursuit of perfection, as opposed to the pursuit for excellence, is more concerned with the chase than the victory—indeed, with many perfectionists there can *never be* a victory, as lurking behind every apparent success is yet another hurdle to jump or obstacle to overcome. As stated by a gifted high school student examining his self-determined academic standards:

> Upon receiving a 90, I'd think, "This is almost a perfect paper I have, but would a college professor have given me the same grade? Or, are their skies different, higher than those of my teachers? If so, I should be his student. . . ." All this happened when I was fourteen and had only just entered high school as a ninth grader.
>
> I wondered daily about college. How high does one have to go to get nineties at this particular college? At Harvard? Yale? Oxford? Could I reach these heights? How much effort would it take? Just how "good" am I? *Just how smart is smart?* The questions constantly plagued me. . . . "How do I become better than the bestest best?" (American Association for Gifted Children, 1978, p. 13)

The issue of perfectionism can appear at a very young age and, according to Dabrowski (1972), is a conflict in a child's mind between "what exists" and "what should be." For example, a 4-year-old gifted child may have created a very intricate story in her mind, involving various supernatural characters and imaginary places, but she is unable to write or type her ideas quickly enough to get them down on paper before they leave her mind. The resulting frustration can end in age-appropriate behaviors, such as crying or tantrums, but the underlying *cause* of such overt behaviors may be the inner anxiety at

Former 1950's TV show contestant from *Quiz Kids* (a *Jeopardy!*-like game with bigger prizes and all child contestants), Claude Brenner, remembers his first real taste of competition and social stereotyping:

> MIT was a chastening experience. When you came having graduated first in your class, you discovered that everybody had graduated first in his class. There were a lot of people who'd never heard of, and didn't care about, *Quiz Kids*. . . . When we would go to a party . . . conversation would cease, there would be whispering, and in would walk Claude Brenner, the Quiz Kid. I wanted to make it with a girl because I was charming and good-looking and debonair and dashing and persuasive and seductive, not because I was a Quiz Kid. I want to be a success because I'm competent in my profession, not because I was a Quiz Kid.
>
> —*Feldman, 1982, p. 131*

not being able to translate into reality what exists in one's imagination. If this one incident is coupled with parents, teachers, and peers commenting on how smart the child is, an inner conflict can result, with the child asking herself, "If I am so smart, why can't I write my story?" The subsequent attempts at hurrying along the physical development of her fingers to match her mental condition lead to even more frustration, with a common response being, "If I can't do something perfectly, then I won't do it at all." As presented in chapter 7, this is yet one more instance of the presence of asynchronous development within a gifted individual.

Another reason for perfection—although the jury is still out on what actually "causes" perfectionistic attitudes and behaviors—is societal reactions to the work of gifted individuals. Take the Olympic Games as an example. Even though the athletes competing are among the most skilled and artistic in the entire world, the only person elevated to the status of "hero," the only individual asked to appear on cereal boxes or as a foot model for Reebok, is the person who rises to the peak of the pinnacle: the gold medal stand. Second place—the silver—is considered the first-place loser. This attitude, repeated daily in academic situations in which the student with a perfect 800 SAT score is lauded while the 750 barely causes a ripple of media interest or in a home where a $2 award is given for every report card A, while a very respectable B+ receives a smile and a pat on the butt to "try harder next time," creates an atmosphere in which the spores of perfectionism are germinated in great abundance. It is no surprise, then, that gifted students, expected by everyone—including themselves—to do "better than their bestest best" find less than perfection an unacceptable standard.

There are those who believe that the pursuit of perfection is a time-honored and respectable endeavor. Roedell (1984) sees perfection as the engine that drives the quest for great achievement, and Robinson and Noble (1991) believe that too much attention has focused on the negative impact of perfectionistic strivings, while ignoring the real benefits of the high self-esteem that is received when someone who sets high goals actually reaches them; it provides fodder to continue to urge to do more and makes one optimistic toward undertaking future challenges.

Perhaps the real issue involves a fine-line distinction between two concepts: excellence and perfection. Galbraith and Delisle (1996),[1] in giving advice to teenagers about understanding this distinction, propose the following:

> *Perfectionism* means thinking less of yourself because you earned a B+ instead of an A. *The pursuit of excellence* means thinking more of yourself for trying something new.
>
> *Perfectionism* means being hard on yourself because you aren't equally talented in all sports. *The pursuit of excellence* means choosing some things

---

[1] Excerpted from *The Gifted Kids Survival Guide: A Teen Handbook* by Judy Galbraith, MA, & Jim Delisle, PhD, Copyright © 1996. Used with permission of Free Spirit Publishing, Minneapolis, MN.

I must use myself as an example [of perfectionism] because I think it shows this tendency very well and was, in fact, a puzzle to me until I understood its origin. Our school was very successful in the early years, when our approach was a more traditional one. It was geared to the expectations of society and expected children to perform in the traditional mold. All this took place within a humanistic framework. . . .

Even though things went well, I felt we were not fulfilling our promise to children, and this in turn created a growing sense of guilt in me. I began to look for an alternate structure to facilitate children's development of the unique self and, at the same time, build a bridge toward society's expectations. Many gifted adults cannot find that "connection," that bridge. My only motivation was the feeling that the education we provided was not perfect—not giving children what they truly needed. . . .

When I finally discovered the open classroom and all its possibilities, I felt a great sense of satisfaction and release. Introducing the open classroom was not easy at first. It resulted in unhappy teachers and the withdrawal of some students from the school. From that perspective, the innovation was not a positive one. From my perspective, it was necessary to open a new door for growth of the children. . . . My motivation did not come from the outside and was not based on approval by others and society, but solely on the desire to create an approach which would allow children to become the persons they really were. Once the change had been made, it became obvious to teachers and parents that it was a positive one.

—*Roeper, 1995, p. 104*

you know you'll be good at—and others you know will be good for you or just plain fun.

Perfectionism means chastising yourself because you lost the student council election. *The pursuit of excellence* means congratulating yourself because you were nominated and deciding to run again next year—if that's what you want. (p. 72)

Like all traits psychological, moderation and selective implementation seem to be the key to success and personal fulfillment when dealing with perfectionism. If what Silverman (1993) contends is true—that "the gifted will continuously set unrealistic standards for themselves, will fight windmills and city hall, will persist when others give up, [and] will maintain their visions of what is possible even in the face of disaster" (p. 58), then adults must help gifted children understand the negative consequences of taking any one attribute too far while showing them the positive features of pursuing dreams and goals with vigor.

There is no GOD, only science reigns true.
Just a lie so that there is something to believe in,
A way to control others,
A refuge of faith for the weak.
In life there is love, happiness, kindness
But also hate, misery, pain
AND lies.
In death there is peace, an escape from Hell
There is no point to life, no reason to prolong it
But do what you can to enjoy it
While you have it.
But never fear death, embrace it
And remember
You're ALL going to die.
My views seem insane to the shallow mind.
Open yours and you might learn something.

—Written by a 13-year-old gifted student,
prior to hospitalization for two suicide attempts.

ISSUE #2: SUICIDE AND DEPRESSION

In Western cultures, there is no more tragic loss than the death of a child. When this death is by suicide—an apparently willful decision to die—and it is compounded even more by the presence of giftedness in the victim, the tragedy seems to deepen even further. "How could someone with so much seem to value his life so little?" is a question that parents and educators ask when they hear of the suicide of a gifted child or adolescent.

There is scant evidence and much folklore about the overrepresentation of suicide and depression among gifted populations. In some cases, the 19th-century notion that giftedness (they called it "genius") was but a short step away from madness (Lombroso, 1891) or that individuals had only so much brain power to use in a lifetime, implying that those who ripened early—the gifted—would also rot just as fast, which gave credence to the belief that highly intelligent people had a higher propensity for mental illnesses and self-destructive behaviors. This myth still prevails to some degree today, albeit in much less incendiary terms, when people talk about the gifted as "weird" or "different" or "too smart for his own good" or "socially inept."

But the incidence of suicide among the gifted population continues to be a matter of rampant speculation. Some have investigated this premise. A study by Lajoie and Shore (1981) examined whether depression and suicide were more prevalent among gifted populations. They came to no such conclusion as regards the number of suicides who would be considered intellectually gifted, but they did find that "the causes of suicide are . . . most accommodating to the idea of overrepresentation of the gifted, especially at college age" (p. 141). Likewise, Delisle (1986) and Leroux (1986) looked for evidence that the incidence of suicide was more pronounced among gifted adolescents than others but could find no such data. Webb, Meckstroth, and Tolan (1982) state an equivocal "perhaps" in answer to the question of whether gifted individuals are more susceptible to suicide but cite no research to justify their cautionary tone. Shneidman (1971), who has researched suicide for decades, presented the case studies of 30 of Terman's subjects to psychologists for their review. After reviewing the life histories of these 30 gifted adults, the judges were able to predict accurately which ones (there were 5) had committed suicide. The clues available through their negative life experiences were similar to those that would be found for many individuals contemplating self-destruction.

The real question is not the actual number of gifted individuals who are among the 6,000 adolescent suicides annually in the United States, but rather, the primary concern should be the prevention of this behavior among *all* adolescents, including those who are especially able. For even more startling than the actual incidence of suicide is the number of suicide attempts annually among adolescents that do not end in their deaths: approximately 400,000! And in this arena, the causes of suicidal gestures, we do find that the gifted offer us some unique vantages from which to view their pain.

Galbraith and Delisle (1996)[1] discuss several factors that seem to enter into the gifted student's decision to end his or her life, including

1. A perception of failure that differs from others' perceptions of failure. (For example, feeling that a B is equivalent to an F if your personal standard of success calls for an A or above.)
2. External pressures to always be #1 and a life orientation that identifies one as a "future leader" or a "mover and shaker of the next generation."
3. The frustration that comes when one's intellectual talents outpace his or her social or physical development. ("For being such a smart kid, I'm awfully dumb at making friends" or "Starting school early and skipping second grade was fine, but now I'm the freak of the locker room—I'm so puny!")
4. The ability to understand adult situations and world events while feeling powerless to affect positive change.

> **COMMONALITIES ASSOCIATED WITH GIFTEDNESS THAT WERE SHARED BY THREE GIFTED ADOLESCENT MALES WHO COMMITTED SUICIDE**
>
> 1. The boys expressed their overexcitabilities even in excess of those of their gifted peers.
> 2. The boys had minimal prosocial outlets.
> 3. The boys exhibited difficulty separating fact from fiction, especially in identifying with negative or asocial characters in books and movies.
> 4. The boys devalued emotional experiences, except for pain.
> 5. The boys engaged in discussions of suicide as a viable and honorable solution to life's problems.
> 6. The boys expressed high levels of development according to Dabrowski's guidelines.
> 7. The boys attended a residential high school as a means of escaping home-based problems.
> —*Cross, 1996, pp. 22–23, 50*

Perfectionism, discussed in an earlier section, combined with a supersensitivity to the world and its reactions to gifted children, may be a predisposing factor to self-destructive behaviors. So, even for those students who appeared to have everything going for them, psychic pain may exist to such a degree that suicide becomes a solution worth considering. Webb, Meckstroth, and Tolan (1982) call this "existential depression," stating that "most teenagers go through periods of

---

[1] Excerpted from *The Gifted Kids Survival Guide: A Teen Handbook* by Judy Galbraith, MA, & Jim Delisle, PhD, Copyright © 1996. Used with permission of Free Spirit Publishing, Minneapolis, MN.

A mother, who had contemplated suicide as an adolescent, writes about her son, who had been feeling lonely and depressed:

> The main point I tried to make (without pounding him over the head with it) was that no matter how awful he felt at night, *he would always feel better in the morning.* I tried to reinforce that during especially difficult times. Over breakfast, I would ask him, "Do you feel better now than you did last night? Even a little?" When he said "yes" (if he spoke to me at all), I would say "Remember that feeling and trust it."
>
> There will probably be times in your life (if you haven't had them already) when you feel hopeless and lonely—maybe even enough to consider suicide. When they happen, always promise yourself at least one more morning.
>
> —*Excerpted from* The Gifted Kids Survival Guide: A Teen Handbook *by Judy Galbraith, MA, & Jim Delisle, PhD, Copyright © 1996. Used with permission of Free Spirit Publishing, Minneapolis, MN.*

questioning their personal values, examining their relationships with others and searching for 'meaning'" (p. 194). However, gifted students often go through this existential depression at an earlier age—sometimes as young as age 8 or 9 and "because it is so unexpected, it may be overlooked, dismissed, and not given the serious consideration it deserves" (p. 195). Thus, left alone once again in a world that seems lacking in peers and personal meaning, some see suicide as a viable alternative.

Several strategies are indicated that may help gifted adolescents—and others—understand that suicide is a permanent solution to a temporary problem. The best and most effective strategies are *preventive* in nature, rather than *crisis oriented,* and can occur before an actual suicidal incident disrupts the relative calm of a junior high or high school. Culross (1982) writes that a developmental approach to guidance and counseling, in which fires are put out before they ever ignite, is most sensible. Thus, reviewing with gifted students the following subjects would be instructive for both their mental health and their daily living:

- reviewing what giftedness is and what it is not, as noted through literature, biographies, or personal experiences
- discussing personal, academic, and societal expectations
- debating the role that perfectionism does (or does not) play in their lives
- acquainting students with resources that they may tap into if they are experiencing emotional turmoil
- role playing what they would do if a friend asked "Can you keep a secret?" and then proceeded to detail a suicidal plan
- introducing students to community resources—confidential hotlines or health clinics, for example—that are available for students in crisis

Many of these strategies would benefit all adolescents, not just those identified as gifted. And that is exactly the point. As stated in an earlier chapter, gifted adolescents need to know that they are much more *a part of* the family of humans than they are *apart from* it. Some of the emotional undergirdings that come with growing up are not due to one's giftedness as much as they are intimately tied into one's humanity. Once this common denominator is discovered, then it is time for gifted adolescents to discover those elements associated with their intelligence that make some of their questions more intense, their emotional needs more pronounced.

Suicide—any suicide—claims more than one victim, and it is, in the end, a selfish act sometimes completed by an unselfish person. The reality of existential depression and the alternatives to suicide that are readily available to the gifted adolescent in pain are issues that we ignore at our children's peril.

ISSUE #3: THE MIASMA OF UNDERACHIEVEMENT

There was some mention in chapter 2 about the cyclical nature of research done on underachievement, starting with Raph, Goldberg, and Passow in the 1950s and reignited again in the 1980s, thanks to the work of Joanne Whitmore. Both of these works are powerful and worth exploring in much greater depth. However, the full picture of research on underachievement is a lot messier than those two renowned studies would imply. Indeed, if there is a more convoluted area of gifted child education than the research and practice that falls under the umbrella of "underachievement," it would be difficult to determine.

> According to the American Psychiatric Association, *Who's Who Among American High School Students' 26th Annual Survey of High Achievers* (1996):
>
> - Suicide is the third leading cause of death among teenagers; the second leading cause of death among college students.
> - Of the 3,351 high-achieving teenagers surveyed in *Who's Who*, 26% admitted having considered suicide and 4% had attempted suicide.
> - According to the Centers for Disease Control, suicide rates for teenagers have risen steadily in the past decades. Between 1980 and 1993, the suicide rate for 10- to 14-year-olds rose 120%; for 15- to 19-year-olds, it rose almost 30%. In this same study, of 16,000 high school students asked about suicidal gestures, nearly 1,400 admitted to an attempt within the past year.

Perhaps an example will put this into perspective. One of the first things parents are told when their child is not doing as well in school as test scores would predict is that "Your child is not living up to her potential." The teacher then goes on detailing, often with minute accuracy, the many instances in which papers are turned in messy and incomplete, if at all, and in which the child's full effort was not obvious. The parents often admit an equal amount of frustration with their child's performance. The "solution" is so universal that it should appear in a cookbook: "Put the child on a contract, begin a homework notebook, ask daily for the child to prove that efforts at school work were made, and remove privileges of fun or athletic activities if the child doesn't cooperate."

The only problem with this solution is this: It doesn't work!

Here's why: First, let us return to the underlying premise of the above solution—"The child is not living up to her potential." A simple follow-up question might be, "And how will we know when she *is* working up to her potential?" At what point does underachievement turn into achievement—when report card grades go from D's to B's? when the child initiates projects without prodding and coaxing? And who is to determine when "potential" is reached? The teacher? parent? child? What if each has different ideas on what level of success is acceptable and, indeed, what *areas* of success are important? By not defining either the terms or the yardsticks of measurement, everyone is at a loss when it comes to reversing patterns of underachievement. Also, if the only way

> Many parents of gifted children are trying to relive their own lives through their children; they push the children to do the things they wish they had done for themselves. This type of behavior frequently alienates the child.
>
> —*Perino & Perino, 1981, p. 62*

to measure success is by someone else's standards—a teacher's, a dad's—then the underachieving child may have little or no personal stake in changing or re-focusing energies in ways that are acceptable to these outside others.

Another related issue, and one that is intimately personal, is to ask *yourself* this question: "Are *you* living up to *your* potential?" Having posed this question to thousands of adults myself, I find that virtually none answers "yes." Instead, people want to know what *I* mean by potential, and whether I mean intellectual potential or success as a parent or athlete or singer. They want to know if *my* standards are the same as theirs before they answer "yes," and they want to know if I am going to ask them to prove their potential has been actualized and, if so, how. In other words, they want me to do what they often do not do with so-called underachieving children: to define my terms and to consider their own personal agendas for living their lives.

This first issue—the definitions of underachievement and potential—is only the tip of the proverbial iceberg when it comes to documenting why so much of the research on underachievement is confusing, conflicting, insulting to chil-dren, and downright wrong. Another problem is attitude. Note how one author (Clark, 1997) introduces the topic of underachievement:

> Underachievement in gifted children is one of the most baffling, most frustrating problems a parent or teacher can face. You can see the child's possibilities, occasionally you're given a glimpse of the brilliance, but then it's gone, replaced by a wall of apathy or seeming unconcern. But all of this may be just a facade, for the underachiever may be even more frus-trated than we are. (p. 490)

A careful reading of these few sentences, which are indicative of many of the descriptions that abound about underachievers, shows that even well-meaning words can carry a cruel message to a student: Underachievement (you) is bad, underachievement (you) needs to be fixed, and underachievement (you) shows a general lack of concern about learning. This attitude is at the same time pater-nalistic and ineffective, as it relies little on what most "underachievers" bring into their situations: high intelligence, passions in *some* area of life or learning which may have little to do with school, and a willingness to listen to and learn from someone who gives you what most adults do not—respect.

The main reason that underachievement "solutions" generally do not work in the long term is that the child is not invested in their success. If grades are raised, or punishments lessened, it is because the child has decided to play the game to win back a privilege. But as soon as the restraints are loosened, the un-derachieving behaviors will return, unless somewhere along the line someone takes the time to ask a simple, two-part question: "What's important to you, and how can I help you learn it?"

Underachieving students—every one of them—are successful at doing some-thing that they enjoy. Underachieving students—every one of them—wake up each morning with the hope that someone will find at least one good thing about who they are or what they do. Underachieving students—every one of them—

are not just "students" but "people"; and until the respect that they deserve for being active, feeling beings is acknowledged more profoundly than their academic actions, they will see little reason to alter the behaviors that cause others to criticize them as baffling or frustrating. Perhaps, to some underachievers, those two adjectives also describe the persons who are trying to change them.

To be sure, there are many respectful attitudes and actions that can help "underachieving" children in their quest for personal meaning and success. A stimulating school environment that is challenging and open-ended can be provided; strengths and interests that belong to the child can be acknowledged and encouraged within the classroom; school requirements can include alternative methods whereby the child can prove competence through various projects; so-called underachievers can remain in the gifted programs for which they qualify even if their classroom grades are so low that others want to change their academic placement.

These ideas are based on common sense and respect, not coercion and contracts. If they work, it will be less because of the actions themselves, and more likely because of the attitude shared by the person working with the "underachiever"; an attitude that respects a child's knowledge and interests.

In other textbooks on gifted child education, many step-by-step formulas and models for changing the behaviors of underachievers are offered. Yet they will not be mentioned here for a simple reason: Doing so would legitimize them as worthwhile when, in fact, most of them are not. With underachievement, however it is defined, changing behaviors is the easy part. But understanding the reasons behind a child's actions, and modifying curriculum or expectations or attitudes based on these reasons, are the true test of an advocate, someone who believes enough in a child to disregard the label and address the individual behind it.

ISSUE #4: THE EFFECTS OF LABELING A CHILD AS GIFTED

The label of "gifted"—indeed, any label—need be nothing more than a tag that indicates to others something that is unique about you. "Tall," "brown-eyed," "athletic": These are all labels, too, yet few people seem to take offense when these terms are applied to them.

"Gifted," though, is another thing altogether, for with it comes all manner of unintended baggage:

> I am constantly being reminded how smart I am and it's getting pretty sickening. (Girl, 11, New York)

> Being called "gifted" is fine, but when a teacher brings it up I feel like an outsider, considering most of my friends aren't gifted. (Boy, 11, Connecticut)

> I don't mind being called gifted as long as I'm not stereotyped as being perfect. (Boy, 9, Georgia)

> Sometimes people think "gifted" means stuck up and they think that you are going to make fun of their grades because they don't make as good grades as you do. (Girl, 13, Mississippi)

> —Delisle, 1984, pp. 15, 17

The reasons behind the discomfort that sometimes accompanies the label of "gifted" have been studied by educators and sociologists alike. Colangelo and Davis (1991) assert that part of the problem is our society's love–hate relationship with giftedness. That is, although Americans love to see people succeed (especially if they had to overcome great odds to do so), too much success, especially if it seems to have been achieved without much effort, goes against the grain of a culture, like ours, that purports to be democratic in both opportunity and outcome. And since the word itself, *gifted,* implies to some that you were *given* something (a "gift") without needing to expend any effort to earn it, our egalitarian culture is uncertain whether this gift is to be lauded or ignored. In a related study on the effects of labeling, Colangelo and Brower (1987) found that family dynamics were affected negatively when one child was identified as gifted and a sibling was not. Although this negative attitude diminished over time, its appearance at all shows that this one word—*gifted*—can send shivers up the spines of both those who wear the label and those who do not.

Barbara Clark (1997), a pioneer in programming for gifted students, provides a poignant example of why the label of "gifted" needs to be explained both to those to whom it is given and others around them who must accommodate it:

> An interesting, though frustrating, experience occurred at our university when we began a General Honors Program for students in their first two years who had shown a great deal of academic potential in high school. Immediately, some professors began shifting their course presentation and requirements, leaving out the basic information and requiring synthesis of graduate-level work. These professors became very disappointed and angry at the students and complained loudly against the program, all because of their expectations of "honors" students. Talking with them about student need or potential ability made no impression. (p. 303)

Thus, one of the major problems of labeling gifted children may not be the word itself (although there appears to be a general consensus, at least among children, that the term *gifted* is more of a burden than a blessing) as much as it is the expectations of others that are layered within it.

Apart from the academic issues surrounding the label of "gifted," it is the social ramifications of this intellectual tag that seem to prey even more wickedly on so-labeled youngsters. As Marya Mannes writes, "In our society, to admit inferiority is to be a fool, and to admit superiority is to be an outcast. Those who are in reality superior in intelligence can be accepted by their fellows only if they pretend they are not" (Galbraith & Delisle, 1996, p. 16).[1] Perhaps this social aversion to being called smart is a natural reaction to a society that says one

---

[1] Excerpted from *The Gifted Kids Survival Guide: A Teen Handbook* by Judy Galbraith, MA, & Jim Delisle, PhD, Copyright © 1996. Used with permission of Free Spirit Publishing, Minneapolis, MN.

thing and then does another in relation to its acknowledgment of intellectual giftedness. In a study titled *Brains, Brawn and Beauty: A Context Analysis of Adolescent Response to Three Superlatives (Intelligence)* (1995), Schroeder-Davis analyzed more than 3,000 responses from teenagers who were asked which they would rather be in their high school: the smartest, the most athletic, or the best looking. Although the results differed somewhat between age groups, with older students being more comfortable with their minds, many of the respondents, whatever their choice, agreed with the following:

- Student athletes are more respected by peers than student scholars.
- The "pure scholar" (the nonathletic academic achiever) is the least popular student in the typical school.
- Intelligent students report doing worse in school subjects than they are capable of doing to avoid being labeled a "nerd" by classmates.
- All students spend more time per week on virtually anything other than schoolwork, including socializing, sports, extracurricular activities, TV, work and listening to the radio.

> The culture tries to make the child with a gift into a one-sided person, to penalize him at every turn, to cause him trouble in making friends and to create conditions conducive to the development of a neurosis. Neither teachers, the parents of other children, nor the child's peers will tolerate a Wunderkind.
> —*Mead, 1954, p. 213*

Given these conditions, both inside and outside of schools, it is no wonder that some gifted students do whatever they can to disguise the fact that they are smart. When being average academically seems to carry more social rewards than being smart, who wouldn't want to cover up their abilities?

If nothing else, these societal misgivings about the label of giftedness and what it implies academically and socially create a natural point of discussion for a group of students who have been identified and labeled as gifted. To address openly, without fear of social ridicule, the high points and hassles of growing up gifted; the unrealistic expectations held by some adults; the cruel comments from classmates who criticize gifted students' high standards yet poke fun at any grade they get that is not an A: These are the issues surrounding the label of "gifted" need to be discussed with children, in hopes that they will grow to see that acceptance of an intrinsic quality like intelligence is really a personal choice that, although guided in part by societal reactions, is ultimately a matter of concern to them as individuals.

ISSUE #5: ATTENTION DEFICIT DISORDER AND GIFTEDNESS

Enter any chat room on the World Wide Web devoted to parents of gifted children and one of the first things encountered is a rash of questions and concerns about the copresence of giftedness with ADD or ADHD. Indeed, enough visits to this Web site might lead browsers to believe that the only *truly* gifted children are those who have problems attending to their school tasks! Without a doubt, the controversial issue of giftedness and ADD/ADHD has been one of the "hottest topics" of this past decade among both advocates and critics of gifted child education.

My struggles aren't over. They began early in my education. I always found it so difficult to understand what was being said in class! For example, when the teacher told us to follow multiple directions ("Fold your paper like a hot dog and then turn it 90 degrees"), I would not have a visual picture of what the final result should look like. Therefore, I would immediately rely on my neighbor's product for clues. I felt like crying knowing I couldn't rely on my own abilities. They were there, but I didn't know how to apply them.

Aaron, age 18
—*Excerpted from* The Gifted Kids Survival Guide: A Teen Handbook *by Judy Galbraith, MA, & Jim Delisle, PhD, Copyright © 1996. Used with permission of Free Spirit Publishing, Minneapolis, MN.*

ADD and ADHD are "the new catch-all diagnoses for children, gifted or otherwise" (Davis & Rimm, 1994, p. 356). They are characterized by such qualities as fidgeting, distractibility, disorganization, excessive talking, and a difficulty in following directions. (The distinguishing mark between ADD and ADHD is that the ADHD child has more "hyperactive" movements than does the ADD child, who handles his deficit more quietly.) Ironically, these same qualities, when they appear in a classroom setting, may also be indicative of a gifted child who is bored! However, if teachers are not aware of this (and many are not), they may look no further than the most convenient label: ADD/ADHD. The end result may be that a gifted child, responding in ways that are perfectly understandable for anyone who exists in an intellectually stifling environment, is seen as the *cause* of the behavior problem; but, indeed, the problem may actually be elsewhere, as in a curriculum that is not appropriately challenging for a child with exceptional abilities (Armstrong, 1995; Delisle, 1995).

Although ADD/ADHD is often treated as a biologic condition, the diagnosis itself is often made informally, by nonmedical personnel—including parents and educators. Frustrated by a child's short attention span or frequent classroom outbursts, teachers often seek out answers to explain these disruptive behaviors, frequently falling on the most common culprit: ADD/ADHD. Parents are called to school for a conference with their child's teacher, and all agree that medical attention should be sought to isolate this condition once and for all. However, if the pediatrician is not aware of the characteristics of gifted children (and, again, many are not), then the symptoms are quickly labeled as ADD/ADHD, and the drug Ritalin is often prescribed.

And, to be sure, Ritalin does have a calming effect on many children's behaviors. In fact, research on Ritalin by Anastopoulos and Barkley (1991) shows that it sublimates behaviors of *all* children, whether they are labeled ADD/ADHD or not.

But the question must be asked: "In getting a more complacent child through medication, what are we losing?" Often, the very sparks that made a child stand out as exceptional—the ebullient child who cannot wait to respond to a friend's or teacher's question, the curious drive to know everything about anything— are driven from a child, replaced by a calm, complacent demeanor that shows few signs of intellectual spunk or creative challenge. Also, some children on Ritalin experience unwanted (and sometimes unseen by others) side effects—social withdrawal, sadness, headaches, and loss of energy. To be sure, the child now appears more able to concentrate in the classroom, but the question must be asked: "Concentrate *on what?*" If the work is still easy for the child to complete, providing little intellectual fodder for the bright young mind, then what have we gained?

The ascription of the label of ADD/ADHD to a gifted student places the child at fault for his or her behaviors. Often, no further explanations are sought to determine why a bright, enthusiastic child is concentrating on anything and anyone but schoolwork. Seldom is the issue raised as to whether the school setting is appropriately challenging or the teacher's personality is at odds with the child's. It is seldom suggested that a change in the child's curriculum (or teacher) might diminish some of these inappropriate behaviors, and there are too few instances of determining the settings in which the child *does* attend, *does* complete work, and *does not* appear disruptive.

In not asking these questions, teachers and parents risk giving the child a label and a medical regimen that are both unwanted and unnecessary. As Thomas Armstrong (1995), a promoter of educating using multiple methods, writes on the situations surrounding the ADD label:

> I'm reminded here of the canaries that were kept by coal miners deep in the mines. If the level of oxygen fell below a certain level, the canaries would fall over their perches and die, warning the miners to get out fast. It's possible that children who have been labeled ADD are the canaries of modern-day education; they may be signaling us to transform our nation's classrooms into more dynamic, novel and exciting learning environments. ADD may, then, be more accurately termed ADDD: Attention-to-Ditto-Deficit-Disorder. (p. 36)

Such modern-day thinking that permeates Armstrong's words is not really that new at all. Reflecting once again on the wisdom of Leta Hollingworth, we find that she wrote about this same situation:

> Where the gifted child drifts in the school unrecognized, held to the lockstep which is determined by the capacities of the average, he has little to do. He receives daily practice in habits of idleness and daydreaming. His abilities are never genuinely challenged, and the situation is contrived to build in him expectations of an effortless existence. (Hollingworth, 1931, p. 5)

The ADD/ADHD appellation to gifted children—indeed, to *all* children—has reached crisis proportions. Ritalin prescriptions for ADD/ADHD have reached epic dimensions, and even groups such as the National Association for School Psychologists

In 1951, as a graduate student learning to do child assessments, my late husband, Hal Robinson, was asked by his professor, Maud Merrill (co-author of the Stanford Binet) to work with a student who was not doing well. Jerry (not his real name) was gawky, myopic, and he stammered when he spoke. He was socially inept, disinterested in school, and flunking fourth grade. Jerry's father, an army colonel, was thoroughly disappointed in his "sissy" son, who wrote poetry and wasn't at all good at games like his younger brother. Despite marked anxiety and what we might now term attention deficit disorder, on the Stanford Binet, Form L, Jerry attained a ratio IQ of 212. On all other measures, his standard scores were 150 upward, and his language and reasoning were strikingly advanced. While matters remained problematic at home, in school Jerry gained support from a by-now more sympathetic teacher who used the diagnostic information to devise more challenging assignments. Jerry immediately learned to multiply, for example, in order to calculate the accelerating path of a rocket.

—Nancy Robinson is a professor, psychologist, parent, and grandparent of gifted children.

have begun to speak out on the misdiagnosis of ADD/ADHD and overreliance on this label. Also, the rampant misdiagnosis of ADD/ADHD does little to help children *truly* afflicted with this disorder; those who are impaired to the point at which, despite environmental modifications, the ADD/ADHD behaviors continue. These children (and some adults) need interventions from the medical arena, and continued research on them to ascertain if the causes of ADD/ADHD may reveal include biologic or neurologic conditions. ADD/ADHD does exist, but it does little good when the diagnosis is so oversubscribed that the very presence of the condition causes justifiable suspicion.

Recently, a rating scale has been developed to assist parents and educators in understanding the causes of children's inappropriate behaviors (Figure 8.1). If used well and wisely, this scale, developed by educational consultant Sharon Lind, may cause adults to see "problem" children in a far brighter and more positive light.

Perhaps, in a decade or so, this extreme emphasis on ADD/ADHD will have passed. But if it does, it could be replaced by some other acronym that seeks to explain why gifted and bright children fail to do well in school. Then again, maybe the acronyms will end and the reforms will truly begin; reforms that look beyond children as the source of problems that may reside not in them, but rather, in the classrooms that they inhabit and the low expectations and substandard curriculum that gifted children often endure.

PART B: OTHER ISSUES RELATED TO THE FRUITION OF TALENTS

ISSUE #6: GIFTED ADULTS

A 15-year-old girl, grade accelerated so that she was already a sophomore in college, was reflecting on her upcoming 16th birthday—the birthday that, to her, meant she was a "grown up":

> There is some correlation between age and maturity, but not really all that much. Just as I am realizing that 16 is an artificial age of maturity that I have created for myself, the age of 18 or 21 is just as artificial. It is an expiration date that the government has placed on all our childhoods, and it is just as exact as those placed by the FDA. Nothing horrible will happen to toothpaste if it sits on the shelf too long, but the FDA has determined that there is a higher chance that it will be ineffective if it is over such an age. The same strategy is used for determining the age of maturity, only in reverse. It is a horrible, inexact method of determining maturity, yet at this age, you are automatically entitled the rights and responsibilities of running the country and being liable for your own actions. Age and maturity shouldn't necessarily be tied, as book and moral learning are quite

FIGURE 8.1

■

Before Referring a Gifted Child for ADD/ADHD Evaluation

Parents and gifted educators are asked with increasing frequency to instruct gifted children to conform to a set of societal standards of acceptable behavior and achievement—to smooth the edges of the square peg in order to fit into a "normal" hole. Spontaneity, inquisitiveness, imagination, boundless enthusiasm, and emotionality are being discouraged to create calmer, quieter, more controlled environments in school. An extension of this trend is reflected in an increase in referrals for medical evaluation of gifted children as ADD/ADHD (Attention Deficit Disorder/Attention Deficit Hyperactivity Disorder). There is no doubt that gifted children can be ADD/ADHD. However, there are also gifted children whose "inappropriate behavior" may be a result of being highly gifted and/or intense.

This intensity coupled with classroom environments and curriculum which do not meet needs of gifted, divergent, creative, or random learners, may lead to the mislabeling of many children as ADHD. To avoid mislabeling gifted children, parents and educators may want to complete the following check list to help them decide to refer for medical or psychological evaluation.

Gifted?	Need More Information	ADD/ADHD?
❐ Contact with intellectual peers diminishes inappropriate behavior	❐	❐ Contact with intellectual peers has no positive effect on behavior
❐ Appropriate academic placement diminishes inappropriate behavior	❐	❐ Appropriate academic placement has no positive effect on behavior
❐ Curricular modifications diminish inappropriate behaviors	❐	❐ Curricular modifications have no effect on behavior
❐ The child has logical (to the child) explanations for inappropriate behavior	❐	❐ Child cannot explain inappropriate behavior
❐ When active, child enjoys the movement and does not feel out of control	❐	❐ Child feels out of control
❐ Learning appropriate social skills has decreased "impulsive" or inappropriate behavior	❐	❐ Learning appropriate social skills has not decreased "impulsive" or inappropriate behavior
❐ Child has logical (to the child) explanations why	❐	❐ Child is unable to explain why tasks, activities are not completed
❐ Child displays fewer inappropriate behaviors when interested in subject matter or project	❐	❐ Child's behavior not influenced by his/her interest in the activity

continued on the following page

continued from the previous page

Gifted?	Need More Information	ADD/ADHD?
❏ Child displays fewer inappropriate behaviors when subject matter or project seems relevant or meaningful to the child	❏	❏ Child's behaviors do not diminish when subject matter or project seems relevant or meaningful to the child
❏ Child attributes excessive talking or interruptions on need to share information, need to show that he/she knows the answer, or need to solve a problem immediately	❏	❏ Child cannot attribute excessive talking or interruptions to a need to learn or share information
❏ Child who seems inattentive can repeat instructions	❏	❏ Child who seems inattentive is unable to repeat instructions
❏ Child thrives on working on multiple tasks—gets more done, enjoys learning more	❏	❏ Child moves from task to task for no apparent reason
❏ Inappropriate behaviors are not persistent—seem to be a function of subject matter	❏	❏ Inappropriate behaviors persist regardless of subject matter
❏ Inappropriate behaviors are not persistent—seem to be a function of teacher or instructional style	❏	❏ Inappropriate behaviors persist regardless of teacher or instructional style
❏ Child acts out to get teacher attention	❏	❏ Child acts out regardless of attention

If, after addressing these questions, parents and teachers believe that it is **not** an unsuitable, inflexible, or unreceptive educational environment which is causing the child to "misbehave" or "tune out," or if the child feels out of control, then it is most certainly appropriate to refer a gifted child for ADD/ADHD diagnosis. Premature referral bypasses the educational system and takes control away from students, parents and educators. By referring before trying to adjust the educational environment and curriculum, educators appear to be denouncing the positive attributes of giftedness and/or to be blaming the victim of an inappropriate educational system.

When deciding to refer, parents should search for a competent diagnostician who has experience with both giftedness and attention deficit disorders. It is never appropriate for teachers, parents or pediatricians to label a child as ADD or ADHD without comprehensive clinical evaluation that can distinguish ADD/ADHD from look-alikes with other causes.

—Sharon Lind, M.S. Ed., 1996

separate, but it is something to think about. ("Elizabeth," personal journal, 1996)

Elizabeth, one of countless thousands of gifted young adults seeking their own place in the ocean of existence, took the time to do what many others sidestep: question her own perspectives on life's meaning. People need to remember that which is often forgotten: Gifted children *do* grow up, and the same fears, joys, and dreams they raised as toddlers they will raise again as grown-ups. The Bogey Man might no longer be lurking in the bedroom closet, but the monsters still exist. More amorphous than before, they can still jump out with little warning, causing startled glimpses of the shabby reality presented by an imperfect world.

So what happens to gifted kids grown up? Not just those famous ones, the subjects of longitudinal studies with noted childhood success, but the everyday gifted students who sit in classrooms everywhere, excelling or not; those who play football at recess and then question the relevance of chaos theory as it applies to faking a pass. Those who shun the word *gifted* yet wallow in the intellectual excesses that this label naturally brings. Those with friends, those seeking friends, those who don't know how to make friends. Brilliant all, and introspective by nature, it follows that they do not stop being so when they graduate from high school or college. Instead, they continue to develop, investigating the world around them with continued intensity. So, who are these gifted adults, and what can others learn from them?

First, the famous. There have been several books and multiple longitudinal studies that have focused on answering the question, "Whatever happened to . . . ?" Subotnik and Arnold (1994) compiled voluminous research on talented children whose lives had been followed through adulthood. The fruition of talents was seen as being the result of several conditions, including

Timing: Accomplished scientists did their first experiments as young children. Talented musicians transformed their ability to "sightread" music into virtuoso musicianship. Indeed, there appear to be ideal times, depending to a good degree on the discipline being explored, when the recognition of talent is essential to its development.

Interests: What children did when they didn't have anyone watching was often a key to identifying "signposts of talent." (p. 438)

Mentoring: "Experts enhance the gifts of the novices they mentor" (p. 439), as they served at least four useful purposes: as role models, emotional supporters, intellectual sparring partners, and professional networkers for the talented young people who sought their guidance.

Family context: The ability and willingness of families to be supportive of their talented children was often a key ingredient to later success.

Felice Kaufmann, in her ongoing study (1981, 1986, 1992) of Presidential Scholars, students who were chosen as part of a national effort begun by President

Lyndon Johnson to honor academic excellence in high school seniors, found that the 1964–68 Presidential Scholars, by the time they were between 26 and 32 years of age, had accomplished the following:

- 97% had received college degrees; 81% had earned advanced degrees.
- 92% had received special classes or opportunities in their education, including gifted programs (as children) or other opportunities, as adults, sponsored by such august groups as the National Science Foundation.
- 76% were employed in high-prestige occupations, including professor (20%), physician (13%), and lawyer (9%).
- 67% reported no participation in organized activities out of work, citing lack of time or not being a "joiner" as their reasons.
- 66% reported that their most significant mentors had been teachers.

In addition to reporting these raw data, Kaufmann also hit some raw nerves, by asking her respondents to reflect on their life satisfaction and happiness through open-ended questions. And although the majority excelled academically and in their chosen professions, some individual comments made by respondents make them appear more fragile than their meteoric rise to success might imply. Some resented that their entire identity was based on their academic prowess, as one subject mentioned poignantly that "when I was little, what I wanted to be when I grew up was to go to college." Further, others questioned why they had been selected as Presidential Scholars in the first place, as no one explained to them why this honor had been bestowed. Still others assumed that their selection as a Presidential Scholar would make for effortless achievement in the future and were disappointed when this did not occur:

> If my childhood hadn't been so idyllic, I wouldn't be so cynical now. I feel I was misled by the nature of life by my parents and teachers—it's much more grim than I imagined. (Kaufmann, 1979, p. 83)

Most, however, expressed that their caustic views may have been based as much on immaturity as disappointment, and that their naivete—even as academically brilliant students—was as rampant in them as in any child of the turbulent 1960s:

> In the '60s, many of us had a grossly exalted view of our own impotence. Today I see an exaggerated sense of importance among the youth which is just as harmful. Whatever happens to me, I doubt that I will succumb to the latter illusion. (Kaufmann, 1979, p. 84)

The Presidential Scholars, those young people whom our nation's leaders chose to put on pedestals, are still being studied today by Felice Kaufmann. As the TV networks say, "stay tuned."

Another view of gifted adults can be seen in an interesting retrospective glance at Terman's study completed by J. Shurkin (1992), who, in addition to reviewing the life accomplishments and failures of *Terman's Kids* (his book's title), also presents a three-dimensional view of the man himself, Lewis Terman. It is not an altogether complimentary view, addressing not only Terman's professional biases but his personal flaws and sexual dalliances with graduate students. Nevertheless, Shurkin points out that Terman's study, despite the flawed sampling techniques to locate potential subjects and his lack of a control group of subjects, has much to relate about the care and feeding of brilliance. For example, Terman's kids, once they matured into adulthood,

- gave proof that extremely intelligent people are not generally eccentric, egocentric, or maladjusted
- proved the value of advanced education, as higher school achievement correlated with greater life successes
- showed that those with the most education also evidenced the most happiness in their lives
- indicated that a close family bond, with a surprisingly strong role played by the fathers, figured prominently in their attributions of their own success
- related that the ability to set goals and the perseverance to achieve them were primary reasons for their success

One nugget of insight that Shurkin (1992) mentions only briefly is the importance of a personal mentor or confidant in the life of Terman's kids. Many of them actually sought out Terman himself, or his colleague, Robert Sears, for guidance or special favors:

> Not all people go through life knowing that when they are troubled, when they need advice, when they need help getting into a school or getting a job, when they need money, no matter how long they live, there is an office and a psychologist they can call and be welcomed. Free. Even if they needed only the therapy of opening their heart to someone by correspondence, the Terman subjects knew where to go. (p. 291)

One could argue that this lifelong closeness bordered more on a familial bond than it did a relationship between researcher and subject. But when someone knows intimate details about you—when menstruation began, or when pubic hair appeared, or whether you were homosexual, happily married, or mentally ill—perhaps one can better appreciate the fondness that Terman's subjects showed their "grandfather." Still, although Terman's interventions were always done to help, his relationships with his subjects may have polluted the cleanliness of his research results, skewing them toward the positive. As Shurkin (1992) says, "The relationship between subject and scientist in the Terman study was entirely understandable, human, unprecedented, and wrong. This does not invalidate all or even most of his results. One could only wish Terman had behaved himself" (p. 292).

Still, the Terman research continues to enjoy tremendous respect in the research community, due, in great part, to the careful records maintained to this day about the comings and goings of psychology's greatest subjects: 1,528 "Termites" who came to the attention of a "round-shouldered, bespectacled, red-haired, forty-four-year-old professor of psychology at Stanford University" (Shurkin, 1992, p. 3) in 1922, Lewis Terman.

There have been other longitudinal and retrospective studies on the making of genius (Vaillant, 1977) and world-class athletes and performers (Bloom, 1985). There was also the quirky but significant study conducted by Goertzel and Goertzel in 1962, in which the basis of their research plan was to "include each person who has at least two books about him in the biography section of the Montclair, New Jersey Public Library if he was born in the United States and all persons who have at least one book about them if they were born outside the United States" (p. viii).

Each of these studies points to a continued fascination with the fruition of talent. The lives of these famous or anonymous people are examined from the framework of both researchers and voyeurs. One must ask if this analysis is done as much for titillation as for knowledge—one eye watching a documentary and, the other, a soap opera. Humanity—theirs and ours—shows through each time the question is asked, "I wonder what ever happened to . . . ?"

In addition to these specific studies of genius-in-the-making, there are those who have examined the emotional characteristics of the general population of gifted adults, and one of the prime clinical researchers in this area is someone whose work was referenced earlier: Annemarie Roeper. Stating that giftedness is a state of being, rather than a switch that can readily be turned on or off, Roeper (1995) sees gifted adults as being an extension of the children whom they once were: complex, introspective, compelling. She believes that gifted adults have an impact on their environment ("Where would we be today without Darwin . . . or Eleanor Roosevelt? Where would we be if there had not been Hitler?" p. 94), and she believes that the environment has an impact on gifted adults ("Unsupportive environments can lead to depression, to the suppression of one's abilities, even to feelings of desperation that could become self-destructive" p. 95).

In elucidating the characteristics of gifted adults, Roeper (1995) emphasizes the following:

- *Gifted adults often feel fundamentally different about themselves than others feel about them:* Normal feelings of inadequacy or anxiety may not be allowed in gifted adults whom others perceive as leaders. They are not forgiven the presence of human frailties.
- *Gifted adults are often driven by their giftedness:* Due to an inner drive to understand one's world and to create a better one, gifted adults operate on overdrive. "They must climb the mountain because it is there" (p. 98).

- *Gifted adults are not necessarily popular:* They may have few friends, but what their relationships lack in breadth they make up for in depth. Again, intensity is real, even in personal communications.
- *Gifted adults are global thinkers:* They can see patterns and trends. The "big picture" takes on much more importance than the small details, often putting them at odds with colleagues whose vision is more myopic.
- *Gifted adults excel in too many areas where they would like to work, discover, and excel:* Getting involved in so many different arenas, they may not do well in any, or conversely, they may struggle to complete everything perfectly, increasing their own anxieties and that of those around them.

Other characteristics—sensing the difference between justice and equality, having a complex sense of humor, difficulty in accepting authority unless it is ethical and honest—can help set apart gifted adults from others, especially in the workplace.

These characteristics, mirroring those of gifted children, have similar implications for everyday life. Gifted adults need to find friends and mentors who are like them in intellect and temperament; they need the freedom to pursue their passions and to change their directions as they gain new and interesting insights; they need to allow themselves the ability to show their human frailties without fear of ridicule that "if you're so smart, why couldn't you . . ." comments, similar to ones they may have heard in grade school when they received an unexpected grade of C on a math quiz.

Ellen Winner (1996), in her review of creative adults, finds that the drive and energy that caused Picasso to create 20,000 works and Edison to obtain 1,093 patents must sustain them through what she calls the "ten-year rule: the dictum that it takes about ten years of hard work in a domain to make a breakthrough" (p. 293). This drive, coupled with an intense, focused attention that often sacrifices comfort, relaxation, and personal relationships in the process, also earmarks highly accomplished creators. Also, unflinching confidence in their own talents, which allows them to be "thick-skinned enough to sell themselves" (p. 295), goes hand-in-hand with societal recognition. As Winner concludes, "Caring about pleasing everyone cannot be a priority for anyone who is going to challenge an established tradition" (p. 296).

. . . And speaking of conclusions, it's time to move on to another topic, even if the world of gifted adults is one that is so rich with depth and contradictions that it makes it an area of study worth pursuing deeper and deeper. Like an artichoke whose heart is buried between tasty layers of greens, the journey to the core is, in itself, an enticing experience.

ISSUE #7: LEGAL ISSUES AND THE GIFTED

A second-grade child is intellectually gifted. The parents say so. The IQ score of 145 says so. The school personnel say so. However, the child is not performing well in school. After much discussion, it is determined that, among other things, the child may be bored in school due to a lack of differentiated program services that address the issues of highly able students.

When the parents request that their child be placed in a gifted education program, they are told that no such services begin until fourth grade. For all manner of biases that are logical only to those on whom they are not inflicted—"We don't like to label children at such a young age" or "All young children have something to learn from their classroom teachers"—the parents are, in effect, told to put their child's gifts on hold for the next 2 years. The parents' response? "We don't think so!"

As the parents turn to the legal system looking for ways to force the issue of gifted programming for their child, they discover several things:

1. Gifted students of any age are not protected by a federal statute that requires schools to identify and address their special needs. (Such laws are available only to individuals with disabilities, including, ironically, *gifted* children with identified disabilities.)
2. Laws in individual states vary widely regarding the education of gifted students, with some states requiring identification and service, some just identification, and several states requiring nothing at all be done for gifted students.
3. Even if educational services for gifted students are provided, they are seldom based on the development of an individual educational plan (IEP) agreed to by educators and parents. In effect, the gifted program, good or bad, becomes the *de facto* service offered all gifted students, despite individual needs that may require other services.

Frances Karnes and Ronald Marquardt—she a professor of gifted education, he an attorney and chair of a political science department—have addressed the issue of gifted children in the law in two books, both published in 1991. In discussing the different state laws and regulations regarding the education of gifted children, they find that parents have been frustrated by the lack of uniformity across this nation. Essentially, the same child can be gifted in Pennsylvania, receiving state-mandated services, only to move to Ohio or New York and find that they may or may not be eligible for gifted programming services! "The transfer (of a student) from one school district to another based on the need for advanced instruction will be a persistent question in gifted education" (1991a, p. 161).

Strongly suggesting that parents look for informal ways to resolve disputes with their child's school before embarking on the "expensive, time consuming, adversarial, and emotionally draining" (1991a, p. 37) costs of litigation within the court system, Karnes and Marquardt cite a sequence of steps that should be taken by parents to gain some satisfaction from their school system. The first step is *conferencing* with the teachers and principal, coming (it is hoped) to an agreement of service delivery options that will satisfy everyone. If that does not work, the next step is a *mediation meeting,* during which time "a disinterested person, usually from outside the district, who is specially trained to help resolve conflict in an informal setting" (1991a, p. 107), is engaged. After hearing all sides of the disagreement, the mediator arrives at a written agreement of who will provide what to the gifted child in question. If the agreement is acceptable to all parties, the dispute ends here, and services begin. Of course, the selection of the mediator is essential in this situation. One does not merely walk down Main Street and ask, "Hey! Are you a disinterested person? We need you to mediate a dispute." Indeed, all mediators are professionally trained to handle this role with impartiality and confidentiality, two prerequisites whose importance cannot be understated.

If the mediator is not able to resolve the differences between the parents and school district, the next step is much more formal: a *due process hearing.* Based on the Fourteenth Amendment of the U.S. Constitution, which requires that no person can be deprived of a "property right" without just cause and a justifiable explanation (i.e., "due process"), the courts have determined that education is a property right of everyone. However, this constitutional "property right" of education does not specifically apply to gifted child education, leaving it up to each state to determine whether they wish to allow this intermediary step between mediation and litigation. To date, nearly half of the U.S. states have granted due process authority to resolve disputes about gifted children and their education. At its initiation, a due process hearing begins with the selection of a due process officer, often appointed by the state superintendent of education (or some other such official). A date is set for a formal hearing, a transcript is made of the testimony given, and a formal, written decision is announced. Parents still dissatisfied with the results may appeal the decision, which often results in the case being heard in a state court.

In various due process cases, parents have both won and lost. For example, in four Alabama cases cited by Karnes and Marquardt, two were decided in favor of the student's placement in a gifted program, one was denied admission based on variances in the child's test score data, and a fourth achieved a compromise, for when the parents sought a private school placement for their gifted child who was not being served in the public schools, the due process officer denied this request but required that the public school hire a gifted teacher or consultant.

Barring any success using the above methods, parents may choose to go through their state court system to resolve their dispute. Typically, though, the length of time required to complete this process is so great that the child in question may be married with two children by the time a decision is reached! Court cases, then, often set precedents for other children, rather than affecting the lives of the specific child in whose name the suit was first proposed. Parents who choose this route very often blaze the path down which others will tread.

Karnes and Marquardt believe that future disputes involving the education of gifted children will include the legitimacy of age of admission criteria to school (both kindergarten and postsecondary); whether a student enrolled part-time in college classes may use these course credits toward high school graduation; whether state law requiring mandatory school attendance applies to students enrolled in a postsecondary institution; and whether students talented in the arts will earn the same legal right to receive an education that is afforded to academic gifts. To answer at least some of these questions, the complementary volume to the Karnes and Marquardt book cited previously presents *Parents' Stories of Hope* (1991b), a collection of negotiated and court-sanctioned solutions to working effectively with gifted students within this system of education that we call the public schools.

A very legitimate question may be asked: "Why does anyone—parent or educator—need to go this far to get appropriate services for gifted children?" The answer (or, at least one answer) is given by Karnes and Marquardt (1991b), who assert that "if gifted education advocates at every level continue to strive for the nation's resources to appropriately assist outstanding students, perhaps in the not too distant future, we will have a federal law mandating appropriate education for America's gifted youth" (p. 154).

An earlier pioneer, a young man who disembarked at Ellis Island in New York Harbor in 1912, wrote a letter home regarding his views of his new home: "Before I came to America, I heard the streets were paved with gold. When I arrived, I learned three things. First, the streets weren't paved with gold. Second, they weren't paved at all. And third, I was expected to pave them." How parallel a route parents of gifted children seem to be paving in their quest for an appropriate education road down which their children can travel. . . .

A STUDENT DISCUSSES HIS OWN HOMESCHOOLING

The best part of being homeschooled is that I can be ME. I don't have to try and fit into some mold that teachers and other kids demand. I remember in first grade when I was doing some rote homework assignment, I asked my mom: "Is this what it takes to get from first to second to third grade, and so on?" I really wanted to understand "school," but it didn't make much sense. I guess even at age five I knew this wasn't learning.

At home I learn about what I am interested in when I am interested in it! Without busy work, I have time to do important things like publish a newspaper for kids and work for world peace. I enjoy spending the school day with my parents, who love and understand me, and spending the afternoons with my neighborhood friends in an unstructured way where we can just have fun.

—Jason Crowe is an 11-year-old who loves homeschooling, playing with friends, helping people in need, and life.

ISSUE #8: HOMESCHOOLING AND THE GIFTED

Writer Laura Ingalls Wilder never met artist Andrew Wyeth. Philosopher John Stuart Mill never had a chat with Franklin Delano Roosevelt. It is doubtful that Pearl Buck ever met Thomas Edison. But if some magical twist in the universe allowed them to all convene for coffee, they would all have something in common to discuss: their experiences being homeschooled.

The homeschooling movement is about as recent an invention as oxygen; it has been around, informally or formally, since parents and children began. But the emphasis on homeschooling as an appropriate intervention for gifted students is a more recent phenomenon. Growing each year, homeschooling is now the education of choice for approximately 1 million children, with an increasing number of these children being identified as gifted or talented (Kearney, 1989).

Why would parents of gifted children choose this time intensive option to educate their progeny? The most common reason, cited by Silverman (1994), is that the public schools are either unable or unwilling to accommodate the talents of its brightest youth. In many cases, then, unable to locate or afford a private school alternative, parents select the homeschooling choice. Actually, "select" may be the wrong verb, as some parents feel that homeschooling is something they do by default, rather than choice.

In the case of Laura Ingalls Wilder, whose mother taught her during times when they were living too far from a school building, or when they were in the migrant mode, traversing the Dakota Territory by wagon train, homeschooling is often done for a period of time rather than for the child's entire school career. Even Lewis Terman, gifted's greatest superstar, homeschooled his son, Fred, for a short period. As reported by Seagoe (1975), "Fred did not learn to read until he was eight years of age. As a child, Fred had many interests and was less dependent than the average boy on the companionship of other children. As a result, his parents did not bother to start him in school at the usual age of six" (p. 37).

Many parents feel more comfortable and confident using homeschooling when their children are younger and the content of their lessons easy for an adult to understand. But as their children age and the questions about their subjects' content get harder and harder, parents often rely on another alternative to homeschooling, even if it is a reluctant return to public schools.

But other alternatives do exist. Winner (1996) describes a young adolescent, Alex, whose parents chose to enroll him in a correspondence course to obtain a

---

JASON'S PARENTS DISCUSS WHY THEY HOMESCHOOL THEIR SON

Weeks after our son's first experience with school, the vibrant, curious, loving, spontaneous child disappeared. When three years of parental and professional advocating produced neither curricular nor learning style modifications, and when Jason started talking about suicide, we knew we had to act. Since there is no school for the highly/profoundly gifted near us, homeschooling was our only option.

Its greatest benefit has been the rebuilding of Jason's self esteem through love, affirmation, and flexibility of hours, subject scheduling and a multi-level curriculum which builds on his strengths. Homeschooling allows time for travel, university lectures, special events of Jason's choosing, and most importantly, time for him to pursue his passion for humanitarian causes.

The major drawback is our inability to provide the amount of intellectual and sensory stimulation needed. Also, Jason is very weak in organizational skills and time management; homeschooling does nothing to improve these areas. Furthermore, it's hard to be both parents and teachers twenty-four hours a day!

Yet homeschooling is worth the sacrifice when Jason reminisces as he did last spring: "The teachers at school never really knew me. They only knew the facade they created, and they didn't even like that!"

—*Dennis and Cindy Crowe are educators and homeschooling parents of a gifted 11-year-old.*

A MOTHER OF A HOMESCHOOLED CHILD SPEAKS OF SOCIALIZATION

Our son, like many gifted children, often feels awkward with other children. Unless we find the magical common denominator between Chris and another child, there is no playing. For a long time, whenever I'd ask my son if he played with anyone at preschool, he'd say "Why do you want me to play with kids so much, Mom? You know I'm not that kind of child!"

. . . Interestingly, I now realize that the best socialization, if we define this by the quality of closeness (i.e., trust, openness, deep communication), takes place out of school. My own deepest, most valuable friendships as a child came from neighborhood pals, and I don't think my experience was uncommon. Long talks on the front steps, building forts in the woods, sleep-overs, all offered the makings for real friendships; it was only outside of school that I had the freedom, the environment and the wealth of time that allowed for the building of intimacy.

. . . A child home with a parent and siblings, or doing errands with Mom or Dad practices socialization all day long. Homeschooled children are often very well socialized, as they come into contact with a much wider range of ages, and types of people, than children spending their days in classrooms of same-age peers.

—*Haydock, 1997, p. 17*

high school diploma. Today, Alex is a successful entrepreneur designing computer graphics. Also, Winner speaks of Peter, a young resident of rural Arkansas, whose mother wanted him to start school at the age of 3 because his quest for advanced knowledge was so strong. She explains that Peter wanted to solve equations "when you don't know the numbers" (p. 237), but the school superintendent advised day care, a place where algebra is generally not taught. Not content with this response, Julia (Peter's mother) convinced the superintendent to give her the kindergarten curriculum, which Peter quickly exhausted. By the age of 4, he had completed the third-grade curriculum.

When Peter was eligible for kindergarten, at least in age, his mother again intervened on his behalf. Rather than place him in a school setting where he would receive a 25-minute period every 2 weeks of a gifted enrichment program (and that not until third grade), she chose to educate him at home, using resources such as a math program developed at Stanford University and excerpts form Alex Haley's *Roots* (1976) and Mark Twain's *The Adventures of Tom Sawyer* (1946) to review history and civil rights. For bedtime reading, Peter's dad read him books such as George Orwell's *Animal Farm* (1946).

By far the biggest concern expressed by opponents of homeschooling is the lack of social opportunities that such a cloistered educational environment affords. However, Kearney (1989) dismisses this concern, stating that "many homeschooled children are more socially adept than their peers in regular schools, because their homeschool programs involve social experiences with people of all ages as well as chronological-age peers" (p. 15). Activities such as team athletics, 4-H, dance or art classes, and religious gatherings in which children are involved all provide opportunities for social experiences in which homeschooled children meet other children of their same age. Further, the increasing use of technology and the World Wide Web allows children to "talk" to one another across town or across the globe, sharing experiences, questions, and concerns that may prompt long-lasting friendships. Although there may be no substitute for a flesh-and-blood friend, the notion that all homeschooled children are social isolates seems more a matter of folklore than reality.

Winner (1996), not a fan of homeschooling ("I would consider it to be a last choice because it means children do not have the experience of being with their peers"— p. 268), expresses another concern about parents of homeschooled children, one that is seldom discussed in polite company and will certainly incur the wrath of those who refute it. She states there is sometimes a narcissistic tendency of parents to think that no educational setting is good enough for their gifted child, resulting in constant admissions and withdrawals from various public and private schools. Thinking no one can do a better job than they as teachers of their children, they opt to educate their children at home. "This way," says Winner, "they can see their children as brilliant victims, and themselves as saviors" (p. 205).

> In the parenting process, I have come to realize the importance of three things. First, helping my children grow toward a sane estimate of their own abilities. We encouraged them to develop, express and apply their gifts at home, school, church, and in their community, while always asking the question, "For what purpose are we doing this?" Second, attaining a balance between unconditional love and their skill development. We were aware that some children feel accepted only by the quality of their performances; we wanted to affirm their value as persons, too. Third, we encouraged our children to take advantage of and develop a grateful attitude toward the special persons and opportunities that helped them along the way. We looked for creative ways to say "thank you."
> —*Judy Oraker is a wife, a mother of three gifted children now grown, and a part-time elementary school teacher.*

One would hope that the type of parent discussed by Winner is in the distinct minority of those who homeschool their children. Her comment does, however, bring up a truth that will serve as this section's conclusion: The homeschooling option for gifted children, as historically steeped as it has been through the centuries, remains a controversial choice that will often be second-guessed by school officials who question the motives of parents who do it. The other reality is this: Until gifted children are given priority status in our nation's public schools, there is little doubt that many of their parents will select the homeschooling alternative and that the number of homeschooled children across America will grow. The "goodness" or "badness" of this situation will likely continue to be a matter of substantial debate among educators, including parents.

SELECTIVE INCLUSION

As this chapter (and book) ends, there are still many topics affecting gifted children that are absent from these pages. Shaking this volume as if to reveal some marginal notes that will fall magically from the book's spine, some readers will be disappointed that among the topics not discussed were allergies and the gifted child, sibling issues when one child is gifted and another is not, birth order and its correlation with giftedness, or ways to establish a community-based support group for gifted children. All these topics are important, and somewhere, in another book by another author, the answers to the legitimate questions and concerns that these issues present can be found.

But books must end somewhere, and if this volume were Cinderella dancing gleefully while the midnight hour approached, the pages would soon turn into pumpkins and a little gray mouse would become the book's narrator.

There you have it: a conclusion to the book that matches the "Once upon a time . . ." phrase that began chapter 1.

Gifted child education is a series of stories—Hollingworth's students' perceptions of school; J. P. Guilford walking across campus with Mary Meeker, discussing SOI; Jason wondering when another McDonald's restaurant will disintegrate—and its leaders are a big group of storytellers. As you reach this book's end, closing its back cover, it is hoped that the "happily ever after" conclusion that accompanies so many of our childhood fantasies will not take full hold of your psyche. For there is still more to read, still more to write, still more to learn, still more to wonder.

The best stories are timeless, our favorite fairy tales filled with truths. May your quest in this land of knowledge about gifted children and their education continue with enthusiasm and renewed passion every time you come across one of "those" kids: the gifted children, the ones who give you goosebumps as you watch in awe at the insights known by kids who are just slightly ahead of their time.

The end.

GUIDING QUESTIONS FOR CHAPTER 8

1. What are some important issues in the lives of gifted individuals that transcend schooling and curriculum?

2. What specific social, emotional, and intellectual needs are often encountered by gifted adults?

3. Do gifted children have any specific legal rights to appropriate educations, and if so, what are these rights?

CHAPTER 8 RESOURCES TO REMEMBER

Feldman, D. H. (1986). *Nature's gambit: Child prodigies and the development of human potential.* New York: Basic Books.

In this book, David Feldman highlights the lives of six child prodigies, providing intimate portrayals of how they are different from and similar to other children who surround their lives. The reading is often mesmerizing; the stories are as unique as the children themselves. Writing from a developmental view of human growth, Feldman blends his expertise in understanding children with the personal flavor of a storyteller. In a word, this book is "compelling."

Sapon-Shevin, M. (1994). *Playing favorites: Gifted education and the disruption of community.* Albany, NY: State University of New York Press.

There has to be one book on this list that is so controversial that you will either recite it as dogma or resent it as propaganda. Sapon-Shevin cites gifted child education as a well-articulated plot to separate the intellectual chaff from the wheat. In doing so, she contends that the entire community of learning is disrupted. She makes some broad generalizations and some precise complaints, but one thing is for sure—when you finish her book, you will know where she stands about educating gifted children.

Walker, S. Y. (1992). *The survival guide for parents of gifted children.* Minneapolis, MN: Free Spirit Publishing.

When parents have questions about raising their gifted children, the best person to turn to is often someone who has "been there"—another parent. In this book, the author (a parent of gifted children and a gifted program coordinator) breaks through the jargon and provides honest, understandable advice to raising gifted children with respect and dignity. Many good resources are included for parents who wish to follow up with even more information.

REFERENCES

Abraham, W. (1958). *Common sense about gifted children.* New York: Harper & Brothers.

Adams, J. L. (1974). *Conceptual blockbusting: A guide to better ideas.* San Francisco: W. H. Freeman.

Adderholdt-Elliott, M. (1987). *Perfectionism: What's bad about being too good?* Minneapolis, MN: Free Spirit Publishing.

American Association for Gifted Children. (1978). *On being gifted.* New York: Walker.

American Psychiatric Association. (1996). *Who's who among American high school students' 26th annual survey of high achievers.* Washington, DC: American Psychiatric Association.

Anastopoulos, A. D., & Barkley, R. A. (1991). Biological factors in attention deficit-hyperactivity disorder. *CH.A.D.D.ER, 5*(1), 15–16, 27–28.

Armstrong, T. (1995). ADD: Does it really exist? *Phi Delta Kappan, 77*(6), 424–428.

Arnold, K. D. (1993). Undergraduate aspirations and career outcomes of academically talented women: A discriminant analysis. *Roeper Review, 15,* 169–175.

Baldwin, A. Y. (1994). The seven plus story: Developing hidden talent among students in socioeconomically disadvantaged environments. *Gifted Child Quarterly, 38,* 80–84.

Barbe, W. B. (1955). Interests and adjustments of adults who were identified in childhood as gifted. *Progressive Education, 32,* 145–150.

Barbe, W. B. (1957). What happens to graduates of special classes for the gifted? *Ohio State University Educational Research Bulletin, 36,* 13–16.

Barron, F. (1969). *Creative person and creative process.* New York: Holt.

Baum, S. (1988). An enrichment program for gifted learning disabled students. *Gifted Child Quarterly, 32,* 226–230.

Belcastro, F. (1987). Elementary pull-out program for the intellectually gifted—boon or bane? *Roeper Review, 9*(4), 208–212.

Benbow, C. P. (1992). Mathematical talent: Its origins and consequences. In N. Colangelo, S. G. Assouline, & D. L. Ambroson (Eds.), *Talent development: Proceedings from the 1991 Henry B. and Jocelyn Wallace National Research Symposium on Talent Development* (pp. 95–123). Unionville, NY: Trillium Press.

Bernal, E. M. (1979). The education of the culturally different gifted. In A. H. Passow (Ed.), *The gifted and the talented* (pp. 395–400). Chicago: National Society for the Study of Education.

Betts, G. T. (1985). *Autonomous learner model for the gifted and talented (ALM).* Greeley, CO: ALPS.

Bloom, B. S. (Ed.). (1956). *Taxonomy of educational objectives—the classification of educational goals handbook I: Cognitive domain.* New York: David McKay Co.

Bloom, B. S. (Ed.). (1985). *Developing talent in young people.* New York: Ballantine Books.

Borges, M. (1997). Millicent Borges describes her education in gifted programs. *Gifted Education Quarterly, 11*(4), 12.

Borland, J. (1989). *Planning and implementing programs for the gifted.* New York: Teachers College Press.

Brown, R. G., Cole, D. B., & Cornell, R. H. (Eds.). (1981). Mathematics. In *Respecting the pupil: Essays on teaching able students* (pp. 63–69). New York: Dell.

Bruch, C. B. (1971). Modification of procedures for identification of the disadvantaged. *Gifted Child Quarterly, 15,* 267–272.

Bruch, C. B. (1975). Assessment of creativity in culturally different children. *Gifted Child Quarterly, 19*(2), 164–174.

Bruch, C. B., & Curry, J. A. (1978). Personal learnings: A current synthesis on the culturally different gifted. *Gifted Child Quarterly, 22,* 313–321.

Burroughs, M. C. (1979). *Restraints on excellence: Our waste of gifted children.* Hingham, MA: Teaching Resources Corp.

Callahan, C. M. (1979). The gifted and talented woman. In A. H. Passow (Ed.), *The gifted and talented: Their education and development* (pp. 401–413). (78th Yearbook of the NSSE). Chicago: University of Chicago Press.

Callahan, C. M., Tomlinson, C. A., & Pizzat, P. M. (Eds.). (undated). *Contexts of promise: Noteworthy practices and innovations in the identification of gifted students.* Charlottesville, VA: University of Virginia.

Chaunchey, H. (1958). Measurement and prediction—tests of academic ability. In J. B. Conant (Ed.), *The identification and education of the academically talented student in the American secondary school.* (pp. 27–35). Washington, DC: National Education Association.

Checkley, K., & Willis, S. (1996). Bringing mathematics to life. *Curriculum Update.* Alexandria, VA: Association for Supervision and Curriculum Development.

Checkley, K. (1997). Problem-based learning: The search for solutions to life's messy problems. *Curriculum Update* (Summer), 1–3; 6–8.

Clark, B. (1988). *Growing up gifted* (3rd ed.). Columbus, OH: Merrill.

Clark, B. (1992). *Growing up gifted* (4th ed.). New York: Merrill Press.

Clark, B. (1997). *Growing up gifted: Developing potential of children at home and at school* (5th ed.). Upper Saddle River, NJ: Merrill.

Colangelo, N., & Brower, P. (1987). Gifted youngsters and their siblings: Long-term impact of labeling on their academic and social self-concepts. *Roeper Review, 10,* 101–103.

Colangelo, N., & Davis, G. A. (Eds.). (1991). *Handbook of gifted education.* Needham Heights, MA: Allyn & Bacon.

Coleman, J. S. (1961). *The adolescent society.* New York: The Free Press.

Coleman, M. R., & Gallagher, J. J. (1992). *Report on state policies related to the identification of gifted students* (grant R206-A00596). Chapel Hill, NC: University of North Carolina. Gifted Education Policy Studies Program. U.S. Office of Educational Research and Improvement.

Coleman, M. R., & Gallagher, J. J. (1995). The successful blending of gifted education with middle schools and cooperative learning: Two studies. *Journal for the Education of the Gifted, 18*(4), 362–384.

Columbus Group. (1991, July). Unpublished transcript of the meeting of the Columbus Group, Columbus, OH.

Comenius, J. A. (1657). *Didactica magna.* Amsterdam, Netherlands.

Council of State Directors of Programs for the Gifted. (1994). *The 1994 state of the states gifted and talented education report.* Austin, TX: Author.

Cox, J., Daniel, N., & Boston, B. A. (1985). *Educating able learners: Programs and promising practices.* Austin, TX: University of Texas Press.

Crawford, R. P. (1978). The techniques of creative thinking. In G. A. Davis & J. A. Scott (Eds.), *Training creative thinking* (pp. 52–57). Melbourne, FL: Krieger.

Cross, T. (1996). Psychological autopsy provides insight into gifted adolescent suicide. *Gifted Child Today, 19*(3), 22–23, 50.

Culross, R. R. (1982). Developing the whole child: A developmental approach to guidance with the gifted. *Roeper Review, 5*(2), 24–26.

Cutts, N. E., & Moseley, N. (1957). *Teaching the bright and gifted.* Englewood Cliffs, NJ: Prentice Hall.

Dabrowski, K. (1979). *Theory of levels of emotional development.* Oceanside, NY: Dabor Science Publications.

Dacey, J. S. (1989). *Fundamentals of creative thinking.* Lexington, MA: Lexington Books.

Davies, P. (Ed.). (1976). *American heritage dictionary.* New York: Dell.

Davis, G. A. (1975). In frumious pursuit of the creative person. *Journal of Creative Behavior, 9,* 75–87.

Davis, G. A. (1992). *Creativity is forever.* Dubuque, IA: Kendall-Hunt.

Davis, G. A. (1998). Identifying creative students and measuring creativity. In N. Colangelo & G. A. Davis (Eds.), *Handbook of gifted education* (pp. 269–281). Boston: Allyn & Bacon.

Davis, G. A., & O'Sullivan, M. (1980). Taxonomy of creative objectives: The model AUTA. *Journal of Creative Behavior, 14,* 149–160.

Davis, G. A., & Rimm, S. B. (1994). *Education of the gifted and talented* (3rd ed.). Boston: Allyn & Bacon.

Davis, G. A., & Rimm, S. B. (1998). *Education of the gifted and talented* (4th ed.). Needham Heights, MA: Allyn & Bacon.

de Bono, E. (1970). *Lateral thinking.* New York: Harper Colophon.

de Bono, E. (1971). *New think: The use of lateral thinking with generation of new ideas.* New York: Basic Books.

de Bono, E. (1983). The direct teaching of thinking as a skill. *Phi Delta Kappan, 64,* 703–708.

de Bono, E. (1986). *Six thinking hats.* Toronto, ONT: Key Porter Books.

de Bono, E. (1992). *Sur/petition: Creating value monopolies when everyone else is merely competing.* New York: HarperBusiness.

Delisle, D., & Delisle, J. (1996). *Growing good kids: 28 activities to enhance self-awareness, compassion, and leadership.* Minneapolis, MN: Free Spirit.

Delisle, J. (1991). Remembering the Roepers. *Advanced Development Journal, 3,* 95–98.

Delisle, J. R. (1984). *Gifted children speak out.* New York: Walker.

Delisle, J. R. (1986). Death with honors: Suicide and the gifted adolescent. *Journal of Counseling and Development, 64,* 558–560.

Delisle, J. R. (1987). *Gifted kids speak out.* Minneapolis, MN: Free Spirit Publishing.

Delisle, J. R. (1992). *Guiding the social and emotional development of gifted youth: A practical guide for educators and counselors.* New York: Longman.

Delisle, J. R. (1994a). National report misses some important issues for educators of gifted and talented students. *Gifted Child Today, 17*(1), 32–33.

Delisle, J. R. (1994b). The inclusion movement is here—good . . . it's about time. *Gifted Child Today, 17*(4), 30–31.

Delisle, J. R. (1995). ADD gifted: How many labels can one child take? *Gifted Child Today, 18*(2), 42–43.

Delisle, J. R. (1996). Ghosts from different nightmares: The unabomber, Jessica Dubroff, and the fate of gifted children. *Gifted Child Today, 19*(4), 20–21.

Dennis, W., & Dennis, M. W. (Eds.). (1976). *The intellectually gifted: An overview.* New York: Grune & Stratton.

Dransfield, J. E. (1933). *Administration of enrichment to superior children in the typical classroom.* New York: Teachers College, Columbia University.

Eby, J. W., & Smutny, J. F. (1990). *A thoughtful overview of gifted education.* New York: Longman.

Educational Policies Commission. (1950). *Education of the gifted.* Washington, DC: Educational Policies Commission.

Elkind, D. (1988). *The hurried child: Growing up too fast too soon.* Reading, MA: Addison-Wesley.

Eysenck, H. J. (1985). The nature and measurement of intelligence. In J. Freeman (Ed.), *The psychology of gifted children* (pp. 115–140). New York: John Wiley.

Fahey, R. A. (1996). A different perspective. *Teacher Magazine, 8*(3), 4.

Falk, F., Piechowski, M. M., & Lind, S. (1994). *Criteria for rating intensity of overexcitabilities.* Unpubished manuscript, Northland College, Ashland, WI.

Feldhusen, J. (1985). *Toward excellence in gifted education.* Denver, CO: Love.

Feldhusen, J. F. (1981). Teaching gifted, creative, and talented students in an individualized classroom. *Gifted Child Quarterly, 25,* 108–111.

Feldhusen, J. F. (1995). Talent development: The new direction in gifted education. *Roeper Review, 18*(2), 92.

Feldhusen, J. F. (1998) Programs and services at the elementary level. In J. Van Tassel-Baska (Ed.), *Excellence in educating gifted and talented learners* (pp. 211–223). Denver, CO: Love.

Feldhusen, J. F., & Kolloff, P. B. (1981). A three-stage model for gifted education. In R. E. Clasen, B. Robinson, D. R. Clasen, & G. Libster (Eds.), *Programming for the gifted, talented and creative: Models and methods* (pp. 39–52). Madison, WI: University of Wisconsin-Extension.

Feldhusen, J. F., & Wyman, A. R. (1980). Super Saturday: Design and implementation of Purdue's special program for gifted children. *Gifted Child Quarterly, 24,* 15–21.

Feldman, D. H. (1986). *Nature's gambit: Child prodigies and the development of human potential.* New York: Basic Books.

Feldman, R. D. (1982). *Whatever happened to the Quiz Kids?* Chicago: Chicago Review Press.

Ford, D. Y. (1994). *Recruitment and retention of African American students in gifted education programs: Implications and recommendations.* Storrs, CT: National Research Center on the Gifted and Talented.

Fox, L. H. (1979). Programs for the gifted and talented: An overview. In A. H. Passow (Ed.), *The gifted and talented* (pp. 104–126). Chicago: National Society for the Study of Education.

Frasier, M. M. (1979). Rethinking the issues regarding the culturally disadvantaged gifted. *Exceptional Children, 45,* 538–542.

Frasier, M. M. (1993). Issues, problems and programs in nurturing the disadvantaged and culturally different talented. In K. A. Heller, F. J. Monks, & A. H. Passow (Eds.), *International handbook of research and development of giftedness and talent* (pp. 685–692). New York: Pergamon.

Freeman, J. (1985). *The psychology of gifted children.* New York: John Wiley.

Friede, K. (1997). The important role of failure. In B. Johnson (Ed.), *From the heart: A Minnesota anthology* (p. 41). Minneapolis, MN: Minnesota Council for the Gifted and Talented.

Gagne, F., Motard, D., & Belanger, J. (1991). Popular estimates of the prevalence of giftedness and talent. *Roeper Review, 16*(2), 96–98.

Gagne, F. (1995). From giftedness to talent: A developmental model and its impact on the language of the field. *Roeper Review, 18,* (2), 103–111.

Galbraith, J., & Delisle, J. (1996). *The gifted kids' survival guide: A teen handbook.* Minneapolis, MN: Free Spirit.

Gallagher, J. J. (1979). Research needs for education of the gifted. In *Issues in gifted education.* Los Angeles, CA: National/State Leadership Training Institute on the Gifted and the Talented.

Gallagher, J. J., & Crowder, T. (1957). The adjustment of gifted children in the regular classroom. *Exceptional Children, 23,* 306–312, 317–319.

Gallagher, J. J., & Gallagher, S. A. (1994). *Teaching the gifted child* (4th ed.). Boston: Allyn & Bacon.

Gallagher, J. J., Harradine, C. C., & Coleman, M. R. (1997). Challenge or boredom? Gifted students' views on their schooling. *Roeper Review, 19*(3), 132–136.

Gallagher, S. (1985). A comparison of the concept of overexcitabilities with measures of creativity and school achievement in sixth-grade students. *Roeper Review, 8*(2), 115–119.

Galton, F. (1869). *Hereditary genius: An inquiry into its laws and consequences.* (1892 ed.) London: Macmillan.

Gardner, H. (1983). *Frames of mind: The theory of multiple intelligences.* New York: Basic Books.

George, P. (1988). Tracking and ability grouping. *Middle School Journal, 20*(1), 21–28.

Getzels, J. W., & Jackson, P. W. (1958). The meaning of "giftedness"—an examination of an expanding concept. *Phi Delta Kappan, 40,* 75–77.

Ghiselin, B. (1954). *The creative process: A symposium.* Berkeley, CA: University of California Press.

Goddard, H. H. (1928). *School training of gifted children.* New York: Harcourt Brace Jovanovich.

Goertzel, V., & Goertzel, M. G. (1962). *Cradles of eminence.* Boston: Little, Brown.

Goleman, D. (1995). *Emotional intelligence.* New York: Bantam Books.

Gowan, J. C. (1972). *The guidance and measurement of intelligence, development, and creativity: A book of readings drawn from the collected papers of John Curtis Gowan.* Northridge, CA: J. C. Gowan.

Gowan, J. C., Khatena, J., & Torrance, E. P. (1981). *Creativity: Its educational implications.* Dubuque, IA: Kendall-Hunt.

Grant, B. (1992, November). *The value of achievement in gifted education.* Paper presented at the meeting of the National Association for Gifted Children, Los Angeles, CA.

Guilford, J. P. (1950). Creativity. *American Psychologist, 5,* 444–454.

Guilford, J. P. (1959). Three faces of intellect. *American Psychologist, 14,* 469–479.

Guilford, J. P. (1967). *The nature of human intelligence.* New York: McGraw-Hill.

Guilford, J. P. (1975a). Creativity: A quarter-century of progress. In I. A. Taylor & J. W. Getzels (Eds.), *Perspectives in creativity* (pp. 37–59). Chicago: Aldine.

Guilford, J. P. (1975b). Varieties of creative giftedness, their measurement and development. *The Gifted Child Quarterly, 19,* 107–121.

Haley, A. (1976). *Roots.* Garden City, NY: Doubleday.

Halsted, J. W. (1994). *Some of my best friends are books: Guiding gifted readers from preschool to high school.* Dayton, OH: Ohio Psychology Press.

Harris, C. R. (1990). The Hollingworth longitudinal study: Follow-up, findings, and implications. *Roeper Review, 12*(3), 216–228.

Haydock, D. (1997). Homeschooling the gifted: A personal introduction. *Understanding Our Gifted, 9*(2), 16–19.

Herrnstein, R. J., & Murray, C. (1994). *The bell curve: Intelligence and class structure in American life.* New York: The Free Press.

Hildreth, G. H. (1966). *Introduction to the gifted.* New York: McGraw-Hill.

Hillesum, E. (1996). *An interrupted life: The diaries, 1941–1943; and, Letters from Westerbork.* (A. J. Pomerans, Trans.). New York: Henry Holt.

Hillman, J. (1996). *The soul's code.* New York: Random House.

Hollingworth, H. L. (1943). *Leta Stetter Hollingworth: A biography.* Lincoln, NE: University of Nebraska Press.

Hollingworth, L. S. (1914). Variability as related to sex differences in achievement. *American Journal of Sociology, 19,* 510–530.

Hollingworth, L. S. (1922). Provisions for intellectually superior children. In M. V. O'Shea (Ed.), *The child, his nature and his needs* (pp. 10–32). New York: Arno Press.

Hollingworth, L. S. (1926). *Gifted children: Their nature and nurture.* New York: Macmillan.

Hollingworth, L. S. (1931). The child of very superior intelligence as a special problem in social adjustment. *Mental Hygiene, 15*(1), 1–16.

Hollingworth, L. S. (1939). What we know about the early selection and training of leaders. *Teachers College Record, 40,* 575–592.

Hollingworth, L. S. (1942). *Children above 180 IQ Stanford Binet.* New York: World Book Company.

Hollingworth, L. S. (1990). The hermit. *Roeper Review, 12*(3), p. 207.

Holmes, E. (1932). *The life of Mozart.* New York: E. P. Dutton.

Isaksen, S. G., & Treffinger, D. J. (1985). *Creative problem solving: The basic course.* Buffalo, NY: Bearly Limited.

Johnson, A. G. (1993). *A rock and a hard place: One boy's triumphant story.* New York: Crown.

Johnson, A. G. (1997). The right questions. *Teaching Tolerance, 6*(2), 62–63.

Johnson, D. W., & Johnson, R. (1987). *Learning together and alone: Cooperative, competitive and individualistic learning* (2nd ed.). Englewood Cliffs, NJ: Prentice Hall.

Jung, C. G. (1954). Psychology and literature. In *The creative process* (p. 229). Berkeley, CA: University of California Press.

Kaplan, S. (1979). *Inservice training manual: Activities for developing curriculum for the gifted/talented.* Los Angeles, CA: National/State Leadership Training Institute on the Gifted and Talented.

Karnes, F. A., & Chauvin, J. C. (1985). *Leadership skills development program: Leadership skills inventory and leadership skills activities handbook.* Buffalo, NY: DOK.

Karnes, F. A., & Marquardt, R. G. (1991a). *Gifted children and the law: Mediation, due process and court cases.* Dayton, OH: Ohio Psychology Press.

Karnes, F. A., & Marquardt, R. G. (1991b). *Gifted children and legal issues in education: Parents' stories of hope.* Dayton, OH: Ohio Psychology Press.

Kaufmann, F. (1976, 1987). *Your gifted child and you.* Reston, VA: Council for Exceptional Children.

Kaufmann, F. (1986). Presidential scholars speak. *Gifted Child Today, 9*(4), 12–13.

Kaufmann, F. (1992). What educators can learn from gifted adults. In F. Monks & W. Peters (Eds.), *Talent for the future* (pp. 109–121). The Netherlands: Van Gorcum.

Kaufmann, F. A. (1979). *A follow-up study of the 1964–1968 presidential scholars.* Unpublished doctoral dissertation, The University of Georgia.

Kaufmann, F. A. (1981). The 1964–1968 presidential scholars: A follow-up study. *Exceptional Children, 48*(2), 164–169.

Kaufmann, F. A., Harrel, G., Milam, C. P., Woolverton, N., & Miller, J. (1986). The nature, role, and influence of mentors in the lives of gifted adults. *Journal of Counseling and Development, 64,* 576–578.

Kearney, K. (1989). The highly gifted: School placement (Part II). *Understanding Our Gifted, 1*(3), 14.

Kearney, K. (1990). Leta Hollingworth's unfinished legacy: Children above 180 IQ. *Roeper Review, 12*(3), 181–183, 186–188.

Kearney, K., & LeBlanc, J. (1993a). Forgotten pioneers in the study of gifted African Americans. *Roeper Review, 15*(4), 192–199.

Kearney, K., & LeBlanc, J. (1993b). Forgotten pioneers in the study of gifted African Americans. *Highly Gifted Children. The Newsletter of the Hollingworth Center for Highly Gifted Children, X*(1, 2), 1, 4, 6–10, 12, 14–15.

Kerr, B. A. (1981). *Career education for the gifted and talented.* Information series 230. Washington, DC: National Institute of Education. (ERIC Document Reproduction Service ED 205 778)

Kerr, B. A. (1985). *Smart girls, gifted women.* Dayton, OH: Ohio Psychology Press.

Kerr, B. (1991). Educating gifted girls. In N. Colangelo & G. Davis (Eds.), *Handbook of gifted education* (pp. 402–405). Boston: Allyn & Bacon.

Kerr, B. A. (1997). *Smart girls: A new psychology of girls, women and giftedness.* Scottsdale, AZ: Gifted Psychology Press.

Keyser, D., & Sweetland, R. (1985). *Test of cognitive skills.* Austin, TX: Pro-Ed.

Knowles, H., & Weber, D. (1978). The school community as a moral environment. *Independent School, 38*(2), 13–17.

Kohn, A. (1996). What to look for in a classroom. *Educational Leadership, 54,* 54–55.

Kolloff, P. B. (1989). A comparison of self-contained and pullout models. In R. Swassing (Ed.), *Research briefs* (pp. 20–26). Washington, DC: National Association for Gifted Children.

Kozik, F. (1958). *The sorrowful and heroic life of John Amos Comenius.* (E. Pargeter, Trans.). Prague: State Educational Publishing House.

Krathwohl, D. R., Bloom, B. S., & Masia, B. B. (1964). *Taxonomy of educational objectives—the classification of educational goals handbook II: Affective domain.* New York: David McKay.

Kulik, J. A., & Kulik, C-L. C. (1982). Effects of ability grouping on secondary school students: A meta-analysis of evaluation findings. *American Educational Research Journal, 19,* 415–428.

Kulik, J. A., & Kulik, C-L. C. (1991). Ability grouping and gifted students. In N. Colangelo & G. A. Davis (Eds.), *Handbook of gifted education* (pp. 178–196). Boston: Allyn & Bacon.

L'Engle, M. (1962). *A wrinkle in time.* New York: Farrar, Strauss, & Giroux.

Lajoie, S. P., & Shore, B. M. (1981). Three myths? The over-representation of the gifted among dropouts, delinquents and suicides. *Gifted Child Quarterly, 25,* 183–243.

Laurie, S. S. (1892/1973). *John Amos Comenius, bishop of the Moravians: His life and educational works.* New York: B. Franklin.

Leroux, J. A. (1986). Suicidal behavior in gifted adolescents. *Roeper Review, 9,* 77–79.

Levin, H. (1992, April). *Toward an evaluation model for accelerated schools.* Paper presented at the Annual Meeting of the American Educational Research Association, San Francisco, California.

Lloyd, M. (1997). In practice—dual enrollment. *Understanding Our Gifted, 9*(2), 13.

Lombroso, C. (1891). *The man of genius.* London: Robert Scott.

Lowry, L. (1993). *The giver.* Boston: Houghton Mifflin.

MacKinnon, D. W. (1978). Educating for creativity: A modern myth? In G. A. Davis & J. A. Scott (Eds.), *Training creative thinking* (pp. 194–207). Melbourne, FL: Krieger.

Maker, C. (1986). *Critical issues in gifted education: Defensible programs for the gifted.* Austin, TX: Pro-Ed.

Maker, C. J., & Nielson, A. B. (1995). *Teaching models in education of the gifted.* (2nd ed.). Austin, TX: Pro-Ed.

Marland, S. P. (1971). *Education of the gifted and talented. Volume 1: Report to the Congress of the United States by the U.S. Commissioner of Education.* Washington, DC: Department of Health, Education, and Welfare.

Mead, M. (1954). The gifted child in the American culture today. *Journal of Teacher Education, 5*(3), 211–214.

Mednick, S. (1962). The associative basis of the creative process. *Psychological Review, 69,* 220–232.

Mee, C. S. (1997). *2,000 voices: Young adolescents' perceptions and curriculum implications.* Columbus, OH: National Middle School Association.

Mercer, J. R. (1977). *Implications of current assessment procedures for Mexican-American children. Bilingual education paper series, Vol. 1 No. 1, August, 1977.* Los Angeles, CA: California State University, National Dissemination and Assessment Center.

Millar, G. W. (1995). *E. Paul Torrance: "The creativity man": An authorized biography.* Norwood, NJ: Ablex.

Minnesota Council for the Gifted and Talented. (1997). *From the heart: A Minnesota anthology.* Minneapolis, MN: Minnesota Council for the Gifted and Talented.

Mitchell, J. O. (1974). *Attitudes of adolescents towards mental ability, academic effort and athleticism.* Unpublished masters thesis. The University of Calgary, Department of Sociology, Calgary, Alberta, Canada.

Moon, S. M., Feldhusen, J. F., & Kelly, K. W. (1991). Identification procedures: Bridging theory and practice. *Gifted Child Today, 14*(1), 30–36.

Munger, A. (1990). The parent's role in counseling the gifted: The balance between home and school. In J. Van Tassel-Baska (Ed.), *A practical guide to counseling the gifted in a school setting* (2nd ed., pp. 57–65). Reston, VA: Council for Exceptional Children.

National Commission on Excellence in Education. (1983). *A nation at risk: The imperative for educational reform.* Washington, DC: U.S. Government Printing Office.

National excellence: A case for developing America's talent. (1993). Washington, DC: Office of Educational Research and Improvement, U.S. Department of Education.

National Society for the Study of Education Yearbook. (1924). *Report of the society's committee on the education of gifted children* (Part I). Bloomington, IN: NSSE.

Newland, T. E. (1976). *The gifted in socioeducational perspective.* Englewood Cliffs, NJ: Prentice Hall.

Nixon, J. (1993). 17 dirty tricks you can play on your kids. *Teaching PreK–8, 23,* 66–67.

O'Callahan, J. (1993). *Orange cheeks.* Atlanta, GA: Peachtree.

O'Neil, J. (1997). Building schools as communities: A conversation with James Comer. *Educational Leadership, 54*(8), 6–10.

Oakes, J. (1985). *Keeping track.* New Haven, CT: Yale University Press.

Olszewski-Kubilius, P. M., & Scott, J. M. (1992). An investigation of the college and career counseling needs of economically disadvantaged, minority gifted students. *Roeper Review, 14,* 141–148.

Orwell, G. (1946). *Animal farm.* New York: Harcourt Brace.

Osborn, A. F. (1953). *Applied imagination.* New York: Scribners.

Osborn, A. F. (1963). *Applied imagination* (3rd ed.). New York: Scribners.

Otis, A. S., & Lennon, R. T. (1977). *The Otis-Lennon school ability test.* San Antonio, TX: The Psychological Corporation.

Parke, B. (1989). *Gifted students in regular classrooms.* Boston: Allyn & Bacon.

Parnes, S. J. (1981). *Magic of your mind.* Buffalo, NY: Creative Education Foundation.

Passow, A. H. (Ed.). (1979a). *The gifted and the talented.* Chicago: National Society for the Study of Education.

Passow, A. H. (Ed.). (1979b). *The gifted and the talented: Their education and development.* Chicago: The National Society for the Study of Education.

Passow, A. H. (1986). Reflections on three decades of education of the gifted. *Roeper Review, 8*(4), 223–226.

Passow, A. H. (1990). Leta Stetter Hollingworth: A real original. *Roeper Review, 12*(3), 134–136.

Passow, A. H., & Rudnitski, R. A. (1993). *State policies regarding education of the gifted as reflected in legislation and regulation.* Storrs, CT: National Research Center on the Gifted and Talented.

Paterson, K. (1977). *A bridge to Terabithia.* New York: Crowell.

Pearson, K. (1914). *The life, letters and labours of Francis Galton.* Cambridge: Cambridge University Press.

Perino, S. C., & Perino, J. (1981). *Parenting the gifted.* New York: Bowker.

Piechowski, M. M. (1979). Developmental potential. In N. Colangelo & R. T. Zaffrann (Eds.), *Handbook of gifted education* (pp. 25–57). Boston: Allyn & Bacon.

Piechowski, M. M. (1991). Emotional development and emotional giftedness. In N. Colangelo & G. A. Davis (Eds.), *Handbook of gifted education* (pp. 285–306). Boston: Allyn & Bacon.

Piechowski, M. M. (1995). Assessing developmental potential in gifted children: A comparison of methods. *Roeper Review, 17*(3), 176–180.

Piechowski, M. M. (1997). Emotional giftedness: The measure of intrapersonal intelligence. In N. Colangelo and G. A. Davis (Eds.), *Handbook of gifted education* (2nd ed.) (pp. 366–381). Boston: Allyn & Bacon.

Piechowski, M. M., & Colangelo, N. (1984). Developing potential of the gifted. *Gifted Child Quarterly, 28,* 80–88.

Piechowski, M. M., & Cunningham, K. (1985). Patterns of overexcitability in a group of artists. *Journal of Creative Behavior, 19,* 153–174.

Piirto, J. (1994). *Talented children and adults: Their development and education.* New York: Merrill.

Piper, W. (1961). *The little engine that could. The complete original edition.* New York: Platt & Munk.

Project now crusade against court-martial. (1997, July 25). *The Sun News,* p. A6.

Purkey, W. W., & Novak, J. M. (1984). *Inviting school success: A self-concept approach to teaching and learning* (2nd ed.). Belmont, CA: Wadsworth.

Purkey, W. W., & Novak, J. M. (1996). *Inviting school success: A self-concept approach to teaching, learning, and democratic practice* (3rd ed.). Belmont, CA: Wadsworth.

Purkey, W. W., & Stanley, P. H. (1994). *The inviting school treasury: 1001 ways to invite student success.* New York: Scholastic.

Raph, J. B., & Tannenbaum, A. J. (1961). *Underachievement: Review of literature.* Mimeo. Talented Youth Project, Horace Mann-Lincoln Institute of School Experimentation. New York: Teachers College, Columbia University.

Raph, J. B., Goldberg, M. L., & Passow, A. H. (1966). *Bright underachievers: Studies of scholastic underachievement among intellectually superior high school students.* New York: Teachers College Press.

Raven, J. (1990). *Raven manual research supplement, 3: American and international norms–neurophychological uses.* Oxford: Oxford Psychologists Press.

Raven, J. C. (1980). *Standard progressive matrices.* New York: Psychological Corporation.

Reich, R. B. (1992). *The work of nations.* New York: Vintage Books.

Reis, S. M. (1983). Creating ownership in gifted and talented programs. *Roeper Review, 5*(4), 20–23.

Renzulli, J. S. (1976a). *New directions in creativity.* New York: Harper & Row.

Renzulli, J. S. (1976b). *Scales for rating the behavioral characteristics of superior students.* Mansfield Center, CT: Creative Learning Press.

Renzulli, J .S. (1977). *The enrichment triad model: A guide for developing defensible programs for the gifted and talented.* Wethersfield, CT: Creative Learning Press.

Renzulli, J. S. (1978). What makes giftedness? Reexamining a definition. *Phi Delta Kappan, 60,* 180–184.

Renzulli, J. S. (1986). *Systems and models for developing programs for the gifted and talented.* Mansfield Center, CT: Creative Learning Press.

Renzulli, J. S. (1991). The National Research Center on the Gifted and Talented: The dream, the design, and the destination. *Gifted Child Quarterly, 35,* 73–80.

Renzulli, J. S., & Hartman, R. K. (1971). Scale for rating behavioral characteristics of superior students. *Exceptional Children, 38,* 211–214.

Renzulli, J. S., & Reis, S. M. (1985). *The schoolwide enrichment model: A comprehensive plan for educational excellence.* Mansfield Center, CT: Creative Learning Press.

Renzulli, J. S., Reis, S. M., & Smith, L. H. (1982). *The revolving door identification model.* Mansfield Center, CT: Creative Learning Press.

Ribot, T. (1900). *Essay on the creative imagination.* London: Kagan & Paul.

Richert, E. S., Alvino, J. J., & McDonnel, R. C. (1982). *National report on identification: Assessment and recommendations for comprehensive identification of gifted and talented youth.* (Contract 300-80-0958). Sewell, NJ: Educational Improvement Center-South.

Robinson, N. M., & Noble, K. D. (1991). Social-emotional development and adjustment of gifted children. In M. C. Wang, M. C. Reynolds, & H. J. Walberg (Eds.), *Handbook of special education: Research and practice, Volume 4: Emerging programs* (pp. 57–76). New York: Pergamon Press.

Roedell, W. C. (1984). Vulnerabilities of highly gifted children. *Roeper Review, 6,* 127–130.

Roeper, A. (1982). How gifted children cope with their emotions. *Roeper Review, 5*(2), 21–24.

Roeper, A. (1990). *Educating children for life: The modern learning community.* Monroe, NY: Trillium.

Roeper, A. (1995). *Annemarie Roeper: Selected writings and speeches.* Minneapolis, MN: Free Spirit.

Roeper, A. (1996). Reflections from Annemarie Roeper: A personal statement of philosophy of George and Annemarie Roeper. *Roeper Review, 19*(1), 18–19.

Roeper, A. (1997, Fall). My hopes and my mission. *Counseling and Guidance Newsletter.*

Ross, P. O. (1994). Introduction to descriptions of Javits grant projects. *Gifted Child Quarterly, 38,* 64.

Roweton, W. E. (1990). Leta Hollingworth: A personal profile of Nebraska's pioneering psychologist. *Roeper Review, 12*(3), 136–141.

Rubin, N. (1994). *Ask me if I care.* Berkeley, CA: Ten Speed Press.

Salinger, J. D. (1951). *The catcher in the rye.* Boston: Little, Brown.

Sanborn, M. (1979). Career development: Problems of gifted and talented students. In N. Colangelo & R. T. Zaffrann (Eds.)., *New voices in counseling the gifted* (pp. 294–300). Dubuque, IA: Kendall-Hunt.

Sapon-Shevin, M. (1994). *Playing favorites: Gifted education and the disruption of community.* Albany, NY: State University of New York Press.

Sapon-Shevin, M. (1995). Towards excellence and justice for all: A response to Schroeder-Davis. *Gifted Education Quarterly, 9*(1), 10.

Schaefer, C. E. (1969). Imaginary companions and creative adolescents. *Developmental Psychology, 1,* 747–749.

Schneidman, E. (1971). Perturbation and lethality as precursors of suicide in a gifted group. *Life Threatening Behavior, 1,* 23–45.

Schroeder-Davis, S. J. (1995). *Brains, brawn, and beauty: A content analysis of adolescent response to three superlatives (intelligence).* Unpublished doctoral dissertation, University of St. Thomas, Minnesota.

Seagoe, M. V. (1975). *Terman and the gifted.* Los Altos, CA: Kaufman.

Shore, B. M., Cornell, D. G., Robinson, A., & Ward, V. S. (1991). *Recommended practices in gifted education: A critical analysis.* New York: Teachers College Press.

Shurkin, J. N. (1992). *Terman's kids: The groundbreaking study of how the gifted grow up.* Boston: Little, Brown.

Silverman, L. K. (1990). Social and emotional development of the gifted: The discoveries of Leta Hollingworth. *Roeper Review, 12*(3), 171–177.

Silverman, L. K. (Ed.). (1993). *Counseling the gifted and talented.* Denver, CO: Love.

Silverman, L. K. (1994). The moral sensitivity of gifted children and the evolution of society. *Roeper Review, 17,* 110–116.

Silverman, L. K. (1995). Foreward. In A. Roeper, *Annemarie Roeper: Selected writings and speeches* (pp. vii–xi). Minneapolis, MN: Free Spirit.

Simpson, R. G., & Kaufmann, F. A. (1981). Career education for the gifted. *Journal of Career Education, 8*(1), 38–45.

Slavin, R. E. (1988). Synthesis of research on grouping in elementary and secondary schools. *Educational Leadership, 46,* 67–77.

Smutny, J. F., Walker, S. Y., & Meckstroth, E. A. (1997). *Teaching young gifted children in the regular classroom: Identifying, nurturing and challenging ages 4–9.* Minneapolis, MN: Free Spirit.

SOI Systems. (1997). SOI/Senate bill 3 passed. *SOI News, 23*(3), 7.

Southern, W. T., & Jones, E. D. (1991). Objections to early entrance and grade skipping. In W. T. Southern & E. D. Jones (Eds.), *Academic acceleration of gifted children* (pp. 51–73). New York: Teachers College Press.

Soviet fires Earth satellite into space; it is circling the globe at 18,000 m.p.h.; sphere tracked in crossings over U.S. (1957, October 5). *The New York Times,* p. 1.

Spender, S. (1954). The making of a poem. In *The creative process* (p. 114). Berkeley, CA: University of California Press.

Stanley, J. C. (1979). The study and facilitation of talent for mathematics. In A. H. Passow (Ed.), *The gifted and the talented* (pp. 169–185). Chicago: National Society for the Study of Education.

Stanley, J. C. (1982, October). *Finding intellectually talented youths and helping them greatly via educational acceleration.* Address presented at the meeting of the Wisconsin Council on Gifted and Talented, Madison.

Starko, A. J. (1995). *Creativity in the classroom: Schools of curious delight.* White Plains, NY: Longman.

Sternberg, R. J. (1988). *The triarchic mind: A new theory of human intelligence.* New York: Viking Press.

Sternberg, R. J. (1996a) Neither elitism nor egalitarianism: Gifted education as a third force in American education. *Roeper Review, 18*(4), 261–263.

Sternberg, R. J. (1996b). *Successful intelligence: How practical and creative intelligence determine success in life.* New York: PLUME.

Sternberg, R. J. (1997, June). Developing your child's successful intelligence. *Parenting for High Potential,* 8–10.

Sternberg, R. J., & Davidson, J. E. (1986). *Conceptions of giftedness.* New York: Cambridge University Press.

Strang, R. (1960). *Helping your gifted child.* Syracuse, NY: Syracuse University Press.

Subotnik, R. F., & Arnold, K. D. (Eds.). (1994). *Beyond Terman: Contemporary longitudinal studies of giftedness and talent.* Norwood, NJ: Ablex.

Tannenbaum, A. J. (1962). *Adolescent attitudes toward academic brilliance. Talented youth monograph.* New York: Bureau of Publications, Teachers College, Columbia University.

Tannenbaum, A. J. (1979). Pre-Sputnik to post-Watergate concern about the gifted. In A. H. Passow (Ed.), *The gifted and the talented* (pp. 5–27). Chicago: National Society for the Study of Education.

Tannenbaum, A. J. (1983). *Gifted children: Psychological and educational perspectives.* New York: Macmillan.

Tannenbaum, A. J. (1997, July). *Special education for the gifted: To be or not to be.*

Paper presented at the twelfth world conference of The World Council for Gifted and Talented Children, Seattle, Washington.

Taylor, I. A., & Getzels, J. W. (Eds.). (1975). *Perspectives in creativity.* Chicago: Aldine.

Terman, L. M. (1905). A study in precocity and prematuration. *American Journal of Psychology, 16,* 145–183.

Terman, L. M., et al. *Genetic studies of genius.* Stanford, CA: Stanford University Press.

   I–Terman, L. M. (1925). *The mental and physical traits of a thousand gifted children.*

   II–Cox, C. M. (1926). *The early mental traits of three hundred geniuses.*

   III–Burks, B. S., Jensen, D., & Terman, L. M. (1930). *The promise of youth.*

   IV–Terman, L. M., & Oden, M. H. (1947). *The gifted child grows up.*

   V–Terman, L. M., & Oden, M. H. (1959). *The gifted group at mid-life.*

Thorndike, R. L., & Hagen, E. (1954). *Cognitive abilities test.* Lombard, IL: Riverside.

Tighe, A. (1997). Being a gifted kid. In B. Johnson (Ed.), *From the heart: A Minnesota anthology* (p. 20). Minneapolis, MN: Minnesota Council for the Gifted and Talented.

Torrance, E. P. (1962). *Guiding creative talent.* Englewood Cliffs, NJ: Prentice Hall.

Torrance, E. P. (1966). *Torrance tests of creative thinking.* Bensonville, IL: Scholastic Testing Service.

Torrance, E. P. (1970). *Encouraging creativity in the classroom.* Dubuque, IA: W. C. Brown.

Torrance, E. P. (1974). *Torrance tests of creative thinking: Norms and technical manual.* Lexington, MA: Personal Press/ Ginn-Xerox.

Torrance, E. P. (1975). Motivation and creativity. In E. P. Torrance & W. White (Eds.), *Issues and advances in educational psychology, 2* (pp. 2–18). Itasca, IL: F. E. Peacock.

Torrance, E. P. (1977). *Creativity in the classroom.* Washington, DC: National Education Association.

Torrance, E. P. (1979). *The search for Satori and creativity.* Buffalo, NY: Creative Education Foundation.

Torrance, E. P. (1980). Assessing the further reaches of creative potential. *Journal of Creative Behavior, 14,* 1–19.

Torrance, E. P. (1995). *Why fly? A philosophy of creativity.* Norwood, NJ: Ablex.

Torrance, E. P., Murdock, M., & Fletcher, D. C. (1996). *Creative problem solving through role playing.* Pretoria, Republic of South Africa: Benedic Books.

Torrance, E. P., & Sisk, D. (1997). *Gifted and talented children in the regular classroom.* Buffalo, NY: Creative Education Foundation Press.

Treffinger, D. J. (1975). Teaching for self-directed learning: A priority for the gifted and talented. *The Gifted Child Quarterly, 19,* 46–59.

Treffinger, D. J. (1995). School improvement, talent, development, and creativity. *Roeper Review, 18*(2), 93–97.

Twain, M. (1946). *The adventures of Tom Sawyer.* Cleveland, OH: World.

US Airways. (1997, October). Tune up. *Attaché,* 14–16.

Vaillant, G. E. (1977). *Adaptation to life.* Boston: Little, Brown.

Van Tassel-Baska, J. (Ed.). (1983). *A practical guide to counseling the gifted in a school setting.* Reston, VA: Council of Exceptional Children.

Van Tassel-Baska, J. (1994). *Comprehensive curriculum for gifted learners* (2nd ed.). Boston: Allyn & Bacon.

Van Tassel-Baska, J. (1995). The development of talent through curriculum. *Roeper Review, 18*(2), 98–102.

Van Tassel-Baska, J., Feldhusen, J., Seeley, K., Wheatley, G., Silverman, L., & Foster, W. (1988). *Comprehensive curriculum for gifted learners.* Boston: Allyn & Bacon.

Van Tassel-Baska, J., Johnson, D. T., & Boyce, L. N. (Eds.). (1996). *Developing verbal talent: Ideas and strategies for teachers of elementary and middle school students.* Boston: Allyn & Bacon.

Verholt, J. K. (1993). *Characteristics of effective teachers for intellectually gifted students, at the college level.* Unpublished senior honors thesis, Kent State University, Kent, Ohio.

Vonnegut, K. (1950). Harrison Bergeron. In *Welcome to the monkey house* (pp. 7–14). New York: Delacorte.

Walker, S. Y. (1992). *The survival guide for parents of gifted children.* Minneapolis, MN: Free Spirit.

Ward, V. (1961). *Educating the gifted: An axiomatic approach.* Columbus, OH: Charles E. Merrill.

Ward, V. (1980). *Differential education for the gifted.* Ventura, CA: Ventura County Superintendent of Schools.

Webb, J. T., Meckstroth, E. A., & Tolan, S. S. (1982). *Guiding the gifted child.* Columbus, OH: Ohio Psychology Press.

White, W. L. (1990). An interview with child I, child J, and child L. *Roeper Review, 12*(3), 228–234.

White, W. L., & Renzulli, J. S. (1987). A forty year follow-up of students who attended Leta Hollingworth's school for gifted students. *Roeper Review, 10,* 89–94.

Whitmore, J. R. (1980). *Giftedness, conflict, and underachievement.* Boston: Allyn & Bacon.

Whitmore, J. R. (1981). Gifted children with handicapping conditions: A new frontier. *Exceptional Children, 60,* 183–184.

Whitmore, J. R., & Maker, C. J. (1985). *Intellectual giftedness in disabled persons.* Austin, TX: Pro-Ed.

Williams, R. L. (1975). The Bitch 100: A culture-specific test. *Journal of Afro-American Issues, 3*(1), 103–116.

Winebrenner, S. (1992). *Teaching gifted kids in the regular classroom: Strategies and techniques every teacher can use to meet the academic needs of the gifted and talented.* Minneapolis, MN: Free Spirit.

Winebrenner, S. (1997). Gifted students learn differently from age peers. *Understanding Our Gifted, 9*(4), 30–32.

Winebrenner, S., & Berger, S. (1993). *Providing curriculum alternatives to motivate gifted students.* Reston, VA: Council for Exceptional Children. (ERIC Document Reproduction Service No. ED0-EC-93-7)

Winebrenner, S., & Berger, S. (1994). *Providing curriculum alternatives to motivate gifted students.* Washington, DC: Office of Educational Research and Improvement. (ERIC Document Reproduction Service No. ED 372 553)

Winner, E. (1996). *Gifted children: Myths and realities.* New York: Basic Books.

Witty, P. A. (1940). Some considerations in the education of gifted children. *Educational Administration and Supervision, 26,* 512–521.

Witty, P. A. (Ed.). (1951). *The gifted child.* Lexington, MA: D. C. Heath.

Witty, P. A. (1955). Gifted children—our greatest resource. *Nursing Outlook, 3,* 498–500.

Witty, P. A. (1958). Who are the gifted? In N. B. Henry (Ed.), *Education of the gifted.* The Fifty-seventh Yearbook of the National Society for the Study of Education, Part II (pp. 41–63). Chicago: University of Chicago Press.

Witty, P. A., & Jenkins, M. (1934). The educational achievement of a group of gifted negro children. *Journal of Educational Psychology, 25,* 585–597.

Witty, P. A., & Lehman, H. C. (1927). The play behavior of fifty gifted children. *Journal of Educational Psychology, 18,* 259–265.

Wolfe, D. (1954). *America's resources of specialized talent.* New York: Harper & Brothers.

Zettel, J., & Ballard, J. A. (1979). A need for increased federal effort for the gifted and talented. *Exceptional Children, 44*(4), 261–267.

INDEX